Public Security and
Police Reform in the Americas

PUBLIC SECURITY AND POLICE REFORM
IN THE AMERICAS

Edited by John Bailey and Lucía Dammert

UNIVERSITY OF PITTSBURGH PRESS

Published by the University of Pittsburgh Press,
Pittsburgh, PA 15260
Copyright © 2006, University of Pittsburgh Press
Manufactured in the United States of America
Printed on acid-free paper
10 9 8 7 6 5 4 3 2 1

Library of Congress Cataloging-in-Publication Data
Public security and police reform in the Americas / edited by John
Bailey and Lucía Dammert.
    p. cm.
  Includes bibliographical references and index.
  ISBN 0-8229-5913-5 (pbk. : alk. paper)
  1. Police administration—Latin America. 2. Police administration—
United States. 3. Police—Government policy—Latin America. 4. Po-
lice—Government policy—United States. 5. National security—Latin
America. 6. National security—United States. 7. Democratization—
Latin America. 8. Law reform—Latin America. 9. Latin America—
Foreign relations—United States. 10. United States—Foreign rela-
tions—Latin America. I. Bailey, John, 1944 Nov. 30- II. Dammert,
Lucía.
  HV8160.5.A2P83 2006
  363.2'098—dc22
                        2005020900

CONTENTS

LIST OF TABLES AND FIGURES   VII

ACKNOWLEDGMENTS   IX

LIST OF ABBREVIATIONS   XI

1 ▪ Public Security and Police Reform in the Americas 1
John Bailey and Lucía Dammert

2 ▪ Brazil's Public-Security Plans 24
Emilio Enrique Dellasoppa and Zoraia Saint'Clair Branco

3 ▪ Public-Private Partnerships for Police Reform in Brazil 44
Paulo de Mesquita Neto

4 ▪ From Public Security to Citizen Security in Chile 58
Lucía Dammert

5 ▪ The Institutional Identity of the Carabineros de Chile 75
Azun Candina

6 ▪ Armed Conflict and Public Security in Colombia 94
Gonzalo de Francisco Z.

7 ▪ Demilitarization in a War Zone 111
María Victoria Llorente

8 ▪ Security Policies in El Salvador, 1992–2002 132
Edgardo Alberto Amaya

9 ▪ Violence, Citizen Insecurity, and Elite Maneuvering in
El Salvador 148
José Miguel Cruz

10 ▪ Public Security and Police Reform in Mexico 169
Marcos Pablo Moloeznik

11 ▪ Local Responses to Public Insecurity in Mexico 187
Allison M. Rowland

12 ▪ From Law and Order to Homeland Security in the United States
205
John Bailey

13 ▪ Police-Community Conflict and Crime Prevention in Cincinnati,
Ohio 225
John E. Eck and Jay Rothman

14 ▪ Assessing Responses to Public Insecurity in the Americas 245
John Bailey and Lucía Dammert

NOTES   263

REFERENCES   291

LIST OF CONTRIBUTORS   313

INDEX   315

TABLES AND FIGURES

TABLE 1.1   General country information, 2002 2

TABLE 1.2   Homicide rates in North and Latin America and the Caribbean, 1984 and 1994 8

TABLE 1.3   Homicide rates in Six Latin American countries and the United States, late 1970s–2000 9

TABLE 1.4   Issues in public and national security 12

TABLE 1.5   National-level responses to public-security threats 16

TABLE 1.6   Police-reform case studies 21

TABLE 2.1   National fund for public security 31

TABLE 6.1   Steps of the drug-trafficking process 97

TABLE 8.1   Victimization rates, 1993–2002 137

TABLE 9.1   Opinions about the PNC, 1995–2000 163

TABLE 9.2   Authoritarian attitudes related to insecurity 164

TABLE 9.3   Opinions about weakness of PNC against crime 166

TABLE 13.1   Combining stakeholder goals with best practices 239

FIGURE 1.1   Trends in trust in Latin America, 1997–2001 10

FIGURE 13.1 Process used to reach an agreement 232

ACKNOWLEDGMENTS

For their generous funding we thank the William and Flora Hewlett Foundation. Additional financial support came from Georgetown University's School of Foreign Service, the Center for Latin American Studies, and the graduate school. The National Defense University, U.S. Southern Command, and the Chilean Ministry of Defense funded the participation of our South American contributors to this volume at the Annual Seminar on Research and Teaching of Defense and Security in Santiago, Chile, in October 2003.

At Georgetown, Martha Carro served as our project administrator in the early months and was ably succeeded by Beatriz Hernández. They attended to correspondence, budget and financial matters, and the tracking of dozens of drafts of chapters—in Spanish and English (and Portuguese, in one case)—from the contributors. In addition, Ms. Hernández supervised the editorial chores for the entire manuscript in both Spanish and English and translated chapters 1, 12, and 14 for the Spanish edition of the book. Gustavo Adolfo Flores helped bring the project to conclusion in the spring of 2005. Rachel Fedewa, Karen Bozicovich, and Hillary Thompson served as research and editorial assistants. Patricia Rosas translated chapters 4–8 and 10 ably, efficiently, and with good humor. José Miguel Cruz produced both the Spanish and English versions of chapter 9, and Emilio Dellasoppa translated chapter 2, which he coauthored, from Portuguese to Spanish. Beatriz Sánchez translated chapter 7. Trish Weisman did an efficient, thorough, and helpful edit that improved the overall manuscript significantly.

We thank our Chilean colleagues Hugo Frühling, director of the Center of Citizen Security of the University of Chile; Jorge Correa Sutil, assistant secretary of the Interior Ministry; and Gonzalo García Pino, head of the Interior Ministry's Division of Citizen Security, for their constant and enthusiastic support for this project. Also, we thank Liliana Manzano, who helped us with editorial chores for the entire manuscript in Spanish.

Working with our contributors, who brought such interesting backgrounds and skills to the task, was both a pleasure and a marvelous tutorial. We especially thank two Argentine colleagues, Máximo Sozzo and Gustavo González, both of the Universidad Nacional del Litoral, for their contributions. They provided lively commentary and good companionship at our various meetings and contributed useful papers. Unfortunately, because of severe space constraints, we are unable to include those chapters in the English edition of the book.

ABBREVIATIONS

ACLU	American Civil Liberties Union
	Unión Americana de Libertades Civiles
AFI	Agencia Federal de Investigación
	Federal Investigation Agency
CAI	Centros de Atención Inmediata
	Immediate Service Center
CBP	Customs and Border Protection
CCAN	Cincinnati Community Action Now
CIA	Central Intelligence Agency
CIEP	Centro de Información Estratégica Policial
	Center for Strategic Police Information
CIHD	Comisión Investigadora de Hechos Delictivos
	Investigative Commission for Criminal Acts
CISEN	Centro de Investigación y Seguridad Nacional
	Center for Research and National Security
CNSP	Consejo Nacional de Seguridad Pública
	National Council on Public Security
COMSTAT or COMPSTAT	Computer Statistics
CPRP	Citizen Police Review Panel
CUSEP	Cuerpos de Seguridad Pública
	Public Security Forces
DHS	Department of Homeland Security
DIC	Departamento de Investigación del Crimen
	Department of Crime Investigation
DIJIN	Dirección de Policía Judicial e Investigación
	Bureau of Judicial and Investigative Police

ELN	Ejército de Liberación Nacional
	National Liberation Army
FARC	Fuerzas Armadas Revolucionarias de Colombia
	Revolutionary Armed Forces of Colombia
FBI	Federal Bureau of Investigation
	Oficina Federal de Investigación
FESPAD	Fundación de Estudios para la Aplicación del Derecho
	Foundation for Studies of Law Enforcement
FMLN	Frente Farabundo Martí para la Liberación Nacional
	Farabundo Martí Front for National Liberation
FNSP	Fundo Nacional de Segurança Pública
	National Public Security Fund
GDP	Gross domestic product
INFOSEG	Sistema de Integración Nacional de Informaciones de Justicia y Seguridad Pública
	National Integrated Justice and Public Security Information System
IIS	Internal Investigations Section
ILO/OIT	International Labor Organization
	Organización Internacional del Trabajo
ISI	Import substitution industrialization
ISPCV	Instituto São Paulo Contra a Violência
	São Paulo Institute Against Violence
IUDOP	Instituto Universitario de Opinión Pública
	Public Opinion Institute of the Central American University
NGO	Nongovernmental Organization
OMI	Office of Municipal Investigations
ONUSAL	Misión de Naciones Unidas en El Salvador
	United Nations Mission in El Salvador
PFP	Policía Federal Preventiva
	Federal Preventive Police
PGR	Procuraduría General de la República
	Attorney General's Office
PNC	Policía Nacional Civil
	National Civilian Police
PNSP	Plano Nacional de Segurança Pública
	National Plan for Public Security

SEDENA	Secretaría de la Defensa Nacional
	National Defense Secretariat
SEGOB	Secretaría de Gobernación
	Interior Ministry
SENASP	Secretaría Nacional de Segurança Pública
	National Secretariat for Public Security
SNSP	Sistema Nacional de Seguridad Pública
	National Public Security System
SSP	Secretaría de Seguridad Pública
	Public Security Secretariat
WHO	World Health Organization

Public Security and Police Reform in the Americas

John Bailey and Lucía Dammert

Insecurity is a powerful force in private life and in politics, and fear and apprehension about crime and violence are driving change throughout the hemisphere. With few exceptions, the general pattern in the Americas was a significant increase in crime and violence in the mid-1980s and again in the mid-1990s. This pattern appeared on a global scale as well, for reasons that are not entirely clear. These trends clearly burdened the economies and societies of the affected countries. They complicated democratic governability as well, although we lack systematic, comparative studies (Bailey and Godson, 2000). The main exception to these trends in "common crime" was the United States, where crime rates peaked about 1990 and then declined over the decade (see Blumstein and Wallman 2000). But the sense of well-being brought by declines in crime was shattered by the terrorist attacks of September 11, 2001. In sum, whether due to criminal violence or terrorism, the issue of insecurity has risen to the top of the public agenda throughout the hemisphere.

This book examines the experiences with public security and police reform of six countries in the Americas: Brazil, Chile, Colombia, El Salvador, Mexico, and the United States. Our selection of cases (see table 1.1) includes countries representing the largest and smallest in size and population, federal and unitary in governmental organization, post–civil war and relatively pacific, in the midst of democratic transition and fairly well consolidated. *Public security*, as we use the term, differs from *national security* in that it emphasizes protection of persons, property, and democratic political institutions from internal or external threats. National security, in contrast, emphasizes protection of the state and territorial integrity from other state actors, as well as from transstate actors, such as organized crime, terrorism, and the like. Apprehension about crime and violence against persons in their daily lives throughout the hemisphere puts priority on public security.

Along with the overviews of public-security challenges and responses, we present examples of police reform drawn from the same countries. The police play a central role in political life, and their roles in democratic systems—as Miguel Cruz emphasizes in his chapter on El Salvador—are especially significant. They are the active, visible presence of democratic governance. Their respect, or lack thereof, for civil and human rights sets the tone of government–civil-society relations. And their effectiveness in preventing and repressing crime is a crucial measure of government competence, which in turn affects the legitimacy of democracy as a political regime.

Police reform refers to improving police forces' operational efficiency and effectiveness in preventing and repressing crime as well as to strengthening their democratic ethos and accountability. Police reform is the most frequent first response to perceptions of increased insecurity, and we present a case for

1.1 General country information, 2002

	Population (millions)	Population growth rate (annual %)	GDP per capita[a] (thousands)	Unemployment rate (rates total)	Poverty level[b] (%)	Gini coefficient (2001)
Brazil	174.5	1.2	4,644	10.5	22	0.59
Chile	15.6	1.1	5,436	7.8	22	0.56
Colombia	43.7	1.5	2,274	15.7	55	0.57
El Salvador	6.5	1.9	1,763	10[c]	48	0.51
Mexico	100.9	1.5	3,713	2.1	40	0.52
United States	288.4	0.9	31,977	5	13	0.41

Sources: World Bank Development Indicators, http://www.worldbank.org/data/countrydata/countrydata.html; International Labor Organization, http://www.ilo.org/public/english/employment/strat/kidm/index.html; Human Development Report 2001, http://hdr.undp.org/reports/global/2001/en; Instituto Nacional de Estadística y Geografía, México, http://www.inegi.gob.nx/inegi/default.asp; Instituto Nacional de Estadística y Censo, Argentina, http://www.indec.mecon.ar; Instituto Brasileiro de Geografia e Estadística, Brazil, http://www.ibge.gov.br; Latin-Focus.com, 2003, http://www.latin-focus.com.
[a]GDP/per capita based on constant 1995 US$.
[b]Data correspond to 2001 for Colombia, Mexico, and United States; 1999 for El Salvador; and 1998 for Brazil and Chile.
[c]Data correspond to 2001, *CIA World Factbook*, 2003, http://www.cia.gov/cia/publications/factbook.

each country that opens a window onto some aspect of governments' efforts to use this instrument. Our selection of police-reform cases was not guided by a single criterion, as, for example, the most typical, most publicized, or most successful. Rather, the cases tell us stories about reform efforts that are interesting in particular national contexts. Our cases cover efforts to demilitarize the police in Colombia, Chile, and El Salvador; the creation of a business-oriented nongovernmental organization (NGO) in São Paulo to promote police reform; community self-help in Mexico to counter a hostile and ineffective state-police force; and a negotiated effort to improve relations between police and the African American community in a U.S. city. The stories illustrate vividly how factors such as political pressures, technology, scandal, leadership, culture, myths, and embedded corruption interact to affect change. Along with the overviews of public-security policies, they provide material to help us extract lessons about the success or failure of policy initiatives.

Although this book is mostly about Latin American countries, we include the United States. As shown in table 1.1, the United States is much more populous, wealthy, and economically equal and enjoys much higher rates of employment. Most discussions of policy problems are premised on the notion that the Latin American and U.S. cases are like apples and oranges. In contrast, we believe that a strength of this collection is to bring the U.S. case into a common framework of public security with other countries in the region. We emphasize two rationales. First, there is little mutual understanding of the different types of public-security challenges faced by the United States and by the other countries of the region. Sheer distance from the terrorist attacks of September 11, combined with a general antipathy in the region toward U.S. unilateralism in foreign policy, especially the March 2003 attack on Iraq, help explain the lack of understanding to some degree. Similarly, the U.S. public—including informed elites—has relatively little appreciation of the severity of crime and violence in the rest of the hemisphere and of their multiple impacts on the polity, economy, and society. For example, as Portes and Hoffman (2003, 70–74) point out, crime and violence have become significant push factors for outmigration from Latin America to the United States. Ignorance about each other's security situation leads the United States and the other countries of the hemisphere to misperceive and misinterpret actions and policies and to "talk past one another." These gaps in understanding may complicate efforts by the American republics to negotiate a successor to the 1947 Inter-American Treaty of Reciprocal Assistance, viewed by many as an outdated relic of the Cold War. In short, the multiple challenges of insecurity in effect compel us to include the United States in a hemispheric context.

Second, Latin American political leaders, under siege from public demands that something must be done about crime and violence, have cast about anxiously for quick answers. Many of their ideas are drawn from the U.S. experience, which is seen to represent something like best practices. Frequently, the transplanted ideas are not well understood, and they may produce unexpected (often unwanted) results. An apt example is zero tolerance (sometimes called broken windows), drawn from New York City's perceived success and considered for adoption in Brazil and Mexico. A better comprehension of the institutions and values that shape U.S. experience can help guide selections, or at least it can illuminate the problems of policy diffusion from one national setting to another.

Dual Transitions and Public Insecurity in Latin America

Beginning in the late 1970s and continuing to the present, most of the Latin American countries experienced profound changes in both economic and political systems. These structural and institutional changes both coincided with and partially account for the upsurge in crime and violence. On the economic side, countries began transitions away from import substitution industrialization (ISI), with its emphasis on market protection and state-led promotion of domestic industry and toward greater emphasis on promoting trade and investment externally and deregulating the domestic market. ISI had been pursued to one degree or another throughout the region since the 1950s. While important advances in industrialization had been achieved by the 1970s, the overarching pattern was one of an inefficient industrial plant, unable to compete internationally in price and quality, and a public sector overburdened by multiple programs of economic promotion, regulation, and social welfare. Without exception, the countries experienced recurring and often severe bouts of inflation, along with balance-of-payments problems and fiscal deficits. The energy crises of the 1970s, with negative impacts on both oil-exporting and oil-importing countries, set the stage for the abandonment of ISI in the 1980s.[1]

The economic transition to more open markets brought pain and sacrifices in the short term (and possibly in the long term as well), along with important benefits. Fiscal crises forced cutbacks in a variety of public programs, which in turn caused layoffs in public employment and the reduction or elimination of subsidies. Governments retreated from industrial-promotion activities and began to sell off assets through privatization programs in, for example, telephones, transportation, agricultural-product processing, and a host of other activities. Reduction in tariffs and other forms of import barriers exposed economies to new pressures across the board, pressures that many domestic industries were unable to absorb. On the positive side of the ledger, most countries reduced fiscal deficits and overall levels of inflation and made progress on a variety of administrative reforms, including decentralization.

At the same time that Latin American countries experienced economic shocks, many of them (with Colombia as an exception) underwent complex transitions from different forms of authoritarianism to formal, that is, electoral, democracy.[2] The routes and circumstances varied. Of the countries included here, Brazil and Mexico followed a more gradual, negotiated path; El Salvador's democracy was negotiated in a formal treaty in 1992, ending its decade-long civil war; and Chile's seventeen years under military rule (1973–1990) ended with a peaceful plebiscite. Whatever the route of the transitions, the forms of democracy that emerged tended to be shallow and fragile (with Chile as an important exception). These democracies (including Colombia's) met the minimum requirements of competing parties, periodic elections that were reasonably clean, and elected leaders that exercised at least some degree of control over their bureaucracies. But constitutional guarantees were unevenly enforced, legislative bodies and courts operated ineffectively, subnational governments (states, provinces, cities) were generally inefficient and starved for resources, and democratic political culture and engaged civil society were generally lacking. Outside of the urban middle and upper strata, law enforcement was typically precarious, perverse, or nonexistent (Mendez, O'Donnell, and Pinheiro 1999).

Guillermo O'Donnell (1994) insightfully characterizes these emerging regimes as a type of delegative democracy. This is a species of democracy that in his view meets minimal criteria of procedural democracy but lacks horizontal accountability in the sense that powerful presidents are not checked by effective legislatures or courts. O'Donnell questions whether these new democracies will naturally evolve toward forms of representative democracy, with better enforcement of constitutional rights, more effective horizontal accountability, and more robust civil societies, or whether they will suffer what he calls a slow death of violence, corruption, inefficiency, impunity, and poor-quality decision making. Some countercurrents, however, such as more assertive legislatures and courts and more active civil-society organizations, suggest a more nuanced picture. Latin American democracies may be moving beyond the delegative image that O'Donnell sketches.

This dual economic and political transition of the 1980s and 1990s coincided with a sharp increase in crime and violence. This, in turn, triggered fear and insecurity, often out of proportion to the situation. Since there appeared to be a near-universal increase in crime and violence (again, with the United States the exception), we cannot assign a direct causal role to the dual transition. Even so, several linkages appear significant. The economic changes that brought greater underemployment in the formal sector, a burgeoning informal sector, and inequality in income and wealth also popularized the consumer tastes of the postindustrial, wealthy countries. That is, men and women lost jobs or endured income losses at the same time that they were bombarded with advertising and images of the good life from advanced postindustrial societies (Oxhorn and Ducatensziler 1998; Portes and Hoffman 2003).

On the political-administrative side, the new democracies inherited feeble state capacity to formulate and implement programs. Weak capacity was further undermined by fiscal crises. Among the feeblest of the institutions were those expected to confront the upsurge in crime and violence: the police, courts, prison systems, and agencies charged with social rehabilitation. In some cases, such as El Salvador and Mexico, the transition to democracy meant challenges to old systems of control in which political elites had negotiated extralegal and corrupt arrangements with police to manage the crime problem.

In all, structural and institutional changes created circumstances that contributed to the upsurge in crime and violence. We should emphasize that crime and violence have long been chronic problems throughout Latin America. The democratic transitions of the 1980s and 1990s created more open political and social systems, and these in turn both magnified perceptions of insecurity and generated pressures on elected officials for prompt solutions. Politicians took up crime control as a campaign banner and competed in offering tough anticrime programs. Perceptions of insecurity were further magnified by mass media, which both enjoyed greater freedom from government control and confronted the pressures of market competition. In this context, crime coverage—especially by television—generally increased in volume and graphic intensity. A nonobvious effect of media coverage was to broadcast the heightened sense of insecurity from the main urban centers—where problems of insecurity were usually more severe—to the smaller towns and countryside, contributing to a sense of insecurity in these areas often out of proportion to reality and unrelated to urban crime and violence (see, e.g., Smulovitz 2003).

Diagnosis of the Problem of Insecurity

A fundamental obstacle to grasping the dimensions and dynamics of the public-security problem in the hemisphere is the lack of accurate, reliable, and comparable data on violence, crime, and fear of crime, along with indicators of their societal-political impacts. The quality of the data is generally poor and unreliable, with relatively few exceptions. One of the several implications of this diagnosis deficit (Llorente and Rubio 2003) is the space it opens for criminal policy to be shaped by ideology, improvisation, or emulation of foreign experience—a theme that recurs in several of our cases.

Lacking standard terminology and data-collection methods about varieties of types of crime across regions and countries, and even within countries, the most reliable estimate for trends in criminality is the homicide rate, taken to mean intended, nonaccidental deaths per one hundred thousand persons. The assumption is that, by and large, other forms of crime tend to covary with homicide. To provide a context by which to interpret the Western Hemisphere, the world average homicide rate in 2000 was 8.8; for high-income countries, it was 2.9; for low- and middle-income countries, it was 10.1. In regional terms, the rate for Africa was 22.2; for Europe, 8.4; and for the Americas as a whole, 19.3 (World Health Organization 2002). Table 1.2 shows that the United States, Anglo Caribbean, and Southern Cone approximate the world average, while the rest of the hemisphere exceeds it by magnitudes between two (Mexico) and seven (Andean region). Homicide rates generally increased throughout the Western Hemisphere from 1984 to mid-1994. With Colombia as the main outlier, the Andean region registered the fastest increase (over 100 percent) and the highest overall rates (51.9), followed by Central America and the Latin Caribbean, up 20.6 percent to 21.1.

Table 1.3 shows that in the countries examined in this book, homicide rates peaked in the early 1990s and subsequently declined (with the exceptions of Argentina and Brazil, which registered considerable increases, and Colombia, which held steady at a rate eight times the world average).

National averages, however, mask important subnational patterns. First, the homicide rates in certain urban regions are far above the national averages. Brazil's national homicide rate was 25 in 1999, but much higher in ma-

1.2 Homicide rates in North and Latin America and the Caribbean, 1984 and 1994 (per 100,000 inhabitants)

Regions	1984	1994
Central America and Latin Caribbean	17.5	21.1
Andean region	25.2	51.9
Anglo Caribbean	5.2	8.7
Southern Cone	5.4	6.2

Source: Arriagada and Godoy (1999, 17); Federal Bureau of Investigation, Index of Crime 1982-2001, http://www.fbi.gov/filelink.html?file=/ucr/cius_00/xl/00tbl01.xls.

jor cities: for example, Recife 65.4, São Paulo 51.1, and Rio de Janeiro 37.8.[3] Second, violence tends to be concentrated among young men in the ten- to twenty-nine-year age bracket. In this respect, Latin America has the world's highest homicide rates, as seen in Colombia (84.4) and El Salvador (50.2) (World Health Organization 2002). Closely related to this is a phenomenon reported by several of our contributors, that is, there are strong indicators of a culture of violence among young, mostly urban, males.

Victimization surveys are a useful tool to assess crime situations cross-nationally and over time. However, for a variety of reasons, such as cost, political sensitivity, and distortion by media, there is little experience with such surveys in the region (with the United States as a clear exception). Lacking reliable comparative data, we can report specific results for national cases, which can provide a partial impression of overall tendencies.

In the countries included in this volume, we have victimization surveys for Chile, Colombia, El Salvador, and the United States.[4] In all of these cases the surveys were done by a government agency. For Colombia, El Salvador, and the United States, the surveys were done nationwide, whereas in Chile coverage was limited to the main urban areas. In Colombia, Brazil, and Mexico,[5] several public-opinion surveys were done by private entities for publication in mass media. Unfortunately, in many of these countries the survey items regarding victimization do not relate to the same types of crimes. Still, there is useful information that allows us to characterize the regional crime problem.

Several trends are apparent: (1) there is an important gap between fear of crime and crime as measured by various means; that is, there is more fear than warranted by reality; (2) victimization is increasing at even higher rates in medium-size cities; (3) only 25 to 30 percent of crimes are reported to the police; (4) ordinary, violent crimes are reported at even lower rates; and (5) one of the main reasons given for not reporting a crime is distrust of the police (with Chile and the United States as exceptions).

Crime and violence have an impact on democratic governability. A key trait of democracies should be trust, not only toward public institutions but also among citizens. Citizens in Latin America evince limited trust in public institutions. A recent survey (figure 1.1) found that between 1997 and 2003 public trust tended to decline throughout the region (Latinobarómetro 2003). Specifically, lack of trust is greatest toward political parties and the two institutions that are keys to public security: the justice system and the police. For example, those expressing trust in the judiciary declined from 33 to 27 percent between 1996 and 2001 (Latinobarómetro 2003).

In general, low levels of interpersonal trust are a defining feature of Latin American political culture (Lagos 2001). The reasons for such low levels vary by country, but they create contexts for the development of more social and territorial segregation. That is, distrust tends to discourage citizens from in-

1.3 Homicide rates in six Latin American countries and the United States, late 1970s–2000 (per 100,000 inhabitants)

Countries	Late 1970s, early 1980s[a]	Late 1980s, early 1990s[b]	1995[c]	2000[d]
El Salvador	—	138.2	117.0	42.9
Colombia	20.5	89.5	60.8	65.0
Brazil	11.5	19.7	19.3	25.0
México	18.2	17.8	15.4	12.5
Chile	2.6	3.0	1.8	1.9
United States	10.2	9.4	8.4	6.1

[a]Arriagada and Godoy (1999, 17).
[b]Arriagada and Godoy (1999, 17).
[c]Pan American Health Organization, http://www.paho.org/Engl; Instituto de Medicina Legal de El Salvador; Ministerio del Interior Chile, www.interior.gov.cl.
[d]Pan American Health Organization, http://www.paho.org/Engl; Ministerio del Interior Chile, www.interior.gov.cl; National Vital Statistics Reports, vol.50, n.16, CDC, United States, 2000, http://www.cdc.gov/nchs/products/pubs/pubd/nvsr/50/50-16.htm.

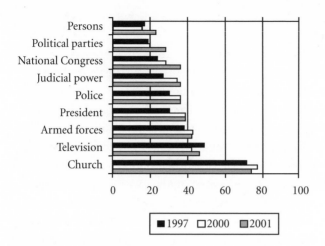

FIGURE 1.1 Trends in trust in Latin America, 1997–2001
Source: Latinobarómetro, 2003.

teracting freely in public spaces, such as city plazas, parks, and commercial establishments, and encourages them to seek refuge in gated communities and fortified homes. The situation is dramatic in countries such as Brazil, in which levels of interpersonal trust were at 4 percent in 2000 (Lagos 2001).[6]

A key issue that characterizes the problem of insecurity is fear of crime. As noted in the literature (Walklate 1998; Rotker 2000), fear of crime is a highly sensitive issue because it affects not only crime victims but also those receiving images about crime, either directly or as filtered by various means. In that sense, a common element of daily life in cities worldwide is the perception of insecurity. Crime in itself cannot fully explain the levels of fear of crime found in most cities. Chile is an excellent example of the role that citizens' increasing fear of violent crime has on setting the public-policy agenda (Dammert and Malone 2003). In contrast to those in Chile, victimization surveys in Colombia show substantial declines in fear of crime. In 1999 about 60 percent of households reported feeling unsafe in their particular city; in 2002 that figure had dropped to 44 percent. The change in Bogotá, the national capital, was most dramatic. Whereas in 1999 Bogotá recorded the highest rate of insecurity, in 2002 measures of perceptions of insecurity declined by half, and the capital ranked last among the major cities (Fedesarrollo 2003). While fear of ordinary crime declined rather steadily in the United States, fear of terrorism—which is both a crime and an act of war—spiked in the aftermath of September 11 and remained at high levels.

Responses to Public Insecurity

While interstate wars—with threats to state institutions and territorial integrity—have diminished in importance throughout the hemisphere, internal and transnational crime and violence of various types increased in the 1980s and the early 1990s. The shift calls attention to challenges to public security, which differs in important respects from national security (summarized in table 1.4). National security focuses on protecting the state or state institutions from both external and internal threats. The external threats are posed by both the conventional military forces of hostile states and transnational actors. Threats to national security may be posed by internal subversion as well. For example, threats posed by organized crime or terrorism can be both internal and external in nature. Responses to these threats usually center on state institutions, especially military forces. Public security, in contrast, involves the protection of persons, property, and democratic political institutions against both internal and external threats of violence or intimidation. In its simplest daily manifestation, public security refers to the physical and psychological safety of persons from threats from natural disasters or from actual physical aggression by others.[7] "Others" may include ordinary criminals or politically motivated terrorists. The primary targets are civilians, although state institutions may be attacked as well. Responses to public-security threats, both internal and external, are led more by police, law enforcement, and intelligence services. Military forces may also play a significant role. Public security emphasizes civil rights and rule of law, which imply both effective governmental law enforcement and citizens' safety from extralegal or illegal coercion by state officials. Finally, public security, like national security in the context of the Western Hemisphere, includes protection of democratic institutions.

Put another way, countries of the Western Hemisphere typically confront a mix of both public- and national-security threats. Both types of threats can take external and internal forms. National-security threats target state institutions and state attributes, such as sovereignty and territoriality, and the responses are typically led by military forces. Public-security threats target individuals, and law-enforcement agencies are the lead responders.

The sources of threats to public security are principally crime, violence, terrorism, and domestic institutions characterized by incompetence, corruption, and impunity. Throughout much of Latin America and the Caribbean, the principal threats are multiple forms of crime and interpersonal violence;

1.4 Issues in public and national security

	Who or what should be protected?	Who or what present threats?	What forms do threats assume?	What are state responses?	What are societal responses?
National Security	• State and key state institutions • Sovereignty and territorial integrity • Political stability and internal order • Democracy and individual freedoms • Economic growth and competitiveness	• Nation-states and state agencies • Trans-state actors, including terrorists, organized crime • Structural, non-actor threats from population movements, environmental degradation, etc.	• Disputes between sovereign states • Aggression by rogue states, especially from weapons of mass destruction • Corruption by organized crime, especially drug trafficking • Attacks by transnational terrorists or by domestic terrorists	• State-centered responses: military, diplomatic, and intelligence • Coalition building • Regional cooperation (bilateral and multilateral approaches to drug trafficking and terrorism, as well as increasing intelligence sharing)	• Mobilization (e.g., citizen support for defense activities) • Vigilance
Public Security	• Personal safety • Personal assets and goods • Rule of law • Democratic institutional development	• External and internal organized crime, especially drug trafficking • Weak internal institutions (e.g., inefficiency, poor training, inadequate resources) • Common crime • Urban violence • Terrorists	• Instrumental, targeted violence and intimidation in public spaces • Diffuse violence by individuals and gangs • Domestic violence • Corruption • Official impunity and predatory law enforcement • Disregard for basic civil and human rights	• Control, prevention of crime • Strengthen army, security forces and police • Outsource security to private sector • Coalition building, regional cooperation • State reforms (e.g., legal framework, police, judiciary) • Increase of prison population	• Citizen participation in public programs • Citizen participation in community organizations and programs • Self-defense and vigilantism • Culture of lawfulness
Citizen, Inhabitant, Human Security	• Economic sufficiency • Physical and emotional integrity • Political, civil, and human rights • Youth and other at-risk groups • Cultural identity	• Poverty • Weak internal institutions • Demographic change and population movements • Resource scarcity • Environmental degradation	• Poor health, malnutrition • Corruption • Targeted and diffuse violence • Emigration/ Immigration • Pollution • Natural disasters	• State reform (e.g., improved efficiency; anticorruption efforts) • Expanded social services (e.g., health and education) • Expanded regulation (e.g., environmental protection)	• Building citizen participation, community organization, culture of lawfulness

these threats peaked in the mid-1990s and have remained at a comparatively high level into the twenty-first century. The region also suffers from corrupt and inefficient law-enforcement and judicial institutions. It is important to differentiate between national and public security in countries that have suffered dictatorships and that are struggling to improve law enforcement and justice administration while also promoting human rights. In the U.S. case, crime and violence were significant issues in the 1970s and 1980s but appeared to diminish in importance in the 1990s. The overriding concern pervading the society is about domestic and transnational forms of terrorism. In the U.S. case as well, the concern is the balance between strengthening security and protecting civil rights.

Responses to threats to public security involve both government and civil society. Typically, governments invest resources in hiring additional police officers, and they may or may not strengthen the judicial system at other stages, from crime prevention through investigation, prosecution, imprisonment, and rehabilitation. Additional efforts go toward improving cooperation among security forces, including police, intelligence, military, and border-control agencies. Governments may also privatize some aspects of police or judicial operations. Since the threats are often transnational, efforts are devoted to international cooperation as well.

Somewhat in contrast to national security, public security places greater attention on cooperation between government and civil society. This can assume multiple forms. Some of these are positive, such as citizen membership on police-oversight panels, neighborhood watch or patrol organizations, participation by service organizations in safety training and crime-prevention measures, and the like. Public security requires active civic involvement and the awareness that a civic culture of lawfulness is needed to complement public efforts to construct a society in which the rule of law can be achieved.

Civic involvement can assume negative forms as well, which can undermine the rule of law. Passive negative forms include the tendency toward self-protection through gated communities, fortification of private homes, and expanded acquisition of handguns and other types of personal weapons. Of greater concern are active-negative forms such as vigilantism or contracting for private justice. Increasingly in the 1990s, instances of vigilantism, including lynchings, were reported in parts of Latin America and the Caribbean. Also, it is not uncommon for government police officers to participate in private security. This can take authorized or tolerated forms, such as moonlighting as private guards. It can also take reprehensible forms, such as violent "cleansing" targeted against homeless indigents, homosexuals, petty thieves, and others perceived as undesirables.

Several other terms frequently appear in the security discourse. Most of these are variations on public security and emphasize protection of persons, property, and democratic institutions. In this volume, *citizen security* is employed in the Brazilian, Chilean, and Salvadoran cases to emphasize protection of citizens from extralegal coercion by state agents. In these countries, which experienced brutal dictatorships, the term emphasizes the legal and real protection of citizens' civil and human rights. *Homeland security* is used in the U.S. case to emphasize that, for the first time since its Civil War of the 1860s, internal security of territory and persons is paramount.

Table 1.5 summarizes the main governmental responses to the threats to public security. Across the board, governments adopted national-level policies, often taking the form of official plans. The general pattern was to adopt tougher, more punitive responses to perceived threats. But a countercurrent of measures aimed at crime prevention and at social rehabilitation was apparent as well.

The federal systems (Brazil, Mexico, and the United States) relied extensively on reorganization and targeted spending to improve federal-state cooperation in law enforcement. Cabinet-level ministries of public security were created in all cases, and national-level police forces were strengthened. This was especially the case in Mexico, as described by Marcos Pablo Moloeznik, which created a new National Preventive Police. National policies in Brazil and the United States were triggered by specific crises. In Brazil's case, Emilio Enrique Dellasoppa and Zoraia Saint'Clair Branco point to the hijacking of a public bus in Rio de Janeiro in June 2000 as a precipitating event. The hijacking was televised nationally and showed, in dramatic fashion, police incompetence and brutality. In the U.S. case, John Bailey emphasizes how the terrorist attacks of September 2001, also televised nationally, traumatized public opinion and led to immediate and extensive federal government responses. The national government reorganized and expanded several national-level police forces, including the Federal Bureau of Investigation, the Transportation Safety Administration, and various intelligence, migration, and border-security forces. Changes also bolstered the U.S. government's access to varieties of private information and eliminated the long-standing separation of law enforcement from intelligence.[8]

In the unitary systems of government (Chile, Colombia, and El Salvador), central government security forces operate directly at the local level throughout the territories. Lucía Dammert stresses the impacts of the perceptions of increased crime on the Chilean public's demands for effective responses. In the Colombian case, Gonzalo de Francisco Z.—who represented Andres Pastrana's government in various negotiations with guerrilla groups in the 1990s—emphasizes the lack of an overall government strategy to combat the guerrilla groups while also repressing violent crime. Edgardo Alberto Amaya shows how the government of El Salvador confronted the task of founding a new democratic system in the midst of economic crisis, profound distrust among various contenders, and an acute wave of crime and violence.

A theme running throughout all the cases is the complicated relationship between the armies and the police forces. In the countries that suffered violent repression by authoritarian governments, the cases of Brazil, Chile, and El Salvador, the recurring theme is separation of the military from police functions and creation of effective civilian oversight, including ombudsmen and other forms of human-rights guarantors. In Brazil, Chile, and El Salvador, however, the army-police relationship remains complex and closely intertwined. In Brazil and El Salvador, the seriousness of the public-security problem and the perceived ineffectiveness of the police are creating pressures to involve the military in police operations. The debate in Chile revolves more around formal authority over the police forces, which in 2004 still reported to the Ministry of Defense. The issue of army involvement in internal security has not been part of the public debate in that country. In Colombia, the continued mix of guerrilla conflict, drug trafficking, and ordinary crime tips the scales toward a close coordination of the national police and the army.

In Mexico and the United States, military involvement in domestic policing has increased in important respects. Problems of police corruption and ineffectiveness throughout Mexico have led policy makers to involve the military directly, for example, in antidrug operations, as well as indirectly, for example, military officers who are retired or on leave staff numerous police commands at various levels. Terrorism is seen by U.S. officials as both a crime and an act of war. Thus, the U.S. military is being assigned new domestic functions to conduct internal defense operations and to support state and local public-safety forces.

Why is involvement of the military in domestic policing a problem? David Bayley (2001, 38–39) summarizes the main points: "The military's mission is so different from that of the police that each contaminates the other. Democratic policing especially is undermined by military involvement, because soldiers take orders from above rather than responding to the appeals of individ-

1.5 National-level responses to public-security threats

Country	National public security policy	Origins of policy	Principal objections	Short-term results
Brazil	National Public Security Plan, June 2000; National Public Security Fund, 2001; regulate portrayal of violence in media	Increase in violent crime; televised scandal of police incompetence and brutality, June 2000	Elaborate decalogue of goals, including coordinate federal- and state-level government responses to violent crime, fight drug trafficking, gun control, repress cargo hijacking, improve public security intelligence	Plan lacks operational objectives and indicators, no evaluation, plan is mainly symbolic, vested political interests shape or resist federal coordination
Chile	Comprehensive Plan for Citizen Security, 1998; Safer Cities Program, 2000; Twenty Measures to Improve Citizen Security, 2001; At-Risk Neighborhoods, 2002	Increase in crime and fear of crime, early 1990s with newly democratic regime	Reduce violent crime and fear of crime, develop long-term comprehensive crime-prevention plan, increase civil-society participation in crime prevention, increase effectiveness of police control strategies	Mix of punitive with preventive policies, growth of prison population, national application of crime-prevention programs, increased role for Interior Ministry in security policy making, no systematic evaluation of public programs, better coordination with police institutions
Colombia	Neighborhood Security Fronts, 1994; Strategy for Coexistence and Citizen Security, 1998; Plan Colombia, 2000	Expansion of guerrilla conflict and drug trafficking, mid-1980s; Increase in "ordinary" violent crime	Combat guerrilla forces and drug trafficking, eradicate crops, strengthen and modernize police and military, improve police technology and management techniques, increase local influence over National Police	Improved training, equipment, and performance of police and military; decline in ordinary crime, especially in Bogotá; weak local-level security planning; weak information system and overall plan evaluation
El Salvador	National Council on Public Security, 1996; Criminal Procedures Code, 1998; Alliance for Security, 1999; National Defense Law, 2002	Increased violent crime following Civil War	Reduce violent crime, corruption, drug trafficking, and weapons trafficking; eradicate kidnapping; increase civil-society involvement	National Defense Law points to return to old notions of national security, with emphasis on state institutions; weak civilian oversight; improved National Police; improved planning (e.g., statements of objectives and indicators for evaluation)

Country	Policy	Context	Objectives	Outcomes
Mexico	National Public Security System, 1995, with subsequent constitutional amendments and administrative changes	Increased violent crime, including political violence (e.g., 1994); Peak crime rate, 1998	Coordinate federal-state government responses to crime and violence, improve database and information, increase budget in public security, regulate private security	Reorganization; creation of Federal Ministry of Public Security, 2000; creation of Federal Preventive Police, Federal Investigative Police; improved national information system; priority investments in technology and hardware (rather than training); increased arrests and prison population; increased role for military; weak plan evaluation
United States	USA Patriot Act, Oct. 2001; Department of Homeland Security, June 2002	Terrorist attacks, Sept. 2001	Reorganize federal security apparatus, strengthen law-enforcement legislation, remove barriers between law enforcement and intelligence, increase public-private-sector cooperation	Extensive reorganization underway, with numerous problems and delays; internal reorganization and reforms to CIA, FBI, and defense; active profiling of immigrant community, especially young Arab males; tensions with civil rights groups

ual citizens; their use of force is much less restrained, and secrecy is a more ingrained mindset. . . . Policing requires mediation skills, the exercise of discretion in the use of authority, and a facilitative style of supervision." Police are expected to know their community and to use street savvy and negotiating skills to manage disputes and serve the public. Army personnel are expected to carry out operations and accomplish assigned objectives with maximum efficiency and effectiveness. Too often, when assigned to police duties, army personnel are not sufficiently trained or supervised to be attentive to civil rights and legal guarantees.[9] The result in many Latin American cases is human-rights abuses. In the U.S. case, the 1878 Posse Comitatus Act limited direct military involvement in domestic policing, although regular military forces have participated in a number of instances. Military involvement in domestic antiterrorism operations is so new, however, that its potential for abuses remains unclear.

The militaries in Latin America have historically played much more important roles as guardians of patriotism and national order than is the case in the United States (see, e.g., Loveman 1999). Armies in that region have long enjoyed special juridical status, including exemptions from civilian courts and justice.

Police Reform as a Principal Response

Feeling threatened and insecure, governments and the public turned first to the instrument most familiar and closest to hand: the police. Their expectation was that a more efficient and effective police force could solve the security problem, and in many cases the public appeared willing to sacrifice some degree of civil-rights protection for greater security. Such willingness is remarkable in those societies that had suffered under dictatorships. Thus, efforts to promote civil rights and government accountability in the new democracies confronted an additional burden.

The focus on the police suggests that there was little awareness by the public that public security as a policy issue is systemic and integrated. The broader policy issue includes programs and agencies dedicated to (1) crime prevention (education, child care and family welfare, recreation, employment, criminal intelligence, routine patrol, community awareness, etc.), (2) crime repression and investigation (uniformed and plainclothes police, criminal forensics), (3) prosecution (public prosecutors, courts, including judges and administrative staff, defense attorneys), (4) prison system (construction, maintenance, staffing), and (5) prisoner rehabilitation (job training, employment, personal and family counseling, drug treatment). To be effective, these agencies should be integrated with other public-sector agencies and with civil society. Relying on greater police presence and more crime repression produced many more convictions—not always of guilty persons—but had the negative effects of overwhelming the judicial process and prison system and of relegating rehabilitation to a mere formality. The overburdened judicial system, in turn, became more vulnerable to inefficiency, injustice, corruption, and abuse. And the overcrowded prison system became more violent and dangerous human warehouses, in which much of the teaching and learning involved advanced criminal skills.

For what is meant by *police*, we follow David Bayley (1990, 7): "people authorized by a group to regulate interpersonal relations within the group through the application of physical force. This definition has three essential parts: physical force, internal usage and collective authorization." Police are the executive agents of force; they are authorized to apply it. Internal usage helps distinguish police from military forces. Authorization "is necessary in order to exclude from the term *police* persons who use force within a society for non-collective purposes" (8), such as, for example, robbers, terrorists, and—on occasion—parents and schoolyard bullies. The key is that the police derive authority from the social units that sponsor them. With the exception of the chapter on Mexico, the focus of this book is on the formal-legal police, especially the uniformed forces.

Bayley's approach signals two recurring themes in the study of the police in the Americas. First, the difference between internal and external security has not been sharply drawn historically in Latin America, and military forces have long played the central role in maintaining order.

Second, as Bayley suggests, where legitimacy and authority are in dispute, the role of the police is complicated. This is most obviously the case in Colombia, with its long-running guerrilla conflict, as analyzed by María Victoria Llorente. But it appears in more complex ways as well. Allison Rowland's chapter on police reform in Mexico and the *policía comunitaria* (village police) in the rural areas of the southern state of Guerrero describes a kind of spontaneous self-help by villagers who deeply distrust state-level authorities. The result is tension and conflict between the semiformal community police and the official state force. Azun Candina shows how Chile's much-admired national uniformed police, the Carabineros, allegedly practice a harsher type of policing with young, poor, urban males. The long history of employing El

Salvador's security forces to protect the interests of wealthy groups, according to José Miguel Cruz, undermined their legitimacy in the eyes of the lower social strata. African Americans in the United States are much more skeptical about the observance of their civil rights in comparison with other groups and much more critical of what they perceive to be police brutality and racial profiling of their community, which is the central theme in the analysis by John E. Eck and Jay Rothman of reform in Cincinnati. In all these cases of deep social, ethnic, and racial divisions, the role of the police is controversial and contentious.

Candina's chapter on Chile emphasizes two main dimensions of police reform: operational capacity (police efficiency and effectiveness) and democratic accountability (police responsiveness to political control and respect for civil and human rights). Table 1.6 summarizes the six cases. All of the federal systems deal with regional, state, or local cases, while the unitary systems examine reforms to the national police forces. With the exceptions of the United States and Chile, police reforms were attempted in strongly adverse conditions: the public was demanding quick relief from a perceived escalation of violent crime.[10]

Our police-reform stories involve three arguably innovative cases, that is, the introduction of new ideas, forms of organization, or techniques. A fourth case is clearly a qualitative change, the introduction of a new police institution. Two others might be viewed as incremental, that is, rather limited adjustments to established practices. Paulo de Mesquita Neto's account of the São Paulo Institute against Violence describes a recently created public-private partnership to improve policing and contribute to crime prevention in a metropolitan area suffering acute levels of criminal violence. Joining together business associations, academic institutions, and communications firms, the institute demonstrates a creative civil-society response to improving police efficiency as well as effectiveness. This is a welcome antidote to despair and *fracasomanía* (the ingrained prejudice that governments will fail, whatever they try) regarding crime prevention and repression.

Rowland describes how several villages in the rural southern state of Guerrero, Mexico, confronting increased violent crime, cooperated to counter what they perceived to be ineffective and sometimes predatory state-police forces. The indigenous communities created a local police force made up mostly of volunteers, whose legality is questioned by state authorities. Rowland assesses both the benefits and problems associated with community self-help.

1.6 Police-reform case studies

Country	Locale and time	Causes of reform	Type of reform	Goals of reform	Short-term results
Brazil	São Paulo metro area, 1992–2000	Business community dissatisfaction with police performance	Innovative; creation of new public-private partnership for police reform	Promote civil-society cooperation and involvement in police reform; improve police efficiency and accountability	Improved civil-society involvement in crime prevention and repression; improved police effectiveness
Chile	National Police, Carabineros, 1990–2003	Democratic transition, 1990; perceived increase in violent crime	Incremental; improve police effectiveness, responsiveness to community	Improve civilian control over police; increase local control; increase transparency	Incremental improvement; Carabineros able to control agenda and pace of reforms, emerge in strong position
Colombia	National Police, 1993–2003	Civilian defense minister, 1991; corruption scandals, 1994	Incremental; purge corrupt officers; introduce management reforms	Demilitarize and democratize the police; improve effectiveness, reduce corruption, increase local control	Limited effects; police resist reforms; reappearance of corruption scandals, 2003; police leadership effectively uses the media
El Salvador	National Police, 1994–2003	Democratic foundation in post-civil war treaty of 1992	Qualitative change; foundation of new national police	Reconstitute national police as part of peace process; demilitarize and strengthen political and citizen oversight of security forces	Improved but declining public approval of national police; reinvolvement of military in policing
Mexico	Guerrero, rural southern Mexico, 1995–2003	Increase in violent crime; fear and distrust of official state police	Innovative; regional indigenous police force	Improve local safety conditions; create local force of volunteer and paid officers	Local community support gained, but opposition by state authorities; improved local security situation
United States	Cincinnati, Ohio, 2001–2003	Allegations of police brutality, excessive force against African American community; racial profiling	Innovative; negotiated agreement to new rules of engagement between police and minorities	Implement problem-oriented policing; create new citizen oversight board; new use-of-force rules	Withdrawal of police and African American representatives from agreement; advances in community dialogue and police practices; increased community involvement in policing

Eck and Rothman analyze a significant reform effort in Cincinnati, Ohio, one in which they played important roles as architects and facilitators. The innovation was twofold in creating a negotiating process that effectively involved the major stakeholders and in introducing a technique, problem-oriented policing, that has been shown to be effective in a variety of settings. The outcome shows that innovations can produce mixed results: the police and African American community subsequently withdrew from the formal agreement, but community cooperation in policing was advanced.[11]

Cruz analyzes the case of El Salvador, in which a wholly new national police force was created as one of the central agreements of the treaty of 1992, which ended a horrific civil war. He emphasizes the ways in which police forces serve political ends. In the old regime, the security forces represented the interests of the upper strata and landed groups. For example, national security forces were used to keep order on coffee plantations at harvest times. In the postwar setting, a new national police was constituted with veterans from the guerrilla forces and from the army, as well as new recruits. The process, though ultimately successful, was flawed, and the high public approval of the national police declined over time. Cruz suggests that the reform of the Salvadoran force, while successful in the regional context, fell short, as seen in the return of the military to assume policing functions.

The cases from Chile and Colombia show reform of a more incremental type. The national police of both countries are distinctive in Latin America in that they enjoy relatively high levels of public approval. Candina shows how Chile's Carabineros cultivated a powerful mystique since their foundation in the 1920s and how they used their quasi-military discipline and esprit to recover public support following their repressive role during the military dictatorship of 1973–1990. Police throughout the region have been able to control external efforts to reform them, but the Carabineros have been arguably the most successful. Their ability to co-opt and redefine the notion of community policing is an apt example. To the Carabineros, protection of and proximity to the community—which they have always practiced—constitutes community policing.

Colombia's national police force experienced a significant turnaround in the mid-1990s. It was able to overcome problems of corruption and demonstrate impressive effectiveness in hunting down notorious drug traffickers. However, as Llorente shows, efforts to improve internal organization and procedures were resisted, and corruption scandals reappeared in early 2003.

Fear and apprehension due to perceptions of increased crime and violence are driving much of public-security policy in the hemisphere. Citizen involvement in democratic processes means that politicians are under acute pressure to craft solutions that are seen to produce results. Acting under pressure and with limited resources, elected officials are forced to improvise, experiment, and treat the symptoms. Even if policy science could produce a consensus on the causes of and remedies for crime and violence, which to date it has not, governments need short-term results that can reassure their publics. Thus, public-security policies in the region reflect complex mixes that lean toward punishment and contain fairly large doses of symbolism, such as highly publicized national plans, special new programs, and the importation of ideas from abroad.

In Latin America, we sense, from polls, media coverage, and informal conversations, that the public perceives that little progress is being made to improve public security and that police-reform efforts do not attack the real causes of police brutality and ineffectiveness. However, this sense of *fracasomanía* may be exaggerated or even wrong. Governments throughout the region have worked rather consistently over the past decade to address problems of public insecurity. The six national cases, with pairs of studies on public-security policy and police reform for each country, suggest that the record is more complex than pessimism warrants.

Brazil's Public-Security Plans

. . . .

Emilio Enrique Dellasoppa and Zoraia Saint'Clair Branco

In 1995 General Nilton Cerqueira, then secretary of public security for Rio de Janeiro, entrusted the task of cleaning up the police force to Hélio Tavares Luz, at that time a candidate for chief of the Civil Police. This dialogue was recorded in May:

> Luz: "General, there is a lot of corruption out there, and I cannot promise you that I'm going to show up and the kidnappings will immediately stop. Even police officers are implicated."

> Cerqueira: "I'm not going to demand short-term results. I only want you to contain the corruption and keep the police department under control. Afterwards, we'll see what measures we have to take." (Benjamin 1998, 53)

Five years later, the Plano Nacional de Segurança Pública (National Plan for Public Security, PNSP), developed by the Fernando Henrique Cardoso administration (1994–2002), was unveiled on June 20, 2000, a week after the hijacking of Bus 174, with these words: "This plan is based on the following principles: inter-disciplinarity, organizational and managerial pluralism, legality, decentralization, impartiality, accountability for actions taken, community involvement, professionalism, attention to particular regions, and a strict respect for human rights. Observing these principles is a condition for success."[1]

The dialogue between Luz and Cerqueira is an example of a minimalist notion of planning, based on a "philosophy of satisficing," which sets deliberately suboptimal objectives and develops a fragmented and antisystemic vision of planning.[2] It is an example of "the science of muddling through," as Charles Lindblom (1980, 67) calls it.[3] In Cardoso's statement, language in effect functions as cover for hypothetical strategic planning for an area that began as Objective no. 28 in the Justice Ministry's *Orientação estratégica do Ministério da Justiça para a elaboração do plano plurianual 2000–2003* (Strategic Guidelines for the Implementation of the 2000–2003 Multiyear Plan; BRASIL 2000). The multiyear plan does not make a single reference to any process under way or about to begin in order to implement the PNSP. The implementation of the PNSP offers a notable example of so-called opportunistic regulation (Donolo 2001), and it suggests the reasons for its predictable failure.

All strategic planning can be categorized as an attempt at regulation, but not all attempts at regulation count as strategic planning. Operation Rio, for example, launched in November 1994, produced no results worthy of mention in regulatory advancement, despite the impact of its implementation.[4]

The Constitution

Article 144 and Amendment 19 of 1998 of the constitution, with their corresponding legislation, currently govern public security and regulate the police forces.[5] However, the regulatory process is not yet complete, and in many cases, it has yet to begin. Fifteen years after the 1988 constitution, the federal police force still lacks framework legislation, as does the civil police force for the state of Rio de Janeiro. Article 144 does not establish a clear and precise definition of the concept of security or responsibility, the latter being attributed to all citizens, with a double sense of both rights and responsibilities.[6] On the Web site for the Justice Ministry's Secretaria Nacional de Segurança Pública (National Secretariat for Public Security, SENASP), the page entitled "Basic Concepts of Public Security" newly defines the terms used in Article 144, notably,

> In the absence of an explicit and unequivocal definition of public security, it is possible to argue from the text of the constitution, that it is a condition or state. It is the government's duty to insure that the nation has it, by providing the services delivered by agencies referred to at the end of the introduction to Article 144. Because of the semantic definition of "security" and the reference to the cited implementing agencies, it seems the "provision of public security" implies the assurance of a state of things in which the Nation will be protected from victimization by crime, violence, accidents, or disasters. It basically falls within the jurisdiction of the federal, provincial, and municipal executive branches to implement the policies, the methods, and the processes needed to provide public security and which are instrumental to fulfill the constitutional requirement.

The lack of precision, both in the constitutional text and its clarifications, is striking. The concept of nation that appears in the clarifications is not defined in the constitution. Also surprising is that the nation rather than citizens is the focus. The texts of the Justice Ministry itself seem to reflect the increasingly ambiguous relationship between the state and civil society. None of these terms has a practical or technical definition in the juridical-administrative field covering public security.

Key Federal Policies and Programs

In the 1990s, during what was characterized as a state emergency and amid plans for reform to improve "publicizing" (a Brazilian version of transparency or accountability) and governability, public security was characterized as exclusive to the government. Public security was considered to belong to an arena of state action responsible for regulation, implementation of actions, and so forth. These topics, accountability and governability, guided the debate and public policies that brought about a partial reform of the Brazilian government in the 1990s.

Managerial public administration had a prominent place in the writing of the Plan Director de la Reforma del Aparato del Estado (Master Plan for Reform of the Government Apparatus), which President Cardoso signed in 1995. The document emphasized the issues of planning and ongoing assessment of material resources, financing, and, in particular, strategic management of personnel. At the same time, under the influence of the Programa Nacional de Publicización (National Transparency Program),[7] social organizations came to play an important role in the implementation of public policies. The *Strategic Guidelines for the Implementation of the 2000–2003 Multiyear Plan* contain no reference to any process already initiated or to be initiated for creating a PNSP. The multiyear plan's first directive for the Justice Ministry is to "create a macroeconomic climate favorable to sustainable growth," and the twenty-eighth objective is to "mobilize the government and society to reduce violence." The multiyear plan's minimal attention to structure and detail is surprising, even given its preliminary character, and it reinforces the hypothesis that the PNSP was prepared in reaction to violent events that had a major impact on public opinion.

The Brazilian people attach great importance to violence and security issues, with only unemployment being of greater concern to them. The PNSP was announced as an action plan, in an attempt to overcome the general perception of inertia by the government in dealing with violence and public security. It is the kind of regulation that is notable for its opportunism, that is, for taking steps based on circumstantial events (Donolo 2001, 37), a distinctive characteristic of public-security planning. Regulations generally do not have the approval of those who are affected by them: that is why policy makers often opt for a technocratic alternative, resource allocation, as Michel Dobry (1986) called it, rather than facing a decision-making process or building consensus, considered politically unviable or harmful to the political interests of the administration in power. Under these conditions, politicians frequently blame a lack of political capital for the failure to implement measures that might imply a possibility for real change rather than a mere "reestablishment of 'business as usual' " (Drucker 1996, 17). The usual policies are recognizably useless except for their media appeal and generally appear in a minimalist, instrumental version: weapons and vehicles.

CARDOSO'S IMPROVISED PLAN FOR PUBLIC SECURITY

The PNSP was the first Brazilian federal-level public-security action plan since 1808, when the Intendencia General de Policía de la Corte y del Estado de Brasil (General Police Administration of the Brazilian State and Court) was created along the lines of the French model. From 1827, when the investigative police force was founded,[8] professionals who were in contact with the public and charged with maintaining public security did not receive any planning initiatives from the federal or provincial governments that would include equipment, financing, or staffing. To some degree, this may justify the Justice Ministry's claim that the PNSP constitutes "the first public security policy for citizens implemented in the country" (SENASP 2001, 8).

The SENASP was created by Decree 3698 (December 21, 2000) to advise the Justice Ministry, to which it is directly subordinated, on the definition and implementation of a national policy on public security. The SENASP's principal task, according to the PNSP, "has been to implement and manage the PNSP, by adapting new procedures as well as by providing new services to the public" (SENASP 2001, 8). The PNSP, created in June 2000, includes fifteen commitments that are to be implemented in 124 steps. It is included in the *Plan Avanza Brasil*[9] and is arranged in four chapters, which outline the commitments that the federal executive is to assume, in cooperation with the other branches of government, the state governments, and civil society. It also specifies the actions to be performed to meet required objectives (Ministério da Justiça 2000, 4).

The PNSP was characterized by an exhaustive decalogue of principles. Its objective was to improve Brazil's public-security system. It proposed to do so by integrating security policy with social policy and community action as a way of preventing and repressing crime and reducing impunity while increasing security, peace for the Brazilian public, and recuperation of confidence in Brazil's institutions. All of this was to be achieved rigorously within the spirit of government reform, as defined by the Cardoso administration. In accord with guidelines in any basic planning manual, the fundamental elements were present, beginning with establishment of objectives so that a strategic plan could be elaborated, which would include policy guidelines about how to pursue public security in Brazil. However, because of the lack of any reference to the plan in the Justice Ministry's original strategic guidelines, one can deduce that the PNSP was conceived, in the best-case scenario, at the beginning of 2000, six years after Cardoso took office, and out of necessity.

To accomplish the intended results, the plan called for the participation of a vast number of agencies: the Office of the President, through the Casa Civil; the Justice Ministry, through its executive secretary; the Federal Police Department and the Department of Federal Transit Police; the Planning, Budget, and Management Ministry; the Federal Economic Fund; the Brazilian Reinsurance Institute; the National Council for Scientific and Technological Development; the Foundation for Coordination and Training of Managers; the National Congress; the Public Ministry; the provincial justice and security secretariats; universities and other institutions of higher learning; and NGOs involved in training and research on police administration.

The PNSP included measures that fell within the federal government arena; these promoted cooperation between the federal and provincial governments and were of a regulatory and institutional character. The federal-level measures took the form of commitments to (1) fight drug trafficking and organized crime, (2) disarm the public and enforce gun control, (3) repress robbery of cargo and improve highway security, (4) implement a system of public-security intelligence, (5) extend witness-protection and crime-victim programs, and (6) regulate the portrayal of violence in the media.

Chapter 2 of the PNSP outlined the measures that the federal government will support, in the sense of cooperating with provincial governments and civil society and stimulating their involvement. Commitment no. 7 mandates reducing urban violence; no. 8, counteracting gangs and fighting social disorder; no. 9, eliminating multiple homicides (*chacinas*) and summary executions; no. 10, combating rural violence; no. 11, strengthening measures in the

National Program for Human Rights; no. 12, providing professional training and equipment for the police; and no. 13, improving the prison system. The regulatory measures called for the government to improve legislation (no. 14) and, as an institutional measure, implement the National System for Public Security (no. 15). Specific PNSP measures included

- creation of the National Public Security Fund, for financing the reequipping, restructuring, and professional training of the police, as well as the actions foreseen in the plan

- support for training of provincial police officers and incentives for community policing, with an eye to supporting and standardizing training for provincial police forces

- programs to support the provincial police, which would provide incentives to launch actions of a social character

- reequipment of the provincial police, making resources available in return for the provincial governments' commitment to and actions advancing the PNSP objectives

- support for the creation of police auditors (*ouvidorias*) as a mechanism of external control and channel for citizens' claims (Serviço de Atendimento ao Cliente [Client Attention Service])

- execution of administrative tasks by external agents in the police force, stimulating the outsourcing of bureaucratic-administrative services[10]

- creation of a special corps to combat impunity

In February 2002, confronting criticism charging that the PNSP was nothing more than a plan for distributing financial resources, President Cardoso claimed that the plan was not only intended to transfer funding to the states but also to create projects of a social nature in the context of training police officers.

The PNSP could not ignore the lack of standardization among the police training programs in Brazil's various states, and it demonstrates clear concern for creating standardized training for civil and military police. The *Balanço de 500 dias de PNSP—Balanço Consolidado de Destaques* (Evaluation of 500 Days of PNSP—Consolidated Evaluation of Achievements; Ministério da Justiça 2001), referring to Commitment no. 7 in Action no. 51, describes as ongoing the implementation of joint courses for police officer training and qualification at all levels in the two agencies, adopting, when necessary, the

Basic Curriculum for Public Security Professionals, developed by the Justice Ministry. Also included here is the implementation of training centers for the two police forces (i.e., uniformed, or preventive, and investigative).[11]

The June 2001 report, *Resultado de um Ano do Plano Nacional de Segurança Pública: Resultado de un Año del Plan Nacional de Seguridad Pública* (National Public Security Plan: First-Year Results), provided descriptive tables on PNSP actions that had been effectively fulfilled and those for which partial results were achieved. The *Informe de Gestión del Ejercicio 2001* (2001 Report on the Management of Implementation) includes a technical file on the Citizen Security Program, a list of seventeen measures that were accomplished, a table summarizing the budgetary line items authorized for SENASP investments, a list of decentralized resources for the provinces and municipalities, and a list of signed accords and other projects. In addition, it includes appendixes with tables on expenditures and additional information on the Sistema de Integración Nacional de Informaciones de Justicia y Seguridad Pública (National Integrated Justice and Public Security Information System), the Federal Training Program for Public Security Professionals, and Financial Flows for Projects Financed with External Funding.

THE NATIONAL PUBLIC SECURITY FUND

The *SENASP Management Report for 2000*, covering the PNSP's first 180 days, was written in February 2001. Action no. 93 established the Fundo Nacional de Segurança Pública (National Public Security Fund, FNSP), whose objective was "to support public security projects that are the responsibility of the provincial governments and the Federal District, and those of municipalities, where municipal police forces exist" (SENASP 2001, 7).[12] In its 2002 budget, the National Treasury allocated approximately US$146.8 million to the FNSP. The fund also financed provincial training programs, but release of the funding was conditioned on recipients' using the *Basic Curriculum for Federal Training Program for Public Security Professionals* and meeting requirements the Justice Ministry had set for the accomplishment of the PNSP objectives.

Table 2.1 compares the investments made in the final years of the Cardoso administration with the investments during the first year of the da Silva administration (2002–2006), based on the per capita value in U.S. dollars by year and by month. (The exchange rate used for the conversion is based on the value of the U.S. dollar at the time the expenditure was approved.) According to information provided by the national secretary for public security,

Luiz Eduardo de Mello Soares, the agency had approximately R$404 million to invest in 2003 (about US$114.7 million or US$0.054 per inhabitant per month) as of July 1, 2003.

The da Silva administration's financial situation is precarious, and strategic planning is based on extremely limited financial resources. At the rate of five cents per person per month, FNSP operates with only about one-third of what was allocated in the previous administration under similar circumstances; thus, it seems realistic to be skeptical about the anticipated results, particularly because the states are not actually using the resources that were freed up by the FNSP during 2001 and 2002. According to Secretary Soares, as of June 30, 2003, 93 percent of the funds made available by the secretariat during those years remained unused.[13] By December 14, 2003, only 14.5 percent of that year's budget was actually spent by the federal government.[14]

THE TASK FORCE ON ORGANIZED CRIME

The Cardoso administration introduced the idea of using task forces to combat violence and organized crime. The first experiment with this was supposed to be in Rio de Janeiro, after a group led by the drug trafficker known as Elias Maluco kidnapped and murdered journalist Tim Lopes. The experiment was not implemented. In both Rio de Janeiro and Espírito Santo states, the task forces were soon forgotten. This was because of the dilution of responsibilities between the provinces and the federal government, which in

2.1 National fund for public security

Per capita allocations (2000–2002) and projected allocations (2003)

Year	Allocation (US$)	Total population (Brazil)[a]	Per capita/year (US$)	Per capita/month (US$)
2000	160,915,634.17	170,143,121	0.946 (5 months)	0.189
2001	207,903,425.51	172,385,826	1.206	0.101
2002	146,813,653.00	174,632,960	0.841	0.070
2003	114,694,526.46	176,876,443	0.648	0.054

Note: The US$/R$ exchange rate is based on the opening rate for the year, with the exception of 2000, when the July exchange rate is used.
[a]Data are from the Censo Demográfico 2000 and from projections by the Popclock of the Instituto Brasileiro de Geografía e Estatística for 2001–2003, http://www.ibge.gov.br.

practice translated into a lack of legal measures for effective implementation,[15] and also because, with growing budgetary problems, political will to implement them was missing.[16]

A wide array of definitions exists for what might constitute a task force. For example, Rio's federal police superintendent Marcelo Itagiba believes that the collaboration of efforts that the da Silva administration is building between the federal and provincial arenas constitutes a new task force. "The task force is like a Brazilian soccer selection, with the best players, that has the best knowledge, and this team is united to play together. I do not see another way of combating crime than by joining forces at a regional and national level, fighting against a common enemy" (*OESP Online*, February 27, 2003).

The fate of the task forces has also been related to their ephemeral character. For example, Secretary Soares recently opposed them precisely because of their impermanence.[17] The ad hoc and temporary nature of the task forces indicates that they were used merely to satisfy public opinion in states facing crises. However, the difficulty in implementing them effectively is also due to the political realities of public-security matters. For example, some politicians are elected in areas controlled by drug trafficking, and the politicians must negotiate with the traffickers. These negotiations would be more difficult if the federal government became directly involved in local law enforcement, because federal officials are less interested in local political realities.[18] Use of task forces would require major political articulations at the federal and provincial levels that would take into account the interests of the many affected sectors, such as local politicians, civil and military police, and the judiciary. The armed forces could provide major political support to the task-force proposal, since that option would remove them from the unwanted complexities of acting as a police force, with the inevitable erosion of their image that this implies. In one police intervention, for example, soldiers killed a school teacher at a checkpoint, under unexplained circumstances. The implementation of the task forces can be seen as a way of dealing with the constitutional question of the attributes of both the federal and provincial police forces.

CIRCUMSTANTIAL MEASURES WITH FEW RESULTS

In addition to the task forces, during the Cardoso administration packages of public-security measures were announced. In general, the purpose was to reduce coordination problems originating in constitutional rules, such as that contained in Article 144, which clearly established different responsibilities for the civil and military police (i.e., investigative and preventive functions, respectively), as applied to each of Brazil's states. As the "unification of the police forces" requires a prior constitutional modification, different sets of more-or-less artificial measures are put into practice, on a case-by-case basis, to try to get around this problem. In each case, practical solutions must be negotiated that take into account the corporate, that is, bureaucratic and institutional, interests of all the involved actors.

The package published on August 9, 2002, included two provisional measures and proposed laws. In the Brazilian system the president can immediately implement a provisional measure, which must be periodically confirmed by the Congress, while the proposed laws on the same matters go through the legislative process. The 2002 package aimed to help the provinces confront public-security problems, the prison crisis (by diminishing organized-crime activities within prisons, some of which are dominated by various crime syndicates that run their operations from jail), and the crisis in various provincial police forces (by preventing local police strikes, which can spread throughout the country).[19]

The Cardoso administration had tried to implement public-security measures in 1997, also at a time that police strikes were occurring in various provinces. However, it could not get the support to get them off the ground because of resistance from a wide variety of sectors, which took the form of defense of either individual rights or corporate privileges. In August 2002, following demands from the governors that the army patrol the streets, Cardoso appointed a cabinet-level commission to try to negotiate a solution to the strikes.[20] The package included an explicit ban on any type of work stoppage on the part of the civil police, daily fines for unions and strike leaders, and prison sentences of one to four years in the case of seizures of police stations or public buildings. Regarding criminal organizations, the package banned cell phones in prisons and required that interrogations of prisoners take place inside jails to impede rescues by accomplices.

Fissures within the National Congress blocked approval of the packages at that time, given that these contentious proposals affected multiple interests. The influential São Paulo chapter of the Ordem dos Adrogados do Brasil (Brazilian Lawyers Association) joined the opposition, and in August 2002 it came out against the government's plan to criminalize police strikes. Timing was another element that made approval difficult: with the presidential term ending, the states knew that the federal government was in no position to demand the implementation of the measures required as a condition for the release of the funds.

POLITICAL DECISIONS AND TURF BATTLES

The Cardoso administration stoically stood by the priorities established in the Justice Ministry's 1999 *Strategic Guidelines for the Implementation of the 2000–2003 Multi-Year Plan*. In January 2002, an internal government meeting discussed the feasibility of creating a special commission on public security, which was to be formed in the image of the Gestão da Crise de Energia Elétrica (Energy Crisis Management Commission), but this option was not approved. At that time, a statement of the minister of the General Secretariat of the Presidency, Arthur Virgílio Neto, revealed an attempt to reiterate the first of the objectives and directives of the strategic guidelines of the Justice Ministry: "No. 1: create a macroeconomic environment favorable to sustainable development. Directive: Reinforce the regulation and monitoring of private actions." Neto stated, "Success in fighting violence depends on stability." Moreover, repeating the discourse of justice minister Aloysio Nunes Ferreira, Neto reiterated that the federal government was not simply blaming the public-security shortcomings on third parties (i.e., the states): "We created the public security plan, we gave money to the states, we equipped the Federal Police, but there is something that we cannot do, and that is to combat criminality directly. That is the responsibility of the [Brazilian] states." According to him, what the executive branch could do at that moment was advise the governors.[21]

Minister Virgílio Neto explained the reasons for the failure of the plan, given the federal government's limited jurisdiction and political resources. Throughout its eight years, the Cardoso administration argued against constitutional limitations and the pressures from the states and various agencies. The administration's policies ended up being limited to the creation of the PNSP, which never got off the ground as a plan and was barely more than a resource-distribution program for the states and a training agency for public-security professionals chosen by their respective institutions. Public security had been emphasized during Cardoso's initial election campaign in 1994. But the plan was not introduced until 2000, two years before the end of his second term. This sort of government inertia is commonplace. "Mr. Cardoso sent various bills to Congress to reform the police and the judiciary, restrict the circulation of guns and so on, but got nowhere. It did not help that he had nine justice ministers in eight years. Without a strong and consistent push behind the reforms, vested interests were able to block them" (*Economist*, February 20, 2003).

Criticism of the PNSP

Criticism of the PNSP and its operations began to grow when it was perceived that its effectiveness, measured in improved crime statistics, was irrelevant, and that reports on it consisted of a presentation of assorted actions and partial results, without any reference to indicators to assess its results. The Internet version of the June 2001 *National Public Security Plan: First-Year Results* is not accompanied by any evaluation from the Justice Ministry or the National Council on Public Security. Moreover, the Justice Ministry never released the 2002 report.

It is notable in the 2001 draft that civil society again is assigned responsibility for security.[22] Also notable are the rhetoric about indignation and frustration and the preference for allocating resources, given the lack of options. In the PNSP's second-anniversary ceremony, the federal government signed accords with ten states, transferring more than US$36 million to the provincial treasuries on the eve of a presidential election. The eighth—and next to last—Minister of Justice under Cardoso, Miguel Reale Júnior, affirmed during that ceremony that "many values go unrealized because of the government's lack of action. A new focus is necessary—one on prevention and the inclusion of the government as conflict mediator." Ironically, in the newspaper *O Globo* are the following items: "Traffickers Close Rio's Municipal Schools"; "Homicides Increase 37 percent between 1992 and 1999"; and "Survey Reveals Serious Increase in Violence."[23] The PNSP is characterized by rhetoric that is out of touch with reality but very sensitive to power relations among the various corporate interests (e.g., lawyers, judges, the army, and federal and state preventive and investigative police forces) and political factions. The rhetoric of indignation led to the resignation of Minister Reale, after President Cardoso decided not to authorize a federal intervention in the state of Espírito Santo, where the state assembly was publicly and notoriously controlled by elements recognized as linked to illegal gambling (*jogo do bicho*) and to organized crime in the state.

Inevitably, a year after this rhetoric advocating prevention, the state of Rio de Janeiro experienced two army operations to control violence. The national secretary for public security in August 2003, Luiz Eduardo de Mello Soares, accurately characterized the situation:

The Secretaria Nacional de Seguridad Pública was created in 1995, but it remained irrelevant until June 2000, when the National Public Security Fund was created. After that, it became a treasury, and therefore important. But it continued to be powerless despite the professional quality of its managers because there was very little that the context could allow. The secretariat functioned as a checkout counter: It received isolated projects from the provinces, which it examined to see if they formally aligned with the Justice Ministry's requirements, and—bureaucratically—it transferred the money. Vehicles and weapons were bought like never before in Brazil without knowing their real effectiveness.

There was no policy, that is, an assessment of problems, identification of their origins, ordering of priorities, rigorous planning, implementation of evaluation mechanisms, and routine dynamics for monitoring. Without those elements, it was not possible to learn from mistakes and construct an institutionalized system of rational practices, with some probability of progressively improving it.[24]

The "Simplified Table on the PNSP's First Year, by Commitments," contained in the PNSP's 2001 report, shows three columns with fifteen commitments. Under PNSP Actions, for the columns Goals Accomplished and Partial Results, no indicator exists that can be used legitimately as an evaluative tool.

Other criticisms of the deficiencies and conceptualization of the PNSP came from the very agencies that are supposed to implement the plan. Meeting in Porto Alegre in August 2001, representatives of the police forces from all the Brazilian states strongly criticized the PNSP, which, according to João Batista Rebouças, president of the Union of Police Investigators for São Paulo, "never got off the ground. . . . It is useless to contribute money for building jails and buying vehicles and weapons if the police are poorly prepared, poorly paid, and lacking in motivation and support." Federal police officers were also very critical about the PNSP, the PNSP's budgetary cutbacks, and the lack of federal intervention in the state of Espírito Santo.

Critical observers of the PNSP's implementation quickly perceived that there needed to be effective monitoring and evaluation of results, as well as effective accountability to society, rather than a bureaucratic management report. Moreover, some weaknesses were already visible: (1) failure to identify all actors involved, (2) lack of unity among those actors, (3) simple lack of knowledge on the part of some institutions concerning their connection to the PNSP, (4) lack of a proactive vision of the institutions in relation to the PNSP, and (5) absence of a managerial focus for the PNSP. Clearly, the shortcomings in the PNSP were very important. Moreover, the incentive system for participation in the PNSP was almost exclusively financial, and this would be

interpreted by the various actors or brokers within the framework of their political culture: state political factions would control financial resources to
improve their political influence as a faction, without much interest in the impact on public security (Donolo 2001, 38). The first four weaknesses indicated that the entire arena of institutional and political mediation between
rules and actors was neglected or was abandoned because the arena lacked
sufficient political backing to require such mediation.

Despite all the intended strategic and planning depth, in both its development and implementation, the PNSP fits clearly within the frame of the regulators' limited rationality. An observer must also recognize that, despite an assumed commitment to more than ten principles and values, the program was
implemented incrementally. At times, it was merely a matter of "muddling
through" (Lindblom 1995), which, in the case of Brazil, implies ongoing commitment, reconciliation with the past, and the maintenance of authoritarian
and corporativist traditions from which it will be extremely difficult to break
free (Debrun 1983).

This issue will reappear, always in new ways, in the implementation of current public-security policy in the da Silva administration. Muddling through
is the way things operate, the way to get the things done. Here we are dealing
with issues that seem to constitute the "the cement of society" for Brazil (Elster 1990) and that determine what the context allows for the conceptualization and implementation of plans in the public-security arena.

New Administration, New Plan

In February 2002, after more than fifteen months of efforts coordinated by
the Instituto Cidadania (Citizenship Institute), President da Silva's Workers
Party announced its public-security plan, which received ample praise from
all political sectors. Under the leadership of justice minister Márcio Thomaz
Bastos, it is being implemented under the logic of corporatist pressures and
existing power relations. Some objectives, such as having the federal police
report to SENASP and the latter's direct connection to the executive branch,
ought to have been discarded right from the beginning. In politics, obviously,
the struggle to define reality does not stop for a single moment, and at every
step, the provisional answer to that struggle determines what the context will
allow.[25]

The philosophy of the Workers Party plan can be summarized in the words
of the national secretary for public security in 2001:

The minimal agenda to formulate a genuine and radically democratic policy, synthesizing the proposed principles, which I presented in detail in my book, *The Jacket I Wear as General* [*Meu Casaco de General*, Soares 2000], [includes]: *modernization* of the security agencies, especially the police forces (*managerially* and *technologically*, with professional *retraining* as a prior condition so that the policy will be viable—making possible consistent data, rigorous assessments, systematic planning, and regular corrective evaluation—and so that application tools exist); ethical training [*moralización*] (through *internal and external controls*, such as an autonomous public complaints office [*ouvidorias*] and unlimited investigative powers, and *positive inducements* as well as *valuing as professionals* police officers, who are frequently subjected to humiliating work conditions and despicable salaries); and social *participation*.[26]

Plans and Justifications

In recent decades, Brazil has been the scene of increasing violence, placing it in a category by itself in Latin America (except perhaps for Colombia). Thus, state agencies face increasing urgency to implement regulatory actions, whether through classic positivist law or in a broader form that would also include public policies or action by the private sector. However, in that context, we encounter a significant issue related to the state's monopoly on legitimate violence in many nation-states of the capitalist periphery (Pinheiro 2001, 297). Anthony Giddens (2001), in his critique of historical materialism, explores these questions in the case of the European nation-state, as does Norbert Elias (1988, 1995, 1997). Sérgio Adorno (2002, 278) sees in Wieworka (1997, 19) a call to pay attention to the loss of efficacy of the traditional Weberian formula in developed capitalist states. But, Adorno continues, "If that argument is acceptable, then how can the state's monopoly on legitimate violence be located in societies that, in their social and political history, never managed to achieve it effectively and certainly shall not achieve it while submerged, as they are, in the avalanche of globalization processes, whatever that may imply?"

This question relates to the complexities and fragility of the democracies that are emerging in Latin America following democratic transition (AAVV, 2000; Debrun 1983; Crozier 1997; Dellasoppa 2000, 2002a, 2002b, 2003; Méndez, O'Donnell, and Pinheiro 2000; O'Donnell 1994, 1997, 1999). To paraphrase Adorno, if we accept the argument of the limited state, how do we situate the problem of the possibility of public-security regulation in societies where the state, either federal or provincial, never achieved a monopoly on legitimate violence within the rule of law?

To conceptualize a plan implies working with a complex set of elements that must be integrated in relation to the regulator's set of values and objectives and put in motion in a process of planning and subsequent execution. Western rationality synthesizes this in a cycle: assessment, planning, implementation, and evaluation. Initially, the rational planner has to assess the situation at hand. As Lindblom (1978, 27) points out, the regulator does not confront a given problem: he or she must identify it and formulate it, which is no simple task. That assessment, in the case of the plans cited above, seems to have been primarily, but in different ways, strongly influenced by the public's perception of insecurity, as expressed in public-opinion polls (*Encuesta datafolha Folha de São Paulo,* March 10, 2002). The Cardoso administration's security plan claimed to have as its objective "the suppression and prevention of crime and reduction of impunity, by increasing the security and tranquility of the Brazilian public." This would be done in order to "reestablish among the Brazilian people a clear idea of security and justice." The plan created by the Workers Party stated that "security is an asset for democratic excellence, legitimately desired by all social sectors, which constitutes a basic right belonging to all citizens, a constitutional obligation of the government, and the responsibility of all of us. Thus, we conclude: either there will be security for all or no one will be safe in Brazil" (Instituto Cidadanía 2002).

The Workers Party plan's implicit rationale is presented as nonideological. It is also an example of an apparently effective response to issues that have no short-term solution but that rank high in the public-opinion polls. From an assessment uniting a set of values with a set of empirical data on the nature of the system that is the object for future planning, there supposedly arises a rational foundation for planning an attack on the causes of insecurity. Once such a rational foundation is identified, it is believed that the groundwork is solidly laid for future collective action that will result from the planning.

President da Silva presented the Workers Party plan as nonideological and nonpartisan, with the purpose of promoting national unity against violence. In the Cardoso administration's plan, the issue of ideology was not even mentioned, perhaps because of the speed with which the plan was finished. Its opening line states, "This is an action plan." In other words, it was not a plan for deliberation or a simple justification for budgetary line items that the interested parties, whether federal or provincial governments or private initiatives, could argue over at the "checkout counter." A little further on, it tells us,

"This plan is based on the following principles: inter-disciplinarity, organizational and managerial pluralism, legality, decentralization, impartiality, accountability for actions taken, community involvement, professionalism, attention to particular regions, and a strict respect for human rights." This contains the reasons for the plan's failure. The relationships among political actors, the political capital of the rational planner, and political will affect the outcome. These components are not the exclusive competency of the rational planner, however, but rather of the complex set of political forces and institutions that must implement the plan, under conditions that the context allows.

To judge by the planners' proposals, it is enough to have a good assessment, rational principles and appropriate values, and political capital and will to manifest the broadest possible national unity in order to combat and defeat the common enemy: violence in all its forms. It showed unwarranted optimism or naïveté to believe that the plan could be imposed on all of society through its rationale and that those elements would be sufficient to build such collective action.

It would seem to be assumed that the weak rationales operating in the social sciences, politics, and society—through various forms, goals, values, and so on—have been suddenly unified in a rationale shared by all political forces, corporate actors, institutions, and even individuals, to lay the groundwork for a broad national consensus against the common enemy. The observed results encourage skepticism.

We need actors—we may imagine state agencies, complex in their various and multiple instances, all the way down to individuals—who would put into practice the actions conceived of through planning according to the indicated rational frameworks. However, the multiple organizations and agencies affected by these proposals have to implement those actions within what is possible according to their own objectives. Organizations do not have objectives as givens; rather, they are always in search of objectives. Government agencies, NGOs, and companies fit this generalization. At the same time, organizations operate in an environment that restricts their freedom, reducing the real possibilities for negotiation and resolution of coordination problems (Crozier and Friedberg 1977, 54). That implies additional difficulties for the creation and development of collective action. Collective action unfolds in a context determined by limited rationality, according to the concept introduced by March and Simon (1958). Actors in organizations do not commonly search for an overarching view of the best solution for a given problem; thus, the ability to optimize performance does not exist. In reality, actors choose the first solution for a specific problem that meets or exceeds their minimal expectations. As Cerqueira explained to Luz, do what you can and we will see where to go from there. In most cases, this process is repeated indefinitely.

In the complex itinerary for regulation, the logic of the free rider holds. All those who share the same conditions generally avoid taking the first step. Moreover, regulations generally do not have the consensus of the affected or interested parties: that is why so frequently the technocratic option is chosen (allocation of resources) as an alternative to a costly and wasteful process of political negotiation that could turn out to be politically unviable.

The definitive form adopted in practice for a regulatory proposal is the result of a political struggle to define reality. The area of public security in its many manifestations, both in institutions and interest groups, as well as in its social representations, is one of these realities, an object of competition over its definition. It is a matter of political struggle, undertaken according to the rules of electoral competition, which transforms plans into arenas of negotiation for internal factions—allies and adversaries—where all who are involved try to minimize the internalization of its negative externalities.

The almost total absence of the time dimension in the planners' plans and in the politicians' speeches should not be overlooked. No one knows how long it will take for the problem of violence and security to be reduced in Brazil to the dimension, for example, of that in the United States. Obviously, there is no rational model capable of providing an answer, or even a good guess. This creates an additional difficulty. In limited cases, within the natural sciences, perhaps in economics within strict limits, the model of rationality may be applied with reasonably consistent results, where time is a basic variable. In the case of politics, time figures in the sense of amplifying results that are generally unexpected, and the plans are overwhelmed by the present moment, to the degree that often they are reduced to simple assets in a negotiation. For example, among the unexpected results it could be that managerial changes and rational professional training for the public-security forces do not produce the anticipated results. Planners in the da Silva administration are aware of the basic problems that remain and that are going to demand an unspecified amount of time to reach their hypothetical solution (Soares 2003).

The results of the public-security plans that have been implemented up until now are instructive. Virtually nothing has been achieved since 2000. At this writing, the plan being implemented cannot be definitively judged, even though events before Carnival 2003, which culminated with the emergency use of the army to keep order in Rio de Janeiro, suggest some signs of what it has represented. The presumed authority of the state over civil society has broken down, the state's monopoly on legitimate violence within the rule of law has failed, and, in some places within Rio de Janeiro state, chaos (or control by drug traffickers) has been imposed as a social rule. Under such a scenario, in crisis situations, the regulator adapts by refusing to intervene or, as in the case of Rio de Janeiro, repeating military intervention (Donolo 2001). Even though the Justice Ministry considered it to be an emergency measure, it clearly shows that there is no hope for short-term control by state-police forces.

We are again faced with muddling through, a contingent adaptation, included within the framework of limited rationales of the involved regulators, both at the federal and state levels. Only now there is no alternative except to increase the intensity of the army's operations (or of some task force that will come to replace them). Once a course of action is adopted, signals are sent that the interested parties immediately decode as they understandably attempt to adapt to new conditions, and that implies increasing difficulties for later interventions. The states of Rio de Janeiro and Espírito Santo will constitute a field of severe trials for the security policy that the da Silva administration is implementing.

The Situation in November 2004

In the state of Rio de Janeiro, former governor Anthony Garotinho developed a patron-client political project that included an extreme politicization of the public-security area. Media impact motivated many actions. The state declined to participate in the national public-security plan, after the governor pledged he would do so. The political rise (and fall?) of exgovernor and exsecretary of public security Garotinho deserves extensive research. As secretary of public security for Rio de Janeiro, Garotinho performed badly, and homicide rates in 2004 were even worse than during his governorship (1999–2002). The press and the public agree that there is no basis for optimism.[27]

In Espírito Santo, President Cardoso's last justice minister, Paulo de Tarso Ribeiro, ordered a "special mission to fight organized crime in the state of Espírito Santo" in July 2002 (following Minister Miguel Reale's resignation). The mission included nearly two hundred police officers, judges, prosecutors, and public officials and prosecuted several influential organized crime figures, including the former president of the state parliament, José Carlos Gratz. The new governor, Paulo César Hartung Gomes, hired Rodney Miranda, a former federal police *delegado* (precinct chief) as secretary of public security, to work with the team of the mission. Miranda was not previously involved in local politics. However, since the mission investigates only federal crimes, the struggle against organized crime in Espírito Santo has barely scratched the surface.

Federal justice minister Márcio Thomaz Bastos declared that "the country lives under the feeling we are at war." He was talking not about Rio de Janeiro or Espírito Santo, but about São Paulo, where kidnappings are increasing at a high rate. In the first six months of 2004, fifty-one cases were reported. "I think we are not losing this war," said the minister (*O Globo*, November 9, 2004). But it is not clear that outcomes will be different under this government.

Public-Private Partnerships for Police Reform in Brazil

Paulo de Mesquita Neto

Since the transition from authoritarianism to democracy in the 1980s, police reform has been high on Brazil's political agenda. Initially, the main objective of police reform was to improve police integrity and legitimacy, compromised after years of authoritarian rule. Reform aimed at reducing corruption, violence, and discrimination in police organizations and rendering the police more accountable to the law, more respectful of human rights, more responsive and transparent to the citizens. In a word, the objective was to make the police more democratic (Bayley 2001).

This remains an important objective of police reform. However, because of the dramatic growth of crime and violence in the 1980s and 1990s (as homicide rates increased from 11.7 homicides per one hundred thousand people in 1980 to 27.0 homicides per one hundred thousand people in 2000), effectiveness in crime control and crime prevention became another important objective of police reform (Waiselfisz 2002; Mesquita Neto 2001).[1] Finally, in the 1990s, as a result of growing concern over inflation and public deficits, efficiency also became an important objective.

Thus, even though directed toward multiple and diverse objectives and depending on the political context and the coalition of actors supporting it, police reform has been on Brazil's political agenda for almost two decades. The difficult questions are: What has and has not been achieved in reforming the police? What strategies have been more successful in police reform? What can be done to consolidate the achievements and strengthen the process of police reform?

It has been increasingly recognized that the police alone cannot solve public-security problems, particularly in countries with high levels of crime and violence. The judiciary, the legislature, other executive-branch agencies, as well as civil society and private organizations have parts to play. Furthermore, since Brazil is a federal system, the federal, state, and municipal governments also have important roles. Yet the police have a constitutional responsibility to prevent crime as well as to detect and apprehend criminals. Police institutions that are legitimate, effective, and efficient can make a positive, sometimes decisive, contribution to crime control and crime prevention. Put negatively, police institutions that are illegitimate, ineffective, and inefficient not only undermine any effort to control and prevent crime but sometimes contribute to the growth of crime, particularly organized crime. Thus, in new democracies with problems of high crime and violence, police reform becomes a crucial component of the process of improving public security and consolidating the democratic regime.

In Brazil's state of São Paulo, the private sector has become involved in partnerships with the government to effect police reform. As Christopher Stone, director of the Vera Institute of Justice, and Chitra Bhanu observed (2003), the success of police reform depends on internal and external support, and "one of the most promising and least studied sources of external support for police reform is the private business community."

Brazil's business community has traditionally opposed police reform. In this sense, it has benefited from, tolerated, and even contributed to police corruption and violence. During the authoritarian regime (1964–1985), some businesses even supported death squads formed by police officers. Since the transition to democracy, businesses frequently seek privileged access to police services and even hire off-duty police officers to provide security for firms and executives. Even though privileged treatment and police moonlighting are illegal, they are tolerated by government and police authorities and widely practiced, with serious consequences for police legitimacy, effectiveness, and efficiency.

To be sure, in Brazil, as in other countries, businesses have indirectly contributed to police reform to the extent that they have organized their own security forces or hired private security companies.[2] By supporting the growth of alternative providers of security services, businesses have, to a certain extent, forced the police to improve their services. The police needed to become more effective and efficient and more responsive to public needs and expectations in order to compete with other agencies for public funding. The movement toward community policing in Brazil and in other countries can be understood in part as a police strategy to compete for shares of government budgets and public resources.

In the 1990s, however, business leaders became increasingly concerned with the problems of crime and violence, as well as police corruption, ineffectiveness, and inefficiency. They came to play an important role promoting police reform, initially joining other civil-society sectors in demanding improvements in police services. In the state of São Paulo, business leaders moved one step forward and created an NGO that not only became a voice demanding police reform but began to support programs and actions to improve police services: the Instituto São Paulo Contra a Violência (São Paulo Institute against Violence, ISPCV).

Public Security and Police Reform

Brazil is a federal political system, comprising twenty-six states and the Federal District. It has three types of police forces: a small federal police force and, in each state, civilian police and military police, which are the main police forces in the country. The civilian, plainclothes police force is the counterpart of the judicial police in other Latin American countries. It is responsible for criminal investigations. The uniformed military police make up the largest police force. Responsible for preventive policing and the maintenance of public order, the military police force was created in 1970, during the authoritarian regime, with the incorporation of the municipal guards into the state's public force. The municipal guards had been responsible for preventive policing, while the state's public force was a military force responsible for the maintenance of public order. As of 2001, in the state of São Paulo, there were approximately thirty-four thousand judicial police officers and eighty-three thousand officers in the military police (see http://www.mj.gov.br/senasp).

During the authoritarian regime, the three police forces were dedicated to the protection of the regime and its governments rather than to the protection of the citizens. In 1982, as one of the first steps in the democratic transition, direct elections were held at the state government level. In the states of São Paulo and Rio de Janeiro, democratically elected governments, led by Franco Montoro and Leonel Brizola, respectively, began to talk about police reform and community policing. In 1985, Tancredo Neves (governor of the state of Minas Gerais) and José Sarney (senator and former governor of the state of Maranhão) were elected to the presidency and vice presidency of the republic. In 1988, to complete the transition from authoritarian rule, the National Congress promulgated a new, democratic constitution.

Despite the transition to democracy and the new constitution, there were few changes in the public-security system established during the authoritarian regime. The federal, civilian, and military police remained the three main police forces. The military police continued to serve as a reserve for and auxiliary force of the army. The armed forces continued to be responsible not only for external defense but also for the maintenance of internal law and order. Many proposals to promote police reform through constitutional changes —particularly the unification of the civilian and military police and the separation and differentiation between the military police and the armed forces— were systematically blocked by the congressional lobbies of the armed forces and the military police. The main constitutional change was the authorization for municipal governments to create municipal guards, which are public agencies responsible not for policing in the strict sense, like the municipal guards that existed before, but rather for the surveillance and protection of municipal property and services.[3]

Absent reform in the 1980s, the new democratic regime inherited police forces with many problems that undermined their capability to control crime and violence and provide security to the citizenry. The population distrusted the police, which lacked general legitimacy. The police were not trained for crime control or prevention and were perceived as ineffective and inefficient. Corruption reached new heights in the police hierarchy. The population and especially the poor suffered not only crime but also police violence and discrimination.

In the state of São Paulo, a turning point came in 1992. In that year, some 1,458 civilians were killed by police officers. In addition, 111 prisoners were killed during a military police operation to contain a rebellion in the Carandiru Penitentiary, in the city of São Paulo, an operation widely publicized in the media as the Massacre of Carandiru.[4] Also in 1992, an internal evaluation conducted by the military police concluded that the organization was obsolete (Aldarvis 2003).

A working group formed in 1993 by military police officers and civilians presented a proposal for "the implementation of a community policing model, in partnership with diverse public and private actors, to search for possible solutions for community problems in the area of public security" (Polícia Militar do Estado de São Paulo 1993). An external evaluation conducted by McKinsey and Company in the following year concluded that the military police had management problems, particularly in the areas of human resources and customer relations, and obsolete processes (Aldarvis 2003).

For the first time, there were indications of support for police reform from within the ranks. The police signaled their growing concern about community problems in the area of public security and about their effectiveness and efficiency in crime control and prevention. New strategies for police reform were discussed, centered on concepts of community policing and involving management and operational changes, rather than constitutional or formal legal changes. Furthermore, these initiatives were appearing at the state level rather than at the national.

Even so, little happened before 1997. The most significant change prior to this was the creation of the Police Ombudsman in the state of São Paulo in 1995, an institution subsequently created also in the states of Rio de Janeiro, Minas Gerais, Rio Grande do Sul, and Pará. The Police Ombudsman is an independent institution responsible for receiving and monitoring the investigation of complaints against police officers. Even though they lack the power to investigate complaints, the ombudsman agencies provided a unique opportunity for the population and even police officers themselves to participate in the process of police reform by providing information on different types of problems affecting both the civilian and military police, problems often unknown to police and government authorities. Despite insufficient resources and strong resistance and even opposition from the police leadership, these ombudsman agencies have gained force and played an important role in the process of police reform.[5]

Media scandal again enlivened the reform process in March 1997. Military police officers were videotaped, on three consecutive nights, threatening, beating, and stealing money from people, even shooting a person, near the Favela Naval, a shantytown in the city of Diadema in the metropolitan area of São Paulo. The videotape was shown repeatedly on national television, and the distrust toward the police reached new heights. A few months later, in June–July 1997, as a result of conflicts over pay, working conditions, and government policies, police strikes erupted in many states and the armed forces had to intervene to restrain police strikes in nine states.

Also in 1997, the governor of the state of São Paulo, Mario Covas, changed the commander general of the military police. The new commander created a community-policing commission, formed by representatives from the military police, the civilian police, and the community, and the police adopted a community-policing philosophy. Furthermore, the military police initiated a total quality management program, providing training in total quality management for police officers.

The São Paulo case illustrates how the coincidence of perception of crisis along with new ideas for remedies can lead to interesting innovations. In May 1997, Globo Television and the Center for the Study of Violence of the University of São Paulo organized an international conference on urban violence in Brazil.[6] The conference produced a report stressing the importance of a series of actions to improve public security, including the creation of a police foundation, capable of mobilizing the business community, to provide support for police reform and improvements in police service. In November 1997, the main business associations in the state of São Paulo joined forces with Globo Television and the Center for the Study of Violence and created the ISPCV.

Public-Private Partnership for Police Reform

The decision of business associations and firms to join forces, to create the ISPCV and play an active role in police reform represented a major change from their traditional investment only in their immediate private security and sporadic demands that the government improve police services to an investment in police reform and public security.

Multiple factors influenced the process that led to this change. First, there were enlightened business leaders who perceived the need for police reform. Their support was crucial for the creation and sustainability of the institute. Second, high levels of crime and violence in the society reduced the incentives for foreign and domestic investments, undermined the foundations of economic development, and aggravated social problems, clearly not helpful to businesses. A study made by the Inter-American Development Bank indicated that the cost of violence in Brazil reached 10.5 percent of the country's gross domestic product (GDP), including 1.9 percent in health costs; 3.6 percent in public and private security and criminal justice; 3.4 percent in reduced investment, productivity, employment, and consumption; and 1.6 percent in losses as a result of robberies, thefts, extortion, and corruption (Londoño and Guerrero 1999; see also Ayres 1998). Third, private security, despite significant growth in the 1990s, remained expensive and hardly up to the task of protecting businesses, business executives, or their families. Fourth, the media and the press increasingly emphasized the social responsibility of businesses in different areas, including the area of public security, and NGOs were created to promote the social responsibility of businesses.[7]

Business associations and firms with different and sometimes conflicting interests, from diverse areas of industry, commerce, banking, insurance, transport, and advertising, among others, had to overcome a collective-action problem to join forces and act together in the area of public security.[8] However, with their willingness to take the initiative to promote police reform and improve public security, the creation of an NGO could produce significant benefits. Businesses could share the costs of participation in the process of police reform. Second, they could increase their legitimacy and political influence. Third—and very important in the struggle against organized crime and police corruption—an NGO provided a certain degree of anonymity and protection for its members against criminals and against police officers not interested in police reform.

The state of São Paulo produces approximately 35 percent of Brazil's GDP. The most powerful business associations and most of the largest private companies in Brazil are located in the state. The private sector grew and modernized under the authoritarian regime, but many business leaders supported opposition parties during the transition to democracy and played an important role in the election of progressive presidents Fernando Henrique Cardoso in 1994 and 1998 and Luis Inácio Lula da Silva in 2002, as well as state governors Mario Covas and Geraldo Alckmin. As the growth of crime, violence, insecurity, and, particularly, organized crime began to undermine the process of democratic consolidation and socioeconomic development, the business community was relatively well positioned to participate in the debate and the formulation and implementation of policies and programs in the area of public security.

THE ISPCV

Even with its strong support from businesses and priority concern with the improvement of police services, the ISPCV is not simply a business coalition for police reform.[9] It is an independent, nongovernmental, and nonprofit organization, formed by business associations, private companies, academic institutions, community associations, and media organizations, with the goal of developing innovative and effective policies, programs, and actions for reducing violence and increasing the security of the citizens in the state of São Paulo.

Among the founders of the institute are the Federation of Commerce, the Federation of Industries, the Association of Banks, the Association of Private Insurance Firms, the Federation of Cargo Transportation Firms, the Association of Public Transportation Firms (all of these at the state level), the National Organization of Business Leaders, the Brazilian Association of Advertising Agencies, the Center for the Study of Violence and Public Health School at the University of São Paulo, the Center for the Study of the Third Sector at the Getúlio Vargas Foundation, the Downtown São Paulo Association, and the Roberto Marinho Foundation, which is linked to Globo Television.

The ISPCV has a council of thirty members, which elects an executive board of eleven members, formed by business leaders, academics, lawyers, and NGO representatives. With an annual budget of US$600,000, the institute develops projects in partnership with federal, state, and municipal governments, as well as NGOs, focusing on four main strategic objectives, which are to seek improvements in

- police services
- the judicial process
- the penitentiary system
- violence-prevention policies and programs, focusing attention on high-risk urban areas and social groups

DISQUE-DENÚNCIA

Disque-Denúncia (Crime Stoppers) was established in October 2000. It is a project sponsored by the business community, through the institute, in partnership with the state secretary of public security, the military police, and the civilian police. It is a crime-stoppers program, inspired by similar North American and European programs. The ISPCV maintains a call center that receives information and tips about crimes and criminals from the public, directs the information to police authorities, and receives information about police actions from police authorities. The caller is not identified by any means, but is assigned a code number to use in supplying additional information and receiving information on police actions.

In three years, Disque-Denúncia contributed to improved collaboration between the community and the police, increased police effectiveness and efficiency in detecting and apprehending criminals, and increased police responsiveness to community needs and expectations. By August 2004, the service had received more than 270,000 calls with information about crimes and criminals and helped the police solve more than nine thousand crimes.[10]

DEMOCRATIC AND EFFECTIVE POLICING

The ISPCV has also supported a series of projects and initiatives aimed at promoting police reform and improving police services. Since 1997 the institute has supported the community-policing program in the military police, participating in the force's Community Policing State Commission and promoting collaboration between the military police and community organizations for the identification and resolution of public-security problems in the state of São Paulo. The institute has supported the total quality management program in the military police, participating in the evaluation of police units competing for the Quality Award of the Military Police in 2001 and 2002.

In 2002–2003, the ISPCV developed the project Policing and Social Expectations, with the objective of identifying different social expectations regarding policing and changes in police practices that were expected by community leaders and police officers in the city of São Paulo. The project included a series of twenty small-group discussions and four larger workshops, with the participation of community leaders and police officers from the military and the civilian police. Despite significant criticism of the police, there was a great deal of agreement on the possibility of improving police services through reforms aimed at the establishment of community policing.[11]

In 2001, the institute participated in a special commission established by the State Secretariat of Public Security to develop strategies to reduce the number of deaths and injuries resulting from police actions. The special commission was composed of representatives from the civil police, the forensic police, the military police, the police ombudsman, the Center for the Study of Violence, and the institute, which represented the NGOs in the commission. The institute also participated in a special council established by the State Secretariat of Public Security, formed by NGOs and academic institutions, to study and develop crime-prevention strategies integrating the police and other state agencies. In both the commission and the council, the institute strengthened the voice of NGOs and, particularly, of business associations in the formulation and implementation of public-security policies.

In 2001–2002, the institute supported the use of computerized crime mapping in the development, monitoring, and evaluation not only of police strategies for crime control but also of crime-prevention strategies implemented by state and municipal governments and NGOs. In 2002, with the Metropolitan Forum for Public Security, the institute mediated an agreement between the state government and the municipal governments of the thirty-nine cities in the metropolitan region of São Paulo. Through this agreement, the state began to provide access to crime-mapping tools and city governments began to use these tools to develop crime-prevention programs (in partnership with the state government and NGOs). By 2003–2004, the cities of São Paulo, Guarulhos, Mogi das Cruzes, Diadema, and São Caetano do Sul had gained access to crime-mapping tools and began using crime-mapping technology to identify high-crime areas and direct public services and crime-prevention programs to these areas, with positive results for public security.

METROPOLITAN FORUM FOR PUBLIC SECURITY

An important facet of the partnership is promoting informed discussion about crime-prevention policies and programs. The ISPCV, in partnership with Globo Television and the Center for the Study of Violence, organized the Metropolitan Forum for Public Security in 2001. The forum is made up of the mayors of the thirty-nine cities in the São Paulo metropolitan region. The mayors meet every three months with representatives of government agencies and NGOs and specialists to discuss and adopt actions to reduce crime and violence, emphasizing preventive actions.

The metropolitan forum has working groups that implement the decisions made by the mayors in five areas: crime information, crime prevention, municipal guards, social communication, and legislation and policies. The institute acts as the forum's general secretary, providing critical organizational support for the functioning of the metropolitan forum and its five working groups. In addition to the agreement on crime mapping, the metropolitan forum has developed a series of crime-prevention initiatives, including a Metropolitan Plan for Public Security; a course on the local management of crime- and violence-prevention policies and programs, in partnership with the World Bank; a course for municipal guards, in partnership with the military police; a journalism prize for reporting on public security; and an annual day of popular mobilization for the prevention of crime and violence (see http://www.forumsp.gov.br).

HUMAN-RIGHTS OBSERVATORIES

In partnership with the Center for the Study of Violence, and with the support of the federal government's State Secretariat of Human Rights and State Secretariat of Social Assistance, the ISPCV coordinated the establishment of a national network of human-rights observatories in 2003. These observatories were formed by youth groups linked to community associations, which were trained to collect and analyze information and produce reports on human rights in their communities, identifying human-rights violations and best practices to protect and promote human rights. The project included the establishment of human-rights observatories in six state capitals.[12]

STRATEGIES FOR POLICE REFORM

Police reform has been part of a larger movement for improving public security by integrating a variety of public and private actors and a series of programs and actions. In the past, businesses supported the police individually by providing money, products, and services for police agencies and individual officers. In this way, they contributed little to police reform, increased the risks of police corruption, and strengthened business control over police services. Ironically, these practices sometimes led to police control over business.

Through the ISPCV, businesses have supported the police collectively by providing economic, political, and technical support for projects that can make the police more democratic and more effective and efficient in crime control and crime prevention. Rather than acting individually, businesses, associations and firms have formed a broad alliance, which also includes other sectors of society, particularly academic institutions, media organizations, and community associations. They are oriented toward police reform and improving police services rather than simply strengthening the police. The new strategy emphasizes the importance of quality over quantity in policing. Businesses have focused attention on reducing crime and violence and on increasing public security, rather than on getting privileged access to police services. The new approach has established more transparent relations with the police.

By adopting a different strategy and establishing a different type of partnership with the police, businesses have made a significant contribution to police reform. Even though the public-private partnership for police reform is new and the results are only beginning to appear, one can say that the police are becoming more democratic (accountable to the law, responsive to the citizens, and transparent). The police are also becoming more effective and efficient in crime control and more oriented toward crime prevention. The police, and also businesses, have gained legitimacy, particularly as a result of the resolution of a growing number of crimes, with the support of information provided by the crime-stoppers program, which is widely publicized in the press. Violent crimes have begun to decline in the state of São Paulo, particularly in the metropolitan region of São Paulo, after years of growth. The homicide rate in the state of São Paulo, which reached 35.79 homicides per one hundred thousand people in 1999, declined to 28.69 per one hundred thousand in 2003 (down 19.83%). In the metropolitan region of São Paulo, where the crime-stoppers program and the metropolitan forum have a strong presence, the homicide rate, which was 52.10 homicides per one hundred thousand people in 1999, declined to 39.19 per one hundred thousand in 2003.[13]

QUALITY POLICING

A strategic choice for businesses and other social actors interested in police reform is between focusing attention on raising the societal demand for quality policing and assisting the government and the police to raise the supply of quality policing. Both demand for and supply of quality policing are important in the process of police reform. However, the willingness and capacity of businesses to invest in raising demand and supply varies across societies and over time and is likely to depend on the nature of public-private partnerships for police reform.

The Global Meeting on Public-Private Partnership for Police Reform, held in Kenya in January 2003, provided an opportunity to compare public-private partnerships for police reform in Brazil, South Africa, Kenya, India, and the United States. In all these countries, businesses are developing partnerships for police reform: Brazil's ISPCV, Business Against Crime in South Africa, Nairobi Central Business District Association in Kenya, India's Merchant Chamber in Mumbai, and the New Orleans Police Foundation, among other police foundations, in the United States.

Comparing different experiences, it appears that Business Against Crime and the New Orleans Police Foundation have a closer relation to the government and the police than do the ISPCV, Nairobi Central Business District Association, and India's Merchant Chamber in Mumbai. The ISPCV has a closer relation to the university and civil-society organizations than to the government and the police. As a result, Business Against Crime and the New Orleans Police Foundation tend to focus attention mainly on the supply of quality policing, whereas the ISPCV tends to focus more attention on the demand for quality policing.

In most countries, businesses know that police reform depends on the supply of and demand for quality policing. It is important to increase the social demand for police reform as well as to increase police capability to provide better police services. The nature and the focus of public-private partnerships do not depend only on businesses' ideas and interests regarding police reform but also on the social and political context in which businesses operate.

In the United States and in South Africa, after its transition to democracy, businesses found the government and the police more open to police reform. The mobilization of businesses for police reform required an alignment with government and police authorities interested in police reform, more than with other social actors. As a result, more emphasis was placed on the supply of quality policing.

In Brazil, businesses traditionally have been aligned with the government and the police, but the government and even less the police have not been open to police reform. The mobilization of businesses for police reform required an alignment with other social actors, particularly university and civil-society organizations, which for a long time were pushing for police reform. As a result, in the state of São Paulo, in spite of the strong effort to collaborate with the police, for example, through the crime-stoppers program, emphasis was also placed on the demand for quality policing.

In São Paulo, the main challenge was not so much to choose between but to combine actions aimed at raising societal demand for police reform and actions aimed at assisting the government and the police to improve police services. As a broad alliance, the ISPCV had to unite groups that had a more adversarial relationship and groups that had a more collaborative relationship with the government and the police. The integration of these groups and their different approaches to police reform was never easy and frequently generated conflicts and crises that undermined the capability of the organization to develop actions either demanding or supporting police reform.

Police reform is only part of the struggle against crime and violence in Brazil. Public-private partnerships are only part of the struggle to reform the police. The business community is large and diverse, and many business associations and firms are not interested in or committed to police reform. However, the experience of the ISPCV in the state of São Paulo shows that, to the extent business associations and firms engage in public-private partnerships for police reform, they can make a significant contribution to this process. A crucial factor is the capability of business leaders and associations to form and maintain a broad alliance for demanding police reform from the government and the police as well as supporting government and police efforts to improve police services.

There remains a question about the impact of public-private partnerships for police reform on the performance of the police. A crucial feature of the police in democratic societies is their responsiveness to the citizens, not the government, and their commitment to equal protection for all citizens. Business support for police reform may help make the police less responsive to the government and more responsive to the citizens, but it does not necessarily help make the police committed to equal protection for all citizens. On the contrary, the police may become more responsive to the business owners and managers than to the workers or the general public. The police may become more responsive to business sectors that are better organized and mobilized in favor of police reform than to business sectors that are less organized and mobilized. Ultimately, the police may become more responsive to the rich than to the poor.

This is not a new problem. Community-policing experiments are frequently unevenly distributed in the society and more oriented toward neighborhoods and social groups that can afford to pay for the infrastructure required to implement community policing and participation in community-policing meetings and committees (Rosenbaum 1994; Greene and Mastrofski 1988). But it is a difficult problem to solve, particularly in highly unequal societies. If unchecked, the unequal distribution of police services, or differences in the quality of police services provided to the citizens, may undermine public-private partnerships for police reform in the same way that they have undermined otherwise-promising community-policing experiments.

From Public Security to Citizen Security in Chile

Lucía Dammert

In Chile, as in many other Latin American countries, security policies have undergone significant redefinition. Thus, these policies have moved from a perspective centered on the criminal-justice system (the police and the judiciary) as a unique actor in the design and implementation of security policy toward a conceptualization that is beginning to include the citizenry.

Particularly in the 1990s, a noticeable increase in reported crime, the use of violence in resolving personal conflicts, and a strong sense of insecurity among the population made it appear that the government was having difficulty confronting these issues by means of traditional methods of control and police repression. Despite the importance of security, advances in state policy in this area have come only slowly and, in some cases, have been contradictory.[1] Remarkably, following Chile's seventeen years of military government (1973–1990), the democratic administrations have found that the public-security debate is still complicated, given that it implies the diminution or regulation of police powers. The questions to be asked after more than a decade of democracy are diverse and complex: In Chilean public policy, what does security mean? Is there consensus around the conceptualization of security? What are the central characteristics of citizen security as a policy focus? What is the role of the police within that focus? What role does the community play? The answers may help to tease out whether Chile's security policy has truly undergone a conceptual shift and, above all, a change in practices, or whether it is merely a discursive strategy that seeks to hide traditional crime-control practices behind a guise of new focus on community participation.

Violence, Crime, and Fear

The issue of violence in Chile is nothing new. To the contrary, several authors have suggested that Chilean society has exhibited clearly repressive and authoritarian tendencies, which would explain the use of violence in various arenas and activities (Oviedo 2002). Because of its multifaceted and dynamic character, the characteristics of this violence are specific to different historical periods. Nowadays, the use of violence is apparent not only in the incidence of domestic violence but also in problems relating to civic coexistence.

Official information shows that crime rates have slowly risen since the mid-1980s, with a clear upward trend since 1997 in property and personal crime.[2] In 1977–2003, property crimes rates trebled while rates of crime against persons doubled. By 2003 crime rates reached a historical high of 2,191 per one hundred thousand inhabitants; information for 2004 does not show an improvement (Ministerio del Interior Chile 2004a).

Furthermore, the first national victimization survey, done in 2003, showed that 45.5 percent of those interviewed or their relatives were victims of a crime during the previous year, while more than 50 percent said that crime increased in the last year and 38 percent said that they are afraid of walking at night in their neighborhood (Ministerio del Interior Chile 2004b).

Also, national public-opinion polls as well as other surveys reveal that public concern over crime has been a priority for Chileans since the beginning of the 1990s (Dammert and Lunecke 2002; Oviedo 2002). For instance, in the early 1990s, public opinion placed greater importance on crime issues than on unemployment, health, or education issues (Frühling 2001).

The impact of fear of crime is an issue highly debated but underresearched in Chile. Undoubtedly, it became part of the political agenda with the transition to democracy, which shows that fear is not always related to a sudden increase in crimes reported to the police. For the first part of the 1990s, the element that was thought to explain this increasing fear was the media. However, although there is an increasing coverage of crime, there is no conclusive evidence of its impact on fear. Some authors highlighted the presence of a political agenda hidden in the media's focus on crime. This agenda was inferred because most media companies are owned by families that were aligned with the previous regime (Ramos and Guzmán 2000). Other studies showed, however, that the media's agenda-setting role is not quite so evident. Although the causes and nature of public fear are still under discussion, the survey data show that a significant portion of the population currently suffers deep anxiety about crime (Oviedo and Abogabir 2000; Dammert and Lunecke 2002).

Security Policies

In general, we can confirm that third-generation reforms (those that follow the initial stages of stabilization and structural adjustment) are essential for the consolidation of the democratic process in Latin America. These third-generation reforms have been placed on the "pending" agenda for most Latin American democracies, given the levels of conflict and controversy that they generate. Among these, reforms focused on security in general and on the activities of the police in particular figure prominently. However, in Chile there is a gradual movement toward redefining security policy, whose core dynamic is evident in three things. One is the decline of political power for the armed forces, which, during 2002–2003, offered an apology to those harmed by the army's conduct during the military regime. This discourse contrasts with the initial stand of the armed forces at the beginning of the 1990s, when they attempted to vindicate their actions as well as their right to impose policies, even against the will of the democratically elected authorities.

A second factor is the change produced in the police, whose role has been increasing as a primary actor in crime prevention and control. Third is the appearance of new actors—such as local governments and organized citizens' groups—which are involved in the design and implementation of security policy. An interesting change is notable in the outlook of center-left political groups, who are appearing as actors interested in opportunities to collaborate and coordinate with the police to overcome (in part) the mutual sense of suspicion and mistrust that came about during the military regime.

In addition to these general changes, security policy in the past thirty years can be analyzed in terms of three key periods: the military government (1973–1990), the transition (1990–1997), and the consolidation of a citizen-security perspective (1998–2003).[3]

Construction of an Internal Enemy

The military dictatorship constructed security policies around an image of an internal enemy that threatened stability and national viability. This promoted a generalized climate of popular suspicion and mistrust and established an official discourse that focused on domestic security concerns. The military government advanced security policies that were directly connected to the National Security Doctrine, used by various military regimes in the region. This doctrine emphasized a militaristic conceptualization of security, and it focused on national defense and maintenance of public order, even to the point of the institutional use of violence. A primary concern of this militarized vision of domestic conflict was the containment and, in some cases, eradication of political and social views that disagreed with the government or questioned its legitimacy. Thus, internal-security policies were given priority over concerns about property crimes; they centered on control of political activity, with the argument that such actions were directed at maintaining national order, even when they threatened human rights.

In Chile the National Security Doctrine included a militarization of police forces, a creation of special units dedicated to repression (including torture), and a definition of the nation as the subject of security. Thus, the military government made a clear attempt to militarize the police, as shown in the transfer of control over the police from the Interior Ministry to the Defense Ministry and the change in 1975 of the Ley Orgánica (Framework Law) for the Carabineros (Chile's national police force), which reinstituted its military character. Ultimately, this dependence on the armed forces made the police the poor cousins of the military regime (Aguila and Maldonado 1996). Not surprisingly, the relationship between the police and the armed forces was marked by the use of the former to repress the civilian population and the involvement of the military in such key areas as the training of police officers and internal organization. In general, during the seventeen years of dictatorship, the activity of the police, according to Hugo Frühling (2001, 28), was based principally on "two strategies: increase in police visibility and arrests without warrants."

Despite the obvious subordination of the police to the armed forces, the 1980 constitution granted the police a significant amount of power, especially in regard to reducing its civilian character, a fact that undoubtedly helped to distort even further its professional role (Aguila and Maldonado 1996, 17). That constitution is still in force, and it covers security in chapter 10, where it establishes that the Carabineros de Chile and the Policía de Investigación (Investigative Police) are the forces charged with maintaining law and order. Both "constitute a public agency and exist to give force to the law and to guarantee public order and domestic security" (Article 90).

During the final years of the military regime, revelations about human-rights violations in which police were implicated increased the public's mistrust toward both institutions, but principally toward the Carabineros. The revelations caused a crisis of legitimacy for the police force that, combined with the secondary role the armed forces had given it, led to a distancing of the top-ranking Carabinero officers from the decision making of the military government (Oviedo 2002).

Urban-development policies also affected security and public trust, since their principal focus was a massive relocation initiated around 1979. More than thirty-five thousand low-income families were removed from downtown Santiago and transferred to the outlying areas, which led to a great sense of isolation for those who had been uprooted (Rodríguez 2001). This policy received significant support from the middle and upper classes, which made a direct connection between poverty and violence (Tironi 1990, 111). Thus, prevention was related openly to the spatial isolation of a significant percentage of the population that was considered prone to violence and crime.

The Transition

Chile's return to democracy presented various challenges related to security policy. The strong presence of a militarized discourse within the police as well as its close relationship to the armed forces gave significant levels of power and autonomy to the Carabineros. Moreover, the public's fragility and sense of insecurity in the face of criminal violence became ever more palpable. Finally, as Patricio Tudela writes (2001a, 92), "security emerged as one of the more important aspects of the media's news coverage."

Consequently, as in the rest of Latin America, debate began over what were the most efficient measures to lower crime rates. The initiatives fell into two groups: those aimed at crime control or repression and those supporting crime prevention. From the beginning, the opposition (center-right) political forces advocated heavy-handed policies that would reinforce the role of the police and strengthen penalties for minor crimes as well as lower the age at which a person could be indicted. The importance of preventive measures for crime reduction entered only peripherally into the discussion.

Security was thus obviously among the main concerns of the transition administrations. However, we can see a change in the topics (from terrorism to common crime) that formed the backbone of their agendas. Thus, for example, during the government of President Patricio Aylwin (1990–1993), the "first task of the transition consisted of achieving the quick and complete return of the Armed Forces to their barracks, and their reinsertion into the democratic political order as essentially obedient, apolitical institutions, professional, hierarchical, and disciplined" (Boeninger 1998, 390). Two central issues were terrorism (by left-wing groups) and ongoing complaints about human-rights violations during the military dictatorship. Regarding terrorism, the government reduced sentences and released prisoners held for their beliefs or for nonviolent activities. The measures adopted were inspired by the idea that security formed part of a process aimed at consolidating and perfecting democracy.

Regarding human-rights violations, the government negotiated the transition so that the traditional power of the armed forces remained intact. Contrary to what the democratic administration had expected, during May and June 1990, terrorist activity resurfaced in Chile, forcing the government to create the Consejo de Seguridad Pública (Public Security Council). One of the principal successes in this period was that President Aylwin "managed to centralize the issue of public security in the Interior Ministry and limit the role of the Armed Forces in domestic security matters" (Tudela 2001a, 94). The central task was to change the doctrine of national security (Oviedo 2002), which meant entrusting the external defense of the country to the armed forces and at the same time moving them away from internal security. Later, the Public Security Council was transformed into the Dirección de Seguridad Pública e Información (Public Security and Information Office) under the Interior Ministry. During the administration of President Eduardo Frei (1994–1999), the political focus began to center especially on the issue of common crime.

JUDICIAL FRAMEWORK

Three categories of citizen-security laws were passed during the transition. One set sought to establish institutions to address citizen-security issues (for example, Law 19212, which created the Public Security and Information Office). Another specifically addressed police operations, including the resources of the police and their role (for example, a 1990 law increased the staffing of the Carabineros to 4,400 positions). The third category was connected to tougher sentences, with two distinct phases: The start of the democratic process was characterized by an attempt to ease penalties and limit punishments for political prisoners (an example was a 1991 law that established the possibility of amnesty, pardon, and even probation for prisoners held for acts of terrorism). The second phase, in the mid-1990s, saw the return to "punitive populism," centered on tougher sentencing for criminal offenders.

SECURITY AS STATE POLICY

During the transition, at various points, political discussion revealed the need for an overarching security policy. The first attempt began in 1994 with the first Plan Nacional de Seguridad Ciudadana (National Plan for Citizen Security), developed by an expert commission of the Coordinating Council on Citizen Security in the Interior Ministry. The media covered the advancement of this plan only minimally, and the public is still uninformed about much of its content and proposals. Despite this lack of information, it is known that the plan established a series of measures to improve police administration as well as interinstitutional coordination, including the need for new coordination mechanisms between the police and government. Serious tension in the political-military relationship impeded the implementation of almost all the proposals. For instance, several members of the Senate who were appointed during Pinochet's regime had clear links to the armed forces and police. Also, the armed forces remained in the hands of military officers loyal to Pinochet and the previous regime. Thus, the first attempt to define a national citizen-security strategy was undone well before a public discussion of its content could occur. In 1996, a package of government security measures was issued that set a specific policy and legislative agenda but lacked a general operational framework (Tudela 2001b).

CONSOLIDATION OF THE ROLE OF THE POLICE

Chile has two police forces operating at the national level: the Investigative Police, dedicated to crime investigations, and the Carabineros, responsible for crime prevention and public order. The centralized Carabineros force has a military, hierarchical, and, with respect to the government, relatively autonomous status (Frühling 2001; Ward 2001).

During the transition, the government strongly supported these forces in their fight against the biggest social problems facing Chileans. Government backing was principally visible in increases in the police budget and personnel. In the national budget, expenditure for both police forces grew noticeably. Thus, for example, the Carabineros budget grew from P\$155 billion in 1992 to P\$204 billion in 1997 (in 2001 Chilean pesos), or approximately from US\$238 million to US\$313 million (in 2001 U.S. dollars).

Although the total number of pesos allocated for security increased notably, the portion destined for the police forces declined. The various justice and security line items indicate the government's priorities for addressing security issues: the percentage destined for both police forces declined from 66 percent to 58 percent of overall justice and security spending.[4] In general, the judicial system had greater priority. The implementation of the penal-process reform included an important public investment in the building of new agencies such as the Ministerio Público (Public Ministry) and the Defensoria Penal Pública (Public Defenders Office).[5]

However, about this same time municipalities began to provide significant financial support, in particular to the Carabineros. In response to residents' demands for more security and police presence, some local governments have begun to provide financing for more infrastructure, vehicles, and technology.

Along with this increase in budget and human resources, traditional operational strategies for the police forces changed to incorporate the goal of involving the community in crime reduction (Frühling 2001; Burgos 2000). Thus, from 1994 on, the Programa Puertas Abiertas (Open Door Program) sought to increase public awareness about the activities at police stations. To achieve that, Carabineros were selected to act as delegates to neighborhood associations, with which they would meet periodically to gather information on major community concerns. Similarly, private citizens and community leaders were invited to Carabineros' headquarters in order to establish more direct relationships and stronger lines of communication. This initiative also resulted in the publicizing of emergency telephone numbers (Sandoval 2002).

Other initiatives were implemented in later years. For example, in 1996, the Programa Seguridad Compartida (Program for Shared Security) had as its principal objective to increase the public's awareness of the importance of its collaboration with the Carabineros. This program had a public-information component and the implementation of joint efforts to renew this relationship. It also sought to better prepare the Carabineros for their work with the community.

PARTICIPATION

In the mid-1990s, community participation in crime prevention appeared as a theme in Chilean security policies. Before that, initiatives were centered on improving police administration; defining a new framework for operations within a democratic system; responding to specific crime issues, such as robberies of financial institutions; and related matters. Nevertheless, the growth trend in reported crime as well as the apparent incapacity of the police to respond to it, or to create a strategy built around crime prevention, showed the need to consolidate and—in some cases—establish mechanisms for community participation at the local level.

Municipalities, beginning in the early 1990s, implemented citizen-security measures that leaned toward private patrolling and neighborhood organizations similar to Neighborhood Watch programs. The presence of municipal initiatives (principally in those cities with governments from the center right) generated a timely response from the national government, which not only proposed community participation as an articulating element in security policy but also emphasized shaping and consolidating of networking over neighborhood watches. Two primary initiatives arose during the transition: the Neighborhood Security Program (1993) and the Citizen Protection Committees (1995). The central government designed and implemented both initiatives with the objective of consolidating existing local networks by developing, and in some cases financing, crime-prevention programs. Thus, the groundwork began to appear for a prevention policy that emphasized local initiatives executed by neighborhood residents.

Emphasis on Citizen Security

Beginning in 1998, the discussion emphasizing citizen security grew stronger until it came to the forefront of security policy. It was visible not only in this period's debates but also in its practical initiatives. President Ricardo Lagos (2000–2005) focused his administration's agenda on the citizen-security issue, but with a new perspective characterized by reform of the justice system, investment in the prison system, and development of crime-prevention programs stressing community participation.

One of the principal policy innovations on the issue of crime control ensures that there exists, in undersecretary of the interior Jorge Burgos's words, full "conviction about the separation between social prevention and police prevention" (2000, 17). Hence, for the government, and especially for President Lagos, there is an explicit preference for prevention, to the degree that this would make it possible to define "citizen security as being the result of actions of various state agencies and sectors of civil society . . . in the framework of a public policy that necessarily must include citizen participation" (speech by Jorge Burgos, August 2000).

Legal Framework

One of the key priorities for democratic governments is modernization of the criminal-justice system. The *reforma procesal penal* (reform of justice procedures) took on a central role in the 1990s. This reform arose from the need to create a more effective and efficient justice system, one more accessible to the public and that takes the rights of victims into consideration. The introduction of oral judgments, as well as the presence of prosecutors and other new actors in the court system, has the potential to improve Chile's justice system. Reform has been implemented slowly and still has not reached metropolitan Santiago (scheduled for June 2005), where most court cases are heard. However, findings from those regions where the reform is in force show a decline in the length of trials.

Another result is the notable increase in reported crimes in the regions where the reform has been implemented. For example, preliminary information from the Interior Ministry shows an increase of more than 50 percent in crimes reported to the police in those regions. This still has not been studied in depth, so it is impossible to guess the causes behind that increase. However, it seems that the reform has resulted in a decline in the *cifra negra* (unreported crimes) as confidence in the criminal-justice system has increased and the perception of inefficiency in the judicial system has declined slightly. Nevertheless, there is still debate over the consequences of judicial reform on the security agenda.

During this period, various laws were also debated that would toughen sentences for lawbreakers. At the end of 2003, a reduction in the age at which one can be indicted was discussed and encountered almost no opposition. Similarly, motions were proposed and approved to increase sentences for certain types of crime.

Beyond the judicial changes enacted in this period, one of the direct consequences of the hardening of the legal framework was the growth of the prison population, which in 2005 surpassed twenty-seven thousand prisoners, an increase of over 48 percent between 1990 and 2002. Attempts to alleviate this resulted in huge public investments in remodeling, maintenance, and construction of new jails (Ramos and Guzmán 2000, 112), as well as a process of privatization in the construction of prisons, which are scheduled to open their doors in the next few years.

Security Plans and Administration

The first attempt to establish a national plan for citizen security came in 1999, but its antecedent was a package of eleven measures announced by President Frei in 1998. The Comprehensive Plan for Citizen Security focused on improving crime-information systems, police administration, and community participation. The Inter-Ministerial Commission on Citizen Security, consisting of representatives from all the ministries and services connected with security issues, was formed to coordinate the various state agencies. Moreover, a process of connecting the commission and the police forces, especially the Carabineros, was strengthened, and the Carabineros established a unitary system for information on crime complaints that allows the government to track crimes reported to both police institutions. This plan progressed for a couple of years, and then it disappeared from public debate without a word about its transformation or demise (Oviedo 2002).[6]

In mid-2001 the División de Seguridad Ciudadana (Citizen Security Division) was established within the Interior Ministry. Its main role was the advancement of citizen-security policies, and it was charged with coordinating with the Carabineros on projects involving nationwide systematization of official crime data. Similarly, the division collaborated on training in general and in developing geographic information systems to analyze crime trends. It was also responsible for community-participation initiatives, which led to the design and implementation of the Comuna Segura Compromiso 100 (Safer Cities Program) and Barrios Vulnerables (At-Risk Neighborhoods), both initiatives that enhanced the role of the citizenship in crime prevention.

In October 2001, President Lagos proposed Twenty Measures to Improve Justice and Citizen Security, which established short- and medium-term goals and objectives to improve security and the criminal-justice system. Most were connected to crime-information collection and improvement of police administration.

At the beginning of 2003, a major debate erupted in the media over whether a national-security policy really existed. The principal policy center on this issue, Fundación Paz Ciudadana (Citizen Peace Foundation), as well as the right-wing opposition's think tank, Instituto Libertad y Democracia (Liberty and Democracy Institute), were among those that claimed that the country did not have a policy that could give substance and coherence to all initiatives in place. The government's response was, in some cases, weak: it claimed that a national-security policy existed implicitly, that is, it contained guideposts for the implemented initiatives but lacked systematization. This debate had a high profile in the media; the criticisms issued by the think tanks were based on interviews and editorials in the main daily newspapers. The disadvantage of the official position is obvious, since the government lacked a communications strategy about citizen security that would allow it to engage the public in a productive debate.

In 2003 the Citizen Security Division also began a process of formulating government policy. This explicitly laid out the guiding principles for various government initiatives as well as the short- and medium-term challenges. Paradoxically, one of the greatest weaknesses in the elaboration of this proposal was the lack of general crime indicators that could help in evaluating information on various issues, such as the effectiveness of the justice system and the police and prison overcrowding. Similarly, no studies were conducted to identify risk factors associated with the recent noticeable increase in the use of violence and in certain crimes. These two fundamental shortcomings led the Interior Ministry to form an advisory committee (in June 2003) composed of sixteen experts on citizen security, which was charged with devising crime indicators as well as a working agenda on possible explanations for the crime rates.

THE ROLE OF THE POLICE

After 1990, the strategy of the democratic administrations was to avoid interfering with the internal organization of the Carabineros. Emphasis was placed on consolidating police operations, maintaining the force's institutional nature, and strengthening its community relations.

Certainly, the role of the police during the military government led the opposition political parties to hold "an understandable and visceral position of mistrust and antagonism with respect to police duties" (Boeninger 1998, 424). However, their attitude changed in the 1990s, from distant mistrust to ongoing collaboration. High-ranking Carabineros played an essential role in defining and consolidating collaborative connections in certain areas of police work. Despite that, major changes are still pending, which have to do with the definition of the Chilean police force.

In general, the discourse of the democratic administrations centered on reforming the Carabineros, strengthening the force's professional character, and attempting to win approval to place it under the control of the Interior Ministry. The latter was stipulated in the Programa de Gobierno de la Concertación de Partidos por la Democracia (Program of Government of the Accord among Parties for Democracy) in power since 1990. That governance program also opened the door to the topic of human rights, with the guiding principle of achieving the common good.

More recently, the Carabineros took a rhetorical turn toward a more professional posture, one that is not political, and a reevaluation of their institutional conduct. However, the force's organization and military structure retain characteristics similar to those established during the previous regime. In August 2003 interior minister José Miguel Insulza gave an important speech that opened the debate over the critical need to create a special ministry of citizen security that would house both police forces, the various corrections agencies, and all preventive programs under its wings.

Despite the presence of a proactive and optimistic vision on the part of the Aylwin, Frei, and Lagos administrations, the armed forces were not subjected to further logistical or bureaucratic restructuring, and significant reductions were not made in their budgetary allocations (Fuentes 2002, 121). Claudio Fuentes (2002) cites four factors to explain why the armed forces were not reformed: (1) the military's autonomy from civilian authority, (2) the political support it gets from the parties on the right, (3) politicians of the center choosing to focus on other goals, and (4) the lack of civilian expertise and technical capacity in military affairs.

The effort to reintegrate the police into the Interior Ministry's sphere of influence did not succeed. The reluctance on the part of the police force itself can explain the government's failure. Top-ranking police officials believed that the Interior Ministry had a direct link to the government's political agenda, so they justified their subordination to the Defense Ministry as necessary to guarantee the political independence of the Carabineros. In addition, political actors on the right worked to prevent the transfer of Carabineros to the Interior Ministry. This opposition was also motivated by the desire to keep the police independent of the highly political Interior Ministry. Nonetheless, the police experienced major modernization, visible not only in technological infrastructure but also in changes in discursive and operational strategies.

Human rights is one area in which major changes occurred. At a discursive level, human rights were defended intensively by the Carabineros' leadership, even to the point of declaring, "We have no choice but to condemn and reprove the illicit acts that Carabineros committed which, far from the doctrine of protecting human life, did everything to the contrary [during the military dictatorship]. Those who behaved in such fashion deserve our repudiation."[7]

In 1998, the Plan Antidelincuencia (Anticrime Plan) was instituted to create mobile police stations to achieve greater involvement of the police in local-level problems. It also emphasized community organization in the poorer sectors of the city and in activities to improve security.

Also in 1998, a pilot program of the Plan Cuadrante (Block Watch Plan) was implemented in the prefecture of the southern zone of the Santiago metropolitan region.[8] The strategy, in brief, consisted of dividing an urban area into quadrants (one square kilometer, or approximately sixty-four blocks), to be patrolled continuously, either in automobiles or on foot. Preliminary internal assessments of the pilot program showed that community-police relations improved and perception of insecurity declined (Ward 2001). Encouraged by those results, the police decided to expand the initiative to the entire metropolitan region in 2000. In mid-2003, the plan was being implemented in various regions of Chile, and it was anticipated that the program would be available nationwide by 2005. Nevertheless, the absence of an evaluation process to measure effectiveness makes it difficult to ascertain the program's impact on the levels of complaints filed, victimization, fear, and other factors.

The police and government also worked to design efficiency indicators to evaluate police administration. These were being implemented in coordination with the Interior Ministry in 2005 and were intended for use in measuring the activity of each police officer as well as the impact of operational strategies.

Finally, Carabineros de Chile began a process of public-accountability reporting in each police precinct throughout the country twice a year. This process not only permitted the establishment of a direct relationship with the local community but also revealed the strengths and weaknesses of police service in specific zones. Lamentably, public-accountability activity did not involve, in most cases, true participation and collaboration with the community. In some cases, these reports were merely formal presentations that did not allow for dialogue to develop between the police and the community. However, some institutional interest, from both the police and the community, exists for improving the possibilities for this kind of dialogue.

All the reform initiatives for operational strategy within the Carabineros had to make room for more fluid accountability and for forging and consolidating collaborations with the community. The community became an important ally of the police for crime prevention, and the role that the community plays in the design and implementation of security policies was recognized. However, the top-ranking Carabinero officials stressed that the force was "charged with social prevention but that is not the sole function of the institution" (Cienfuegos 2002a, 1). The institutional mission was redefined so that the "principal duty is police prevention, that is, to guarantee public order and public security" (Cienfuegos 2002a, 2); the community was left with a narrowly circumscribed role in police crime-prevention policies.[9]

The Barrios Vulnerables united initiatives for police control and intelligence with social prevention and investment in neighborhoods suffering from high levels of crime, violence, and—in particular—drug trafficking. This program sought to disrupt the networks of microtrafficking existing in certain neighborhoods as well as to increase the presence of the government through social investment. As of mid-2003, only four neighborhoods were covered, all in metropolitan Santiago. Preliminary results varied, and an evaluation had yet to occur on the program's impact in each of these neighborhoods. However, this method demonstrates a real possibility for combining the police's repressive control actions with a focused investment in social programs and for consolidating neighborhood networks that collaborate with the government to improve the local situation.

The budgetary allocations trends of previous periods continued. In general terms, public spending for both police forces continued to increase from 1990 to 2003, reaching P$311 billion (in 2001 pesos), or US$509 million. Also, the percentage of total spending on security remained at about 6 percent of total government outlays from 1998 to 2003, but within the amounts allocated to security the percentage dedicated specifically to both police forces continued to decline, as in the transition period, dropping to 55 percent by 2001. Thus, while the total amount of pesos allocated for security continued to increase, the relative portion destined for the police forces declined. Thus, allocations continued to decline for the reform of the justice system that faced the greatest challenge of all: that of the metropolitan region of Santiago, the locus of more than 40 percent of total crime reported to the police in the country.

COMMUNITY PARTICIPATION

In this period, the priority given to the issue of community participation made it a focal point for local prevention policies. Thus, at the beginning of 1998, citizen-protection committees formed in various neighborhoods of metropolitan Santiago to implement security measures, such as installing alarms or community-alert systems (Araya Moya 1999), with support from the Secretaría General de Gobierno (General Government Secretariat). The secretariat implemented training programs for local leaders that stressed prevention and encouraged the creation of connections based on trust between neighbors and Carabineros and the municipal government. Although the national government encouraged the formation of these committees throughout the country, they had their greatest impact in metropolitan Santiago. Despite the absence of an evaluation of the program, it is understood that the failure of neighbors to meet regularly was one factor that may have caused the program's lack of continuity (Araya Moya 1999). Subsequently, the program was terminated.

In mid-2000 the Interior Ministry, together with the Citizen Peace Foundation and the Chilean Association of Municipalities, formed the Safer Cities Program, which encouraged community participation and development of participative social networks for crime prevention, as well as the consolidation or development of local social capital. The goal was to construct a local alliance, which would translate integrally into the Neighborhood Councils for Citizen Security and would open access to grant competitions to finance prevention programs in those communities.[10] As of January 2004, this program was in its fourth phase of implementation, involving fifty-six communities nationwide, or more than half of the national population.

Unfortunately, the role of the community lacks definition. Until now community involvement has been limited to neighborhood watch and similar projects and has not developed into an agenda of community or social prevention.

Toward Citizen Security

Since the beginning of the 1990s, and despite ups and downs in public debate, a new view of security has slowly gained ground in Chile. It is changing policy priorities and establishing a requirement for mechanisms to respond to crime that include participation of the public as well as an increase in government investment. Three trends are clear: First, security as state policy in Chile responds to a paradigm that increasingly approximates citizen security or democratic security and is moving further away from practices connected to the National Security Doctrine. Second, a consensus exists on the importance of security for the public agenda as well as on the need for effective measures to limit the growth of victimization and, above all, the use of violence to resolve community problems. Third, police forces have followed a path of incremental change that has made it possible to include discussion of topics such as community policing and management indicators in the government agenda.

The process of redefining security policy has plotted a new course and is clearly advancing. However, the definition of a policy of citizen security still faces at least four main challenges in the coming years. First is the need to establish interinstitutional coordination mechanisms to make it possible to focus efforts, diminish duplication of initiatives, and—above all—consolidate a public consensus in the discourse on security. Such coordination not only should be realized within various national-level government agencies but also should include the regional and local governments.

Although the relationship of the police to the Interior Ministry has been strengthened over the years, it is essential to continue to insist that the police forces be made subordinate to the Interior Ministry rather than to the Defense Ministry. This move would not only deepen the modernization process for the police but also incorporate governmental control mechanisms to ensure efficiency and effectiveness.

Another challenge is community participation in crime prevention. A positive attempt has been made to include the community in various initiatives. However, that is a double-edged sword since, on one hand, it increases the public's expectations about the government's actions, and, on the other, it introduces conflicting conceptualizations of the role of the community in the design and implementation of prevention initiatives.

Finally, the greatest challenge for citizen-security policies relates to the unstable equilibrium between prevention and control. The public demands more patrolling, more control, and longer sentences for criminal acts, but the government—without overlooking the component of crime control—must have the capacity to establish medium- and long-term goals with emphasis on social prevention and community participation as cornerstones for a national strategy for citizen security in Chile.

The Institutional Identity of the Carabineros de Chile

Azun Candina

The fifth stanza of the anthem of the Chilean Carabineros (Chile's national police force) goes:

> Sleep peacefully, innocent little girl
> Don't let the brigand worry you.
> As you smile sweetly in slumber,
> A loving Carabinero watches over you.

The child sleeps peacefully, unafraid of outlaws, while the Carabinero, feeling special affection for her, stands guard. That is the purpose of the police. The watchful Carabinero/sleeping innocent relationship is not the only one in the anthem. There is also the response to evil and outlaws:

> If evil stalks the peaceful nest
> Where innocence took shelter,
> Let us, the protectors of the weak,
> Fearlessly pursue the outlaw.

The anthem describes the police, those who are between the innocents and the Others: "We are the sun that burns brightly, Carabineros of the Nation." The fourth stanza adds:

> The people live in peace,
> Enjoying happiness and pleasures,
> As we pursue the palm frond
> That we shall win with our sacrifice.

On one side are serene shadows, where those who sleep peacefully lie (Us); on the other side are threatening shadows, evil lurking in the darkness (the Others). The Carabinero is the one who stops the Others from reaching Us. The Carabinero is a continuous light in the shadows. The Carabinero is guard and guardian, even to the point of self-sacrifice. Indeed, he belongs neither to the world of Us nor to that of the Others.

A Unique Public Servant

Although police officers are public servants and officials, they have certain characteristics that distinguish them significantly from others in that category. As Katharine Kravetz writes, "Undoubtedly, we appreciate, fear, and at times, detest the police. We appreciate them when they bring to justice someone else, someone who has hurt us or who frightens us. We fear them when we are the objects of their authority, whether we are caught speeding or are murder suspects. And we hate them when we feel that they have infringed on our rights, by exceeding their authority and stepping on us" (1998, 176).

The police constantly walk a tightrope between order and violence, between the fearful and the angry, between the accuser and the accused. As Claudio Beato and Luiz Antonio Paixao claim, the modern state has found a tool in the police to resolve the problem of instrumental use of violence in social interactions, "the coercive imposition of rules regulating behavior, which guarantee the peaceful dream of Adam Smith's business owner and reduce the risk of violent death that struck fear in Thomas Hobbes" (1997, 2).

The Carabineros share these characteristics. They are public servants, and the central government, with some contributions from local government, provides their funding, salaries, and material resources. However, Carabineros are also markedly different from other public servants. They wear uniforms, they study in special schools for police officers, and they swear to give their lives when necessary to fulfill their duty. They are responsible for an array of functions, including control of demonstrations, vigilance and patrol duty, delivery of court orders, crime prevention, traffic control, personal protection, border patrol, emergency services, and—for special units—investigative duties, drug-trafficking control, and intelligence gathering. Other government agencies typically do not have martyrs or, if they do, we do not hear about them.[1] A Carabinero may not participate in party politics, form a union, or go out on strike. Thus, the Carabinero anthem, more than a mere poem, appears to be a key to decipher the uniqueness of police work.

Police Studies in Latin America and Chile

It has become a cliché to say that studies on policing in Latin America are in short supply and inferior to what is available for Europe and North America. In the most general terms, the treatment of Latin American policing falls into two categories. First, we have studies on the increase in insecurity and crime at a hemispheric level, especially in the fields of sociology, public administration, and political science. For those who have tried to propose alternative solutions to the disturbing increase in crime during the last third of the twentieth century, the police institution is an actor that can hardly be ignored, and it is, indeed, the institution that most frequently receives the blame or the credit for increases or decreases in crime rates.[2] These studies have reached several broad conclusions:

1. Latin American police forces, for the most part, are poorly paid and poorly trained, come from a military and authoritarian tradition, and have little legitimacy in the eyes of the public. Consequently, they have been poorly prepared to confront the increase in crime and violence.

2. To make these police forces a useful instrument for—rather than an obstacle to—democratic consolidation will require major reforms. Broadly, these would involve two core changes: decentralize, make flexible, and modernize structures, personnel, and strategies, and create an opening for community involvement. Those steps would create a respected, effective, and honest police force of the type that is needed.

3. The mechanisms and proposals for reform have come primarily from the North American and western European experiences and models of policing, which sometimes are modified and adopted as their own models by local actors. Community policing, zero tolerance, front-line policing, problem-solving strategies, and techniques such as crime mapping and victim surveys are among the ideas that have circulated most widely. To the degree that these new paradigms have been internalized in public-security and justice systems, it should raise us to better levels of objective and subjective security while contributing to democratic consolidation in Latin America.

The second trend in police-force studies also relates to democratic consolidation, but from the perspective of research and proposals to denounce authoritarianism and human-rights violations and to fight against corruption in

Latin America. The Latin American and international human-rights movements have embraced these studies and declarations, which present these findings:

1. Latin American police forces participated—and in some countries and regions, continue participating—in human-rights and citizen-rights violations, and this unacceptable conduct has undermined their legitimacy.

2. It is necessary to launch public campaigns, undertake legal actions, and build institutions that can expand and improve the methods of control over police behavior, punish abuses, and optimize channels for reporting unacceptable activity.

3. The principles and procedures to achieve these changes are an extension of the tools designed for other issues, such as the fight against ethnic or gender discrimination. In broad terms, we need to educate people about their basic rights, create or support private or semipublic (comprising both government and citizen members) organizations to control police behavior and disseminate their results, reform police training, and encourage legal changes to protect citizens against situations that could lead to abuse, such as concealment of information, arbitrary detentions, or imprecise definitions of crimes, such as torture, unnecessary violence, and police abuse.

The separation between the social-science and human-rights categories is, of course, abstract. In reality, initiatives tend to appear in clusters, with one aspect or another having greater weight depending on local or national reality. Nevertheless, differentiating these categories makes sense because the predominance of one or the other leads to marked differences in how police reforms are undertaken.[3]

Finally, two characteristics of these proposals stand out: First, they are exogenous in terms of Latin American reality; in practice, none of these proposals has arisen from an internal effort, whether by the police forces, the government, or local intellectuals. Second, these proposals share an evolutionary vision of government institutions. This is apparent in the supposition (often implicit but easily deducible in the texts) that police forces can evolve from being traditional or even backward (purely repressive, authoritarian in character, isolated from society, and unprofessional) to being modern or more advanced (preventive, professionalized, democratic, and transparent).

The Chilean Carabineros as an Exception and Contradiction

Existing studies have evaluated the Carabineros positively in some aspects but negatively in others. They are considered to be one of the least corrupt police forces in Latin America, especially in comparison to the high levels of corruption and public scandal of Argentine, Brazilian, and Central American forces. As Christopher Stone and Heather Ward note, "Chile's largest police force, the Carabineros, has a reputation among Chileans for being clean, honest, and disciplined. Some Chileans say it ranks just below the Catholic Church as the most trusted social institution. . . . The Carabineros are proud of their clean hands" (1998, 1–3). Yet this study emphasizes that the starting salary for a Carabinero is approximately equivalent to that for a Russian policeman, with the cost of living similar in both countries. The Russian police force, however, is notorious for its corruption and organized-crime connections.

The image of the struggling Carabinero, proud of his profession, also exists in the ranks. A 1996 study showed that most of those who enter the force— especially high-ranking officers—are motivated by relatives who are already in the service, by a deep respect for the uniform, and by a desire to serve the community. Job stability is also cited, even though it is clear that money is not a primary motivation. As one interviewee said, "One's calling in life? You don't do it for money" (Sepúlveda 1996, 29). Hugo Frühling's studies also emphasize the positive image of the Carabineros in the Latin American context, even though this police force does not have the level of trust that forces in other regions of the world enjoy (2002).

Nevertheless, the Carabineros have been criticized. Perhaps the most important complaints have been the institution's isolation from civil and external controls over operations and development of operational strategies and the implication of Carabinero officers in abuse cases. Claudio Fuentes's study on police abuse in Chile from 1990 to 2001 focuses on the Carabineros (2003). He concludes that the Carabineros commit (or reportedly commit) an average of one abuse per day, and this unacceptable behavior is centered in urban areas, against young, poor males. Along with this, there are testimonies of "social hatred" toward the Carabineros. A Centro de Estudios Sociales SUR (Center for Social Studies SUR) study of Santiago's young street vendors clearly indicates that this group has a very negative image of the Carabineros:

> Young street vendors express their daily relationship to the rest of society in a
> language of violence, which they also use to describe their relationship to the po-

lice. The vendors, who have been the victims of police abuse, declare their hatred for the Carabineros, and when a Carabinero is killed in an attack, the vendors recount it with glee. It's not just that street vendors are taken prisoner and fined, but that the Carabineros beat them until they are black and blue, demand bribes, and even frame them, to make it appear that they are selling stolen merchandise. (Martínez and Palacios 1996, 94)

When about twenty groups took part in a contest for young rappers from Santiago's poor neighborhoods, each performed at least one song criticizing the Carabineros (Guzmán 2000, 96). This is a contradictory reality: on one hand, a police force praised for its integrity and uprightness and on the other, a force criticized for abuses against the poorest members of society, or even for abuse against its own officers.

The Origins of the Carabineros

The Carabineros de Chile national police force was founded on April 27, 1927, during the dictatorship of General Carlos Ibáñez del Campo, one of the most difficult political and economic moments in twentieth-century Chile. Ibáñez took power in 1927; an economic crisis and a broad-based popular movement led to his ouster in 1930. Although he was a repressive leader, he also founded important institutions that survived the fall of his administration. The Carabineros were among them. Institutionally, the force has conserved a positive image of the Ibáñez administration and of its founder.

The last chief of the regiment popularly known as the Cuerpo de Carabineros (Carabinero Corps) was don Carlos Ibáñez del Campo, who was then a colonel in the army. He was a man of great vision and statesmanlike qualities who, after assuming first the post of minister of the interior and then of vice president of Chile, promulgated Executive Decree Law No. 2484 on April 27, 1927. The decree merged the military unit with the revenue and municipal police forces. The duties and powers of the uniformed police were thus centralized in one institution, which has since been the only police force in Chile (see www.Carabineros.cl).

Thus, the Carabineros are a military organization charged with fighting crime. Going back almost seventy years, the *Revista de Carabineros* (*Carabineros Magazine*) contains praise, similar to that on the force's Web site, for General Ibáñez's administration and his role as founder of the national police and unifier of the Carabineros. The magazine—a revealing source for studying the discourse that the police institution and its members invoked—

describes the founding moment: "Our current president [Ibañez], with a clear and broad vision for the interests of the nation and for the progress of our institutions, issued the April 27 Decree Law. . . . We, the longstanding police . . . have given all our love and affection to the new Green Flag. . . . Our current Chief did well in uniting the two healthy and robust forces so that they may work together for the same ideal and hope" (*Revista de Carabineros* 1927a, 36).

From the outset, the Carabineros force identified with the government that had created it. Thus, not surprisingly, Ibáñez's violent fall led to expressions of popular hatred toward the members of the institution that he himself had founded and had used to repress his political adversaries. Clotario Blest, distinguished union leader of the twentieth century, recalled those distant events: "I recall the many demonstrations against the Ibáñez regime. . . . It was a silent war that killed him. It reached the point that when Ibáñez fell, the Carabineros went into hiding for a month. They could not come out in public because they would be killed. Unfortunately, I once saw how they slashed a cop; he was cut to shreds. That was the level of hatred that existed" (quoted in Echeverría 1993, 125).

During the early years of consolidation, the Carabineros viewed themselves as soldiers—soldiers of a special stamp, "an armed citizenry," but one that adhered to martial principles of daring, discipline, and bravery. As would continue to occur, the Carabineros favored the military code that their origins in the armed forces had bequeathed to them, understanding it as part of necessary police discipline and training (*Revista de Carabineros* 1932, 71–72).

A few years after the unification, a debate began about the Carabineros' role as teachers of the general population and examples for the nation's youth, one of the central characteristics of the force:

> Today's Carabinero is not what the police of the past were nor what the former Carabineros themselves were. A new activity has been added to the mission of maintaining domestic order and public security. . . . It is perhaps the most important and significant development for the immediate and future well being of the Republic. . . . It consists of making the Carabinero into a true guide and teacher for the general public, someone who is their best friend, and their most loyal defender and counselor, always effective in stopping anything that might disturb public order (*Revista de Carabineros* 1927b).

That step was part of the development of the institution's complexity and sense of patriotic duty. In an affirmation that would hold true over time, the

Carabineros define themselves as the force that is "always everywhere" and that fulfills a mission when other public officials do not or cannot.

Similarly, the Carabineros fully accept their repressive role in society and do not view it as a contradiction of their duties in the legal, welfare, and social-education arenas. Faced with the 1938 Seguro Obrero massacre, a public scandal that cast a shadow on the final year of the Arturo Alessandri administration, the Carabineros institutionally vindicated their position: repression was their duty, and they obeyed orders.[4] "The services offered during strikes, rallies, and other public demonstrations are not, as one might believe, special tasks above and beyond our duty; to the contrary, these services are part of our basic and unavoidable responsibilities" (Arriagada 1938, 16).

Early on, Carabinero leaders and officers adopted a clear policy position in the face of riots and social protests spilling into the streets: rejection of doctrines fomenting social disorder and support of orderly governments, such as that of General Ibáñez's administration. Present also was fear of the agitators and of the harm they might inflict, directly or indirectly, on the institution's members:

> If it happens that they take power, those who call us "Brother Carabineros" will not hesitate to offer us up as a sacrifice to the insatiable appetites of vengeance. They will massacre us pitilessly for having been "the oppressors of the people," since one of the basic principles of their dissolute doctrine is suppression of the Carabineros in order to replace them with the destructive regime's praetorian security guard. Carabineros, should you under any circumstances receive letters, pamphlets, or pieces of subversive propaganda, even if it only hints at this, you should courageously report it to your superiors. (Bettancour 1937, 83)

The Carabineros have a clear definition of who they are and who are the Others: the Carabineros are soldiers with military training and a hierarchical structure, who defend and protect good citizens and the state by prosecuting crimes and maintaining law and order in the face of onslaughts from the Others. Whereas the government and good citizens respect orderly control and welcome the assistance of police power, the Others infringe on the law and spread the doctrine of social agitation. The Carabineros, along with their duty to uphold the law and combat subversion, are public servants and teachers of the general population.

Permanence over Time

This basic identity has not changed significantly over time. In 1965, during an altercation between Argentine gendarmes and the Carabineros in the Laguna del Desierto border region, Lieutenant Hernán Merino Correa was shot to death, making him one of the best-known and emblematic Carabinero martyrs. Coming thirty years after the institution's founding, the statements about Lieutenant Merino reveal that the image of the ideal Carabinero—one who embodies heroism, devotion to the homeland, and self-sacrifice (even to the point of dying)—had been successfully maintained:

> As the son of a distinguished Chief of the Carabineros, you possessed the magnanimous and brave temperament that the noble profession you embraced required of you. . . . [You did this] in the face of the sacred mandate of our nation: "To give one's life if necessary in defense of order and the Homeland." The men who forged their flesh into steel in the Carabineros of Chile never waver. . . . Behind them, one sees a calendar imbued with spotless tradition, a martyrology ennobled over a hundred tours of duty, and an institutional umbrella whose folds safeguard trustworthy proof of heroism and sacrifices. (*Revista de Carabineros* 1965, 38)

After Merino's death, condolences arrived at Carabineros headquarters from all the important places: the executive branch, Congress, all of the press, public and private institutions, and even the Federación de Estudiantes de Chile (Student Federation of Chile), all came forward with tributes to the assassinated officer (*Revista Carabinero* 1965, 24).

Eight years later, on September 11, 1973, the coup d'état would give the Carabineros a new and more important role in Chilean society. The Carabineros, together with the three branches of the armed forces, participated in the military junta that governed the country for seventeen years. The Carabineros' experience of autonomy and of governing alongside the armed forces reinforced their pride in the military character of the force. Even though the separation between the armed forces and the police is acknowledged, both institutions continue to view each other as reciprocal and complementary in their grand objective of ensuring national security:

> Whereas it is true that the duties of the Armed Forces and the Police Power are different, they are not completely separate. On the contrary, according to the circumstances . . . they must complement each other since External Security and Internal Security are each a branch of National Security. Consequently, both forces

are integral parts of the National Security Council. It has already been explained how reciprocal complementarity is produced, as when the Carabineros participate in the defense of the borders. Moreover, according to Art. 15 of its Charter, it can be partially mobilized to supplement the Armed Forces in case of war, when equivalence of hierarchical grades acquires force. For its part, the Armed Forces, in cases of emergency, grave disruptions of the law and order, and threat or danger to national security can perform the duties of domestic security. (*Revista de Carabineros* 1981, 17)

In the mid-1980s, the Carabineros had to confront strong waves of urban social protest against the dictatorship. The economic crisis that exploded in 1983 aggravated the situation. The Carabinero position was clear: all protesters were enemies. As the police saw it, these protests were part of a subversive plot against the government, and they threatened not only domestic peace but the Carabinero institution itself:

> The implicit objective of the mass movements is to gravely disturb the peace, which constitutes a direct and unrestrained attack on the system of government. The police force is assaulted physically and verbally, to make it react with maximum energy and if possible, in an uncontrolled manner, so that it can be accused of all sorts of abuse—that for which the term "Police Brutality" has been coined, when referring to repressive operations. This not only discredits the government but also the Carabineros and is an attempt to besmirch the moral authority of both. (Donoso 1985, 33)

In *Revista de Carabineros*, the statements of General Rodolfo Stange about democracy and Marxism are also clear: democracy involves more than just voting for and electing officials, political pacts have little value, and dialogue with sectors of the Marxist Left are useless or unthinkable.

> A general misperception exists that democracy consists only of voting to elect officials to the executive branch and Congress. This is "one" of the "expressions of democracy," but it is not the most important. . . . Clearly, all dialogue with Marxist-Leninist communism is impossible or useless. . . . One must not forget that violence plays a preponderant role within that doctrine. . . . No one is fooled, the terrorist is not an idealist; he is a social disease that survives by violence, without distinguishing between civilians and those in uniform, between men, women, or children, between the sacred and the profane. To help the terrorist is a "Social Crime." (*Revista de Carabineros* 1987, 23)

References to the public's rejection, however timidly made, are always present. Rejection is attributed to the public's failure to understand the institution; people don't really "know" the Carabinero or understand what he or she does. Since it has a complicated, sometimes tutelary role, the force is easily misunderstood, given its ongoing contact with the public. Moreover, people have "an exaggerated idea of their rights" (Delgado 1985, 22).

New Models of Citizen Security

The issues of security, police, and public policy created an especially complex triad at the beginning of the new democratic era in Chile. The armed forces and the security and order forces (that is, the Carabineros de Chile) relinquished power in 1989, following the first free and democratic elections in seventeen years. A militarized, hierarchical, and legalistic police force served the era of dictatorship, but these traits do not mesh well with democracy. The publicity about increasing crime rates (especially for murders, assaults, armed robberies, and sex crimes) strongly influenced the public's agenda. The government and the parliament were obliged to respond to the increase in crime, and the issue of citizen security became the subject of editorial commentary in the media. The Carabineros, in turn, had to speak out on these issues.

CARABINERO DEPENDENCE ON CIVIL AUTHORITY

The early years of the Concertación, a coalition government made up of center-left parties—the Aylwin administration (1989–1994)—were marked by conflicts between the government and the Carabineros because of the institution's recent relationship with the military dictatorship and its implication in political violence. The Aylwin administration convened the Truth and Reconciliation Commission to investigate deaths and disappearances from 1973 to 1990, and it found Carabineros to be directly implicated in many of these cases.[5] Although the institution seemed disposed to help clear up cases in which its personnel may have been involved, then–director general Rodolfo Stange declared that these revelations could damage the image of the Carabineros as public servants and might even expose certain officers to revenge (Araya, Frühling, and Sandoval 1998, 45). Moreover, just before leaving power, the military government had approved a new framework law for the Carabineros, which established that the president of the republic could demand the retirement of a Carabinero officer only if the institution's director general proposed it—a serious diminution of presidential powers (42).

In a much longer-lasting conflict, the democratic government initially proposed fully subordinating the Carabineros to the Interior Ministry, as they had been from 1927 to 1973. Then the military government moved the force to the Ministry of Defense to avoid potential political manipulation by the executive branch. By a 1992 Supreme Decree, Interior assumed the coordination of all tasks relating to law and order, but no bill was passed to subordinate the Carabineros to it. The list of Concertación efforts to achieve this is long: one attempt in 1991, one in 1993, four in 1998, and one final one in October 2001.[6] Congress rejected or tabled all of these bills.

In a document focused on the organizational status of the Carabineros, Carabinero inspector general Iván González Jorquera declared, "Carabineros de Chile is a permanent institution of the *Chilean state, and as such, it transcends the transitory power with which an administration is vested so that it can, for a determined time, run the institution"* (González Jorquera 2001, 2).

According to González Jorquera, the Carabineros force is a state entity, like the Finance Ministry, the Central Bank, and the armed forces, and not an ordinary public service. Public services are administrative organs charged with satisfying collective needs in a regular, ongoing way, and each is subject to the policies, plans, and programs of the ministry to which it reports. The Carabineros de Chile organization, however, is not subject to the ministry to which it reports, because the constitution establishes the duties of the force, it is governed by its own constitutional framework law, and it interacts directly or indirectly with all ministries, "thus surpassing the concept of public service" (González Jorquera 2001, 3). It is difficult to imagine a clearer declaration of institutional autonomy from governmental political power.

Finally, González Jorquera emphasizes that such status results from the autonomous position that the Carabineros force has and because of the social work it performs: "The importance that the legal system has awarded it is not by chance nor is it due to the economic and political support it has received. It comes instead from *social empowerment* achieved during its 74 years of existence within *Chilean society,* which has granted that empowerment to it, in virtue of the institution's professional performance and development, carved out by the efforts of its men and without dependence of any kind or to any organization to which it might have to report" (González Jorquera 2001, 6).

These words evidently refer not only to the legal or constitutional role of the Carabineros force but to its historic and social development as an institution, which has culminated in its present autonomy. The refusal to return to being a highly politicized police force, with its attendant loss of legitimacy in the eyes of the public, seems deeply embedded in the perspective of the institutional leadership, which is keen to defend the institution's identity.

INSECURITY, THE POLICE, AND COMMUNITY

At a conference in November 2002, undersecretary of the interior Jorge Correa Sutil stated that, although the democratic administration had taken sound initiatives in the areas of housing, health, and the economy, in the area of public policy relating to crime and policing, it had made little progress. During his first two years, the security issue had suddenly and aggressively surfaced (Correa Sutil 2002).

An obvious issue is the shortfall in police manpower and needed equipment. From 1937 on, the ratio of Carabineros to the population declined steadily: 1:244 in 1937, 1:338 in 1959, 1:356 in 1973; and 1:427 in 1989 (Araya, Frühling, and Sandoval 1998, 59). The Aylwin administration started a process of budget increases for the force, sending bills to Congress to increase the Carabinero force by 4,400 officers over a period of four years (beginning in 1991). Congress approved the measures, mandating an increase of US$25 million in the institution's annual budget.

Along with this, both the government and the Carabinero leadership agreed that the institution should modernize its administration, training programs, and structure. New models of police work were gradually beginning to arrive in Chile. The notion of security as a quality-of-life issue and a citizen right, as well as the distinction between objective and subjective insecurity were added to earlier concepts of ensuring respect for the law and maintaining law and order. A good example of these changes and the new content is the concept of human security, embraced by the United Nations Development Program (see UNDP 1998, introduction). Thus, security stopped being an issue only of obeying the law and was transformed into an item on the social agenda of government administrations. In that framework, the citizenry in its entirety—the government, lawmakers, and civil society—has the right and the duty to participate.

The government created new departments within the Interior Ministry and Secretaría General de Gobierno (Presidential Secretariat) dedicated to designing public policy and mechanisms for participation in public security and crime prevention (see Dammert 2002, chap. 3). Similarly, private centers, such as the Fundación Paz Ciudadana (Citizen Peace Foundation), and NGOs, such as SUR Profesionales, and Centro de Estudios para el Desarrollo (Center for Development Studies), among others, have developed research studies and issued opinions on topics such as crime statistics, crime prevention, and the role of the police in a democratic society.

NEW MANAGEMENT AND RESOURCE ADMINISTRATION REFORM

The Carabineros organization has positioned itself for modernization and established operational mechanisms and institutional relations to achieve reforms in security concepts and policing strategies. First, the Carabineros have not abandoned their self-perception of being a total police force, that is, an institution that covers the entire country and that must be available for any situation—especially emergencies—even when a situation does not fall within the constitutional definitions of its duties. On one hand, they have accepted that their officers should focus specifically on police work and that their structure and management must be more flexible. However, frictions with the investigative police over Carabinero involvement in investigations, maintenance of the institution's hierarchical and strongly centralized structure for dealing with its own personnel, and resistance to accepting municipal police forces as potential local police forces all show that the Carabineros are ready to undertake some reforms but not a managerial revolution.

Several events illustrate these realities. First, an unusual and perhaps unprecedented event in the (public) history of the Carabineros was the street protest by Carabinero wives and relatives in April 1998, on the anniversary of the institution's founding. Protests were ignited specifically by salary increases benefiting (in the opinion of the protesters) the top brass more than the rank and file. Candlelight vigils and *cacerolazos* (banging of kitchen pots and pans in a street protest) took place in communities where the police officers live. When the demonstrations began to spill over into downtown Santiago, the demonstrators were arrested. A sergeant went so far as to testify on television about the poor work conditions and abuses that personnel suffer at the hands of their superiors, but high-ranking officials curbed the demonstrations and arrested the sergeant (Maldonado 1998, 1). This tip of the iceberg of the internal conflicts between the rank and file and high-ranking officers disappeared from public view and has not reappeared.

The Carabineros have also encountered increasing security initiatives taken by the municipalities. In some cases, this has benefited the Carabineros. According to data produced by María Pía Guzmán, congresswoman from the Renovación Nacional Party (one of the principal opposition parties), the annual budget for the Carabineros increased by as much as 20 percent, thanks to the special contributions from municipalities as well as regional governments and private companies (Maldonado 1998, 9).[7] Nevertheless, while some mayors limited themselves to donating certain items, such as police cars, creating citizen-security offices, and participating in government crime-prevention initiatives, others were more aggressive with their initiatives and demands, which generated protest by Carabineros.

On September 1, 1998, the mayor of Las Condes municipality, Joaquín Lavín, created the Uniformed Municipal Inspectors Corps, composed of thirty-six officers patrolling in eighteen automobiles belonging to the municipality.[8] These officers, as former uniformed Carabineros, were allowed to carry weapons, and their vehicles sported emergency warning lights even though only authorized emergency vehicles are permitted to have these. The Carabineros reacted, sensing a usurpation of their functions, and the municipal vehicles were fined. When the mayor complained about continuing high crime rates in Las Condes, despite resources that the municipality had given the Carabineros, the commandant in charge responded that the Carabineros are a police force for all the nation's people, not just those of Las Condes. If it were necessary, he would return the municipality's donations.

A similar situation arose over external advisors and academic centers that were participating in the new management of the Carabineros. In a lecture in Santiago, the head of the Chilean Carabineros Planning Office, Major Jorge Villaroel Altamirano (2002), discussed the challenges and benefits that had arisen from researchers and police collaborating on studies for future reforms. That collaboration started in 1995, when the Carabineros began to formulate plans to modernize, working with institutional experts in their own ranks and external consultants, with whom they signed agreements. Among the institutions participating were the Programa Interamericano de Preparación (Inter-American Training Program), the Universidad Católica (Catholic University), and the Fundación Paz Ciudadana, and two unidentified universities evaluating data on the Plan de Vigilancia por Cuadrantes de Carabineros (Block Watch Plan). The major noted that the Carabineros must accept that their vision is not comprehensive and that researchers must accept that their experience is theoretical. The police must be open with the researchers, and the researchers must be objective in analyzing their information.

Major Villaroel's comments highlight a central characteristic of the modernization of Carabinero management: it is a self-directed process. The institution itself has assumed the leadership and construction of the modernization process. External participation has been at the behest of the institution, and it is the institution that has announced to the outside world both the methods to be used and the time frame for changes.

CARABINEROS DE CHILE AND COMMUNITY

Perhaps one of the most important changes is the Carabineros' understanding of concepts such as community policing. Community policing is more than just a way of increasing involvement with the community. The Spanish term—*policía comunitaria* (community police)—is less precise than the English term because Spanish does not have a verb "to police" (hence "policing" does not exist). The label community police refers to an activity, a way of being police. It is, indeed, a different model, based on a horizontal relationship with the community and a problem-solving orientation. It proposes, as a central objective, a decentralized police force with a predominantly civil character, flexible structure, and adequate funding, which would rely on studies of police efficiency, not just effectiveness.[9]

The Carabineros de Chile, as an institution, is a centralized, hierarchical police force, with a militarized command. Thus, the Carabineros have interpreted the term community policing in their own unique way. The Carabineros have affirmed that they have always been a community police force, because they have always been a supportive police force, ready to help people in emergencies, to help the poor, and to help those who need assistance and comfort and those who cannot or do not know how to turn to anyone else. As the current director general of the Carabineros affirms, "History shows that since its founding, the Carabineros de Chile have been a police force that is close to the people. That is, it has been close to the community. By transcending its doctrine of service [in regard to] the duties that the law accords it, and interpreting fully the spirit of those laws, it has performed broad social actions, especially directed to our most underprivileged fellow citizens" (Cienfuegos 2002a, 4).

Referring to a 1928 flier, the director general emphasized the true social doctrine that is the Carabineros' mandate: they carry out tasks that include, among other things, building shelters for homeless children, organizing adult education classes, providing lunches for children, giving talks on hygiene to workers, and so forth (Cienfuegos 2002a, 4). That definition is consistent with the concept the institution has of its relationship to the rest of the world. What the Carabineros understand as community and as acting *comunitariamente* (in a community-minded fashion) means fulfilling that part of a role that is historical and not legal: to be available for people even to the point of self-sacrifice.

Without abandoning that perceptual framework, the Carabineros have taken some strategies from the original community-policing model and adapted them to their professional services. The most important is the Block Watch Plan, whose pilot program began in 1998. In broad terms, the Block Watch is a strategy for police surveillance, in which the responsibility for guarding an urban area is assigned to a specific detail of police officers. The institution has defined this initiative as "preventive patrolling practices in co-ordination with the community" (see www.Carabineros.cl). As Hugo Frühling (2002) has noted, the Block Watch Plan is not exactly a neighborhood watch program. However, it involves novel elements, such as the division of the city and the assignment of resources according to a quantitative assessment, and it generates a closer relationship between the police and the members of the community. Each block officer carries a cell phone that people can call to talk directly with the Carabinero in their neighborhood.

As noted in Frühling (2002) and other documents from the institution it-self, the Block Watch Plan has been complemented by other initiatives aimed at enhancing community relations, such as "open-door" police stations and the Carabineros' invitation to youth and other community members to get to know them and to participate in crime-prevention initiatives. An Office of Community Relations and Criminal Analysis recently opened to coordin-ate operations responding to citizen demands, complaints, and suggestions. Carabineros also attend meetings on the government's new municipal-level citizen-security plan, Plan Comuna Segura Compromiso Cien (Commitment 100 Safe Municipality Plan).

The Reassertion of Identity

An internationally held, evolutionary vision of reform sees police forces evolv-ing from traditional (authoritarian, isolated from society, inefficient) to mod-ern (democratic, efficient, and open to citizen control) institutions. The two axes of this evolution are administrative modernization and democratization, both in doctrine and in the treatment of the public.

The Carabinero force itself does not entirely accept this evolutionary model. As an institution, it is proud of its social work and history, high ap-proval ratings, and efficiency. Thus, the Carabineros accept the first axis as a timely necessity, related to unavoidable technical changes, but they do not see a need for self-questioning introspection or institutional reform. Because they are a first-rate police force, the Carabineros must familiarize themselves with and adapt to new technology and operational tools for their professional activities. They are willing to use these techniques and tools only to the degree that they do not call into question—but rather are coherent with—the basic institutional identity of the Carabineros de Chile. That institution is autonomous, unitary, national, and hierarchical. It resolves its problems internally and provides society with answers—not questions. In these respects, the force demonstrates a powerful coherence across time. Despite transformation of language (each period has its own style and manner), a line of thought and a construction of identity have been passed down over the years, with few changes or contradictions. Even the silences are silences inherited from times past.

These silences relate precisely to the second axis of reform, and they pose a paradox for the Carabineros. Responses to protests, accusations of abuse, and political maneuvers have been weak. Neither the police institution itself nor the government leadership has been able to fully accept the need to examine issues such as repression when it goes beyond crime control, internal conflicts, and accusations of police abuse. These are taboo subjects for the Carabineros de Chile as an institution. It is as if the relationship with Us—children who visit police stations, neighbors concerned for security, slum dwellers affected by storms—can come out into public view and be photographed—while the relationship with the Others—the suspects and criminals, underprivileged youth whose attitude and style of dress defy authority, street vendors, and subversives—must remain hidden and buried in a dark land where only the Others and the police can go unless scandal attracts the media and draws international condemnation.

Daniela Sepúlveda (1996) sheds some light on this through interviews with Carabineros. It is evident that few of them feel regret, pain, or compassion when, for example, a criminal is injured. As one officer notes pointedly, "If it involves a criminal, he probably deserved it." In contrast, the reaction when a companion is harmed is strong and demonstrates tremendous loyalty:

> If the injured person is a colleague, I'm terribly upset and repulsed. We live together, we eat together, at least, those of us who are single do. It feels as if they have hurt or killed my brother.
>
> If they beat a Carabinero, 10 cars will arrive, and the Carabineros will get out and not very politely either. When a Carabinero radios for assistance, within three minutes, the street is full of cars coming to the rescue. (Sepúlveda 1996, 52)

A grave issue of transparency and discrimination is still pending in the political and parliamentary debate in Chile. Certainly, the Carabineros can feel pride for their social and educational efforts over the years, for their capacity for self-renewal and adaptation to new operational tools and technologies, and for the high esteem in which the Chilean public holds them. Nevertheless, we clearly need public debate, transparency, and openness about how the institution achieves its effectiveness, how it manages disciplinary controls, and how it could maintain a sense of honor and commitment to its work that would be tied to a respect for human and citizen rights, so that this institution could be truly nondiscriminatory and responsive to society in a transparent way.

This task does not belong solely to the police. We need to define our position as a nation on issues such as human rights for everyone, the limits to the use of violence, the peaceful resolution of conflict, and the rejection of authoritarianism, corruption, and secrecy about the activities of public officials. Here, the Chilean press could have an important role, if it abandons its sensationalistic approach to citizen security and helps to create a more critical public opinion.

It is not surprising that a police officer would feel much angrier about harm done to a colleague than about harm done to a prisoner, especially if that officer has been trained as a member of an institution that is also a family, with comrades sharing their entire lives, not just their work. However, it is profoundly disturbing that the justice system, civil society, and the media react alike or have no reaction at all, which amounts to almost the same thing. Indeed, we should not be surprised that any institution would prefer to keep confidential its internal audits, its problems with its own officers, and its shortcomings. What should surprise and concern us, however, is that we consider this to be normal.

Armed Conflict and Public Security in Colombia

Gonzalo de Francisco Z.

In recent decades, Colombia's national police force has evolved in response to challenges specific to that Latin American nation. The struggle against drug trafficking, its special role within the country's armed conflict, and the quest for citizen security—all framed in a society with a strong democratic foundation—have shaped the current characteristics of an institution that has won the respect of most Colombians.[1] It is not a question of whether the national police force has taken an inappropriate role in the fight against drug trafficking, the guerrillas, and the paramilitaries. This is the reality that Colombian society and the government have imposed on the police. This is what has shaped the response capacity of the force in its quest for security, understood broadly.

According to Jaume Courbet (1983), the objectives of police work include crime prevention, immediate response to incidents that directly threaten the security of citizens, investigation of all crimes and accidents in a given jurisdiction, and traffic control. The magnitude of Colombia's armed conflict, involving the guerrillas, paramilitaries, and drug traffickers, require the Colombian police to exceed those objectives, which fall within the framework of the quest for citizen security. However, the activities of the national police, particularly in the fight against illegal drugs, have strengthened the agency's capacity to respond to Courbet's objectives.

The Importance of the Armed Conflict

The national police were directly involved in the conflict between the Liberal and Conservative parties during *la violencia* (the violence), from 1930 to the end of the 1950s. Consequently, the force suffered an acute crisis over its role in society. As a police force of civilian character, subordinate to the Government Ministry (which Colombians frequently call the Ministry of Politics), the national police responded to partisan interests and became a significant actor in that phase of Colombian history (for more information on the period, see Guzmán 1986). After the Frente Nacional (National Front) superceded *la violencia* and the dictatorship of General Gustavo Rojas Pinilla (1955–1958), the national police were limited to managing the growing problem of citizen security in an eminently rural country and were subordinated to the armed forces in the Defense Ministry. The national police were about to face a new phase of armed conflict, characterized by guerrilla warfare carried out by revolutionary organizations of a Marxist character.[2]

Unlike in most Latin American countries, the subordination of Colombia's armed forces to civilian control is more the product of the role the army assumed during *la violencia* than of the military's control of the government. Since the cessation of the mid-twentieth-century violence, Colombian society has been predominantly civil or civilian in nature, as demonstrated by the clear rejection of any possibility that the military might control the government.[3]

In the second half of the twentieth century, the national police had a special role characterized by their low profile. Militarized primarily because of *la violencia*, and now liberated from partisanship, the force concentrated its activities in the cities. It addressed the guerrilla conflict only tangentially, since the armed forces primary handled that task. The national police were subordinate to the armed forces because of both the strength of the operational-command concept and the fact that the Defense Ministry, in which the armed forces and national police were located, was led by the top army general until 1991.[4]

During the 1960s and 1970s, guerrilla warfare had typically been rural, isolated from social conflict, and powerless to destabilize society more generally. By the early 1980s, it had become highly mobile, covering the entire nation and employing criminal activities that affected all of Colombian society as its principal source of resources for its maintenance and expansion. By 1982, the Fuerzas Armadas Revolucionarias de Colombia (Revolutionary Armed Forces of Colombia, FARC) and the Ejército de Liberación Nacional (National Liberation Army, ELN) had approximately 19 guerrilla fronts with 1,400 men, operating in six regions of Colombia (Echandía 1999a, 55–63). In 2000, there were 107 fronts and 21,025 men with a presence throughout the entire country, including the areas surrounding all major cities (data provided by Sala de Estrategia Nacional, Presidencia de la República, July 2002).

Analyzing why this evolution occurred would require more space than is available here. In addition to the FARC's and ELN's political and strategic decision to expand, five possible explanations can be offered, none related to Colombia's social situation and poverty. The principal factor is drug trafficking, whose evolution unfolded in two distinct phases. The first, between approximately 1980 and 1993, was characterized by the presence of major cartels, primarily dedicated to importing coca base from Bolivia and Peru, which they used in the manufacture of cocaine that they would directly transport to the major centers of drug consumption throughout the world. The second phase, between 1990 and 2003, was characterized by extensive cultivation of coca in Colombia and by the appearance of small drug-trafficking organizations that manufactured cocaine for eventual delivery to the international cartels, which took charge of transporting it to the consumer.

This second phase had a major impact on the growth of guerrilla warfare, by facilitating access to incalculable economic resources that financed the guerrilla expansion. From a strategic point of view, the question is not whether a guerrilla will become a drug trafficker. There are approximately seven steps in the drug-trafficking process, from planting the crop to shipping the cocaine out of Colombia, and for each the FARC and the ELN can demand payment (see table 6.1). It is probable that this model, which has many variations depending on the region and the moment in time, constitutes one of the most successful criminal schemes that has existed in recent decades anywhere in the world.

The second explanation for the growth in guerrilla forces is the presence of additional financing, gained from extortion and kidnapping. Drug trafficking is basic to the expansion of guerrilla fronts, while kidnapping and extortion are useful for consolidating a front's presence in a given area. Kidnapping and extortion are decisive from a strategic point of view because they affect the highest levels of Colombian society (Pizarro 1991). However, this last claim is debatable on two points: extortion and kidnapping arise from a real need for economic resources, and these crimes indiscriminately affect all segments of society, including the poorest. The obvious fact is that kidnapping increases as the presence of guerrilla forces increases.

The other fundamental explanations for the growth of the guerrilla forces are geography, negotiations with the guerrilla groups, and society's and the government's lack of clear purpose.[5] The lack of a government strategy to con-

6.1 Steps of the drug-trafficking process

Agrochemicals	Herbicides, insecticides, and fungicides for cultivation
Cultivation of coca leaf	Carried out by "raspachines" that are commonly organized by a single person
Chemical Inputs	Gasoline, cement, and sulfuric acid to produce the coca base in "kitchens"
Sale of coca base	The portion of profit that the guerrilla takes is called "gramaje"
Laboratory	Converts cocaine base into cocaine; requires security squads
Chemical precursors	The principal one is potassium permanganate
Sale of cocaine	This is the purchase of what will be shipped
Clandestine runway	Not all laboratories have a clandestine runway

front the guerrillas is evident. Missing from the public-policy agenda was comprehensive, ongoing strategy, supported by all institutions and Colombian society itself, which could have impeded the growth of the guerrilla forces.

This last factor, combined with kidnappings and indiscriminate extortion, laid the groundwork for the paramilitaries, which are also a characteristic of the Colombian conflict.[6] Faced with the government's inability to stem the increase in guerrilla forces, a minority in Colombian society—the direct victims of kidnappings and extortion—decided to form a series of organizations to confront the guerrilla forces, using methods and tactics, such as executions and deportations, copied from the guerrillas themselves. The evolution and crisis of the paramilitaries were closely associated with the growth in illegal crop cultivation, the tool the drug traffickers were using to consolidate their position. Rather than counteracting the guerrilla forces, the paramilitaries became an additional source of illegal activity, that is, criminals. In short, they exacerbated the armed conflict rather than resolving it. For government agencies, in particular, the armed forces, and the national police, the paramilitaries were a double challenge, both because of their criminal activities and because they distracted the security forces from their real task of addressing the guerrilla threat.

The national police in rural areas had to confront the FARC's strategic decision to wipe out police stations in its quest to consolidate territorial control.

By 2003, the police force had withdrawn from 157 *cabeceras municipales* (similar to county seats). This retreat highlights the immense difficulty of the government's deploying more personnel than would normally be required for patrolling and citizen-security tasks in these sparsely populated areas. Only by deploying more manpower will it be possible to prevent or respond to guerilla attacks.

In confronting the guerrillas, the national police are really confronting criminal organizations that commit felonies, such as kidnapping and robbery, which require a police mentality to counteract. The force has also fulfilled the role of supporting the efforts of the army, whose essence is mobility. What is important, however, is that the national police force, as an institution identified as a security agency, has not been able to achieve clarity about its strategic role within the armed conflict with the guerrillas and the paramilitaries.[7]

The Police and the Drug Traffickers

During the 1980s, the Colombian drug traffickers reached the peak of their powers, to such a degree that they threatened the legitimacy of the Colombian government itself. The importers of coca base and the exporters of cocaine, who were concentrated particularly in the Cali and Medellín cartels, began as a small group of newly rich high rollers, tolerated by a permissive society. But they were to become the leaders of immense armed organizations, controlling large rural areas and ruthlessly eliminating anything that stood in their way.

The huge revenues generated by drug trafficking created a growth dynamic that left the government powerless to respond. The most serious drawback, however, was not a lack of resources to stop the problem at its inception, but rather the inability to visualize the dimensions that drug trafficking would reach over time. At the end of the 1970s, there was no clarity about which agency should take charge of confronting the proliferation of marijuana crops along the northern coast of Colombia. Despite an understandable reluctance on the part of army officers, this force was chosen to be responsible for confronting the incipient drug-trafficking organizations and destroying the crops (interview with armed forces officers, Curso Integral de Defense Nacional, Escuela Superior de Guerra [War College], April 2001).

As the 1980s progressed, the growth of the business and the immense accumulation of wealth led the drug traffickers to do two things with long-term consequences: create an armed apparatus, based in multiple organizations, and pursue political and territorial control. Once the first alarms were raised about the dimensions of the drug-trafficking phenomenon, and when the international community began to call the attention of the Colombian government to this phenomenon, the drug traffickers began expanding into something more than mere organizations dedicated to trafficking in narcotics.

Because the cartels lack any regulation, all their transactions are based on what Colombians call the *palabra del gallero* (the promise of a bettor on cockfights, a popular rural pastime). The failure to honor one's word is tantamount to asking for violence. Anyone involved in drug trafficking is, in general, subject to violence and even death. Consequently, the growth of illegal crops is related to the increase in the homicide rate, even though, obviously, it is not the sole cause.

Territorial control also goes hand in hand with drug trafficking. The impressive estates from which Gonzalo Rodriguez Gacha and Pablo Escobar administered the activities of the Medellín cartel are notorious. Political control, in contrast, originates with the need to block the inevitable response from the government and society. Notably, political control by means of corruption was always severely limited by the presence of government and social actors who energetically opposed the cartels. The use of armed apparatuses became the tip of the lance to silence that opposition, whatever form it took. It led to the use of hit men. In this way, the drug traffickers became the greatest threat that the Colombian government has faced since at least the mid-twentieth century.[8]

Resolution 2743 of April 1981 assigned lead responsibility in the fight against drug trafficking to the national police by creating an antinarcotics unit in its Dirección Operativa (Operations Bureau). From that moment, the unit began to receive U.S. support; this was cautiously limited to a few teams and sporadic training courses. Only at the end of the 1980s, when the Virgilio Barco administration (1986–1990) ordered the national police to confront the hit men, did this assignment become a major function for the national police (Pardo 1996). The power of the drug traffickers quickly brought them into a fierce confrontation with the guerrillas. Pablo Escobar and Gonzalo Rodriguez led armed organizations that were so immense it was unnecessary to make pacts with the guerrillas for protection, even of laboratories and airstrips. Assassinations by the drug traffickers became daily fare for not only all who were associated with the guerrillas but also those who represented leftist or progressive positions. The mass murder of the members of Unión Patriótica, the leftist coalition consisting preponderantly of Communist Party members, was one of those unfortunate events. For the Barco administration, the situation was untenable, even more because the so-called paramilitary groups began imitating the activities of the hit men. Moreover, targeted murder extended to any who opposed the interests of the drug traffickers, such as journalist Guillermo Cano and presidential candidate Luis Carlos Galán.

Decree 814 of April 1989 created the Cuerpo Especial Armado (Special Armed Unit), placing it directly under the supervision of the national police. Its principal task was to dismantle the gangs of hired assassins. Within months, however, it became apparent that the drug-trafficking organizations were behind these groups. This ultimately led to reinforcing the Dirección Nacional de Antinarcóticos (National Antinarcotics Bureau), which had evolved out of the original unit in the Operations Bureau (Decree 423 of March 1987). This shows how the government was building an administrative model based on the circumstances as they arose rather than on a strategic plan with short- and long-term goals. Undoubtedly, the government's lack of financial resources and its overall failure to prepare the defense sector for the evolving threat from the drug traffickers, guerrillas, and paramilitaries were primary reasons.

Notably, the police responded to the challenge by becoming the primary agency responsible for confronting the Cali and Medellín cartels. The Antinarcotics Bureau thus came to the forefront and began creating a new generation of officials, specialized in the detection and removal of drug-trafficking groups. The cost, nevertheless, was heavy in human life. Hit men assassinated more than two hundred police officers during the dismantling of the Medellín cartel. At the beginning of the 1990s, Escobar targeted the police for destruction, and the size and criminality of his organization became highly visible. Clearly, drug trafficking had become a genuine threat to the government's survival. It reached the point that Escobar even jeopardized Colombia's institutions, outmaneuvering them by subjecting them to negotiations that defied Colombian law.[9]

Although the government responded, it did so without a long-term vision. It averted a total crisis, but it failed to gain the initiative. With the escape of Escobar following his brief incarceration, the César Gaviria administration (1990–1994) took a positive step by creating the Bloque de Búsqueda (Search Bloc), a coordinating mechanism for Colombia's crime-fighting agencies. Participating in it were the armed forces, the national police, the Administrative Office on Security (the intelligence agency under the control of the presidency), and the Public Prosecutor's Office, which had been created in the 1991 constitution to direct criminal investigations. The Search Bloc was not, in itself, synonymous with weakness: many countries rely on interagency coordination when confronting specific criminal phenomena. However, at that moment in Colombia, the bloc was an extraordinary mechanism, which revealed the ad hoc way in which the government was preparing itself to confront the drug traffickers. On the positive side, it generated a new experience, which enabled various agencies, particularly the police, to become familiar with advanced operational methods and technologies for intelligence gathering, all a product of U.S. support.

Pablo Escobar was murdered on December 2, 1993 (Bowden 2001). The final operation, supported by the Public Prosecutor's Office, was almost entirely the responsibility of the national police. However, this does not imply that the Search Bloc failed or that the army's role was insignificant. To the contrary, Escobar's death can be attributed—although not exclusively—to a systematic and coordinated effort on the part of all the agencies. This was possible because of the personal commitment of the commander of the army and the chief of the national police, who monitored, day after day, the joint work of their subordinates. For the first time in a mission of such broad scope, these two forces worked together, without one taking precedence over the other in the operational command and with the novelty of having a civilian defense minister.[10] Clearly, both the army and the national police tended to specialize, yet each did so without excluding the other: the army focused on territorial control and rural operations, and the national police focused on citizen security, based in Medellín and the surrounding metropolitan area.

The Search Bloc did not endure as an administrative mechanism nor as an operational model. One reason lies in the special nature and purpose of each force. Another is the rivalry inherent among these institutions, which does not appear so much at the operational level, as is sometimes believed, but rather manifests itself in public relations, that is, in claims made in the media. The Search Bloc was so successful that the country's leaders used its name to respond to the public during security crises in certain regions. This was so obvious that during the Ernesto Samper administration (1994–1998), one frequently heard that the Bloque de Búsqueda army unit or the Bloque de Búsqueda police unit had received orders to deploy somewhere, phrases that patently indicated that the concept of a joint and coordinated bloc no longer existed.

The dismantling of the Medellín cartel evolved into the dismantling of the Cali cartel. This latter group had a distinct way of operating. Its security-and-protection scheme was based on institutional corruption rather than on squadrons of paid assassins, even though hit men continued to be the base supporting illegal activities. Combating the Cali cartel proved to be more suited to police work than the Medellín anticartel operation had been, and it required a transformation of the national police, including the dismissal of a large number of the officers.[11] The result of the transformation was the capture of the Rodríguez Orejuela brothers and the general dismantling of the Cali cartel.

However, the drug-trafficking problem did not disappear; instead, it was transformed. The major cartels importing coca base and selling cocaine on the street in the major centers of drug consumption transformed themselves into small organizations that exported cocaine made from coca base available from the huge coca leaf plantations within Colombia itself. Thanks to interdiction, planting of illegal crops declined in Peru and Bolivia, but it increased in Colombia.

The National Police and Plan Colombia

The rural nature of the drugs and violence phenomena and the learning, even if at an operational level, as with the Search Bloc, led the Andrés Pastrana administration (1998–2002), with U.S. support, to take a new step: Plan Colombia. Also, the political crisis of the Samper administration had revealed —from a different perspective than that of the violence of the Medellín cartel's assassins—the degree to which drug trafficking could affect society. (For more on the Samper administration's crisis, see Vargas, Lesmes, and Téllez 1996.)

The hour had come to confront the drug traffickers, not just to impede their development but rather to eradicate them from Colombian society. The national police had the capacity to identify and dismantle the drug-trafficking organizations. But these would never be thoroughly destroyed until the problem of the illegal crops was resolved. The approximately 166,000 hectares under cultivation provided an ongoing encouragement to the small cartels as well as being a major source of funding for the guerrillas and the paramilitaries, who were also engaged in drug trafficking.

Plan Colombia, rather than a plan in a narrow sense, as of early 2005 is the implementation of a government strategy aimed at confronting the primary causes of violence in Colombia. To combat drug trafficking, which is one of its four components, the strategy is to put the pace of crop eradication above that of crop planting, which requires major advances in forced eradication (fumigation with herbicides), interdiction, and social action.[12] The fumigation policy has long been criticized because it failed to stem the spread of illegal crops in the 1990s, leading to the theory that destruction in one place only leads to planting somewhere else. Plan Colombia seeks to change that by increasing the capacity for fumigation; performing interdictions on land, rivers, sea, and air; and promoting social action toward a new productive apparatus that could support as many as 150,000 families, those who had been surviving by cultivating illicit drugs. Drug trafficking has moved from being an organized-crime issue to also being a social problem.

Plan Colombia resulted in a new strengthening of the national police force in its confrontation with the drug traffickers. Added to its capacity to dismantle crime organizations was major capability for crop destruction. In 2003, twelve thousand hectares per month were being eradicated. For its part, interdiction, which had only been partially pursued, now included the participation of the army's Brigada Contra el Narcotráfico (Antinarcotics Squad); the navy, at sea and on the rivers; and the air force. The decline in crop cultivation shows that Plan Colombia's Initiative against Drug Trafficking is succeeding; that is, it is on its way to achieving its aim of complete eradication of illegal crops and dismantling of the organizations dedicated to drug trafficking.

This overall effort has created a police force that is competent and has the best antinarcotics agents. Indeed, I believe the Colombian police today know more about the distinct facets of international drug trafficking than any force in the world; consequently, the force is one of the most renowned anywhere. Nevertheless, the fight against drug trafficking has been more than a matter of gaining international recognition: above all, it has demonstrated to Colombians themselves the force's usefulness as an agency and its capacity to respond to challenges such as those that society faces from drug trafficking. The antinarcotics fight has enabled the national police to train, modernize, and gain prominence. But the fight has also produced a new generation of senior and midrank officers and patrolmen, who, little by little, have been transmitting their new knowledge of method, intelligence, and operational doctrines to the other issue that is their responsibility: citizen security.

The National Police and Citizen Security

While the guerrilla forces, the paramilitaries, and the drug traffickers expanded alongside each other beginning in the 1980s, a socioeconomic and cultural process was also under way: Colombia was becoming urban.[13] Citizen security emerged as a quality-of-life issue for all urban inhabitants. Crimes such as assault, residential burglary, vehicle theft, and bank robbery, among others, became relevant because they increased as cities grew. In Colombian society, pressure quickly built, driven above all by the mass media, and the public began to demand that the government respond. The guerrilla warfare also became urbanized, as some armed forces chose to approach urban centers. Moreover, trying to sustain themselves, the FARC and ELN began to use kidnapping and extortion in the cities and even began to commit such crimes as bank robbery and car theft.

In the past ten years, the national police have experienced two interconnected processes of institutional change: the so-called 1992 reform and the Cultural Transformation of 1995–1999.[14] Both were in response to the pressing need to prepare the force for the antinarcotics fight and the quest for citizen security. Both required major changes and sought resolution for internal problems related to efficiency and effectiveness in police work and to structural problems including, most importantly, corruption. Nevertheless, these reforms should not be viewed, either separately or together, as marking an end or a beginning, because rather than generating a process, they were the manifestation of something more significant: the preparation of the national police to confront the challenges of drug trafficking and citizen security.

Notably, both reforms tried to go beyond what the institution was able to do and society to assimilate. Both, in themselves, were signs that the government and the national police had responded and were seeking to perform better in the antinarcotics and citizen-security arenas. Significantly, the fight against drug trafficking led to modernization and an effort to become current, which made possible important advances. With citizen security, the issue was and remains more complex.

It is reasonable to ask whether the national police force ignores citizen security because it is preoccupied fighting drug trafficking and the intense armed conflict. The answer is no. The fight against drug trafficking was a stimulus for the role of the police in society, and it was a mechanism to introduce new management models that influenced essential matters, such as operational formats and intelligence. The armed conflict, in contrast, has not involved the national police in an effective role, apart from serving as one of the restraints keeping the guerrilla forces out of populated areas. Despite the resources that are allocated to controlling the armed conflict and drug trafficking, citizen security has not deteriorated more than in other Latin American countries (Acero 2002).[15]

Colombia is not atypical within Latin America in citizen-security matters, as can be seen in the recent halt in growth trends for routine crime. However, Colombia has one of the highest homicide rates in the world, with seventy-three deaths per one hundred thousand inhabitants, on average from 1994 through 1997. These high rates are largely caused by criminal organizations—guerrillas, paramilitaries, and drug traffickers. Even so, in 1998 estimates showed that 60 percent of all murders in Colombia were committed in fifty-nine municipalities (mid- and large-sized cities that account for fewer than 6 percent of all Colombian municipalities), with 55 percent of the population (Consejería Presidencial 1998, 30). Undoubtedly, that alone makes homicide a citizen-security problem.

Besides structural issues such as income inequality and poverty, two factors partially account for high homicide rates in urban areas. First, as a study on Bogotá showed, there is a clear relation between homicide and the presence of organized crime (Alcaldía Mayor de Bogotá 2000). Second, the government has not implemented a clear gun-control policy. In 1998, nearly 80 percent of the 23,133 murders were committed with firearms. The national police, along with mayors and opinion leaders, support a gun-control measure, but they have been unable to convince the government to establish tighter controls even in urban areas.[16]

Two other citizen-security strategies were initiated by the executive branch: Seguridad para la Gente (Security for the People, 1993), a significant part of the Gaviria administration's Estrategia Nacional contra la Violencia (National Strategy against Violence), and the Pastrana administration's Estrategia para la Convivencia y Seguridad Ciudadana (Strategy for Coexistence and Citizen Security, 1998). Both focused on such things as local security plans, which encourage greater collaboration between mayors and the police, and the search for new managerial tools. Examples of the latter include the 1998 implementation of closed-circuit television in the streets of major cities and the establishment of the Centro de Información Estratégica Policial (Center for Strategic Police Information, CIEP). These two strategies indicate that the civilian authorities support the work of the police.

However, the argument that the national police have responded to the challenge of citizen insecurity is based more on the stimulus the institution received through its participation in the antinarcotics fight and on the reforms and changes it has instituted. The two executive-branch strategies had an impact and made progress possible, but they were less significant within the larger national agenda, which is dominated by the armed-conflict and drug-trafficking issues. Obviously, the Defense Ministry, continuously focused on the armed conflict, cannot give priority to crime prevention.

In attempting to improve citizen security, the lack of resources, particularly manpower, is the biggest constraint on the national police and the government. The Community Policing Program is an example of the problems caused by a shortage of officers. Pressure from the president and the desire of the police leadership to encourage state-of-the-art service led to implementation of nonmotorized patrols to increase community contact. However, it was impossible to select only certain urban areas in which to apply the model, so service was provided everywhere. Thus, the patrol officers have ended up covering such an extended area that it is beyond their ability, for example, to appear personally and regularly at each household. A key feature of the service is thus lost.

Local Security Strategies

To improve citizen-security management, the government must take greater advantage of the human capital and expertise within the national police, which have been gained primarily from the drug-trafficking fight. Because of its national-level strategies, Colombia has only limited experience in elaborating and implementing local security plans. These involve defining goals and specific measures as well as full collaboration between police leadership and local governments. Only Bogotá has experimented for several years with joint efforts between the local government and the police, and it is thus possible to claim that a local security plan exists, although it may not exist as a written document.

The weak connections between city government and the national police are the origin of this problem. In Colombia, the mayor is the highest-ranking police official in a city and thus supposedly controls the actions of the national police. However, the appointment and control of a police commander for a city falls to the director general, who in turn answers to the Defense Ministry and the president. It would not appear expedient to change this as long as guerrilla warfare and drug trafficking continue to be prevalent in Colombia. Consequently, an additional incentive must fill the gap, and the best choice for this is enhanced funding. Experience shows that when a city allocates funds for policing, it invigorates collaboration between the police and local officials, making it more feasible to develop a plan that establishes goals and specific activities.

The Fondos Locales de Seguridad (Local Security Funds), originally established in 1996, are the only tools mayors have to support the national police in their cities. This funding is a percentage of the government allocation for public works, which means the amount available varies year to year. When the public-works budget shrinks, something that happens frequently, the funding for the Fondos Locales shrinks as well. Thus, not only are the Fondos Locales poorly endowed, but their variability makes planning based on them almost impossible. The Fondos need to be strengthened in the future so that city contributions can influence the size of the local police force.

Policy and Institutional Priorities

The national police force needs to create a statistical database to monitor crime, which could be put to immediate use in police planning. However, maintaining up-to-date records is not enough. Since the 1990s, police forces in cities around the world have implemented COMSTAT (computer statistics), which subjects statistical information to ongoing, interinstitutional assessment as a tool in planning and targeting police action. Recently in Colombia, CIEPs have been set up in six police-department headquarters. These centers provide digital mapping of the respective cities. However, these centers are not a meeting place where police and local officials can outline a security plan, monitor daily trends in crime statistics, and, ultimately, assess the functioning of the plan itself. CIEPs must form part of a technological triangle that would include the Centros Administrativos de Despacho (Administrative Bureau Centers) and closed-circuit television monitoring. It is estimated that today only 10 percent of the surveillance cameras needed in Colombia's major cities are operating or are in the process of being installed.

Despite its advances, Colombia still needs to create a penal system that gives the public prosecutor exclusive responsibility over an investigation, with specialists assisting in the work. The challenge is to strengthen the role of the Dirección de Policía Judicial e Investigación (Bureau of Judicial and Investigative Police, DIJIN) as the agency with primary responsibility for criminal investigations. A clarification of the respective responsibilities of the Cuerpo Técnico de Investigación (Technical Investigative Force), in the Office of the Prosecutor General, and the DIJIN is called for. The DIJIN should either take full charge of this work or disappear. The latter option is not attractive, however, given the agency's accumulated knowledge and experience.

With the dual objective of achieving greater rapport with the community and encouraging police–civil-society collaboration, the national police created the Frentes de Seguridad (Neighborhood Security Fronts) in 1994. These organize neighborhood residents and, using multiple alarm systems, enable them to warn each other while simultaneously communicating with the nearest police station. This mechanism is applied primarily in middle-income and poor neighborhoods, and it mimics similar police experiments worldwide.

The success of the Neighborhood Security Fronts is still under discussion. There are those who claim that results have been insignificant because of a lack of investment for communication systems and the police force's poor response capacity, due to manpower shortages. Initially, the public was enthusiastic, but over time its disillusionment has led to a decline in community participation. However, if the performance were really so poor, there would not have been a 268 percent increase in the number of fronts: by November 2001, 12,972 fronts were operating.[17]

Security is important; so too is the perception of security. Despite inadequate resources, the Neighborhood Security Fronts enabled the national police to build a relationship with the public, which has increased the public's level of confidence in the force and even in their own neighborhoods—no small achievement. As of 2005, the fronts remain merely an exercise, far from being a central foundation for urban police administration. They are merely a complement, whose virtue lies in their preventive nature. Despite conditions in Colombia, the policy of the national police is that the public should not arm itself and should only count on means for communicating with the police.

The Neighborhood Security Fronts will be very useful as the national police implement the policies of the administration of President Alvaro Uribe (2002–2006), which encourage greater involvement by the general public in security matters, including issues relating to the guerrillas, paramilitaries, and drug traffickers. An important topic of debate is the national government's encouragement of informants, who receive money in exchange for information leading to the capture of a criminal. This has generated a major controversy because it entails paying for what is a civic duty and because, potentially, it involves collaborating with people who have ties to criminal activity. The Neighborhood Security Fronts have enabled the national police to declare that citizens without criminal connections are providing information without asking for a reward.

COMPREHENSIVE POLICING

One policing issue in major cities that causes great mistrust—or perhaps frustration—is that patrol officers do not provide all the services for which the agency is responsible. The issue goes beyond the four duties mentioned by Courbet (1983). The national police, probably at the insistence of the executive branch, have created a lengthy list of services that the police on the street are required to specialize in. This has reached the point that an officer often ignores anything that is outside his or her area of specialization. The most radical case is in cities, where most police officers are assigned to traffic control. Too often, the citizen who asks a police officer about a security issue remains perplexed when the patrol officer insists that he cannot help.

The solution is not to remove the innumerable armbands that national police officers must wear. This has to happen, but only as the culmination of a process of training and preparation that would provide sufficient knowledge of criminal investigations to fulfill the duties that Courbet listed. Providing child-protection services, customs and airport policing, and policing for the diplomatic corps and tourists, among other things, could continue, but only if these services do not detract from the public's evaluation of the national police.

The answer to this challenge lies, above all, with the legislature and the executive branch. To achieve comprehensive policing in all areas of responsibility requires reforms that would assign, for example, traffic control throughout the nation and would provide the funding and manpower necessary to meet that objective. The responsibility of the national police is to call attention to the need to reform its services.

RELATIONS WITH THE UNITED STATES

A complex issue facing the national police force is its relationship to the United States. In confronting a phenomenon like drug trafficking, which has threatened the future of the Colombian state itself, it has been expedient to receive incentives and encouragement to meet the objectives of the police, the government, and society. It is also expedient to be exposed to new procedures and technologies. It is inexpedient, however, to create the kind of dependency that appears when things are done or encouraged only because of the availability of resources from the United States. Such impractical behavior originates with the government and society but also, undoubtedly, with the national police force itself. In the future—once the illegal crops are eradicated—it will be necessary for U.S. support to go beyond the issue of drug trafficking to focus on the concept of prevention, which likely will require a lot of technology and very little herbicide.

CORRUPTION

Corruption within the national police is minor in comparison to other agencies within the Colombian government, and its level is similar to, or below, that found in other Latin American police departments. The involvement in fighting drug trafficking also provides experience in fighting corruption and the development of counterintelligence operations.

The advances achieved invite us to continue to pursue the goal of reducing the impact that corruption has on citizen security. This raises the issue of the position of police commissioner, created in the 1992 reforms, which, in the hands of a civilian, should constitute a channel for processing citizen complaints. The national police have resisted this new position, with the result that it has had only minimal importance. The problem is not, however, that the police are not ready to fight corruption or that they resist any type of reform. The agenda of the national police—that is, the tasks of confronting guerrillas, paramilitaries, and drug traffickers and of addressing citizen-security issues—and the limited resources to perform the work create a problem that leads the commanders of the national police to demand that they be given internal control of the institution, without delegating any responsibility to the general public. The police leaders are convinced that, in light of the tasks they confront, it is a strategic error to place the management of the problem of corruption in the hands of a third party, because it weakens their authority and responsibility.

Demilitarization in a War Zone

María Victoria Llorente

The current debate on public security in Colombia does not address police reform in the terms originally posed more than a decade ago. A process of institutional change began in 1993 with an effort to demilitarize and democratize
the police based on principles found elsewhere in Latin America and community-policing concepts in vogue internationally. Nevertheless, possibilities for
reform have been limited. A principal obstacle has undoubtedly been Colombia's domestic conflict, which has kept the government and its police force
under continual tension, particularly in regard to restoring law and order in
the country while addressing the general public's demand for security and
peace. This tension has shaped the development of Colombia's police force in
recent decades, making it only intermittently possible to advance the separation of the police from the military. Today, confusion remains about the responsibilities of each institution.

The repugnance the Colombian people feel toward the activities of illegal
armed groups—particularly, rejection by those guerrilla groups of the generous peace offers by the Andrés Pastrana administration (1998–2002) and
the growing, indiscriminant use of terrorism and kidnapping—have tipped
the balance toward the public's plea for a heavy hand. The upturn in violence
late in the 1990s can explain the overwhelming public acceptance of Alvaro
Uribe's Democratic Security proposal, which helped him to win the presidency
in 2002.

From that proposal, the Uribe administration (2002–2006) has developed
a security policy that clearly diverts the police from normal anticrime functions to a role in the counterinsurgency strategy that aims to regain and consolidate the Colombian government's control over vast areas of national terri-

tory now under assault by guerrillas (Presidencia de la República 2003a). Despite the effect of this policy on the path the police followed in the past decade, no one today in Colombia is asking if it is necessary or even possible to continue to demilitarize the police and to construct a more civilian institutional identity for it. The absence of public debate on this issue is notable, as is the lack of civilian leadership that might reinitiate police reform based on democratic principles, particularly those centered on serving the needs of the public and making the agency more transparent and responsible to society (Bayley 2001, 13–14).

Profile of the Colombian Police

The Colombian police force has its origins in the National Police Corps, founded in 1891 under the Ministry of Government to maintain law and order in Bogotá. It has evolved into a modern police force only during the past forty years. The first decades of the force's existence were punctuated by periods of partisan conflict, in particular, the Thousand Days War in the early twentieth century and *la violencia* (the violence) in the mid-twentieth century.

During those times, the police were involved in partisan struggles, and the solution chosen by the governments in power was to place the police force under the Ministry of Defense (at that time, the Ministry of War), reconstituting it with new personnel, most of whom were drawn from the army and were untrained (Torres 1994; Llorente 1999). The government lacked sufficient resources to expand law-enforcement coverage into Colombia's many regions, so there also existed police forces in the Colombian *departamentos* (provinces) and municipalities. These local police forces were subordinate to governors and mayors, and they operated in relative autonomy from the central government. They were politically partisan, mainly because their personnel lacked technical training and were recruited from among the followers of regional and local political bosses (Torres 1994, 182; Pardo 1996, 338; Llorente 1999, 400).

With the installation of the military government (1953–1957) and the Frente Nacional (the bipartisan agreement in force from 1958 to 1978, which enabled Colombia's two traditional parties to alternate in power at the national and regional levels), the country was pacified. In that context, it was possible to reconstitute the police force as a centralized public entity. During the military government period, the army took administrative control of the police force, including the recruitment and training of personnel (Pardo

1996, 338).[1] Early in the 1960s, the unruly departmental and municipal police forces were nationalized and subordinated under the Policía Nacional. In only three years, nationalization—which had been attempted during the military regime without much success—was finally achieved, making the departmental and municipal police forces dependent on the reestablished Policía Nacional for salaries, training, and logistics (Torres 1994, 183; Llorente 1999, 403). At the same time, the Policía Nacional force began to regain its autonomy from the military and chart its own course, even though it remained under the Ministry of Defense, with a military character that survives to the present.[2]

Colombia's first police school was founded in the 1930s, but professionalization only took off once the force had been consolidated as a national-level service. The career ranks of high-ranking and midlevel officers were reorganized in the mid-1950s, according to military norms. One objective was to give high- and midranking police officers parity with army officers (Echeverri 1993, 227–28). During that period, the military tribunal had jurisdiction over trials of police officers. While the structure of police careers changed after the reforms of the 1990s, military jurisdiction over the police has continued and was legitimated in the principles of the 1991 constitution.

In contrast, there were efforts to construct a professional identity more oriented toward law enforcement and less toward the military. For example, a disciplinary process was introduced in the 1960s, based on a special (that is, nonmilitary) regulatory body for the police. The trend was also visible in training programs for higher-ranking officers introduced during the same period, which, while still containing components on military strategy, armaments, and counterinsurgency, also included courses on police tactics, criminology, law, and administration (Torres 1994, 186).

Specialization in law-enforcement organization has been a complex process, given the rise since the 1960s of multiple guerrilla groups in Colombia, and it has not been achieved yet. The first concrete step in this direction was the creation of the judicial police between 1964 and 1966.[3] Nevertheless, the government's plan in the 1960s to expand the police in order to reduce urban crime was countered by the argument that the capacity of the police to support the army in its mission of national pacification in rural areas was more important than fortifying the Policía Nacional as a crime investigation organization (Torres 1994, 185). Thus was born a semispecialized police force, oriented toward, on one hand, complementing the army's counterinsurgency work in rural areas, and on the other, expanding the law-enforcement activities appropriate to urban environments, such as patrolling and crime investigation.

Throughout the 1980s, the image of a police force whose function was urban protection and crime control came into sharper focus, and the organization moved in the direction of providing those services. The Policía Nacional grew in size in order to increase its urban presence, a need associated with increasing urbanization and the growing rates of crime in Colombia's major cities (Torres 1994, 187). There were also important operational enhancements aimed at making the police more responsive to the urban public. These included the creation of metropolitan police departments, the implementation of Centros Automáticos de Despacho (Automated Dispatch Systems), and the establishment of Centros de Atención Inmediata (Immediate Service Centers, CAIs).

The metropolitan police departments were created at the beginning of the 1980s to offer law-enforcement services in Bogotá, Medellín, and Cali, Colombia's three principal cities. At the same time, automated dispatch systems were introduced in these and other large cities to modernize the handling of the emergency calls and speed up the dispatching of patrol cars (Londoño and Diettes 1993, 341–42). The CAIs were created near the end of the 1980s, first in Bogotá and soon in almost all Colombian cities.[4] These centers, which deployed officers in posts at multiple points around a city, were the main initiative of the Policía Nacional to improve community relations through decentralization of basic police services (Camacho Leyva 1993, 280). The CAIs were the first evidence in the operational arena of a shift to an emphasis on attending to the needs of the public, as the chief task of police work. This emphasis was one of the pivotal moments for the reform process of the 1990s.

During this period, the first specialized units to fight organized crime and for assault and rescue operations also appeared. Antinarcotics police units, antikidnapping groups, and the Elite Corps—responsible for dealing with highly dangerous organizations, such as the so-called death squads, gangs of hit men, and paramilitary groups—were all created.

Current Structure and Functions of the Policía Nacional

The current shape of the Policía Nacional is the result of the reorganization process initiated in the mid-1950s. The force has evolved uninterruptedly since then, and in 1991, the new constitution defined it as a standing armed civilian body that reports to the national government and is part of the Fuerza

Pública (that is, the Armed Forces and the National Police).[5] It is a central-ized, national-level organization subordinated to the Colombian president. Its structure is part of the Ministry of Defense, and its chief commander re-ports to the minister of defense. The Attorney General's Office oversees the investigative tasks that are constitutionally in its jurisdiction. The force is di-vided into units corresponding to Colombia's *departmentos* (provinces), and its three largest cities have metropolitan police departments; the governors and mayors supervise these forces, which are at their disposal as mandated by the constitution. In practice, however, many limitations are imposed by the national and centralized structure of the police (Casas 1994), as well as the governors' and mayors' only incipient institutional competence to address public-safety issues in their jurisdictions (Comisión Consultiva 1994, 144–152; Acero 2003, 41–44).[6]

The size of the Policía Nacional has grown in a sustained manner since the 1960s, both in absolute terms and in relationship to the country's popula-tion.[7] By the end of 2003, the force had almost one hundred thousand sworn officers, equivalent to twenty-three officers for each ten thousand inhabitants —a ratio that is reasonable even by international standards.[8] Nearly 80 per-cent of its personnel are professionals who have graduated from the police-training schools. Five percent of these career officers are women. The force also has twenty thousand nonprofessional *auxiliaries de policía* (police assis-tants), that is, high school graduates and nongraduates doing their manda-tory military service in the national police, as well as six thousand civilian em-ployees who perform a variety of administrative tasks.

The Policía Nacional force exhibits a complex hierarchical structure that employs military ranks and yet includes standard international police career paths. On the one hand, it has three career tracks equivalent to those of the army: *oficiales* (high-ranking officers, including generals, colonels, majors, captains, and lieutenants), *suboficiales* (midlevel officers, including sergeants and corporals), and *agentes de policía* (police agents, the rank-and-file sworn officers). A fourth category, called the *nivel ejecutivo* (executive level), was created in 1993 to fuse into a single career track midlevel officers and police agents. This has yet to be fully implemented. The organization has a pyra-midal structure where 4 percent of its members are high-ranking officers, 20 percent are in the middle or supervisory ranks, and the remaining 76 percent are the rank and file. This last category includes a large proportion of career officers and, to a lesser degree, nonprofessional police assistants, who account for 24 percent of the rank and file.

The police are preponderantly deployed in urban areas, which is not surprising given the accelerated process of urbanization that Colombia has experienced in recent decades. By 2002, at least 75 to 80 percent of the force was concentrated in urban areas, where almost the same proportion of the Colombian population lives, while in rural areas the police presence was precarious. Moreover, 15 percent of Colombia's municipalities—all of them in rural areas—had no police presence whatsoever.[9] These ratios of police presence in urban areas versus rural areas are common by international standards. Nevertheless, Colombia's rural areas, although the least populated part of the country, represent the largest expanse of territory and are the primary site for the armed conflict. Indeed, one of the focal points of the government's current security strategy is to resolve this precarious situation by broadening the base of the Carabineros, part of the police force specifically trained for the rural context, and complementing them with police assistants and so-called *campesino* (peasant) soldiers (Presidencia de la República and Ministerio de Defensa Nacional 2003).[10] With the current efforts to increase police presence in rural areas, as of 2004 there were no *municipios* (townships) in these areas without police protection, and at least 30 percent of the force was assigned there.

Finally, considering the Colombian police in terms of their current duties, patrol officers make up a major part of the force (80 percent). These are uniformed officers performing such varied tasks as routine patrolling; responding to calls from the public; enforcing national, departmental, and municipal police statutes; providing traffic control in some cities; patrolling national highways; guarding dignitaries (e.g., judges, politicians, and public officials), protecting economic and services infrastructure as well as national parks and natural reserves; serving as riot police and juvenile police (Llorente 1999, 445–49).

In contrast, only 10 percent of the personnel are involved in crime-fighting activities: the *policía judicial* (judicial police), this is, plainclothes officers performing criminal investigations, represent 4 percent, antinarcotics agents 3 percent, the intelligence police (also plainclothes officers) 2 percent, and antikidnapping units 1 percent. By international standards, and compared with other police forces that also exercise the dual function of patrolling and crime investigation, the scarcity of specialized personnel for the latter is surprising. For instance, in English-speaking democracies and Japan, between 14 and 20 percent of police personnel are assigned to criminal investigation (Bayley 1994, 25).[11] The remaining 10 percent of the force includes police officers doing paperwork at the national headquarters (5 percent) and uniformed personnel in training schools (5 percent).

The Police Crisis of the 1990s

After two decades of uninterrupted institutional growth, Colombian society once again began profoundly questioning the police in the early 1990s. The public's confidence level in the police was no greater than 35 percent, whereas confidence in the army was closer to 50 percent (Lemoine 1997). The level of confidence in the police dropped to 21 percent in 1993 (Lemoine 2003), a critical year marking a significant rupture for the organization. Colombia's principal analysts on defense and security matters during that period argued that the basic problem was an increasing divorce between the public and the police (Comisión de Estudios sobre la Violencia 1987; Camacho and Guzmán 1990; Camacho 1993, 1995; Leal 1994). This had its origins in the militarization of the police force, due to its previous institutional development under the army's control. The analysts also pointed out the obvious national weakness in formulating security policies to address diverse challenges, particularly the absence of a government policy delimiting citizen security in the overall national security picture.

Militarization had impeded creating a closer relationship with the community, but only in that institutional framework had it been possible to keep the police out of political conflicts and give the force the stability necessary for its professional development (Pardo 1996, 338–39). A more accurate hypothesis is that the absence of a coherent security policy provided the space for organized violence to flare up, with deep repercussions for the police. Until the early 1980s, successive administrations put priority on the counterinsurgency issue and battling nascent drug-trafficking organizations, which meant a delay in addressing the issue of common crime, something overlooked to an unacceptable degree in the country's primary cities. Consequently, the public ended up seriously doubting the ability of the police to control crime.

EFFECTS OF THE FIGHT AGAINST DRUG TRAFFICKING

Beginning in the 1980s, the police became the primary tool in the government's antinarcotics fight and were called upon to track down kingpins and control illegal crops.[12] Leading analysts on defense and policing issues argued that this focus affected the relationship of the police with the public (Camacho 1993).[13] This was apparent in the main urban areas. For instance, during the fight against Pablo Escobar's cartel (late 1980s to early 1990s) in Medellín, the police were perceived by both the community and the local authorities as part of the problem of violence affecting that city, and this led to tremendous public distrust. A survey done in Medellín in early 1993 showed that 50 percent of the interviewees from all strata felt distrust, fear, and hatred toward the police, while only 16 percent felt protected by and respectful toward the institution (Universidad de Antioquia 1994, 53). During this period the municipal authorities repeatedly asked the national government to remove the Policía Nacional from Medellín so that a local force could be created.[14] Not only did many officers die in that conflict, but in some areas of Medellín, the police had to retreat in the face of targeted attacks, ordered by the cartel capos.[15] Criminal gangs took over, and in response to the growing anarchy, people began organizing *milicias populares* (popular militias), some of which were ultimately confused with urban guerrilla cells, also called *milicias*.

The war against drugs had devastating effects on the integrity of the National Police. Some officers were implicated in human-rights violations, most of them related to police retaliation against the Medellín cartel's persecution of them (Americas Watch 1990, 19–28; 1993, 127–29). Moreover, several cases of police officers—even high-ranking officials—linked to the drug-trafficking cartels were revealed by the press. Thus, for example, at the end of the 1980s, information published in a leading news weekly implicated two Policía Nacional generals in the activities of the Medellín cartel.[16] Unholy alliances between police officers and the Cali cartel, forged as the police carried out their war against the Medellín cartel, also came to light (Velásquez 1993). The involvement of officers in the complex crime morass in Medellín, fueled by the drug traffic, was also public knowledge (Pardo 1996, 340). By the mid-1990s, it was also revealed that the Cali cartel had deeply infiltrated units in Valle Province and in its capital, Cali. After a list of payments from that organization to the Valle Police Department was found, sixty-four officers were dismissed, all of whom had ties to the mafia.[17]

EFFECTS OF THE INTERNAL CONFLICT

Although traditionally the army led the counterinsurgency effort, the police always played an important role, particularly because of their presence throughout much of Colombia. As the guerrilla groups began an aggressive strategy of expansion and territorial control starting in the mid-1980s (Echandía 1999b), lack of police preparation to meet the growing threat was apparent. The basic problem in this case was both the lack of manpower in rural areas—the main location for the conflict—and the political establish-ment's lack of clarity about the role of the police in restraining the guerrilla advance (Llorente 1999, 457).

Police weakness was visible in the number of officers who died in guerrilla attacks on police stations.[18] The difficulties the police faced in defending themselves from these attacks led to a gradual withdrawal and regrouping into smaller, but better manned, posts (Pardo 1996, 339). According to police data, from the 1980s into the early 1990s, the force withdrew from almost thirty rural stations.

Pressure from the guerrilla threat also affected the government's decisions on police deployment. For example, in the César Gaviria administration (1990–1994), expansion of the police force was a key policy to strengthen the institution. In 1992, almost 80 percent of that increase was destined for the so-called Plan Energético Vial (Energy Delivery Plan), which was designed to protect the nation's energy and highway infrastructure, which had become the object of guerrilla attacks (Llorente 1999, 452). Thus, in practice, the nec-essary increase of police personnel during the 1980s and the beginning of the 1990s did not result in coverage of more territory or better protection for the public.

No systematic documentation exists on the impact of the police force's re-treat from certain municipalities and its scant presence in others. Even so, it is reasonable to suppose, and evident in a variety of media stories, that the withdrawal left the population either at the mercy of the violent struggle be-tween the guerrillas and the paramilitaries for territorial control or under the domination of one of those actors, in many cases because of police and mili-tary powerlessness, neglect, or complicity.[19]

POWERLESSNESS AGAINST GROWING CRIMINALITY

By the beginning of the 1990s, the urban population was strongly criticizing the police force for its lack of effectiveness and transparency in its daily crime-prevention work. Between 1985 and 1995, victimization surveys in var-ious cities showed a troubling increase in property crimes, particularly those involving violence, such as armed robbery—generally the most prevalent crime (Rubio 1999, 48–54). Between 1983 and 1992, a steady and unprece-dented increase in homicide rates also occurred. During that same period, homicides in Colombia more than doubled, rising from thirty-two to seventy-nine homicides per one hundred thousand inhabitants. Furthermore, public criticism of police involvement in illicit activities also grew, as police gangs formed in several cities to carry out armed robberies and "social cleansing," that is, the selective killing of criminals, prostitutes, beggars, and the mentally ill (Camacho and Guzmán 1990; Amnesty International 1994; Rojas 1996).

The CAIs, the force's flagship community-relations program, was in clear decline. The few assessments on these centers agree that the rapid multiplication of police posts, based more on the political interests of the municipal authorities than on sound planning, hurt the program, both in personnel and allocations of resources (Pardo 1996, 339–40; Llorente 1999, 416–19, 429–30). Paradoxically, the deterioration of the CAIs, which the police had enthusiastically launched in their attempt to rescue their institutional image, was the first evidence of a crisis that had overtaken the Policía Nacional: the situation with the CAIs revealed problems in the quality of rank-and-file personnel and the low ratio of supervisors to police officers, which, according to high-ranking officers, was at the root of the internal-control problems.[20]

The police crisis of the 1990s was directly associated with successive government administrations' failure to establish policies responding to public-security challenges, among them the implementation of police reforms. The growing threat of armed illegal organizations (guerrillas, drug traffickers, and paramilitaries) overwhelmed the Colombian law-enforcement establishment as a whole, and particularly the Policía Nacional, which were further weakened by their inability to prevent common crime. Just before the reforms that would start in 1993, the principal challenge for the police was to introduce organizational changes that would enable them to address adequately both the needs of the general public and those of the government, as they faced the threat of increasing activity by powerful armed organizations operating outside the law.

The Reform Agenda in the 1990s

During the Gaviria administration, an attempt was made to change the focus of public-safety policies at the national and local levels: civilians were called upon to be more active in the design of public policies on national defense and citizen security, as well as in the related planning and allocation of resources. At the presidential level, a discourse unfolded that began to differentiate between citizen security and national security. For the first time, the government established a strategy that clarified the state's objectives and its internal-security policies, as well as a plan to develop the security forces.[21]

This strategy represented an initial attempt by civil authorities to try to delimit the roles of the armed forces and the police and to consider a reform of the criminal-justice system.

Significantly, the government strategy also introduced an approach to decentralizing the management of citizen security, which proposed that regional and local authorities show some leadership and take a more active decision-making role. It also envisioned a decentralization of police services based on local-level security priorities. Various regulations were established to modify regional and local decision-making mechanisms to pave the way for municipalities to increase the availability of police personnel, both career officers and police assistants, based on local needs.[22]

The appointment in 1991 of a civilian defense minister, after forty years of army control over this office, was particularly relevant for wresting the police from the military line of command. This step would grant the police greater operational autonomy from the army. Notably, one of the first measures adopted by the first civilian minister of defense was to regulate the use of operational control over the police by the military, limiting it to specific cases authorized by the minister (Pardo 1996, 336–37).[23] The police also gained greater control over their budget, which formerly was allocated by the military as part of the overall defense sector.

Although the police crisis in the early 1990s made major reforms unavoidable, another factor that undoubtedly helped lay the groundwork was the government's new approach to the management of public safety and citizen security, with an increased role for civilians. The police reform was launched with an initial phase in 1993–1994, led by the newly appointed civilian minister of defense. In 1995, a second stage began, which lasted until the late 1990s and was under the exclusive leadership of the police force's chief commander.

NONREFORM

The 1993 reform represented a milestone in that it generated internal and external debates about the police force and its role in Colombian society. Indeed, the government appointed two commissions to propose reform measures: an external one, comprising civilians (congresspersons, mayors, governors, union representatives, and a variety of associations), and an internal one, made up of members of all the ranks in the force.[24]

The principal motor for this reform was the need to emphasize the civilian character of the police force, that is, to deepen its separation from the military. Three basic elements were considered: (1) the creation of mechanisms to promote greater civilian control over policing and to provide incentives for citizen participation in police matters, (2) a structural reorganization to respond in distinct ways to the demands for citizen security and national security, and (3) the introduction of a new professional career track aimed at creating a less hierarchical command structure and increasing the ratio of supervisors to the rank and file.[25]

On the first point, a major development was the introduction of regulations strengthening the governors' and mayors' constitutionally granted control over policing in their jurisdictions. Also significant was the creation of the national police commissioner, a civilian who headed an external office, which would be responsible for monitoring the disciplinary system and handling complaints against the police.[26] The creation of a Sistema Nacional de Participación Ciudadana en Asuntos de Policía (National System for Citizen Participation in Police Matters) would open the way for various sectors of society to express their concerns about the police and to guide and supervise the relationships among the police, the public, and local authorities. Moreover, an Office of Community Participation was to be opened within the police to support and promote the development of the national system, among other functions.

On the second point, structural reorganization, an institutional framework was planned, to be built around three specialized branches: urban policing, rural policing, and criminal investigation. The primary aim was to draw a sharper line between an urban force, with its more civilian profile, and a rural force, trained especially to maintain order in regions where guerrillas and paramilitaries operate. Institutionally, this meant the creation of two new offices, one responsible for the development of the urban police and the other for the rural police, the Carabineros.[27] In practice, every city with more than fifty thousand inhabitants supposedly would have an urban police force trained to respond to public demands and the security challenges of the urban environment. In rural areas, there would be a corps of Carabineros, conceived of as a strike force to maintain public order and control areas affected by the armed conflict.

To address the third point, a new career track was introduced, the *nivel ejecutivo* (executive level), into which midlevel officers and police agents would gradually be absorbed. The long-term goal was a flatter command structure, one less like the military and better aligned with international trends that were moving toward a simplification of hierarchies and shrinking of lines of command in police departments (Bayley 1994, 60–66). The national police would have only two levels: a career track for high-ranking officers—with ranks equivalent to those found in the military—and the executive level, with only five ranks. The latter would enable personnel to rise rapidly (after five years as patrol officer) to middle management and supervisory positions, which would serve to increase the ratio of supervisors to rank-and-file police officers.[28]

In practical terms, none of these reform initiatives flourished, largely because of institutional obstruction and poor planning. In some cases, these proposals mandated measures that were obviously complicated. For example, the National System for Citizen Participation in Police Matters could not operate without convening a National Commission, comprising twenty-three members from varied backgrounds. Moreover, the force's leadership, in general, was unwilling to accept these reforms because most of the recommendations came from outside the organization.[29] For instance, a special concern of the minister of defense at the time was the proposed reorganization into urban, rural, and criminal-investigative branches, which never materialized. Instead, the urban orientation, which the police had been developing since the 1980s, remained predominant. Under the Uribe administration new provisions have been made to increase the number of Carabineros as part of the counterinsurgency effort rather than as a planned structural reorganization. Meanwhile, the enhancement of an urban-oriented police identity remains the sole interest of its commanding officers.

Measures aimed at expanding civilian control over the police also did not succeed. This was not only because they sparked resentment among the police leadership but also because of shortcomings in planning, as, for example, in the creation of the *comisionado nacional para la policía*.[30] As could be predicted from similar efforts elsewhere in the world (Goldsmith 1991), the Policía Nacional did not embrace this idea. More importantly, perhaps, improvisation in the design and implementation of this office blurred its preventive goals while generating resistance among the institution's leadership, which viewed this office as nothing more than another *procuraduría general de la nación* (national procurator general).[31] The failure to implement an internal mechanism for disciplinary control, to complement the Office of the National Police Commissioner, was yet another shortcoming. In contrast, rather than fitting it into the new scheme, the Office of the Inspector General was abolished, which undoubtedly generated more institutional resentments. In 1995 the inspector general was reestablished, but with reduced disciplinary powers. The *comisionado*'s office remained open but was never able to accomplish its disciplinary and anticorruption tasks.

Not even the new *nivel ejecutivo* career track developed as planned by the 1993 police reformers. Today, the old career paths for midlevel and rank-and-file officers still operate because not all officers wanted to take the steps to move to the new track, but it is apparent that the numbers in all the ranks under the *nivel ejecutivo* have grown, while the numbers remaining in the old ranks have declined. The most significant effect of this measure has been the change in the pyramidal structure of police command. By 2002 the ratio of supervisors to rank-and-file officers had changed dramatically compared with a decade before, from one supervisor for every thirteen police agents and assistants in 1990 to one for every four rank-and-file officers in 2002. Even though this ratio falls within international standards for forces with more civilian command structures, this change did not improve the levels of supervision as originally intended.[32] The *nivel ejecutivo* failed to meet this objective because of poor planning; especially significant was a failure to include special training in management to earn promotion within this career track (Misión Especial 2004, 32–35). For the past few years, high-ranking officials of the Policía Nacional, including the chief commander, have been complaining about what they believe to be an excess of supervisors to rank-and-file personnel (interviews with high-ranking police officers, December 2002). They argue that this supervision is costly and ineffective because the new midlevel personnel were never properly trained. Also, it is an obstacle to the government's objective of increasing police presence in rural areas.

CULTURAL TRANSFORMATION OF THE POLICE

The arrival of the Ernesto Samper administration (1994–1998) meant substantial changes concerning the participation of civilians in security matters. One clear repercussion was that the 1993 reform was buried in favor of another one, promoted and guided by the new police chief commander. The political crisis at the start of the new administration—caused mainly by a scandal over illegal campaign contributions from drug traffickers—meant a loss of some of the progress the previous administration had made in paving the way for civilian initiatives on security. This was obvious for both the military forces and the Policía Nacional (Dávila 1999, 307–10). In the case of the police, the situation was aggravated when General Rosso José Serrano, an internationally renowned figure in the antinarcotics effort who enjoyed credibility with Washington (which President Samper lacked), took over as head of the force. Upon assuming his post in late 1994, Serrano indicated that his priorities would be "fighting drug trafficking and police corruption, adopting citizen security strategies, and encouraging institutional reform."[33] With this development, the police leadership took the reins and initiated a new phase of reform. The earlier reform process, although largely dead, had nevertheless laid the groundwork for a significant internal rethinking about how to adapt the institution to the needs of the public.

One of the most relevant institutional developments arising from General Serrano's priorities was in the antinarcotics area. National and international media widely heralded the success of efforts carried out by the restructured Central de Inteligencia de la Policía Nacional (Police Intelligence Agency), which had led to the capture of high-profile drug-trafficking capos, including the heads of the Cali cartel, in the mid-1990s.

Also notable was the process of internal cleansing, which used discretionary powers granted in 1995 by presidential decree and made possible the expeditious dismissal of any police personnel implicated in illegal activities.[34] To implement this measure a small internal affairs office was opened within the new Police Intelligence Agency. During Serrano's tenure (1995 to mid-2000), almost eight thousand officers of various ranks were removed through this measure—11 percent of all sworn officers (averaged across that period).[35] These figures do not necessarily correspond with the anticorruption efforts during this period, since most of these officers were not prosecuted, nor were there records of the reasons they were removed from the force. Nevertheless, Serrano used them to show the extent of his achievements in police integrity, as well as to question the need for external control mechanisms, such as the comisionado's office. In fact, Serrano publicly argued, "Now, we (the police) no longer require other controls. Public opinion is our best judge, and I can assure you that the Policía Nacional has developed the necessary integrity in order to exercise internal control, with the support of the President and the Minister of Defense" (*El Tiempo*, February 1, 1996, quoted by Goldsmith 2000, 185).[36]

At this point, apparently there was no more room for an office under civilian leadership aimed at increasing police accountability. Furthermore, President Samper's dislike of the comisionado experiment became public knowledge when he labeled it "a monstrous control" and stated that "we (the civilians) should let the police regulate itself."[37] The open hostility of the police toward this external control mechanism crystallized in severe budgetary cutbacks in 1995 (Goldsmith 2000, 184) and in an attempt to close the office in 1997 by a presidential decree (ruled unconstitutional in 1998). As of 2004, even though the national police commissioner office continues to operate, it does not have the profile intended at the time of its creation.[38]

There is no straightforward answer as to whether the internal cleansing process led by Serrano reduced police corruption or even helped to control it. There is no way to confirm if the officers removed by discretionary powers— almost 8,800 by 2002—were involved in illicit activities. Moreover, supposing most of these dismissed officers were truly corrupt, these figures could be interpreted in contradictory ways: On one hand, it could be an indisputable indication of institutional healing, but on the other, it could be a symptom of the high levels of corruption present in the force. In favor of the first interpretation is the fact that during Serrano's term there were very few complaints about police corruption. Nevertheless, between 2002 and 2003 an avalanche of scandals linking police officers of various ranks with criminal activities suggested that the anticorruption effort launched six years earlier probably was not as effective as first publicized, or had ephemeral effects.[39]

It appears that, with the departure of General Serrano in mid-2000 and the changes at the top of the force, internal controls have been relaxed, and the discretionary measure may have slowly fallen into disuse (Torres 2002; interviews with high-ranking police officers, December 2002). Whatever the case, the use of these powers as the core of the force's anticorruption strategy was further questioned by a special commission appointed in late 2003 by the minister of defense to analyze the functioning of the internal and external police control mechanisms and to make recommendations to enhance them (Misión Especial para la Policía 2004).[40] This commission also pointed out its concern for the lack of a comprehensive police integrity policy, which should be the motor of any police accountability reform (Misión Especial para la Policía 2004).

Another critical institutional reform proposed by General Serrano was the Plan for Cultural Transformation, which was implemented since 1995. It was aimed at fortifying the civilian character of the police through involvement in measures such as the introduction of new leadership and management models, personnel training, and development of client service precepts.[41]

Perhaps the most substantive part of the cultural transformation was the modernization of management. Advances were achieved principally through the adoption of a strategic planning process to define priorities and institutional goals and to assess results. Annually since then, the top commanders of the police have established a Plan Estratégico Institucional (Strategic Institutional Plan), which outlines specific plans for the various national and regional departments. To consolidate this new culture of strategic planning internally, an educational process was launched to develop managerial and leadership skills in police officials. Through contracts with various Colombian universities, professional training courses have been made available principally to high-ranking officers (interviews with police officials, December 2002, February 2003).

A new organizational structure was also mandated. Although the organizational changes introduced in 1993 were reversed and the force largely reverted to its pre-1993 structure (Llorente 1999, 413–15), the proposal sought a renovation of human-resource management by replacing the quasi-military model with one based on more horizontal relations and the assignment of responsibilities based on an officer's abilities. Concrete advances and results have yet to be documented for the objectives of this organizational reform, but it would appear that the discourse about a more level structure and assignment of responsibility on the basis of a person's capabilities has not taken root among officials and even less so among most of the midranking and lower-level officers.

This lack of penetration is mainly due to the still-prevalent culture in which the high-ranking officers feel they must maintain their distance from the mid- and lower-ranking officers. Indeed, the main training associated with the new management culture concentrated on officials, who took coursework at business schools in several Colombian universities. In contrast, the respective police schools offered supervisory personnel and lower-ranking officers revamped professional training, which tended to focus on the idea of client service while reducing military-style training (interviews with police officials, December 2002).

Another significant aspect of the cultural transformation was the proposed rapprochement between the police and civil society. Activities were developed to open the institution to citizen participation, in an attempt to refocus service to respond to public demands and to incorporate the citizenry in the reform of the police force. One initial measure was to take surveys in the three largest cities to get a more precise idea of how the public perceived the police and the services they provide, as well as to identify public needs. Another important activity involved collaborating with national and local business organizations, to gain support for the work the police do and for the managerial reforms under way.

Perhaps the most popular facet of public outreach was the promotion of partnerships with average citizens to engage them in crime-prevention initiatives within their communities. To achieve this, the police, inspired by the Neighborhood Watch programs that have spread throughout Great Britain and the United States, promoted similar community organizations called Frentes de Seguridad Local (Local Security Fronts) and Escuelas de Seguridad (Security Schools). From 2,700 fronts organized in 1995, the program grew to 6,800 in 2001, with almost half a million citizens from various Colombian cities taking part.[42] According to a study done on Bogotá, where the program began, the initiative has had an impact on the number of people that the police have been able to rally, but its results for crime prevention seem to be less than hoped for (Sánchez et al. 2001). This has been true as well for the Neighborhood Watch programs (Bayley 1994; Sherman et al. 1997).

Community-policing initiatives were also launched, with a pilot project starting in Bogotá in 1998. Preliminary assessments of that project note its fidelity to the philosophy for this type of policing, as well as some positive results in improving the public's image of the police in sectors of the city where community policing is available (Llorente 2004). Nevertheless, this project has not been widely implemented, primarily because it was not developed as an integral reform of the Colombian policing model. Thus, it ended up as a set of public-outreach activities that the police had already been performing for some time—among them, notably, the Local Security Fronts and the Security Schools (Llorente 2004).[43] Later, General Serrano's original idea from 1999 of broadening Bogotá's community-policing project to other regions of the country was implemented to some degree, but these efforts were less in accord with the philosophy of this policing model (interviews with police officials, February 2003).

Effects of the Reform Process and Current Challenges

One of the most obvious effects of the reform in the 1990s was the consolidation of an institutional identity that is more appropriate to urban policing. This shift in identity first began to appear in the 1980s, but the urban-rural balance inclined in favor of urban security issues during the second half of the 1990s. At that point, unprecedented increases in guerrilla attacks on rural police posts, combined with a lack of military support, led the police to withdraw from a number of positions in guerrilla-dominated zones.[44] For better or worse, that process represented a significant change in the separation of the police from the military and the development of a more civilian-focused concept of Colombian policing. Nevertheless, there is still far to go, particularly in civilian control of, and public participation in, police matters.

The very evident change in the public's perception of the police may also be associated with the 1990s reforms. At the end of 2002 the Policía Nacional had a high level of public trust: 57 percent of Colombians had confidence in the institution, a notable contrast to only 21 percent exactly ten years before (the average for Latin America as a whole barely exceeds 30 percent; Lemoine 2003). Compared with other Colombian government institutions, the police had the largest increase in public confidence for the past decade, with the Armed Forces coming in a distant second (Lemoine 2003).[45] Ironically, citizens also identify the police as one of the most corrupt institutions in the country. For instance, in a survey on corruption, also conducted at the end of 2002, 85 percent of the interviewees thought that the police were corrupt.[46]

There are three possible interpretations. One is that the 1990s reform process delivered its promised effect of restoring the institution's conventional crime-fighting image. In this view, the process of constructing a more civilian identity that responds to public demands, plus the internal cleanup and greater orientation toward urban policing, ultimately increased the effectiveness of the police force in its fight against common crime. Arguing in favor of this interpretation is the continuous decline of property crimes between 2000 and 2002. According to official records and victim surveys for Colombia's five largest cities, these are the crimes that affect the largest portion of the population, at least in urban settings.[47] During those years, the sense of security among the residents of the five major cities increased substantially (Fedesarrollo 2003). How closely related these changes are to the activity of the police has yet to be explored adequately, but striking correlations exist between the reform process, growth in public trust in the police, decline in common crime, and increase in public perception of security.

A second possible interpretation is that the increase in public trust in the police has less to do with the reforms and their possible effects on urban crime and instead is related to the image of General Serrano, who headed the Policía Nacional between 1995 and 2000, and the prestige garnered from capturing the Cali cartel capos in the mid-1990s. Arguing for this interpretation is the fact that General Serrano consistently had a public approval rating of almost 80 percent (*Revista Semana*, May 5, 1997), and this might have influenced the public's perception of the institution under his command.

Moreover, by 1996, only a very short time after Serrano's reform began, Colombians' confidence in the police had already grown to a level of almost 50 percent (Lemoine 1997). The very visible results in the fight against the drug cartels came at precisely that time.

However, this interpretation is more applicable to the changes in perception in the short and medium term, because it is unlikely that a high level of institutional credibility could be maintained for several years after the successes against the cartels and the departure of General Serrano. Undoubtedly, there must be a more solid reason for the change in public confidence in the Policía Nacional. This is also likely because the police corruption scandals in 2002 and 2003 did not have an immediate effect on public confidence in the institution (Llorente 2003).

The third interpretation is that regard for the police is directly associated with the hard line that the Colombian people are taking toward crime and violence, particularly in regard to guerrilla groups. This may also explain the increased confidence levels for the armed forces and the widespread support for the current administration's proposals.

The most plausible interpretation, however, is one that blends these three possibilities: Initially, General Serrano's prestige, combined with the successes in the war on drug-trafficking cartels, may have launched the growth in public confidence in the police. Then, the discourse about opening the institution to the public and about community relations, combined with declining property-crime rates, consolidated the shift in perception while creating an impression that the improvements in containing crime were directly related to the reforms. Thus, in a context in which the public is calling for a heavy hand, a recently reformed police force that apparently is getting results seems even more attractive. This argument would largely explain the absence of public debate about police reform in Colombia during the past few years.

This way of thinking, however, is extremely superficial. Significant doubts have arisen about the path the Policía Nacional may take under the new security policies advocated by the current administration. The priority of those policies is to regain control of national territory as a function of a counterinsurgency strategy, and within that, the police are called upon to play a fundamental role that involves retaking the rural areas from the guerrillas, and, in general, fortifying the force's presence in the countryside. Indeed, between 2002 and 2003, a plan was implemented to achieve accelerated growth in manpower. An additional twenty thousand sworn officers and assistants were enrolled in only one year.[48] Of these, 20 percent were assigned to the country's three principal cities, and the remainder (eight thousand Carabineros and eight thousand assistants) were deployed on the principal highways and in rural areas affected by the armed conflict (*Revista Criminalidad* 2003, 9–20).

Clearly, this refocusing on a counterinsurgency strategy diverges from the path that the Policía Nacional took as an institution during the 1990s. Regardless of the appropriateness of the current administration's policies, in institutional terms, it remains an open question what effects this new focus will have on the identity of the police, on which so much effort was expended in recent years. Moreover, the rapid increase in force size has been achieved at the expense of halving the length of officer training—from one year to only six months—coupled with a considerable increase in the number of nonprofessional personnel, police assistants, who receive only a three-month training program before being sent to the new rural posts (Misión Especial para la Policía Nacional 2004, 34). Unarguably, this poses enormous institutional challenges. Also, recent police corruption revelations once again threaten the credibility of the Policía Nacional.[49]

As expected, the recent scandals made integrity problems the main public concern in Colombia regarding policing, and steps to deal with this situation were taken in late 2003 by the Uribe administration. These included the removal of police leadership (five generals, including the chief commander) and the appointment of a special external commission. In contrast, there is no public debate about the institutional change of course that will result from the development of the current government's policies. In sum, the demilitarization of the police—instituting more civilian control over the force and more civilian participation in police matters—is not the issue today that it was ten years ago.

Security Policies in El Salvador, 1992–2002

Edgardo Alberto Amaya

Security is one of the most sensitive subjects in El Salvadoran political and so-cial history. The founding and consolidation of the Salvadoran state was char-acterized by the systematic use of state force as an instrument to discipline, dominate, and control the population and, especially, to contain societal con-flict (Alvarenga 1996). The instrumental use of security agencies provoked so-cietal resistance of varying intensities. The strongest of these took the form of an armed rebellion that challenged the government during a twelve-year civil war (1980–1992).

On January 16, 1992, the government of El Salvador and the combatant Frente Farabundo Martí para la Liberación Nacional (Farabundo Martí Front for National Liberation, FMLN) signed peace accords. In the decade follow-ing, the security issue figured prominently in the national political agenda as common crime increased and new security models inspired the creation of in-stitutions such as the Policía Nacional Civil (National Civil Police, PNC). The coexistence of democratizing and authoritarian tendencies in El Salvador in this period was an important influence on public-security policy.

Historical Background

The National Guard, the National Police, and the Treasury Police, militarized forces subordinate to the Ministry of War (later renamed the Ministry of De-fense), operated in El Salvador during most of the twentieth century. These *cuerpos de seguidad pública* (public-security forces, CUSEP) played a major role in repressing and controlling social conflict. The National Guard, in par-ticular, was deployed in El Savador's rural areas, and, under an explicit legal mandate, it assisted large landowners and agricultural interests in repressing labor sectors that resisted the existing work conditions.

The recruitment of civilians to monitor and inform on people was a very important government measure to control the population by providing the CUSEP with a nationwide network. At their most advanced, at the end of the 1970s, these civilian groups formed parapolice forces and paramilitary structures and took part in persecutions and political repression, with the support and acquiescence of the government. Patricia Alvarenga (1996) argues that much of the geographic coverage and coercive capacity of the security forces was made possible largely by these mechanisms of cooptation and collaboration.

Although El Salvador experienced a period of relative political stability at the start of the twentieth century, it was interrupted in 1932 by two major events. The first was the coup d'état by General Maximiliano Hernández Martínez, who installed a military-type government that would launch an almost fifty-year political tradition. The second was the peasant uprising, incited by the Salvadoran Communist Party, which government forces crushed with substantial assistance from the CUSEP, leaving an estimated ten thousand dead.

A military-controlled government strengthened the security institutions and increased their profile as instruments of political control, to the detriment of their responsibility to provide security (Amaya and Palmieri 2000, 88). As has occurred in many Latin American countries, the so-called doctrine of national security was implemented, according to which institutions formulated their policies on domestic security in the face of foreign threats, subversive ideologies, or internal protests against the status quo. This transformed the armed forces into the guarantor of that security, placing those forces even above the law (Ellacuría 1991). A public policy that should have served citizens and their need for protection instead benefited an abstract entity, the Salvadoran state.

In this scenario, the military created a model of violent and arbitrary use of power that shaped the country's political culture (Amaya and Palmieri 2000, 91; Ranum 2000, 2002). During the armed conflict, the CUSEP carried out low-intensity warfare. The Truth Commission, created by the peace accords, issued a report covering the period between 1980 and 1990, which showed that Salvador's armed forces, the CUSEP, and the so-called death squads perpetrated 95 percent of the violent acts reported to the commission (Comisión de la Verdad 1993, 41).

The Peace Accords and the Transformations in Public Security

Starting in 1989, in the midst of the armed conflict and during the Alfredo Cristiani administration, the United Nations mediated a negotiation between the government of El Salvador and the FMLN, which produced the peace accords in 1992. A basic objective was the demilitarization of Salvadoran society, and one measure to achieve that called for replacing the CUSEP with a new, civilian security force under the command of civilian authorities and adhering to a new democratic doctrine that would include respect for human rights.[1] That reform had profound significance since it was not limited merely to the construction of a new police force but also involved a radical break from security policy as practiced prior to the accords. In response to that radical change, however, those who had used the CUSEP as a tool of political control sabotaged and distorted the reforms. This was visible in the resilience of the government and allied elites, as they worked to create a new security model, and in their preference for forms of security administration that would be more manageable politically and would have fewer limits and controls (Spence et al. 1997, 20; Costa 1999).[2]

A visible increase in ordinary crime occurred in the postwar transition. El Salvador's crime levels rank it among the most violent countries in Latin America. This was excused as an effect of the postwar era, caused by the temporary vacuum created by the departure of the CUSEP and the inexperience of the PNC (Cruz 1997, 984). The alarm over insecurity was one of the arguments conservatives used to sabotage and distort the new security model. For example, personnel with military backgrounds were appointed to leadership positions in the new police force, and experienced personnel, brought in from the CUSEP, headed the criminal-investigation units. The argument was that, given the increase in crime, it would be imprudent to start at square one with totally inexperienced personnel (United Nations 1997; Costa 1999, 402).

A favored strategy was to increase the size of the police force and its geographic coverage of the country. But expansion neglected important issues, such as technical training for police personnel and the need for sound planning to manage institutional operations (CNSP 1996, 14; 1998, 2–5; United Nations 1997; FESPAD 1998, 67). Also overlooked were prevention policies and mechanisms of internal control over police operations and criminal investigations (FESPAD 1998, 12).[3] The ineffectiveness and weakness of control mechanisms contributed to high levels of human-rights violations and a growth in public distrust toward the new institution (Aguilar and Amaya

1998a, 371).[4] The institutional response to the role of the police in the growing human-rights issue was weak and largely negligent and, in some cases, even complicit. The Fundación de Estudios para la Aplicación del Derecho (Foundation for Law Enforcement Studies, FESPAD) came to view it as an institutionalized and structural problem for the PNC, one that would lead eventually to a new institutional crisis (FESPAD 1998, 69; Aguilar, Amaya, and Martínez 2001, 61). However, the actors who were directly involved did not necessarily perceive this as a problem. Instead, they may have considered it as a normal way of conceiving security management.

In 1996, at the urging of the United Nations, the Consejo Nacional de Seguridad Pública (National Council on Public Security, CNSP) was created as a government entity to serve as the president's main adviser on security matters (United Nations 1997). CNSP produced major research and discussion papers that, for the most part, agreed with other documents and recommendations that the United Nations had previously proposed and that revealed some of the main institutional weaknesses in the public-security sector. However, even though the minister of public security presided over the council, and despite its position as the government's main adviser, its recommendations were rarely implemented, which demonstrates the prevalence of political and discretionary criteria in the management of public-security matters.[5]

The government addressed the problems of crime and violence reactively and with little strategic planning (United Nations 1997, 94). CNSP acknowledged this, even officially (1997, 3; 1998, 2–5). A principal critique on security matters was that decision making was based solely on political criteria and perceptions rather than on clear indicators of need and potential. This failure on the part of the security agencies to provide information and accountability made possible, and even strengthened, reactive discourses. The absence of analyses and assessments was a barrier to creation of a vision for the development and rational operation of the PNC and security policy generally, and that made them vulnerable to law-and-order campaigns.

Moreover, even though the constitution established a clear division between the army and the police, after the signing of the peace accords, plans for highway and rural patrolling by the army were implemented. With the deployment of the PNC, Grupos de Tarea Conjunta (Joint Task Groups) were created, consisting of patrols with personnel drawn jointly from the police and the army and under the command of a member of the PNC. Although this was criticized as a violation of the constitution, the official explanation excused it, claiming a need for personnel to cover the national territory while the PNC was being organized. However, until 2003—ten years after the initial deployment of the PNC—the number of grupos continued to grow, directly alongside the expansion of the PNC (FESPAD 1999, 24; 2001, 33). The continuing use of the military for public-security work is evidence of the government's warlike approach to confronting the issues of crime and violence in Salvadoran society, but it has also served to justify the expense and activity of the army in peacetime.

New Perspectives on Violence and Crime

The counterinsurgency model of security management from the previous decades became obsolete with the end of the armed conflict. However, the increases in violence and crime, unprecedented in recent times, generated a new paradigm for the security and justice agencies. Public demands for security reinforced strategies and policies that tended to rely on the police and courts to control the problem, instead of other, less violent methods.[6] The postwar problems were foreseeable, but government measures were not in place to prevent them. For example, in 1991, the United Nations Technical Mission tasked with the creation of the PNC noted that to develop the new police force successfully would require disarming society (Rodés 1991, 37). That never occurred. Consequently, the PNC had to deploy under violent conditions that negatively affected its development.

In the eyes of the public, crime was one of the principal problems, possibly the most pressing, for El Salvador (Cruz, Córdova, and Seligson 2000), and it became a permanent part of the agenda for the media and the national government. According to some interpretations, the end of the armed conflict as a central focus of national life changed the perception of the existing social order to reveal a new order, which, in reality, had only been hidden during the war (Cruz and González 1997, 960). The end of the conflict presumed a transformation in the rules governing violence and their readjustment to a new stage, one without war and with new actors.

In 1998, following a substantial process of judicial reform, a new Criminal Code and Criminal Procedures Code went into force, radically altering the existing form of criminal-justice administration. This new legislation was widely rejected, by, among others, the leadership of the security agencies, who blamed the new laws for being too soft and thus causing crime rates to increase (FESPAD 1999, 62–71). These new conditions transformed public opinion. At the beginning of the postwar period, the public had blamed structural factors, such as socioeconomic conditions or institutional weakness, for the increase in crime rates. After 1998, the public began to think that the new legislation was a factor in the growth of ordinary crime, and that perception led to a major shift in public support for authoritarian postures (IUDOP 1998, 798–99; 1999; Cruz, Córdova, and Seligson 2000, 143–80).

But public perceptions of insecurity did not coincide with trends in crime as reported in victimization surveys. From 1993 to 2001, the rates of victimization, that is, the percentages of those surveyed who reported being a victim of a crime during the preceding period, declined almost continuously, from 34.3 to only 16.1 percent (see table 8.1). Thus, the 2001 rate was half the 1994 rate, although, oddly, it spiked again in 2002 (IUDOP 2002). These figures show that the persistent perception of insecurity, which has justified reactive security policies, does not necessarily reflect reality, since victimization has not increased (with the exception of 2002). Rather, insecurity reflects the absence of transparency, accountability, and systematic planning on crime issues by official agencies. Also, government decision makers employ public fears as a political tool.

Further, the decline in victimization rates shows little correlation to the criminal-law reform, which began only in 1998, four years after the rates peaked. Instead, the decline has multiple explanations. The slow advances in the peace process and the consolidation of certain institutions, such as the

8.1 Victimization Rates, 1993–2002

1993	34.3
1994	39.5
1995	—
1996	29.5
1997	31.1
1998	21.2
1999	23.4
2000	17.3
2001	16.1
2002	19.7

Source: Public Opinion Institute, Universidad Centroamericana, cited in IUDOP, various years.

PNC, are some of the factors that help to explain the phenomenon of falling victimization rates, but these are not the only causes.

This real decline notwithstanding, the perception of an increase in crime had a direct effect in the political arena.[7] It led to a combining of security policies with legislative reform that moved toward tougher sentences and broader coercive police powers. In this way, a major legal component was added to this repressive form of security management when the president sent it to the Legislative Assembly.[8] According to Elin Cecilie Ranum, "Institutional weakness has contributed to the high levels of violent crime. The weaknesses of the National Civilian Police and the judiciary have reduced the state's capacity to combat the problem. The state has not paid sufficient attention to the problem, and its focus on the legal aspect of crime prevention has not been successful in deterring violent behavior" (2002, 115).

The executive branch reduced the problem of crime and violence to a legal issue and proposed to resolve it by a stronger application of institutional violence, that is, by broadening the powers of the police and the courts. In this framework, violence was both the problem and the solution (Amaya and Palmieri 2000, 82). Part of this strong legalistic influence over security policy was due to conceptual confusion present in the official discourse on crime and violence (Amaya 2002, 38). Moreover, political payoffs redounded to those who promoted such legislative responses.[9]

We cannot relate the decline in victimization rates directly to the application of a specific security policy or legal reform, since the explanation lies in other factors of a social nature. To the contrary, the presence of a significant spike in the 2002 victimization rates calls into question the real influence of the government's security policies.

Public Security, 1999–2002

With the inauguration of President Francisco Flores Perez in 1999, the security agencies (i.e., CNSP, PNC and its inspectorate, Ministry of Interior, and National Academy for Public Security), underwent a significant institutional transformation, particularly in administration (FESPAD 2001, 9–13; 2002). President Flores's first public address presented his policy on public security, which foreshadowed the significance the issue would have for his administration. One of the key points in Flores's campaign platform was security, for which he had developed a special document, the Alianza por la Seguridad

(Alliance for Security) as part of La Nueva Alianza (New Alliance) program (Government of El Salvador 1999).[10] The Alliance for Security had four parts: public security, judicial security, security and national defense, and citizen security. In the area of public security, the plan proposed three strategic objectives: reduce crime rates, encourage citizen participation, and improve job conditions for police officers (Government of El Salvador 1999, 4).

Despite the presentation of these objectives, the presidential address discussed only the first goal, crime reduction. Notable among the proposed targets were a 50 percent reduction in violent crime and a 60 percent reduction in ordinary crime, both to be achieved in only three years, and a 50 percent reduction in organized crime, to be achieved in only two years. This is clear evidence of a strong preference for coercive measures to address the problem of crime, and in light of the utterly unrealistic nature of these goals, it is also evidence of a major planning failure and a complete lack of technical understanding.

Presented along with the Alliance for Security was a strategic plan, which had been circulated for comments among various government offices and cooperating agencies. However, CNSP had not been included in that consultation process, and this omission was widely criticized (FESPAD 2001, 9). Nevertheless, the initiation of a process of security administration with specific objectives and institutional planning mechanisms, and accompanied by quantitative goals, has made overall policy stand out as one of that administration's most positive achievements, even though its goals and objectives were unrealistic. This made it possible to elevate the debate on security administration even as the levels of public transparency and citizen involvement in security agencies continued to be tenuous and arbitrary (Aguilar, Amaya, and Martínez 2001, 112–13; FESPAD 2001, 118).

In its adjustments in the public-security sector to comply with the Alliance for Security, the government of El Salvador changed the profile of CNSP, assigning it operational tasks in the preventive area, a topic that until then had been absent from the security-policy debates. It charged CNSP with implementing a long-term program, Prevención Social de la Delincuencia (Social Prevention of Crime), which focused on offering educational, recreational, and work opportunities for at-risk youth, those who were marginalized or living in poverty-stricken conditions, which are fertile grounds for violence and crime. As the critics of these methods note, however, it is questionable to pay special attention to one sector of a nation's population when it is the government's duty to provide services to all its citizens. The project did little to assist Salvadoran youth and had few effects on the government's broader security policies (FESPAD 2002, 10).

Technical weakness in the original Alliance for Security document quickly caused doubts both within and outside of the public-security sector because of unresolved gaps in defining goals and in aspects of interinstitutional coordination. Thus, in 2000, the government issued a reformulated Alliance for Security plan:

1. Within the framework of current law, guarantee the public the conditions necessary so that they may fully enjoy their rights, take full advantage of opportunities arising from national development, and fulfill their duties.

2. Place priority on reducing to a minimum, and fostering the eradication of, social violence, corruption, drug trafficking, weapons trafficking, and environmental crimes.

3. Reduce rates of social violence by 60 percent by 2002.

4. Eradicate kidnapping in 2001. (PNC 2000, 9–10)

Following the customary government path, security policy again was oriented predominantly toward directing the police to combat crime—specifically, certain types of crime. Once again, the expectations were highly unrealistic and biased toward fighting specific types of crime. As Paul Chevigny notes, it is a mistake to focus crime-reduction efforts exclusively on police involvement without taking into account the presence and role of other criminal-justice institutions, because this ultimately undermines and weakens the police force itself (2002, 60). The government of El Salvador's management of security policy emphasized crime repression, particularly police operations focused on specific types of crime and socially disadvantaged demographic sectors or those areas suffering urban disturbances.[11] All of that was given priority over prevention and alternative ways of dealing with social conflict.

From 1999 to 2002, security strategies were imported through cooperation with the U.S. Justice Department's International Criminal Investigative Training Assistance Program. This was manifested primarily in the establishment of a Patrullas de Intervención Policial Comunitarias (Community Police Patrolling) system and the EFICACIA program, which copied, to some degree, what is known as COMPSTAT (computer statistics) in the United States.[12] This involves the use of computer statistics to aid in planning operations aimed at lowering crime rates, as well as to improve police response to all kinds of conflicts, including low-intensity ones. It also includes record keeping on suspects. These measures follow zero tolerance models (Wacquant 2000).

A perverse effect of this management tool was that the indicators of success were statistics that would emphasize a reduction in crime events and an increase in arrests. Regional police chiefs were evaluated, positively or negatively, by the data they presented, and the resulting focus on increased arrests led to arbitrary detentions and data manipulation (FESPAD 2001, 27).

According to PNC data, in 1999 the police received 53,413 complaints and made 22,047 arrests; in 2000, these figures were 61,545 and 33,607, respectively. In 2001, reported crimes dropped to 52,957 but arrests increased to 41,831.[13] According to these data, between 1999 and 2001, the PNC almost doubled its ability to arrest suspects (FESPAD 2002, 8). This was due to the new techniques instituted in police operations as well as to the increase in police powers of arrest granted by the amended criminal code. Those amendments were made at the request of the PNC and conservative business sectors (FESPAD 2001, 121; 2002, 81–83; Marchelli and Martínez 2002, 62; Martínez 2002, 93).

The effects of this power to arrest were rapidly felt in other parts of the criminal-justice system, in particular the prisons. In April 1998, before the 1998 changes to the Criminal Procedures Code, the prison population was 9,219 (151.86 per one hundred thousand Salvadorans). That number was reduced and contained, thanks to a series of mechanisms introduced by the new criminal code.[14] Only six months after those laws took effect, the number of prisoners dropped 24 percent, to 7,207, or 119.49 per one hundred thousand citizens (Amaya 1999, 21; FESPAD 1999, 69; Martínez 2000, 17). However, in September 2002, following multiple reforms to the criminal code, the number of prisoners rebounded to 10,476, or 160.73 per one hundred thousand citizens (Ministerio de Gobernación 2002). Saturation and overcrowding have become a source of conflict within the prisons. After 2001, the number of prison riots and brawls increased notably (FESPAD 2002, 39).

SECURITY MANAGEMENT IN AN INTERNATIONAL CONTEXT

El Salvador's public-security policies copied models applied in other contexts, including in the international arena. Here they incorporated the hemispheric security interests of the United States antinarcotics efforts, trafficking in people (illegal migration), and—since September 11, 2001—the war against terrorism. The strengthening of institutions to combat drug trafficking and money laundering, recently linked to antiterrorist campaigns, was evident in the cooperation with the United States. The government even signed a treaty to allow the United States to establish a military base in El Salvador for airspace monitoring, as part of the anti-drug-trafficking effort. There was strong support for the creation of money-laundering laws, and a special division in the attorney general's office was created to address this issue. The events of September 11 and the actions taken by the United States led to emergency measures in El Salvador, especially on border and airport security. Initially, this occurred through the army's control over the borders, but later police permanently replaced military personnel.

In the local arena, one of the perverse effects of this phenomenon was to banalize the category of terrorism and its self-serving uses. The Salvadoran legislation recognized terrorism as a crime but regulated it in a broad and ambiguous manner. Consequently, the police justified arrests in cases as dissimilar as juvenile gangs caught with homemade explosives in their possession (FESPAD 2002) and unionized government employees involved in violent labor protests, with the argument that, legally, these constitute acts of terrorism. However, such actions can be interpreted as a manipulation of labels to invent enemies who did not exist before.[15]

NEW SIGNS OF AUTHORITARIANISM

In 2002, the Legislative Assembly passed the National Defense Law.[16] From the start, it was strongly criticized, particularly by human-rights organizations. According to the president, the law's purpose was to carry out the constitutional mandate on national defense that until then had lacked implementing legislation. The criticism focused on a series of terms and concepts that were highly ambiguous and confusing, the interpretation of which might enable the armed forces to intervene eventually in domestic-security tasks, even though the text of the law authorized this only in case of public disturbances.

The National Defense Law returned to the concepts of national security and national defense, transverse axes of government activity, to which are attached such labels as "the fundamental objective of the State." At the same time, it mixed domestic and external security, since the law included within the duties of national defense involvement in the domestic arena and in government civilian institutions, even to the point of creating an ad hoc structure with various ministries and government institutions.[17] Despite criticism from opposition political parties, the media, and human-rights organizations, the law was passed and implemented. Only a few modifications were made, to preserve press freedom, but the original scheme of broad and ambiguous categories was retained. The National Defense Law could become an instrument of social repression and an opening to military involvement in control of the public and in operations to repress social conflict.

Citizen Participation in Security Policy

Citizen participation should not be confused with public opinion. The latter is useful only when crime ranks among a nation's top problems, calling for drastic measures as part of a set of solutions that could be termed punitive populism. Participation of civil society in security matters needs to be developed to give citizens a voice and decision-making power in security matters that affect them. To some degree, this would make it possible to seek alternative forms of management that would fit the country's limited budget.[18]

Some local police headquarters initiated community-security plans, but these were not part of the PNC's institutional program. The plans never got beyond the experimental stage since they lacked institutional support, a clear and operational definition of community relations, and experience in the planning, supervision, and evaluation of such initiatives (Neild 2002). In 1998, CNSP, along with a group of official institutions and civil organizations, launched a consultation and planning process for a pilot experiment in community policing, with the hope that it would become a comprehensive strategy for the PNC. The experiment was based on the idea that the community had very precise needs and opinions about security management, and so it was necessary to include the public in planning at the local level. However, with the presidential transition of 1999 and the transformation of CNSP, the process was aborted.

After 1999, the PNC began to take steps toward rapprochement with the community, but the objective was to improve the image and presence of the police in specific regions. A series of citizen meetings were also arranged to create tools to assess performance in security matters. However, according to the critics, community opinion did not translate into concrete actions on the part of the police force, which continued to operate according to its institutional program, without effective feedback. This was because the planners had a misconception of what community policing really means (Aguilar, Amaya, and Martínez 2001, 129). Nevertheless, this activity, with its limitations, was recognized as a positive initiative for police conduct based on public input (Neild 2002).

Security policy has always been set centrally. However, currently there is growing interest on the part of governments in various Salvadoran cities to outline a local security agenda. The PNC's centralized organization and its internal politics have been barriers to creating a coordination mechanism linking local governments, the police, and other centralized institutions to orchestrate efforts to prevent and treat local problems (Aguilar, Amaya, and Martínez 2001, 93; Neild 2002).

External Controls on Security Policies

The Legislative Assembly's presence, through the Comisión de Seguridad Pública (Public Security Committee), was weak and failed to exert control over the police and address accountability issues. This was because the committee included representatives from the various political factions, and in the assembly a simple majority of the parties on the right was enough to block important initiatives for legal control in security matters. Nevertheless, the committee was effective in resolving problems of a political nature involving public-security institutions, and it maintained communication with the various components of the security sector.

Salvadoran society was immersed to some degree in the discussion on security issues thanks to the efforts of journalists and the media. They revealed issues relating to daily insecurity and fear of crime, and they discussed problems within the security institutions themselves, such as the lack of institutional transparency, corruption, and excesses and abuses committed by police and other security officials.[19]

The Procuraduría para la Defensa de los Derechos Humanos (Office of the Ombudsman for the Defense of Human Rights), which investigates reports of police violations of human rights, was, despite ups and downs, an important source of oversight and critiques of police performance. Nevertheless, the ombudsman's resolutions and reports were not well received by those who administer security policy. NGOs also worked on human-rights issues, and they produced studies and research on the performance of the country's public-security institutions and even documented relevant cases to show police abuse. Moreover, several research institutes produced studies on the impact of violence on Salvadoran society, which carried this discussion into the field of security policy. A coherent public critique developed to observe and evaluate security efforts and policies. Nevertheless, these proposals and criticisms rarely received an official response (Neild 2002).

State management of security matters has traditionally responded to political interests or to media perceptions rather than to concrete societal needs. The government managed little or no long-range planning. The lack of an explicit policy implied an implicit one. The reactive, discretionary, or nontransparent management of security issues corresponded to a specific way of making and administering policy. The consequences of this were manifested in inconsistencies in the government's responses to insecurity, as well as to unproductive investments made in the security sector, which receives a large chunk of the national budget.

The government's 1999 initiative must be acknowledged as a major advance. It created mechanisms to outline a course of action based on strategic and operational planning, and it built an information system to track efforts and results. However, low levels of transparency (Aguilar, Amaya, and Martínez 2001) and citizen participation again distanced security policies from democratic public-policy models that view security as a service rather than as an exclusively discretionary power of the state. Instead, there still persisted obvious signs that political criteria predominated in decision making in the security arena. The reform of the criminal code, as an example, was promoted primarily by the executive branch to create new categories of crime and to broaden police and prosecutorial powers. The government rationalized this as a necessity to contain the high crime rate, at the same time it was heralding the success of its security policy.

Another example was the focus on gun control. In 2001, various sectors came out in favor of banning firearms in public places and toughening gun-permit laws for private individuals. These proposals relied on data released by the PNC, which showed that almost 70 percent of the homicides committed in 2002 involved firearms (UNDP 2003, 164). Most of these murders had motives that were not strictly criminal but resulted instead from routine conflicts that turned violent. PNC headquarters and CNSP were among the government institutions that favored these proposals. However, both President Flores and the then minister of public security and justice were opposed, arguing that people had a right to carry arms for self-defense. This again reveals the preference for violent responses. Sanctioning the use of firearms and awarding permits to individuals to use weapons in self-defense directly transfers to citizens themselves part of the state's responsibility to provide security.

The preference for institutional coercion in the criminal-justice system has at its root a model of authoritarian political culture that carried considerable weight in the government's decision making on security matters (Ranum

2000, 18). This is true even though the expressions of that model were being combined with new techniques and were connected to external interests promoted by globalization and a hemispheric security agenda. As of 2003, there was evidence that Salvadoran security policy was beginning to show some signs of authoritarianism. One factor was the preference for state coercion through the use of reactive police responses to violence and crime and, more recently, particularly to social protest and public demonstrations. Additional evidence is found in the legal-reform process that broadened the spaces for the state to criminalize activities and institute tougher sentences. Finally, the National Defense Law was passed, permitting a mixing of the tasks of national defense, national security, and public security and capable of being interpreted as permitting the involvement of the armed forces in the domestic arena. However, this process did not respond exclusively to local requirements or self-interest. Instead, it was combined with a broader trend, brought about by the war on terrorism and globalization, that undermined international norms for human rights.

Security policy should involve a variety of actors and include alternative or parallel projects to reduce crime, such as prevention plans and alternative conflict-resolution schemes, allowing for more active and decisive participation by the community and local governments. However, the security policy of recent years has been conceived of in a reductionist manner, which is visible, ever more strongly after 1999, in the focus on the police as the implementer of this policy, with a special emphasis on the reduction of crime statistics.

According to Joan Botella (1996), the legitimation of new institutions in the democratic transition depends on the capacity of state agencies to respond to specific social demands and not only to the democratizing motivations from which those institutions arise. In turn, much of that response capacity is conditioned by the shaping of an agenda that includes a broad plurality of societal groups. Edelberto Torres Rivas (1996) classifies as "incomplete transitions" those in which a major influence from the authoritarian legacy remains. To be complete, a transition must consolidate a new relationship between the government and civil society, one that differs radically from the past.

In the Salvadoran case, the length of time for the transition, the significant increase in crime in the postwar period, and the societal demands for security demanded that the public-security agencies show an accelerated response capacity. But the process had perverse effects, as it played down the democratizing inspiration of the security model proposed in the peace accords. Moreover, as of 2003, the management of security still had not articulated an agenda that was inclusive and broadly embraced a variety of social actors. To the contrary, that agenda remained under the control of decision makers and the dominant economic and political elites. Thus, following Torres Rivas's schema, even though the demilitarization of public security was an indisputable triumph for the peace accords, security policy in El Salvador continued to maintain a relationship between the government and civic society that was distant and even contradictory. This relationship was radically different from what existed before the peace accords, which was the main achievement of those agreements. Indeed, the transition did witness a new balance of power, due to the appearance of new actors and a greater public interest in security matters. Even so, the relationship between decision makers and the beneficiaries of security policies was still asymmetric, and manifestations of authoritarian initiatives of a new type were becoming visible.

Violence, Citizen Insecurity, and Elite Maneuvering in El Salvador

José Miguel Cruz

Police reform in El Salvador came as part of a broader package of institutional reforms that accompanied the peace accords of January 1992 that ended the twelve-year civil war. The changes in public security brought new principles and procedures to police institutions; they also signified the dismantling of the old public-security apparatus, namely, the Policía Nacional (National Police), the Guardia Nacional (National Guard) and the Policía de Hacienda (Treasury Police). At the same time, the PNC was created, with a fundamental purpose of centralizing all policing functions under civilian command instead of under the military, as was the past practice. The task of managing internal security was finally separated from the army, which had held it since the twentieth century.

The deployment of a new police force was one of the more visible processes of the political transition, as it established the bases for setting up a democratic regime. The assessment of the success or the failure of the peace process and the subsequent democratic transition has to consider the implementation of this new institution in the realm of public security.

However, as soon as the civil war ended, and with the simultaneous dismantling of the old system and construction of a new one, Salvadoran society faced one of the biggest waves of criminality and violence of its history—and of that of the entire Western Hemisphere as well (Buvinic, Morrison, and Shifter 1999). In a short time, as Salvadorans recovered from more than a decade of political conflict, they found themselves plunged into new sorts of violence and crime. Meanwhile the authorities of the new—and therefore vulnerable—set of institutions were still learning how to manage the country's new circumstances while undertaking a difficult transition from authoritarian to democratic governance.

Complicating both efficiency and democratic norms, the peace agreement established that no more than 20 percent of the members of former security agencies could join the new police. Therefore, the PNC began with little practical experience but still with substantial risks of authoritarian contamination. This is because most of the old regime's personnel had been trained for political repression rather than crime prevention or investigation. Thus, useful crime-fighting experience was largely lacking in the new police forces. As new forms and levels of violence provoked strong feelings of insecurity, and as negotiation between the political elites was taking place, the public demanded quick and effective results from the new public-security system. In addition, the new climate of insecurity fostered an ideological debate over the correctness of integrating the military and police leadership from the old regime into the new democratic system.

Theoretical Framework

Five ideas are fundamental to understanding the importance of the police reform in El Salvador (and throughout Central America). First, the police constitute a key institution in the development of democratic governability in societies that are emerging from authoritarian regimes because they help provide the basic conditions to make governance possible.[1] Second, democratic transitions must entail a reform of the official coercive apparatus, the police, to ensure an effective transition from authoritarian rule. Third, in foundational democracies, such as the Central American ones, the crucial challenge is not to reform institutions but to create fundamentally new ones.[2] The fourth point is that transitions entail basic change, and therefore some degree of social disorder is inevitable (Marenin 1996). This means that the state's police institutions are central to managing the implications of that change in the streets in daily life; they are called on to control the very disorder that can threaten the broad course of the political transition. Finally, the police and judiciary are more closely involved with the common people and with the different sectors of the civil society on a daily basis, so their performance is a kind of window for the people to see how well or badly the new political system is working.

Police institutions play a fundamental role in creating democratic governability (Bailey and Godson 2000, 9). The police represent the use of legitimate coercion within the society; they guarantee a basic level of order in public life. They also enforce the laws and ensure that the people observe these to an acceptable degree. Moreover, the police are key actors in resolving conflicts between the members, groups, or sectors of society. Police may not be legally charged to resolve conflicts for themselves, but they play an unavoidable role in their settlement. In short, policing institutions have enormous significance in social and political life. The police are, therefore, the key state apparatus for maintaining social order, and they act to protect certain groups, values, and ideologies (Marenin 1996). This may be true in every state, but it is especially true in authoritarian regimes, where policing can assume perverse forms of abuse of basic human and civil rights. In a democratic society, police behave according to the predominant values of the ruling elites, but they operate with a certain degree of respect for the laws and democratic methods. In an authoritarian regime, on the other hand, police use their coercive faculties to impose, subdue, and repress social dissent, often by using force in indiscriminate and extreme ways and without regard for human and civil rights.

Democratic transitions must entail a reform of the coercive apparatus: the police, among others. A society in transition from an authoritarian to a democratic regime (or to one less authoritarian) usually faces the problem of transforming its repressive apparatus as one of the main challenges of democratization (Whitehead 2002). In the case of El Salvador—and in several other Latin American countries as well—this means the demilitarization of the public-security forces (see Sieder 2001). Thus, police reform is linked in various Latin American countries with the process of political transitions, be this the foundation of a democratic form of government, the return to democratic rule, or the marginal reform of an existing democracy (see Garretón and Newman 2002). But even in the case of democratic foundations, as in Central America, the issue is not the reform of the police, but rather the creation of new institutions. This is because the former police were so corrupt and so compromised with the old regime that only their elimination can open the way to the foundation of new, democratic, and uncorrupted police (Costa 1999).

Moreover, transformation of the police implies institutional change within systemic change. This represents a dual process. The reform of the police, the judiciary, and the coercive apparatus is a result of the political change, but it is also a process that will affect the broader democratic transition while it simultaneously protects the transition. That is, the police are reformed as a product of democratic transition, but the transition itself has to be guaranteed by the performance of the new forces of order (Marenin 1996). The way this challenge is resolved in the medium and long term can determine the success of both the political transition and the police reform. Under these circumstances the degree of social unrest generated by common violence and crime becomes especially pertinent. Crime and violence can undermine the course of police reform by eroding its credibility, even when the reform effort contributes to the political legitimacy of the broader process (Neild 2002). Thus, citizen insecurity spawned by common violence can not only threaten the reform of police and security forces but also erode the institutional basis of the political transition. Fear of crime tends to generate public demands for a tougher system of policing, regardless of due process and human rights (Rauch 2000; Chevigny 1996; Call 2000). Therefore, the police start to find themselves under pressure to revisit some of their old methods to handle disorder; instead of concentrating on fighting crime, they may regress into violating human and civil rights, whose protection should be central to democratic transition.

The importance of police is not limited to democratic accountability or related systemic issues, but also directly involves the population with which it interacts. There are few state institutions of more direct importance or frequent contact with the public than the police. As Rothstein and Stolle (2002) note, the police connect directly with the people more often because they have to solve everyday inquiries and, in doing so, they perform a socialization role: they teach the people how the system works and how fairly it responds to public requests. Also, police are used to transmit the cultural values and norms prevailing in the society, including its political system. The way policemen or public officers relate to the public reflects how democratic the institutions are and how efficiently the system responds to citizens' demands. This is all very significant because when evaluating the institutional performance of the regime, citizens put priority on the institutions they see every day in the streets: the police.

In sum, reforming the police goes further than satisfying the institutional requirements for control and order in society. This process contributes fundamentally to the building of democratic governability in countries undergoing democratic transitions.

Violence and Insecurity in Post–Civil War El Salvador

It is well-known that postwar El Salvador confronted an enormous upsurge of violence. According to various sources, after the civil war and during the development of the new police, El Salvador faced one of the highest crime rates in the Western Hemisphere in recent years. There has been much debate about the validity of official statistics. Some estimates suggest that rates increased to as high as 130 homicides per one hundred thousand population (Cruz and González 1997; Buvinic, Morrison, and Shifter 1999); others suggest lower rates. There is little doubt that during the years following the signing of the peace accords, the rates reached a minimum of approximately 80 homicides per one hundred thousand population, which is a quite severe problem. In addition, all the studies show that levels of crime, again expressed in homicide rates, peaked from 1994 to 1997 but began a slow decline in 1998 that remained constant until 2002 (Cruz, Trigueros, and González 2000; IUDOP 1998; Aguilar 2002). A series of polls conducted by the Public Opinion Institute of the Central American University during the early years of the posttransition period (IUDOP 1993a, 1994) reveal that nearly 34 percent of Salvadoran families were victims of one or another type of crime. But, in contrast to the violence that prevailed during the civil war or even before it, the postwar violence was not predominantly political but rather common and crime related. With the exception of some assassinations that occurred between 1993 and 1994, with clearly political implications, most of the violence after 1992 was apparently not politically motivated. The mechanisms set up by the peace accords successfully ended the major part of the political violence that had afflicted the country for years, but they failed to prepare for the crime wave that surged in the postauthoritarian years.

Several studies have attempted to explain the phenomenon of postwar violence in El Salvador.[3] Among the factors identified as causes of the violence are a culture of violence exacerbated by the conflict (Huezo 2000); the problem of guns and other weapons left over from the war (Cruz and Beltrán 2000); the structural economic problems of poverty, inequality, and social exclusion (Ramos 2000); and the weakness of the institutions that deal with the problem, namely, the police and the courts (Amaya and Palmieri 2000; Cruz 1997). Although there is common acknowledgment that, in practice, all those factors—and several more—interact to exacerbate violent crime, there is also general recognition that one of the most important problems is weak institutions.

One argument for why common violence became so widespread in the early postwar years is that Salvadoran society lacked an effective public-security agency. With the dismantling of a policing system that resisted demobilization, but that lacked real expertise in dealing with crime, and with the creation of a new police force that was barely learning how to function—while simultaneously being undermined by members of the old system—it is hard to imagine that the country had a operating system of public security. On this point, Stanley (1996) has stressed the impact that the end of the war and the withdrawal of the military forces had on maintaining security: control forces quickly dropped from seventy-five thousand men (army, guerrillas, public-security corps, and village patrols) to around six thousand men, who made up the new PNC and the holdover National Police. Also, the reform of the public-security system did not entail a similarly rapid reform of the judicial system, and the new police force found itself trying to confront crime under a new vision and doctrine that was not prevalent in the courts or within the political establishment more broadly. These factors, taken together, undermined the capacity of the new system to repress crime.

The problem of violence did more than overwhelm the new public-security system. The police also found themselves overwhelmed by the public's demands for security, and this tension led to a series of important errors. The ways people perceived the violence and the extent to which they felt threatened by it were important influences on police reform.

As with the violence itself, Salvadorans' sense of insecurity increased after the signing of the Agreement of Chapultepec. Polls conducted between 1986 and 2000 show a trend in which crime and violence become the second-ranking national problem for Salvadorans in 1993, just a few points below economic problems, and they become the top-ranking problem around 1996. Prior to the accord, the main problems cited by citizens were the economy (poverty, unemployment, inflation, economic injustice, etc.) and the war— usually in the form of political violence. The accords had the immediate effect of ending the war, and public concern over the war and political violence began to recede in 1993. Nonetheless, even as the war receded from people's minds, it was replaced immediately by anxiety over violence of another kind: crime. Between 1993 and 2001, crime vied with economic problems for the top spot in the public debate (Cruz 2003).

Public concerns about the direction taken by Salvadoran society were dominated by the panic provoked by the violence, and this fear influenced public views and debate about the police reform. From 1993, and even more clearly after 1996, Salvadoran media made crime the principal topic of coverage. With the surge in violence after the war, the public's sense of insecurity also increased, and the heightened fear would remain even after the crime rates began to decline.[4]

Police Reform, Violence, and Citizen Insecurity

In an environment marked by violence and by heightened public feelings of insecurity, various mechanisms operated to undermine the overall police reform in El Salvador. First, the political elites used violence to resist changes in the public-security system, and this posed a major obstacle to creating a more professional and transparent police force. The elites did not commit violence, but they blamed criminal violence for the need to postpone changes in the policing system. Second, violence and insecurity significantly eroded the trust of the population in the police and in the whole project of reform. Finally, insecurity encouraged public support for authoritarian responses to repress crime. These responses challenged the legitimacy of the new public-security system.

VIOLENCE AND EFFORTS TO BLOCK REFORM

The most significant attempts to disrupt the reform came at the very beginning of the reform process, and they became significantly harmful to the whole project. The concrete process of Salvadoran police reform was far from smooth. Although the peace accords established many of the features of the new system of public security, including steps toward dismantling the old forces and for the deployment of the PNC, the obstacles to implementing the agreements appeared even before the new police force was created. The entire process, from signing the accords up to the actual deployment of the new force, ran up against exceptions, delays, and sabotage. These were caused mostly by the government's maneuvers, although the FMLN was responsible for a few of them as well.

The earliest problems stemmed from a lack of resources for the transition project. The new police academy failed to provide enough police officers in the first stages of deployment because the government did not supply an adequate site for its establishment early on; it was not until considerable pressure was exerted that the military provided some facilities for the academy.[5] Also, the military refused to transfer the equipment of the former public-security forces to the new police officers. Basic items such as radios, cars, and guns had to be provided by international assistance, because the armed forces command was reluctant to cooperate.

Those problems exemplified the government's reluctance to accept the military's withdrawal from the realm of public security. As observers of the Salvadoran police reform have reported, the government opposed disbanding the former police agencies and favored keeping the military involved in public-security tasks (Stanley, Vickers, and Spence 1993; Costa 1999; Stanley 1996). One of the first government countermeasures was to postpone the gradual demobilization of the old police. The government attempted instead to incorporate the National Guard and the Treasury Police into other units of the Army, although they kept their uniforms, weapons, and facilities (Costa 1999).[6] This maneuver produced the first crisis of the implementation of the accords: in response, the guerrillas refused to demobilize the initial 20 percent of their forces as scheduled in the accords. This led to the first rescheduling of the peace accord by the United Nations.[7]

Even though the government later on started disbanding the National Guard and the Treasury Police, President Alfredo Cristiani decided to transfer a large number of personnel from these agencies to the National Police force, which was also supposed to be dismantled. More than three thousand National Guard soldiers and Treasury Police officers were transferred to the National Police just two months after the implementation of the peace accords; in addition, a short time later, the government transferred personnel from army elite battalions to the National Police. Throughout this time, the old police academy continued working, graduating an average of one hundred police officers per month, thereby reinforcing the ranks of the National Police.[8]

All these measures, adopted more or less in open contradiction to the peace accords, were justified by the government as necessary to confront the criminal violence that had begun to affect public opinion. In addition, the government announced that if the crime wave continued, it would be necessary to deploy army patrols to combat delinquency. At the end of 1992, President Cristiani's government launched the Plan Grano de Oro (Gold Grain Plan), which assigned to the military security tasks in the countryside where coffee was collected.[9] The FMLN and opposition parties criticized this plan, and consequently it was limited to the annual harvest season. Then, in 1993, the government announced the Plan Vigilante, which tasked the army to patrol roads and rural areas to assist the National Police and the PNC. The opposition parties also rejected this plan. Finally, in 1995, President Armaudo

Calderón Sol's government launched the Plan Guardián (still in effect as of February 2003), by which the military and the PNC deployed small units to patrol the countryside more generally.

The efforts to resist the transition to new policing institutions did not end there. Apart from attempts to preserve the old structures and to employ the military in police tasks (e.g., patrols), when the formation of the new system seemed inevitable, the strategy shifted to incorporating members from the old system into the new police force. Between 1993 and 1994, there were several attempts to integrate former officers of the National Police into the PNC. Several members of the old police were sent to the academy even though they did not meet all the standards to join the new institution. Costa (1999) claims that this was possible because the government was keen to control the new system and because the former guerrilla leaders were careless in their oversight once their own combatants were integrated into the new civilian police.

Also, the government attempted to place trusted holdovers from the old regime in key posts to control the new structures. Hence, independent civilians were excluded from those posts to make way for military officers. By the end of 1992, it was discovered that eleven out of the eighteen executive candidates presented by the authorities came from the army and the other former public-security institutions and not from the National Police, as had been originally agreed. However, it was too late to rectify the errors because the candidates were already receiving training in Puerto Rico and Spain.

According to Costa (1999) the most obvious attempt to shape the new institutions and the major challenge to the overall reform were posed by the integration of the Comisión Investigadora de Hechos Delictivos (Commission to Investigate Criminal Acts, CIHD) and the Unidad Ejecutiva Antinarcóticos (Executive Antinarcotics Unit) into the PNC, and the appointment of a former military officer to the key post of deputy director for operations in the PNC. The inclusion of these unreformed units presented a double challenge. First, their numbers exceeded the agreed 20 percent limit on former government forces in the new police. Second, these units were involved in the cover-up of important cases of violations of human rights during the war, and they would be in a position to exert significant influence over the new institution. Further, the selection of a new subdirector coming from the army threatened to remilitarize the civilian police. In fact, not long after his appointment, concerns arose that this subdirector was reproducing a "military style of organization and conduct at the PNC" (Stanley, Vickers, and Spence 1993, 15) and that he was refusing to accept supervision and help from the UN mission in El Salvador and its police division (Costa 1999).

In the end, pressures led to the resignation of the officers involved and to a long and awkward process of dismantling these units within the PNC. It was later revealed that many of the personnel from these units were involved in organized crime, were responsible for assassinations of former guerrilla leaders, and were unable—or unwilling—to confront organized crime. The infiltration of elements of the old structures also took place at top executive levels. The president's principal advisors for public-security issues were military. In addition, in 1994, the vice minister of public security of the Calderón Sol administration included former members of the CIHD and antinarcotics units as his advisors and as parallel structures with the police; formally, they were not members of the police, because they had not graduated from the new academy, nor did they report to the director of the police, but rather to the minister. The minister, however, considered these units to be part of the police (Stanley, Vickers, and Spence 1996). Some of these integrated units were dedicated exclusively to investigating kidnappings, and they operated both autonomously from the PNC and with the financial support of a group of businessmen. Despite complaints by the United Nations and by civil-society organizations about the existence of these units, the ministry refused to dissolve them. In 1996, Stanley, Vickers, and Spence concluded that the minister's actions seriously undermined the development and institutionalization of the PNC (27).

All these problems weakened the capacity of the police to build an effective and professional organization to confront the problem of organized crime. Following the recommendations of the Grupo Conjunto (Joint Group), a unit called the Departamento de Investigación del Crimen Organizado (Department for Investigation of Organized Crime) was created to investigate organized crime.[10] This group was formed with officers trained in the academy, with good credentials; however, once they started to work, they faced a lack of resources and interference from the Departamento de Investigación del Crimen (Department of Crime Investigation, DIC), the unit formed by the personnel of the CIHD. In spite of this, the organized-crime unit solved some important criminal cases and showed up the lack of effectiveness of the DIC. Therefore, it demonstrated that with some political will, the new police force was capable of confronting crime.

Nevertheless, political pressures and resistance by representatives of the old order to the establishment of the new, more democratic order depleted police capacity to confront the problems of violence and crime that were growing within Salvadoran society. Different students of El Salvador's police reform agree that, even though the crime wave after the peace accords was severe, the attempts to obstruct the deployment of the police force, to infiltrate its structures with holdovers from the old system, and to subordinate it to political interests weakened its capacity to fulfill its duties. Confronting these, the PNC could not become the body that society needed during a period of such change and disorder.

Another implication of these problems at the very outset of the institution was that the PNC failed to develop its internal disciplinary mechanisms, something that would have negative consequences for its subsequent development. The institutional design of the new system entailed both internal and external control mechanisms. Stanley, Vickers, and Spence (1996) argue that the structures of discipline and internal investigations provided the tools to fight against corruption and abuses within the police force. Nonetheless, the disciplinary mechanisms failed to work in a timely and effective manner.

The institutional design of the PNC established an Inspectoría General (General Inspectorate), which remained under the control of the vice minister of public security and autonomous from the chief of the police, but on the other hand the inspectorate was part of a structure formed by units within the police force: the Unidad de Control (Control Unit), the Unidad de Investigación Disciplinaria (Disciplinary Investigations Unit), and the Tribunal Displinario (Disciplinary Court). The latter units operated directly under the command of the director of the PNC. They were charged with investigating, prosecuting, and penalizing misconduct by police units or personnel, while the inspectorate functioned as a supervisory body over those corps. At the same time, the overall process was supervised by the human-rights ombudsman (Aguilar, Amaya, and Martínez 2001).

Despite its importance, the PNC's General Inspectorate and the disciplinary units did not begin work until more than a year after the deployment of the new police force. Their debut was rocky. The first chief of the inspectorate was dismissed after just six months because of his lack of leadership and effectiveness in building up the inspectorate, and the agency remained without a head until August 1995—two years after the deployment of the police force. In fact, the inspectorate's investigative personnel did not start to work until 1996, fully three years after the launch of the new force. Neild (2002, 4) states that "because of pressures of rapid deployment of the police and limited resources, little attention was paid to the disciplinary system." This led to ineffective handling of disciplinary problems. Also, the role of the investigative units was unclear, and the overlap of functions between the units became a recurring problem. Furthermore, because the local commanders did not want to deal with minor cases of misconduct, the disciplinary units found themselves overwhelmed with a workload they could barely manage, given their limited resources, personnel, and experience.[11] Thousands of cases were sent to the disciplinary units. Some of them were quite serious, although most involved trivial misconduct by police officers, which the disciplinary units refused to handle.

In practice, several cases of serious misbehavior and even delinquency began to take place within the police, and some citizens started to distrust the new institutions. The most shocking case occurred in 2000, when the media reported a kidnapping perpetrated by uniformed police officers, using their equipment and cars. In response, the police authorities created yet another new unit, the Unidad de Asuntos Internos (Internal Affairs Unit), to work in coordination with the Attorney General's Office. They also amended the basic police law to empower the local chiefs to handle disciplinary matters and to stress the role of the inspectorate in the overall functioning of the system. However, the changes also put the General Inspectorate under the direct control of the director of the police, thus eroding its autonomy and authority as an external disciplinary unit.[12]

By the end of 2000, more than 1,900 police officers, nearly 11 percent of the active-duty personnel, were purged from the force through a set of special edicts. Almost two thirds of these were removed by emergency procedures— procedures that went beyond the original legal sanctions.[13] As Neild (2002) has noted, it is not clear whether these methods will be useful in correcting the problem and whether they constitute a lasting improvement to institutional disciplinary mechanisms.

All these problems have shaped an institution that, even though it is considered to have undergone the most successful reform in Central America, continues to experience serious difficulties with criminal-investigation capacity and with creating effective mechanisms for discipline and transparency.

These problems were not all directly provoked by the violence and insecurity that followed the 1992 peace accords. Nevertheless, the government used insecurity to resist and to undermine the negotiated police reforms. Given the pretext of the priority to fight crime more efficiently, it was relatively easier for the government to alter the original accords to maintain elements of the old system within the new one. The government was astute in using public concerns with crime to block change; it not only succeeded in infiltrating the new police but also managed public opinion in its own favor. The government encouraged a sort of nostalgia in some sectors of the population that undermined the legitimacy of the new police force. The opposition political forces were unable to challenge most of these attempts because, after signing the peace accords, they focused more on their political performance in the public-opinion surveys. Thus, they were more anxious to gain spaces in the political sphere than to strengthen the institutions they helped to create in the peace agreement. Resistance to some of the government's measures came only when those actions represented an obvious threat to the former guerrilla forces, and resistance was successful only when the international community pressed both sides to comply with the original accords. The UN office in El Salvador, under the lead of Enrique Ter Horst played a significant role in these efforts.

National organizations echoed the public's insistence on fulfilling the agreements. Organizations such as the Institute of Human Rights of the Central American University and FESPAD were the most prominent from civil society. The government's maneuvers were also fiercely criticized by the Office of the Human Rights Ombudsman, under the leadership of Victoria de Avilés. All these institutions and organizations—as well as the Washington Office on Latin America and Hemisphere Initiatives in the international arena—denounced the ploys of the Salvadoran government to undermine the process within the police and helped to create an external environment where the elites had less space to corrupt the reforms.

DECLINE OF TRUST IN THE POLICE

The second mechanism by which violence and insecurity affected the reform process was the erosion of the image of the police as a crime-fighting agency. Salvadorans started to distrust the police once they realized that the new institutions were not capable of providing security.

Generally, the Salvadoran public was unaware of the police-reform initiative within the text of the peace accords because they were more concerned with ending the war and rebuilding the country's economy. In a national poll conducted by the Central American University in January 1992, 40 percent of those surveyed said the most important agreement of the peace treaty was the end of the war; 16.4 percent mentioned the socioeconomic agreement, and the rest mentioned such topics as the demilitarization of the country, the integration of the guerrillas into society, and the establishment of the new civilian police force. Although these three last points have to do with the new public-security system, fewer than 8 percent of the people specifically pointed to the issue of a new police force (IUDOP 1992). Nonetheless, the Salvadoran public soon started to recognize the importance of the civilian police force, although their approach to it was definitely shaped by concerns about public security triggered by the problem of postwar violence.

In 1993, a poll revealed that approximately 57 percent of those surveyed indicated that the deployment of the new civilian police force would reduce crime and violence significantly. Only 4 percent indicated that those problems would increase, and 11 percent stated that delinquency would remain the same, with the rest undecided. The deployment of the police force raised expectations among Salvadorans. Because threats of human-rights abuses by the military were reduced by separating soldiers from the tasks of public security, the basic concern for Salvadorans was not whether the new police institutions would respect human rights. The question was whether the police would be competent to manage the problems of security that most of the people perceived as overwhelming. This did not mean that the issue of human rights was unimportant, but the wave of crime and violence that erupted just after the end of the war led the public to give priority to efficiency and effectiveness (IUDOP 1993a).

The early public assessments of the civilian police, as measured by opinion polls, were extremely positive in the regions where the first battalions were deployed. A poll carried out in Chalatenango, Cabañas, and Usulután at the end of 1993 showed that 70 percent of those interviewed evaluated the performance of the police as good or very good, 20 percent said that its performance was fair, and only 1.5 percent said the police work was bad or very bad (IUDOP 1993b). In 1995, when police were finally installed across the entire country and the violence was reaching a crescendo, the public assessment was less positive. Even so, the mainstream opinion of the population remained optimistic: 48 percent viewed the new police force positively, 30 percent considered their performance fair, and 21 percent evaluated it negatively. When people were asked the reasons for such opinions, in every case they pointed to the fight against crime and violence. For instance, those who said that the police were performing well pointed to the fact that the police were fighting violence, while those who believed that the police were not doing well pointed out the lack of success in fighting crime; only 11 percent of those who were concerned with the work of the police gave abuse of human rights as the main reason (IUDOP 1995).

Public concerns about police performance were much less affected by the issue of human rights than by issues of crime. The same survey taken in 1995 showed that Salvadorans tended to see violence as the major threat to human rights rather than state agencies' performance (IUDOP 1995). Police efforts to control violence were seen as one of the main guarantors for human rights in El Salvador, just points below the Office of the Human Rights Ombudsman. It is paradoxical that at the same time, the ombudsman's statistics were showing that more than 55 percent of the complaints of human-rights abuses were against the police. By June 1996, the new civilian police force was the organization with the most human-rights abuses registered against it, but simultaneously—in fighting insecurity—they were seen as the protectors of the population.[14]

Over time, the persistence of crime in Salvadoran society started to erode the perception of police as protectors. A 1998 poll about crime and insecurity revealed that people who were victims of crime had less trust in the police than those who had not experienced such victimization in the period just prior to the survey. Moreover, those who had been victims of serious crime had even less confidence in the police than did the general population (IUDOP 1998).

In the long run, the public perception of the police became more cynical. A comparison of the results of surveys regarding performance of the new PNC in contrast to that of the former National Police, as shown in table 9.1, suggests a slow process of deterioration of the image of the police up to 2000. In 1995, almost half of those polled indicated that the PNC was better than the old National Police; this opinion reached a low point in 2000, with less than one-third of respondents supporting such a view. In contrast, those who indicated that the PNC was doing worse than the old police increased from 18 to 38 percent. However, a recent survey about public insecurity showed that the acceptance of the police among the public improved from 2000 to 2002 (see FUNDAUNGO and IUDOP 2002).

In spite of this, a comparison between the public confidence in the police force and other national institutions reveals that the police force remained as one of El Salvador's least distrusted institutions. Overall, this has been one of the more constant trends in public opinion. Organizations such as the National Assembly, the courts, the executive, and the army receive lower levels of public approval; the police—and the human-rights ombudsman—stood on top.

The erosion of public confidence in the police created doubts that the new

9.1 Opinions about the PNC, 1995-2000 (percentages)

Is the current National Civilian Police better or worse than the old national police?

	Year		
	1995	1998	2000
Better	48.6	44.5	31.2
Similar	26.3	19.9	26.3
Worse	18.0	30.0	38.5
Don't know	7.1	5.5	3.9

Source: Figures extrapolated from data from IUDOP.

institution would fight crime effectively; more disturbingly, it awakened a nostalgia for the old authoritarian methods of fighting against social disorder. Public insecurity, and the awareness that the police were overwhelmed by crime, revived some remnants of authoritarian attitudes that undermined the legitimacy of the new model of policing by stressing extralegal responses and the return of the military to public-security functions.

VIOLENCE AGAINST VIOLENCE

One problem with feelings of insecurity among the population is that these tend to stimulate extralegal responses to crime. This can take two forms. First, if people think that the police are overwhelmed by crime, some of them begin to think about protecting themselves: taking justice into their own hands. Second, beyond self-protection, some people start to claim that police should act without regard for due process and human rights. In these circumstances, some condemn the rights and protections that guarantee due process, and some come to view human rights as a major deterrent to an efficient fight against crime.

These attitudes are not new. They are the legacy of a political culture developed under authoritarian rule. The democratic transition does not completely change them, and insecure conditions bolster them at a time when society is trying to build a new set of relationships between the people and the state.

A study conducted on insecurity and crime (IUDOP 1998) showed that a little more than half of the population responded positively to the statement,

"Given that the government is not capable of combating crime, citizens have the right to take justice in their own hands." The study also found that almost 50 percent of Salvadorans would support the creation of groups of armed neighbors to fight crime and that a little more than a third approved of illegal cleansing groups. Moreover, the study illustrated that these kinds of attitudes were expressed more frequently by those who felt very concerned about crime (see table 9.2). The overall results point to the resilience of some elements of authoritarian culture.

These opinions were registered at a moment when the issue of crime had peaked in the public discussion. The study coincided with the launch of a public campaign for legal reforms intended to give the police more effective tools to combat crime. The aim of the plan was the passage of the Ley de Emergencia contra la Delincuencia y el Crimen Organizado (Emergency Law against Delinquency and Organized Crime), which was approved in mid-1998. The law sought to strengthen anticrime procedures; some provisions were clear contraventions of constitutional guarantees (see González 1996). At the same time, the minister of public security was lobbying for the approval of Juntas Vecinales (Neighborhood Councils), reminiscent of the vigilante groups used by the authoritarian regimes to control the population. Even though some of the juntas were actually formed, internal and external pressures led to their rapid demise. Finally, by mid-1998, public opinion was also following the Sombra Negra (Dark Shadow) case. This illegal paramili-

9.2 Authoritarian attitudes related to insecurity (percentages of those who agreed with each item)

Item	All respondents	High concern about crime (%)	Low concern about crime (%)
Support citizens' right to take justice in their own hands	51.9	55.3	44.4
Support groups of armed neighbors	49.9	41.9	37.8
Support illegal cleansing groups	36.9	43.3	24.3

Source: IUDOP (1998).

tary group appeared in the eastern part of the country to socially cleanse those considered to be delinquents. The group was dismantled soon thereafter as a result of the investigations of the PNC.[15]

These cases illustrate how attitudes were linked with what was happening in Salvadoran society and how the attitudes were both stimulated and used by the establishment, even if they represented a major challenge to the institutionalization of the new police. From the very beginning the government tried to undermine the reform by appealing to problems of insecurity and by using remnants of authoritarian values among the population, made vivid by insecurity.

But attitudes of insecurity and authoritarianism, in several cases orchestrated by the government, also affected the institutional behavior of the police. After the complete deployment of the new police, when it was no longer possible to restrain the scope of the new institution, the government assumed an ambiguous position toward judicial reform. A reform process was under way to adapt the legal codes to new social conditions by adopting laws more protective of civil rights and due process. However, leaders of public-security agencies (the minister of public security and the director of the PNC) managed to blame the lack of success in combating crime on these legal reforms. This discourse depicted the reformed codes and laws as more concerned about the rights of the criminals than the rights and security of the law-abiding population.

In fact, a 1996 survey found that 69 percent of the population agreed with the idea that "human rights give preference to delinquents and with those (rights) it is hard to combat (delinquency)" (IUDOP 1996). The 1998 study on insecurity and crime revealed that almost the entire sample (90.6 percent) agreed there was a need for tougher laws to combat crime. The same study asked an open-ended question about why the police were unable to fight against crime; the responses are shown in table 9.3.

It is striking that, even though most of the responses refer to the police themselves, the most common single response pointed to soft laws. Nevertheless, it is significant that in some ways, the rest of the sample indicated problems related to the police: poor training, scarcity of resources, few policemen, and vested political interests. But those sampled appeared unconcerned about the police force's lack of investigative capacity and its problems of discipline. The official discourse appeared to undervalue these problems publicly; rather, it directed public attention against laws that emphasized due process.

Finally, the most striking effect of this idea of the need to get tough on

9.3 Opinions about weakness of PNC against crime

Reasons	Percentage
Soft laws	35.1
Policemen are not well trained	25.2
Scarcity of resources in the police	13.9
Few policemen	13.4
Political interests within the police	6.6
Other responses	3.1
Don't know	2.7

Source: IUDOP (1998).

crime is the notion that, under certain circumstances, the police can justly break the law to fight crime. Literally, this is to break the law to enforce the law. In 1996, the Estudio sobre Normas y Actitudes sobre la Violencia (Study on Norms and Attitudes about Violence), on several cities in Latin America, sponsored by the Panamerican Health Organization, revealed that in San Salvador, 17.1 percent of residents agreed with the opinion that police torture is justified if it helps to fight crime, 12 percent agreed that the police should invade households without legal authorization if looking for suspects, and 27 percent declared themselves in favor of arresting people simply because they looked like criminals. Moreover, the favorable responses for San Salvador were higher than for other cities included in the study (Briceño-León, Carneiro, and Cruz 1999).

Some authors consider the Salvadoran police reform to be fairly successful, despite its many problems (Neild 2002; Call 2000). This is hard to dispute if the Salvadoran case is compared with other police reforms in Central America. Certainly, contrasted with the latest developments in Guatemala and Honduras, police reform in El Salvador remains one of the most serious efforts to institute a different notion of public security. However, there are serious problems that remain unresolved, and others have appeared with the attempt by the police command as of February 2003 to concentrate and control the agencies intended to watch over the police, to avoid public accountability, and to resort to a reactive style of confronting security issues (despite the alleged program).

Viewed as a single case of police reform, El Salvador is also an exceptional example of how a significant project can be resisted and weakened by representatives of the old regime, who use insecurity to manipulate and exacerbate public attitudes of authoritarianism. Violence has played a major role in this dynamic, because it has allowed part of the old elites to limit opportunities for change in the system. Yet it would be a mistake to ascribe the problems of police reform to a simple relationship between violence and feelings of insecurity or simply to the effects of the authoritarian cultural values. In fact, we are in a situation where, as Menéndez Carrión has proposed, "It is, rather, the complex interplay and outcome of the interactions among the diversity of power struggles, situations and events in the global/regional/local arenas that produce or deny the conditions of possibility for the realm of attitudes and orientations to eventually become relevant" (2001, 255–56).

Salvadoran elites—namely, those who were linked to the old security regime—who opposed the changes in the public-security sector by invoking the threats posed by crime, did not do so because they were truly concerned about the violence and crime in the country. Rather, they were concerned about losing one of their most significant tools of political control. By denouncing crime and playing upon people's insecurity, they found perfect justification for defying the agreements on transition and regaining control over changes they feared. Also, the elites' counterpart in the agreement, the FMLN, was sometimes more concerned with acquiring political positions through direct negotiation with the government than with empowering the institutions of public security. It was international pressure, combined with political forces within the country, that barely neutralized the counterreform. The role of the United Nations as the overseer of the process was extremely important.

Crime remained high as a result of ambiguities and limitations imposed by the political maneuvering after 1992. It has been argued that, whatever the case, crime rates would have increased after the war and that violence was an inevitable consequence of the process. Costa (1999) emphasizes that this argument is debatable. Indeed, crime would have increased in some measure, but it is likely that it would not have reached such levels had the authorities acted more in accordance with the roadmap drawn by the peace agreement, rather than attempting to preserve the old structures. This is, obviously, the realm of counterfactual interpretation, but it is hard to conclude that—given clear policies to strengthen investigative capacities and disciplinary mechanisms, with ready access to the resources to be turned over by the old system, and with a clear commitment by the authorities to fight against impunity—

the result would have been more violence than El Salvador actually experienced.

With widespread electoral abstention and political cynicism, a constant flow of emigration, increasing inequality, and persistent problems of public insecurity, it is hard to assert that El Salvador is in a steady process of democratization. One of the most urgent needs of Salvadoran society now is to ensure public security, not only as a matter of economic development, but also—and more importantly—as a matter of respect for human rights. The police should contribute to this by becoming an effective agent of democratic governability. But we still see mixed signals. The civilian character of the police reform seems firmly established, and there are no public attempts as of spring 2003 to appeal to the military. Also, the PNC seems more effective in combating crime than in the past. On the other hand, indications persist of problems of transparency and concentration of power, along with a repressive and reactive style of confronting crime.

The future of democratization in El Salvador depends in important measure on the way the police resolve these predicaments: becoming a transparent, law-abiding, efficient, and accountable institution for society or returning to the methods of assuring social order and control with less regard for the rule of law.

Public Security and Police Reform in Mexico

Marcos Pablo Moloeznik

Article 21 of the Mexican constitution (2002) states that "public security is a duty of the Federal Government, the Federal District, the states, and the municipalities, in their respective jurisdictions as established by the Constitution." This involves overlapping jurisdictions shared by three levels of government, which, for law enforcement, implies a decentralized model. The implementing legislation treats public security as "a duty of the government, which has as its goals to safeguard the integrity and rights of individuals, as well as to preserve public liberty, order, and peace" (Ley General de Seguridad Pública 1995, art. 3). Mexico's current president, Vicente Fox Quesada (2000–2006), recognizes that public security is "the government's primary and essential responsibility. Protection and guarantee of the population's patrimony are the bases for solid economic and political development and are necessary to achieve confidence, order and stability" (Poder Ejecutivo de la Federación 2001, 147).

Constitutional Article 21 also distinguishes between two types of organizations that respond to the public demand for justice. One type is justice administration, which involves hearing cases and imposing sanctions, an area that belongs solely and exclusively to the courts. The other type is law enforcement —preventing or investigating and prosecuting crimes. The investigative functions are the responsibility of the Ministerio Público (Public Ministry), which is aided by a police force under its supervision. Justice administration is located within the judicial branch, while the Public Ministry is an executive-branch agency, in the regular line of administrative command, and thus lacks autonomy (Ley de la Procuraduría 2002, art. 1 and 67). This is the case even though, by virtue of the regulatory framework, the Public Ministry simultaneously represents both government and societal interests (Ley de la Procuraduría 2002, art. 4; Programa Nacional de Procuración de Justicia 2002, 107). Upon taking office, Fox appointed army general Marcial Rafael Macedo de la Concha as attorney general to head the Public Ministry. The appointment signified an expansion of military involvement in public security and law enforcement at the federal level.[1]

Protection of basic rights in Mexico is exercised by more than just the judicial system. In 1990, the Comisión Nacional de Derechos Humanos (National Human Rights Commission) was established to ensure that the authorities observe and respect such rights. Subsequently, in January 1992, a constitutional amendment provided for the creation of organizations to protect human rights by responding to complaints about acts or omissions of an administrative nature on the part of public agencies or officials. "[These organizations] shall formulate for the respective authorities independent, public, non-binding recommendations and charges and complaints" (Constitución 2002, art. 102b). Each of the Mexican states and the Federal District has its own organization, empowered to receive complaints from citizens about human-rights abuses by government officials. (The electoral, judicial, and labor areas are exempt from human-rights legislation.)

The nature of the ombudsman has changed radically since its inception. It has been separated and distanced from the regular administrative secretariats, as reflected in the greater involvement of the Congress in appointing its management. Law 1999 is significant in shifting the appointment authority from the president to the Congress. Specifically, the Senate elects, by two-thirds majority of the members present, ten advisers and the president of the National Human Rights Commission Advisory Council.

Nature and Dynamics of Crime in Mexico

Between 1995 and 1997, both the rate and absolute number of reported criminal acts increased in Mexico. The trend was reversed between 1998 and 2000, but available information for 2001 again shows an increase. This is why, at the end of his administration, then-president Ernesto Zedillo (1994–2000) acknowledged that "for many Mexicans, a grave problem is the lack of public safety arising from ordinary and organized crime, which is becoming more and more sophisticated and aggressive" (Presidencia de la República 2000). Particularly during the early years of the Zedillo administration, public security deteriorated. Crime rates reached a high point in 1997, with a little more than a million and a half reported crimes, or 16.4 crimes for every one thousand inhabitants. Most were property crimes, but violence also increased consistently.

Of all crimes reported in 2003, approximately 95 percent are classified within the *fuero común* (under the jurisdiction of the states). The remainder are in the *fuero federal* (federal jurisdiction). Of *fuero común* crimes, the most serious are robbery in all its forms, which accounts for 37.2 percent of all reported crimes; bodily injuries, 17.9 percent; and property damage, 9.8 percent. Regarding *fuero federal* crimes, 31 percent fall into the category of crimes against health, or those related to production, trafficking, and consumption of illegal drugs. Next most numerous are violations of the Ley Federal de Armas de Fuego y Explosivos (Federal Law on Firearms and Explosives; Programa Nacional de Seguridad Pública 2003, 31–32). The Secretaría de Seguridad Pública (Public Security Secretariat) has put priority on five federal crimes with major social significance: kidnapping, highway robbery, trafficking in undocumented migrants, and weapons and drug trafficking.

The Mexican state apparatus is marked by overwhelming complexity and limited operational capacity, which limit its ability to guarantee public security. Impunity, taken to mean the government's inability to administer justice, can be measured as the sizable gap between the number of crimes reported to authorities and the number actually prosecuted and decided by the courts. For example, between 1995 and 2000, sentencing occurred in only twenty-eight out of every one hundred cases tried in lower courts (Poder Ejecutivo de la Federación 2001, 148–49). Thus, impunity is a central problem for public security in Mexico, since only 10 percent of the reported crimes are punished, and 75 percent of the arrest warrants go unserved (Zepeda 2002, 63–64).[2]

A basic question is why most victims fail to report crimes to the authorities. Impunity casts doubt on justice and the public's access to it. Complicating this is the public's near-total ignorance of the law. For example, a recent poll indicated that most Mexicans were unaware of their constitutional rights (Secretaría de Gobernación 2001). Nor is respect for the law a value common among Mexicans. The same poll asked, "Who do you believe respects the law the least: government officials, the citizens, or both?" Almost half those polled thought that neither the government nor citizens respect the law. One in every three thought the government respected the law the least, and most respondents agreed that one should not obey a law that is unjust. These results are worrisome if, in the words of Federico Reyes Heroles, "No modern, just state can grow strong if the validity of the rule of law is not fully established among its citizens" (1999, 161).

"Crime has grown radically, strengthening criminal organizations in which corruption and institutional inefficiency create a low-risk scenario for those who commit crimes" (Programa Nacional de Seguridad Pública 2003, 14). Thus, it is unsurprising that Mexico's 2004 Corruption Perception Index was 3.6, putting it in sixty-fourth place among the 146 countries ranked, and below seven other Latin American nations.[3] Corruption has become an entrenched subculture, which undermines public and private institutions and has even "infiltrated police forces" (Poder Ejecutivo de la Federación 2001, 5; Programa Nacional de Seguridad Pública 2003, 19). The basic problem is lack of citizen trust in the public sector, which is reflected in public opinion. In a 1999 poll, 54 percent of those interviewed cited corruption as the principal reason for not paying taxes, and 55 percent indicated that they saw no benefit in complying with their fiscal obligations (Latinobarómetro 1999).

Moreover, Mexico fails to comply with a fundamental condition of the rule of law: respect for basic rights and freedoms (Díaz 1985). A recent Amnesty International report denounced impunity reflected in arbitrary detentions, torture, abuse, disappearances, extrajudicial executions, and assaults on defenders of human rights and journalists (Amnesty International 2002). Also, an analysis of statistics from the National Commission for Human Rights and the state-level organizations protecting basic rights reveals that most complaints for alleged human-rights violations are filed against members of the public-security forces at the three levels of government as well as against agents of the federal and state Public Ministry offices.

Shortly before President Vicente Fox took office, a poll revealed that the primary public demand on the new administration was "to improve public security" (BANAMEX-ACCIVAL 2000, 465). The Plan Nacional de Desarrollo (National Development Plan) 2001–2006 puts priority on the need to prevent crime, combat impunity and corruption, and guarantee public order, with respect for the liberties and the rights of Mexicans within the framework of the law (Poder Ejecutivo de la Federación 2001, Área de Orden y Respeto). A more recent poll (Berumen y Asociados 2002) confirmed that the central concern of citizens continues to be public insecurity and crime.[4]

Income Distribution, Poverty, and Social Rigidity

Mexico continues to have major problems structurally, particularly with regard to the scourge of poverty, which afflicts nearly half the population. A recent study by the United National Development Program notes a polarization in distribution of national income: in 2000, the poorest 30 percent of the population had only 8 percent of the national wealth, whereas the richest 20 percent had 55 percent (UNDP 2002).

Also, economic crises—particularly that of 1994—had devastating effects on employment and real wages. Quality of life deteriorated for wide sectors of the population, straining the social fabric and contributing to an increase in crime and public insecurity (Programa Nacional de Seguridad Pública 2003, 4, 11, 12). Thus, it can be concluded that "public insecurity is the indicator that best reflects structural disequilibria and, consequently, it is a social compass used to put government social policy back on course" (Programa Nacional de Seguridad Pública 2003, 11). Poverty and inequality also help explain why most prisoners are confined for robbery, a principal type of property crime.

Marked social rigidity and apathy accompany these negative trends in income distribution, quality of life, and protection of fundamental rights. Although Mexico has become democratic in the sense of alternation of parties in power, political culture has not evolved at the same pace. For example, the citizenry is not noted for its high level of membership in social organizations: according to an official poll, only 15 percent of those interviewed claimed involvement in any sort of social organization (Secretaría de Gobernación 2001). Moreover, in the area of public security, the three levels of government fail to encourage citizen participation, and most initiatives come from civil society at the neighborhood level.

Security as Public Policy

Given the realities and perceptions of insecurity, the government is designing and implementing various types of policies to confront crime and reestablish the credibility of Mexico's basic institutions. Several pillars of public security and law enforcement underpin these efforts: (1) designation of organized crime as a threat to national security and, consequently, the involvement of the armed forces in combating it; (2) an attempt to improve coordination by creating a Sistema Nacional de Seguridad Pública (National Public Security System, SNSP); (3) creation of the Policía Federal Preventiva (Federal Preventive Police, PFP); (4) establishment of the Secretaría de Seguridad Pública (Public Security Secretariat, SSP); and (5) transformation of the Federal Judicial Police into the Agencia Federal de Investigación (Federal Investigation Agency, AFI).

The development of organized crime "involves criminal groups acting in an equipped, ordered, and disciplined structure, subject to rigid rules, and [operating] without borders" (Programa Nacional de Seguridad Pública 1996, 13). Thus, drug trafficking, money laundering, illegal arms trafficking, and terrorism are "modern threats to national security" (Poder Ejecutivo de la Federación 1995). "Drug trafficking and organized crime represent one of the principal sources of violence and insecurity for society and are a threat to institutions. Additionally, they cause corruption, tarnish the national image, and erode confidence and prestige, both nationally and internationally, which affects sovereignty and damages our international relations" (Poder Ejecutivo de la Federación 2001, 128, 130).

According to President Fox's first state-of-the-nation address (September 2001), an international consensus exists that transnational organized crime, because of its resources and capacity to benefit from globalization, constitutes the gravest emerging threat to the security of nations. That appraisal justifies the active participation of the military in combating drug trafficking, even surpassing the efforts of the Procuraduría General de la República (PGR), the agency legally responsible for investigating and prosecuting drug trafficking and abuse. Thus, the Programa Nacional de Procuración de Justicia (National Program for Law Enforcement) 2001–2006 provides for a strategy of collaboration among the navy, national defense, and public-security secretariats and with the PGR and its field offices in the states. This collaboration calls for appropriate information and ample state-of-the-art tools, equipment, and technology to intercept illegal drug trafficking on land, air, and sea (Programa Nacional de Procuración de Justicia 2002, 117). Given the PGR's lead role in the formal-legal sense, it is surprising that the armed forces are not formally assigned ancillary roles, as are the PGR's state-level field offices, the PFP, the police in the various Mexican states and municipalities, and experts in law-enforcement organizations at the state level (Ley Orgánica de la PGR 2002, art. 20).

To provide a legal framework, lawmakers devised legislation in 1996 that elaborates a concept of organized crime.[5] This law distinguishes between crimes that involve administration, leadership, or supervision and those that do not. The 1995–2000 period also saw the creation of the Fiscalía Especializada para la Atención de Delitos contra la Salud (Special Prosecutor for Health Crimes), the Unidad Especializada en Delincuencia Organizada (Special Unit on Organized Crime), and the Unidad Especializada contra el

Lavado de Dinero (Special Unit against Money Laundering). Despite success-ful operations directed by personnel in the Secretaría de la Defensa Nacional (National Defense Secretariat, SEDENA), the office of the special prosecutor for health crimes was abolished at the beginning of 2003 when evidence sur-faced that it had been infiltrated by organized crime. The other units contin-ued to operate.

As of December 2004, the role of the military was expanding deeper into the war on drugs. For example, in the second half of 2003, the secretary of defense was responsible for 93 percent of the total amount of cocaine con-fiscated, 83 percent of the marijuana, and 70 percent of all firearms, as well as for the eradication of illegal crops on more than 70 percent of the total amount of land previously used for that purpose. All of this signifies that in Mexico, the weight of the war on drugs was falling on the shoulders of the armed forces (Presidencia de la República 2003a, 478).

THE NATIONAL PUBLIC-SECURITY SYSTEM

Article 21 of the Mexican constitution was amended in late 1994 to establish a national public-security system to integrate the federal, state, and local levels of government; the Mexican Congress simultaneously implemented author-izing legislation establishing the bases for cooperation among them (Con-stitución 2002, art. 73, sec. 23). In other words, this is a true constitutional mandate to establish a national public-security system to achieve the most efficient and effective collaboration possible in the area of public security. Given the model of decentralized security—in which federal, state, and mu-nicipal authorities are responsible for maintaining security in overlapping jurisdictions—coordination is essential.

Notably, in light of the overlapping public-security jurisdictions, an execu-tive-branch resolution (Acuerdo del Poder Ejecutivo 1994) created the Coor-dinación de Seguridad Pública de la Nación (National Public Security Office). Its significance was demonstrated in the suggestion that the president him-self head such an office.

Implementing legislation passed in 1995 established the basis for the SNSP, in which the federal government, the Federal District, the states, and the municipalities must guarantee a consistent and coordinated policy in this area. Among other things, this system provides for compiling a nationwide information system on criminals and police forces, decision making on pub-lic-security policy, coordinating human and material elements for crime fighting and prevention at the various governmental levels, implementing collaborative activities and operations, training a critical mass of personnel, and developing a new kind of relationship with civil society.

Thus, the SNSP's database includes a National Registry for Public-Security Personnel that contains *claves únicas de identificación permanente* (permanent individual identity numbers). By mid-2002, that registry contained more than 174,000 individuals, with the photos and fingerprints of personnel in the PFP, the PGR, the state-level prosecutors' offices, various police forces, and state prison guards. This was more than 53 percent of the 325,816 personnel on active duty in these areas (Secretaría de Seguridad Pública 2002a).

Article 3 of the 1995 law sets out a systemic view of public security, instructing that the relevant authorities employ prevention, prosecution, and sanctioning of misdemeanors and crimes as well as the social rehabilitation and reintegration of criminal and juvenile offenders. Similarly, the law calls for a state-level campaign against the causes that foment crimes and antisocial behavior and for the development of policies and programs to foster cultural and civic values conducive to respect for the law in society. The principal innovation in this regulatory framework therefore resides in the introduction of a systemic concept of public security, a paradigm that goes beyond the traditional view centered on the police.[6] It is a new model of public security with a comprehensive approach (Ley General 1995).

In 1999, through the creation of the Fondo de Aportaciones para la Seguridad Pública (Fund for Contributions to Public Security) in the Mexican states and the Federal District, the Consejo Nacional de Seguridad Pública (National Public-Security Council), the top entity coordinating the system, increased resources allocated to security policies. In 2000, the "equipment, technology, and infrastructure" line item represented approximately 48 percent of public-security funding. Training accounted for only 1.5 percent, and community participation only 0.6 percent (Presidencia de la República 2000). A year later, 72.4 percent of the resources went to "equipment, technology, and infrastructure" (including improvement of prison infrastructure). This reveals a pattern of targeting of the government's priorities (Presidencia de la República 2001).

As a result of the punitive policies reflected in the SNSP, the prison population grew 81.1 percent between 1994 and 2000 (Presidencia de la República 2000). This trend continued, and, at the end of 2001, the prison population stood at 31,120 prisoners, almost 20 percent over physical capacity. This indicates that the prisons were not complying with their constitutional mission of reintegrating former prisoners into society. Instead, they were becoming "centers of confinement and socialization in practices that reproduce criminality, with deficient systems of supervision and guards, where overpopulation reigns, provoking riots and high levels of corruption" (Programa Nacional de Seguridad Pública 2001–2006 2003, 5).

Also notable among the SNSP's mandates are the regulation and supervision of private security services, which are listed in the National Registry of Private Security Companies. In 2000, this registry contained 2,581 member firms (Presidencia de la República 2000). This trend of privatizing security has accelerated since the beginning of the new century, with the enrollment of 2,332 new companies, of which 2,098 are local (Programa Nacional de Seguridad Pública 2001–2006 2003, 41).

The SNSP's basic objective is to coordinate policies and programs aimed at preventing illegal activities and combating the commission of crimes and misdemeanors, through effective collaboration among the three levels of government.

TOWARD A MODEL OF MILITARIZED POLICE

The PFP was created in 1999 as a subdivision of the Secretaría de Gobernación (Interior Ministry, SEGOB).[7] The intention was to combine the Federal Highway Patrol (previously within the Commerce and Transportation Secretariat), the Revenue Police (Treasury and Public Credit Secretariat), and the Immigration Police (National Migration Institute in the SEGOB). It proved impossible to incorporate the latter two police forces, but the PFP did absorb the Federal Highway Patrol (which was abolished) and the intelligence arm of the Centro de Investigación y Seguridad Nacional (Center for Research and National Security, CISEN), which reports to the Interior Ministry and has functions similar to the U.S. Central Intelligence Agency, as well as military personnel from SEDENA.[8]

According to the 1999 law, the PFP's most important duties are domestic security and intelligence, which had been the exclusive reserve of the armed forces and CISEN. The PFP's most basic duties in domestic security are the preservation of freedoms and public peace and order. Thus, at the request of state and municipal authorities, it collaborates to protect individuals' physical well-being and preserve property in situations involving violence or imminent risk. At the request of the same authorities, the PFP collaborates with civil-protection services in cases of public calamities, high-risk situations, or natural disasters. It establishes policies and strategies to guarantee the security and functioning of strategic installations in the case of natural or intentional events that pose risks. In addition, the law integrates various specialized units (called Central Administrative Units) into the structure of the PFP. These handle matters such as terrorism, rapid response, special operations, and surveillance and protection of strategic installations and services, traditionally the exclusive reserve of the military.

The PFP is charged with obtaining and processing information as well as implementing crime-prevention methods either directly or through coordination mechanisms set out in relevant laws. Accordingly, one of its administrative units is the Coordinación de Inteligencia para la Prevención (Central Office on Intelligence for Prevention), which the commissioner defines as the brains of the organization, since he sees intelligence work as the base on which to design and implement specific operations.[9] This central office has approximately seven hundred former CISEN agents, each with a minimum of five years of experience in intelligence work. Their role is to design and operate systems to collect and process information and to compile a nationwide database to support development of plans for crime-prevention operations (Reglamento de la Policía Federal Preventiva 2000, art. 14, sec. 2). These agents also coordinate analyses of information to generate operational intelligence aimed at identifying individuals, groups, priority zones, and modes of operation for purposes of both crime prevention and repression. They coordinate specific police operations to procure information to identify and combat the commission of various crimes, including organized crime. Two priority targets are weapons and drug trafficking.

The internal order of 2000 required each regional command to have an intelligence headquarters for prevention matters. This reflects the importance placed on the initial task of securing information for subsequent analysis and use, that is, its conversion into intelligence. This means that the PFP has the unique quality of combining deterrent and investigative roles. As a corollary, since the creation of the PFP in January 1999, CISEN has relinquished operational and law-enforcement functions. Its role is limited to producing strategic national intelligence for decision making at the highest levels of political leadership (CISEN 2002).

Another essential aspect of the PFP's structure involves the trend toward presidentialism and militarization. Presidentialism was apparent from the start in the decision to make the appointment and removal of the commissioner a presidential prerogative. Although the PFP was a subunit of the SEGOB, the president rather than the secretary appointed and removed the

PFP director. With the creation of SSP and the integration of the PFP into it, the situation has not changed significantly: although the head of the new secretariat can nominate the PFP commissioner, the president has the final word on appointment and removal.

In the current legal framework, the commissioner holds the highest rank in the PFP and exercises the powers of command. This explains why Alejandro Gertz Manero, the first secretary of public security, decided to assume the leadership of the PFP directly rather than nominating a candidate to be appointed by the president.

The militarization of the PFP is apparent in its structure and organization, which were designed in SEDENA's image. This is particularly true for the PFP general staff, which is the responsibility of the Chief of Staff. Beyond the military structure of this new police force, militarization is also visible in the composition of the Coordinación General de las Fuerzas Federales de Apoyo (Federal Support Forces Office), one of the central administrative units of the organization. Concretely, and because of an agreement between the SEGOB and SEDENA in 2000, 4,899 soldiers from the Third Brigade of the military police were lent to the Federal Support Forces.[10] The objective of their participation is to manage crises, protect people and government property, guard strategic installations, and take part in antiterrorist operations (Presidencia de la República 2000, 39). The particular aim of the Federal Support Forces, led by a retired brigadier general, is to assist the various federal, state, and municipal authorities and to strengthen their reaction and response in crisis management using specialized personnel.

Even the PFP training centers have not escaped militarization. Currently, a retired military officer, the ex-director of the military college, heads the PFP's Central Office for Police Training. That office even encourages military personnel from SEDENA to relinquish their positions in the military and to join the PFP (Secretaría de Seguridad Pública 2002b). In particular, experienced personnel from SEDENA or the navy are approached to occupy key posts in the Federal Support Forces Office. They are also sought for the Federal Support Forces, to be deployed throughout the country to combat crimes in the *fuero federal* and to maintain order (Secretaría de Seguridad Pública 2002b).

The military model is present throughout both the law and the regulations. For example, the PFP's notion of task forces and its hierarchical arrangements are borrowed directly from the military task force (defined as a group formed to undertake a specific but not ongoing mission), as are the organization's thirteen hierarchical ranks ascending to commissioner. The PFP even borrows the army's differentiation between armed and support services for combat, which, for the PFP, are designated as divisions and services.

This trend toward the militarization of public and domestic security in Mexico is not a new phenomenon. The active participation of the armed forces in missions and roles appropriate to these two dimensions of security underscores that this is not an unusual situation.[11] Moreover, Mexico's standing armed forces are legally empowered to participate in public-security enforcement: SEDENA and the navy are included on the National Public Security Council (Ley General de Seguridad Pública 1995, art. 12). In five separate opinions, the Mexican Supreme Court held that the three armed forces (army, navy, and air force) "can participate in civil actions in support of public security, assisting the civil authorities" (Suprema Corte de Justicia de la Nación 1996). Nevertheless, as one expert notes, "The PFP must be sufficiently effective to free the military from highly visible roles in the area of public security, since such missions reduce popular support" (Turbiville 2001, 57). That is, the government should demilitarize public security and make a commitment to professionalizing the police force.

THE PUBLIC SECURITY SECRETARIAT

Another significant innovation is the creation of the SSP, which has responsibility and duties of a law-enforcement nature, including the organization and supervision of the PFP, which until the end of 2000 had been part of the SEGOB. "In the Secretariat of Public Security, the executive branch will have, in one single entity, the vehicle through which to propose the required reorganization and specialization in the design and focus of federal criminal policy. The objective is to emphasize standards of specialization and professionalism as well as use of scientific tools and suitable techniques" (Cámara de Diputados 2000, 3).

Thus, the creators of SSP foresaw its responsibility to take the lead in developing public-security policies and proposing criminal policy in the federal arena. Other substantive areas under its jurisdiction are responsibility for presiding over the National Public Security Council, nominating and removing the executive secretary of the SNSP, organizing and supervising the PFP and its career officers, establishing a criminal intelligence system, administering crime-victim support services, licensing and supervising companies providing interstate private security services, executing sentencing for federal-level crimes and administering the federal penitentiary system, and administering the federal system for juvenile delinquents.[12] The secretary of

SSP appoints the commissioner of the PFP and may in fact occupy both positions, as was the case in 2001–2004. In sum, the secretary of public security is, like the Holy Trinity, three essences in one, by unifying in his person the head of SSP, the commissioner of the PFP, and the executive secretary of the SNSP.

In addition, for the first time in a sectoral program on public security, indicators are being used to evaluate public-security and law-enforcement strategies. These include socioeconomic impacts of crime, anticorruption activities, the social rehabilitation of federal prisoners, activities of citizen-participation committees, and certification of private security service companies (Programa Nacional de Seguridad Pública 2003, 45–46). Additional indicators concern actions against impunity, respect for human rights, crime-victim services, crisis coverage and response training, and employee professionalization (Programa Nacional de Procuración de Justicia 2002, 123).

In summary, the spirit of the reform is that the SEGOB should concentrate on tasks appropriate to democratic governance, while the new SSP should dedicate itself exclusively to functions related to public security. This puts an end to the political/public-security duality in the former arrangement, in which the political functions of the SEGOB might be perceived as distorting its anticrime functions.

FROM THE FEDERAL JUDICIAL POLICE TO THE FEDERAL INVESTIGATION AGENCY

The National Development Plan makes a commitment to law enforcement that is speedy, expeditious, and respectful of human rights. Given these guidelines, it is necessary to plan strategically. It is also necessary to construct strategic performance and outcome indicators because law-enforcement policy calls for institutional reform and innovation, which requires systematic evaluation to ensure quality and efficacy in decision making and operations (Poder Ejecutivo de la Federación 2001, 149).

The AFI is the operational arm of the PGR. It replaced the Federal Judicial Police, which were generally perceived to be both corrupt and inefficient. Article 21 of the constitution establishes four basic principles for police conduct: legality, efficiency, professionalism, and integrity. Beyond these, the code of conduct for AFI agents calls for certainty, objectivity, and impartiality in the performance of duties as well as conduct that respects human rights and demonstrates efficiency in the procurement of justice.

The attorney general appoints and removes the head of the AFI. With respect to internal organization, the AFI headquarters is responsible for general policies on performance. The Police Planning Office is empowered to design and execute the AFI planning system. The Police Investigation Office assists the Public Ministry in its investigation and prosecution of crimes. The Office for Tactical Analysis is authorized to design and operate the systems for collection and analysis of law-enforcement information. It is empowered to analyze and identify the structures and modes of operation of criminal organizations. The Office of Regional Police Deployment is in charge of assigning AFI officers to respond to patterns of crime. Finally, the Office for Special Operations is charged with implementing searches, bodyguard escorts, arrests, transfers, witness protection and relocation, and personal protection for PGR officials.

As the legislators themselves put it, "The foregoing [reorganization] is not a mere name change but responds to an entirely new structure that seeks to substitute the model of criminal prosecution for a genuine framework of scientific research based on the most advanced technologies" (Cámara de Diputados del H. Congreso de la Unión 2002, 8).[13] Thus, the vision for AFI is to select able, professionally trained, and ethically principled officers who will employ modern, effective techniques in a framework of legality and respect for human rights.

The AFI is composed of both career and special agents. Emphasis is on developing the career category, which comprises recruitment, development, and service-termination stages. AFI agents have several key duties: First, agents must obey all legal orders and fulfill all duties that conform to the law. Thus, adherence to the law is mandated and obedience based on personal loyalties is rejected. Second, agents must maintain confidentiality on matters about which they have knowledge as a consequence of the performance of their duties. That is, they must maintain confidentiality about investigations, which is made easier, in part, by an operating model based on compartmentalized structures. Investigations are carried on in successive steps by different offices, which reduces the risk of corruption incurred when one officer or a small group manages an entire investigation. Finally, in performing duties, they must abstain from seeking assistance from people not authorized by the law. Thus, this helps to avoid illegal use of the so-called *madrinas*, extralegal assistants employed by the federal police. Failure to perform one's duties or being found liable in a lawsuit can result in disciplinary actions, the most severe of which are reserved for investigative police.

The shadow of presidentialism is also spreading over the federal Public

Ministry. Key PGR officials, such as the deputy prosecutors and inspector general, are to be appointed and removed at the pleasure of the president, following nomination by the attorney general. The law also proposes an entirely new structure and organization, based on a system of specialization and geographic and functional decentralization.[14] The AFI is a response to a new law-enforcement model that privileges "legal effectiveness and the use of scientific research against illegal activities" (Programa Nacional de Procuración de Justicia 2002, 105).

EVALUATION OF SECURITY AS PUBLIC POLICY

The Mexican criminal-justice system retains weaknesses in many areas:

1. Lack of respect for the law. There is a deep gap between reality and legality in Mexico. In most cases, informal political forces are imposed over the established laws, which are systematically broken.

2. Absence of autonomy for the Public Prosecutors' Office. Justice enforcement is hampered because this office is integrated into the executive branch. This complicates the office's functions as it attempts to defend the interests of both the state and civil society.

3. Corruption and penal justice. Justice has a price, and everything can be bought. The delinquent with resources can, besides hiring the best attorneys for his defense, resort to corruption of prosecuting attorneys and judges.

4. Biased justice. Most of the prison population is made up of impoverished people or members of the most vulnerable social sectors, such as ethnic minorities. Equality before the law remains a distant goal.

5. Mediocrity in justice administration. The district attorneys, judges, and magistrates are not the best attorneys in Mexico. Although by law these are merit appointments, in practice powerful people, family ties, and friendships work to install less-capable people.

6. Excessive formalism and slow procedures. The slowness of the justice system is due, in great measure, to anachronistic or obsolete processes, especially to written, rather than oral, procedures.

7. Limitations of the human-rights commissions. The agencies that protect basic human rights can only issue nonbinding recommendations. The power of the commissions is limited to their appeal to the public conscience.

8. Impunity and injustice. Impunity conveys three meanings: the inability of

the state to solve crimes and to sanction the delinquents, because of institutional weaknesses; the daily violations of human rights perpetrated by public institutions and authorities (especially those in justice enforcement); and the privileged status of the wealthy and politically powerful, who enjoy virtual immunity and can act in the knowledge that they are not subject to legal prosecution.

9. Militarization of public security and law enforcement. Because of the low level of police professionalism, public opinion supports the expansion of military involvement in police and justice administration. In the Fox administration, a two-star general was appointed as attorney general. One of the likely implications is that the attorney general remained subordinated to the secretary of defense, a four-star position.

10. Politicization of criminal justice and public security. The long arm of the political parties reaches throughout the criminal-justice system. Everything is susceptible to politicization, from appointment of officials to the design and execution of overall policies. Partisan needs prevail over legality and best practices.

Change or Continuity?

During the administration of President Zedillo, the problem of public insecurity exploded in Mexico. It reached a high point in 1997, when crimes reported to the authorities far surpassed the government's law-enforcement capacities. There were various causes for this security crisis. Noteworthy was the severely unequal distribution of wealth and increasing poverty, products of decades of mistaken economic policies. Another cause was the weakness of coordination mechanisms among the three levels of government and among the three branches of government, as well as lack of government capacity and low levels of professionalization among government workers, which contributed to impunity. Other factors included public and private corruption; disequilibria among the various public-security forces, prosecuting attorneys, and specialized personnel; growth of transnational crime; failure of social readaptation programs; obsolescence of the judicial framework; and the progressive loss of public confidence in the institutions responsible for overseeing public security and law enforcement.

To confront the challenges that had become the primary concern of the average Mexican citizen, the government implemented a series of innovative measures. Notable among them were (1) legal reforms to crime-prevention and law-enforcement instruments; (2) militarization of the war on organized crime, particularly against drug trafficking; (3) creation of the entirely new, comprehensive SNSP; (4) increase in prison capacity; and (5) creation of the PFP, a militarized police, which fit the model of an intermediate force between a regular police force and a military institution. In other words, throughout his administration, President Zedillo responded to the challenge of crime and social vulnerability with measures of a punitive nature. The Zedillo administration also created, on November 30, 2000, SSP, which assumed some of the duties that had belonged to the SEGOB. This separated SEGOB's political functions from law-enforcement functions, which passed to the SSP.

With the election of Vicente Fox, the public's demand for security and justice continued unabated. It was an unavoidable challenge deeply rooted in the collective imagination. Given this situation, the new administration decided to extend the process of militarization beyond the public-security arena and into law enforcement proper. The perceived corruption in the PGR and the federal police, in contrast to the credibility and discipline of the military, contributed to the expansion of military influence. As a counterweight, detailed indicators were constructed to facilitate an ongoing evaluation process. The new SSP oversees the PFP, the federal penitentiary system, and the National Public Security Council.

The Fox administration chose to continue the previous administration's security policies, which established a comprehensive model of public security to undergird the SNSP. Even though the approach was comprehensive, the punitive aspects were emphasized. This was reflected in budget outlays, which assigned top priority to prisons and other detention facilities, along with tools and materials for law-enforcement agencies. Moreover, both the Fox and Zedillo administrations emphasized quantitative indicators, which are relatively easy to measure, and minimized qualitative considerations. Examples of quality considerations include leadership, selection requirements for new recruits, training and education, codes of police ethics, law-enforcement doctrines, and internal-control mechanisms and procedures. Paradoxically, as Mexico experiences the transition from authoritarianism to democracy, we have a situation marked by deficits in professionalization and quality of personnel in charge of public security and law enforcement. The gaps and deficits largely explain the dominant trends toward militarization of public police and privatization of personal security.

The political leadership as of late 2004 envisions change in only three areas. First is the creation of the AFI, to replace the Federal Judicial Police as the investigative police of the PGR. The objective is to clean up the investigative police branch and develop a scientific capacity to help overcome the backlog of cases and reduce the high levels of official impunity. Second is the design of indicators to evaluate strategies in both policing and law enforcement. Third is the establishment of a career law-enforcement service for the PFP and the AFI, the two most important federal police forces, and the establishment of clear rules and procedures to encourage citizens to choose a career in policing.

A common denominator for the Zedillo and Fox administrations was their choice of the punitive model, which inherently rejects citizen participation. The limited civic involvement is apparent in both the discourse and framework of traditional corporative organizations, which usurp a social role for themselves that should belong to the citizenry. Finally, for the past decade, government policies have constituted the antithesis of the recommendations of the United Nations Development Program (UNDP 2002). Recent administrations militarized both their public-security and law-enforcement functions, and they have expanded the role of the military. This implied rejecting the model of community policing, minimizing the importance of police professionalization, underestimating and discouraging citizen participation, and overlooking human-rights violations when these were seen to promote greater police efficiency and effectiveness. This militarization and the acceptance of the punitive model show that Mexico, under the administration of Vicente Fox, continued to experience continuity—not change—in the public-security and law-enforcement arenas.

Local Responses to Public Insecurity in Mexico

Allison M. Rowland

Mexico, like the rest of Latin America, has been hit hard since the mid-1990s by a rise in crime and violence, and government measures designed to slow this trend have been largely ineffective. Much of the analysis of the public-security problem in Mexico has centered on large cities, which have suffered the greatest impact of the crime wave in numbers of victims and monetary losses. However, rural areas throughout the country also have been affected by armed banditry, smuggling (particularly drugs and arms), and violence, often with the complicity of police forces and the military. This rural violence is an especially complex issue in the country's southern states, given the long history of political repression in these areas (whether directly sponsored by the government or simply tolerated), particularly where residents are primarily members of indigenous groups. The *policía comunitaria* operate in villages of the southern state of Guerrero, a region traditionally neglected by state and national authorities. The experience of the *policía comunitaria* points up the difficulties of applying a single model of policing, imposed by a uniform legal framework, in a vast and diverse country.

Interest in indigenous forms of policing has increased around the world in recent years for several reasons. On the one hand, it forms part of broader attention to the problems of governance for regional minorities and ethnic groups in liberal democracies. The growing salience of human rights in international law has led to studies of systematic discrimination against disadvantaged groups, including their access to justice, and has come to form part of the agenda for government and democratization in Latin America (see Méndez, O'Donnell, and Pinheiro 1999).[1] These issues came to special prominence in Mexico as a result of the Ejército Zapatista de Liberación Nacional

(Zapatista National Liberation Army) uprising in the state of Chiapas in 1994, which centered worldwide attention on the struggles of indigenous peoples for respect for their basic rights. On the other hand, soaring crime rates in the developing world in the 1990s, combined with the difficulty of identifying successful public policies to combat crime, have engendered efforts to adapt findings about crime and policing from decades of research in the United States, western Europe, and other liberal democracies to different institutional and cultural settings (see Bayley 2001; Fajnzylber, Lederman, and Loayza 1998).

Policía comunitaria can be translated as community police, but I prefer to avoid the term in English because it could be misleading and it downplays some important elements that distinguish the former from more familiar types of police organization present elsewhere in Mexico and in other countries. Apart from the rural and small-town context of this *policía comunitaria*, which contrasts markedly with the big-city emphasis of much of the community-policing literature in the United States and elsewhere (Lyons 1999; Skogan and Hartnett 1997), the organizational structure that supports these officers also plays a key role in the administration of justice. This includes the weighing of evidence and eyewitness testimony, the determination of a suspect's guilt or innocence, the type of punishment to be meted out in the case of guilt, and the degree of rehabilitation of the accused. The term *policía comunitaria* has become common in Mexico, and is used to describe a wide variety of policing strategies. I refer here only to the *policía comunitaria* of the Costa Chica and Montaña de Guerrero regions.

At the same time, the *policía comunitaria* present in the municipalities of Azoyú, Malinaltepec, Metlatónoc, and San Luis Acatlán should not be confused with systems of indigenous justice such as those that operate in some parts of the states of Oaxaca and Chiapas (Collier 1995; Nader 1990) and elsewhere in Latin America. In this area of Guerrero, the focus is on criminal justice and public security rather than civil disputes. The norms regarding appropriate judgment and punishment for suspects in the Costa Chica and Montaña system, including respect for the human rights of suspects, are the subject of serious consideration and debate among participating communities.

Unlike municipal police officers, agents of the *policía comunitaria* of the Costa Chica and the Montaña de Guerrero do not answer directly to municipal administration, but rather to the Coordinadora Regional de Autoridades Comunitarias de la Costa-Montaña (Regional Coordinating Committee of

Community Authorities). Thus, the *policía comunitaria* are not employees of the government, or members of police forces at any level, which makes the fact that these officers carry guns another distinctive, and controversial, aspect of their operation.

Scope and Limits of Mexican Local Policing

Mexican government at all three levels (central, state, and municipal) was initially slow to react to the crime wave of the 1990s. While its attention to the matter has increased dramatically in recent years, measures designed to combat insecurity have been dominated by agencies at the national level, for both personnel and budgets. A modest number of states have taken their own initiatives in this matter, but with even more meager results.

Meanwhile, *municipios* (local governments) all over the country are struggling to improve their response to the crime wave, under conditions of severely limited resources and experience. Paradoxically, as I argue elsewhere (Rowland 2003a), although local government action is necessary in Mexico to improve crime prevention and address the public's perceptions of insecurity, the very institution charged with this task in Mexico—the *municipio*—is ill suited for the job in the vast majority of cases. The product of this dilemma, thus far, has been a proliferation at all levels of government of public policies formulated to fight crime, an enormous increase in the public resources dedicated to this task, and little, if any, evident progress. Unfortunately, incessant attention in the media and by politicians, combined with few positive results, is beginning to lead to public disenchantment. This may endanger recent gains in democratization and decentralization in Mexico, as voices in favor of *la mano dura* (a hard-line approach) by central government gain ground. Thus, effectiveness, or even simply perceived effectiveness, is a key element in the success of any police-reform policies.

The scope and restrictions on local policing in Mexico are defined in the national constitution, specifically in Articles 21 and 115. In essence, municipalities are charged with ensuring local public safety and preventive policing, which is interpreted to include public-order maintenance and the interruption of crimes in progress, with the detention of those responsible, when possible. Municipal police departments are not permitted to engage in investigative work (which is reserved for state and federal ministerial police), nor do they generally work closely with their state prosecutor's offices, although Article 21 mentions the need for coordination among the distinct levels of government involved in public security. Indeed, particularly from the late 1960s to the early 1990s, the role and importance of local policing in Mexico diminished, as government functions generally became more centralized. This tendency toward centralization has been reinforced by the crime wave currently sweeping the country, and has led to calls for national action and high-profile policing modeled on the Federal Bureau of Investigtion (FBI) in the United States and other well-regarded national agencies from elsewhere.

To complicate the panorama, since the mid-1980s, many municipalities, particularly those whose jurisdiction includes major cities, have rapidly increased their administrative and governance capacities (Cabrero 1996; Guillén 1996; Ramírez Saíz 1998; Ziccardi 1995). These local governments have begun to insist on greater responsibilities and more local control of activities—including local policing—that are constitutionally assigned to them but that had been assumed by national or state levels. This process of decentralization by demand of the municipalities is linked to improved oversight and the growing competitiveness of local elections in most parts of the country.

Progress in municipal administration has varied greatly by region, however, and rural areas and towns still generally lack the experience and qualified personnel to successfully carry out even a limited range of services (Cabrero 1995; Díaz Montes, Zafra, and González Mechor 1994; Rowland 2001). In addition, the single national legal framework under which all municipalities are governed—regardless of size, resources, or administrative capacity—fails to recognize that the approaches to policing appropriate for large cities may have limited relevance in rural municipalities. For example, the types of crime in rural areas may be different from those common in cities (livestock rustling, vigilantism, highway banditry), the substantially larger geographic territories of rural areas may require that more resources go to the acquisition of hardware (particularly trucks and communications systems), it may be more important to train police officers as generalists rather than specialists, and sensitivity may be needed for dealing with closer-knit and more traditional communities in rural areas.

Still, as many municipalities are beginning to discover, not only is there much scope for improvement in the limited police functions allowed to local government, but basic reform in policing and police services is a complex and expensive task (Rowland 2003b). Furthermore, municipal administrations are realizing that better performance by local police requires not just improved training and equipment, but also constant contact with, and consensus from, the local population. This is another new and difficult area of local-government activity, since traditional forms of interactions between citizens and local government in Mexico tend to follow clientelist and corporatist patterns.

Rural *municipios* face some difficulties quite unlike those of their urban counterparts, especially in availability of public resources and of experienced administrators. Because of their relatively small political and economic significance for state and federal politicians, they may also find it harder to call the attention of authorities to their plight, although such neglect could be considered a mixed blessing in some cases. However, especially where local areas are homogeneous in ethnicity and cultural norms, certain types of public-security programs may actually be more feasible in small communities and rural areas than they are in cities. In particular, community-based efforts to improve the monitoring and control of activities that violate local standards of behavior (e.g., theft, vandalism, public disorder, domestic violence) may work much better in rural settings than in cities.[2]

Although local crime prevention and public order are constitutional responsibilities of municipal authorities in Mexico, in rural areas and state capitals, state governments often maintain large and active police forces of their own, and these answer directly to the governor. These are often the source of controversy, and allegations are common that state-police forces overstep the limits of their formal responsibilities and impinge upon activities of the municipal forces. They are frequently cited for human-rights violations as well (PRODH 1995, 1997). Their supporters defend their presence by citing municipal incapacity to provide adequate local police protection.

The *policía comunitaria*, which operate in several municipalities in the southern state of Guerrero, are especially interesting. These organizations were formed during the mid-1990s as a local response to growing criminal violence, increased reports of abuses of local residents by police and military agents, and the perceived inattention of state authorities charged with overseeing public security in the region. The efforts of the *policía comunitaria* in the Costa Chica and Montaña regions of Guerrero present a novel and apparently successful approach to local public-security problems, to the extent that they have achieved community approval as well as some degree of effectiveness at a very low financial cost. However, not only do these officers undertake their duties with uncertain levels of legal protection (both from suspects and from various branches and levels of government), but they also run serious risks of injury or death because of lack of coordination with the activities of other security forces.

The *Policía Comunitaria* of Guerrero

The *policía comunitaria* discussed here are currently active in the villages of four rural municipalities of the Costa Chica and the Montaña de Guerrero, two regions located on the eastern side of the southern state of Guerrero, which together were home to more than 703,000 people in 2000. These are some of the poorest and most remote zones in all of Mexico, whose residents survive principally on subsistence agriculture, small-scale cash crops (coffee and fruits), livestock (pigs, chickens, and goats), and the sale of woven palm hats.[3] In the dry season, the landscape in the Montaña is barren and harsh, and access to water determines survival. As in other parts of the country, the most fertile and arable lowlands tend to be private plots owned by mestizos, while the indigenous villagers have title to common plots (under the *ejido*, or communal, legal regimes) on higher, less accessible, and less fertile grounds. On the Pacific Ocean side of the Sierra Madre del Sur, in the Costa Chica and a few Montaña municipalities that straddle the mountain divide, water is more abundant year-round, but cattle production by mestizo elites is expanding and causing friction over land rights. The population in the larger towns in both regions is ethnically diverse, but the villages are principally home to indigenous peoples of Mixteca, Náhuatl, Tlapaneca, and Amuzga ethnicities. These govern themselves with a mix of traditional and modern Mexican practices, including councils of elders and community assemblies, as well as *ejido* and municipal authorities.

Throughout modern times, the state of Guerrero has had a reputation for *caudillismo*, intolerance of opposition and political violence (Bartra 1996; Calderón 1994). The Costa Chica and Montaña regions have been especially fraught with conflicts among rival groups for control of economic resources and political power. Most recently, during the 1970s, guerrilla warfare and violent repression of organized dissent (known as Mexico's Dirty War) shook the region, and even nonviolent organizations and peaceful electoral competition were discouraged. Recent changes in the country's political system have slowly come to be echoed in the Costa Chica and Montaña, however, as opposition electoral victories at the municipal level were grudgingly ceded, particularly since the end of the Carlos Salinas administration (1988–1994).[4] Thus, while reports of ongoing human-rights violations in the region are troubling, the fact that these are registered and protested through official channels is a welcome indication of political change in this region.

The growing number of violent crimes at the beginning of the 1990s, however, marked the proliferation of a different form of assault on the region's residents, with armed robbery, rape, kidnapping, and murder becoming more prevalent, and not necessarily tied to political issues. Local residents tend to blame difficult economic times and a lack of opportunities for young men, and this may be a reasonable conclusion, given that demographic growth in the region has not been accompanied by an increase in the number or types of productive activities available. Indeed, in some areas, young people are not integrated as owners of communal lands for agricultural production because there is no additional arable land for them to work. In the traditional rural context, this implies exclusion from the local social and political structures as well. One result is that seasonal migration, both to the United States and to other parts of Mexico (especially to the states of Baja California, Sinaloa, and Sonora) has grown rapidly in recent years as a response to local stagnation. Return migration by young people who have absorbed different cultural values, including a dependence on cash transactions, may have contributed to the rise in crime in previously tranquil communities.

Another factor in increased criminal violence in the region may be the influx of guns and narcotics traffic in the 1990s. Shipments of cocaine from South America allegedly are delivered along the relatively unpeopled Pacific coast; some local residents, as well as outsiders, are involved in the transportation of these either along the coast toward the United States or across the mountains toward Mexico City. While this activity is not necessarily a source of local violence, it probably adds both to the number of people in the region who do not have ties to local communities and to the availability of arms that can be used to commit crimes. In addition, many peasants were reportedly lured into marijuana and heroin poppy production in the 1990s, and traffickers are reported to give guns and cash as part of their payment, since this valuable crop requires substantially more protection than corn and other subsistence crops.

Finally, in spite of some advances toward democracy, police and military agents are commonly perceived by local residents to contribute both indirectly and directly to the rise of violence and crime in the Costa Chica and the Montaña. On the one hand, the state of Guerrero's police officers play a role in the security operations of most rural areas of the state, ostensibly in support of municipal forces that are often too small and underfunded to carry out their duties effectively. In addition, they are charged with the investigation of crimes reported to the state prosecutor's office. Ironically, to the extent state officers are involved in these activities, their efforts are commonly criticized for being insufficient for the size of the problem.

This scarcity of state police may, however, be a mixed blessing, since the police units (both in Guerrero and in other Mexican states) are often accused of corruption and involvement in organized crime. Mexico's military have traditionally been considered free from corruption, but this has begun to change in recent years with accusations of involvement in drug trafficking and consumption becoming more common. In addition, on several occasions firefights and other incidents have broken out between municipal police forces and either soldiers or state police, with each side claiming that the other was discovered as it engaged in illicit activity.

Police and military presence rose sharply in these regions after the beginning of the Zapatista uprising in Chiapas in 1994, ostensibly in response to several minor guerrilla organizations that made their appearance during the following years. The largest was the Ejército Popular Revolucionario (Popular Revolutionary Army), but none ever achieved the prominence and public support that the Zapatistas did in Chiapas. Meanwhile, complaints to human-rights organizations of illegal detentions and searches of residents and their property, commonly accompanied by beatings and torture, rose sharply from 1994 to 1996, as national military and police forces, joined by the state police, purportedly attempted to thwart guerrillas in the region (Amnesty International 1999; Centro de Derechos Humanos, Tlachinollan 1995, 1996; Human Rights Watch 2001; PRODH 1997). Tales of disappearances and summary executions during these years persist, adding to the climate of fear and vulnerability among residents, regardless of the veracity of any particular case.[5]

This panorama of crime and violence, in which the line between criminals and government is not always clear, is the setting for an innovative experiment in community-based police, begun in 1995. One of the interesting elements of these *policía comunitaria* is that, while they do not attempt to address the underlying causes of crime in the region (and it is not clear that either local groups or higher levels of government could do so, even if they were so inclined), they do appear to have fomented perceptions of increased personal security among residents. Their methods have been dismissed as quaint by some critics and unconstitutional by others, but they fill a vacuum that municipal government is incapable of handling and that state and national government do not appear to take seriously.

ORIGINS OF THE *POLICÍA COMUNITARIA*

The *policía comunitaria* force was formally constituted in 1995, in the village of Santa Cruz en el Rincón, in the Montaña municipality of Malinaltepec, during a meeting of thirty-two elected *comisarios municipales* (village officials) from this municipality as well as Acatepec and San Luis Acatlán in the Costa Chica.[6] These were joined by a number of locally based social organizations, including producer unions, indigenous associations, and representatives of parents and teachers at primary schools. The group made its intentions public and official through registration of their single page of agreements with a notary public from San Luis Acatlán. Their central concern, as expressed in this document, was to put an end to the hundreds of robberies, sexual assaults, injuries, and murders that had taken place over the past few years on rural roads used by villagers to get to markets, schools, and health centers. They complained that in spite of formal reports that victims and their families had filed with the "corresponding authorities," nothing had been done by governments to address the problem.

The group based their decision to form a local, volunteer police force on their interpretation of the newly modified Article 4 of the Mexican constitution, which defends the autonomy and self-determination of indigenous communities and regions, as well as Convention number 169 of the International Labor Organization (ILO), which protects traditional methods of dealing with offenses committed by members of indigenous groups and has been ratified by the Mexican national government.[7]

The original agreement of the group assembled in Santa Cruz en el Rincón was to assign members of the *policía comunitaria* to guard the rural roads connecting their villages with other communities, to coordinate the actions of each village force with the others, and to make it possible for agents of the *policía comunitaria* who did not have firearms of their own to be able to borrow those of others, with the serial numbers of these weapons recorded by the municipal registrars.

Subsequently, and in spite of the lack of official approval, the new *policía comunitaria* were implicitly recognized by Governor Ángel Aguirre Rivero (1996–1999), who provided money and some equipment for their use. Observing the success of these early efforts, other indigenous communities in the region began to follow suit, and by 2001, forty-five villages in three municipalities (Azoyú, Malinaltepec, and San Luis Acatlán) had generated agreements between municipal officials, traditional authorities, and the majority of community members to establish their own *policía comunitaria*.

The municipal governments of these communities have not only accepted this form of local policing but have supported it actively through the contribution of federal funds and equipment earmarked for public security (part of the program for direct federal transfers to municipalities, known as budget section 33). Municipal officials also occasionally solicit the services of the *policía comunitaria* to help undertake operations in the villages where they exist. Indeed, both the municipalities concerned and the leaders of the *policía comunitaria* report good working relationships with one another and offer no complaints about their counterparts. Their success has led to calls to expand these organizations to other municipalities in the region, and in early 2003, several villages in the municipality of Metlatónoc approved their creation. In addition, municipal officials there joined with the other three local governments to inform neighboring communities and officials in the municipalities of Alcozauca de Guerrero, Atlixtac, Copanatoyac, Tlacoapa, and Zapotitlán Tablas about the potential for *policía comunitaria* in their jurisdictions.

The degree of support and cooperation between municipal authorities, whether indigenous or mestizo, and the *policía comunitaria* makes sense, considering the lack of municipal capacity to provide public security and police services. The four municipalities where the *policía comunitaria* now exist have smaller budgets per capita than most Mexican municipalities (in spite of federal transfers), because their impoverished populations limit the potential size of the local tax base.

The administrative limitations of local governments in the Montaña and Costa Chica, as well as their lack of confidence in state authorities, can also be observed in the fact that none of these four submitted their Programa de Seguridad Pública (Public Security Program) to state officials.[8] My colleagues and I were not able to obtain official or unofficial municipal documents of this nature either. This absence is hardly unusual in rural municipalities throughout the country, but the fact that officials of the current state administration use this as an excuse to condemn and dismiss the *policía comunitaria* underlines the difficulty of coordinated government action in favor of residents of the region. Within the region, however, changes in the political sphere have helped support the *policía comunitaria*: municipal officials of all three major political parties are involved in promoting it, and they take pains to describe it as a nonpartisan issue.

ORGANIZATION AND PRACTICES OF THE *POLICÍA COMUNITARIA*

As of 2003, the *policía comunitaria* were active in forty-five communities in the municipalities of Azoyú, Malinaltepec, Metlatónoc, and San Luis Acatlán. Each village names between six and twelve officers, depending on its size and local perceptions of need, and each group is headed by a local commander. Officers volunteer for one-year terms of service or are named by the local council of elders, as a part of their routine, unsalaried *cargos* (community duties), which also may include tasks such as hosting the village's annual feast or serving as village treasurer. Incoming members are trained by village elders and current officers to undertake duties such as maintenance of public order and basic police intelligence work, as well as the apprehension and detention of suspected criminals.

The governing body of the village police forces is the executive committee of the *policía comunitaria,* which consists of five commanders elected from among the participating communities. This committee is responsible for maintaining the radio communication system that ties the villages together, raising money from government and other sources, and representing the *policía comunitaria* in dealings with municipal and state authorities. The whole system is organized under the rubric of the Coordinadora Regional de Autoridades Indígenas de la Montaña y Costa Chica (Regional Coordinator for Indigenous Authorities of the Montaña and Costa Chica), a loosely knit group of regional political and social leaders, which designed the program and is headquartered with the Executive Committee, in the town of San Luis Acatlán. In these offices, thirty-five employees work full-time, with their activities paid for through the municipality's section 33 funds.

While the issue of financing the *policía comunitaria* is of constant concern, the broader efforts to keep money from contaminating both the policing and the administration of justice related to it speak volumes about local perceptions of crime control in the region. Active officers of the *policía comunitaria* are not paid salaries for their services, although they are excused from other community duties and payments. The underlying premise is that money—and in particular, the opportunity to buy one's way out of arrest and prosecution—should be separated from policing. In addition, opponents to paying a salary maintain that to do so would attract careerists who are not fully integrated into the social life of the village and who therefore would undermine the premises of self-policing upon which the *policía comunitaria* are based. However, as is evident from the case of several villages in Malinaltepec, where families of officers do receive cash payments from the municipality's section 33 funds, consensus among residents on this issue does not exist. Those who argue in favor of salaries emphasize the precarious financial situation of most families involved and point out that, during their time of service, officers have less time to devote to their households' agricultural activities.

Because no salaries are paid and only rudimentary equipment is provided, the entire budget for the services provided by the *policía comunitaria* is minimal. The four municipal governments where the *policía comunitaria* are active provide some financial support via their section 33 funds, and during the term of the previous governor, Angel Aguirre Rivero, money and training were also occasionally available. In addition, the Instituto Nacional Indigenista (National Indigenous Institute), a semiautonomous federal agency that operated until 2003 under the auspices of the Secretaría de Desarrollo Social (Social Development Ministry), provided resources for training workshops on penal procedures, human rights, and the rights of indigenous peoples for members of the *policía comunitaria*. It also loaned money for the purchase of radios and antennas for the village groups and has played a role in promoting the *policía comunitaria* generally. Thus, the *policía comunitaria* exhibit no small degree of financial precariousness; it could be argued, though, that in this sense they are little different from other actors involved in service provision in rural Mexican municipalities.

Suspects apprehended by the *policía comunitaria* are turned over to the Executive Committee, which organizes a community assembly (presided over by members of this committee, as well as representatives of the Coordinadora Regional) to determine guilt or innocence. In these assemblies, authorities explain the circumstances of the arrest and the charges against the suspect; the suspect, joined by family and friends, is allowed to present a defense. However, no lawyers are allowed, because of local perceptions that these also lead to corruption and inequitable treatment of suspects.

Members of the assembly vote on the proposals for punishment and reparations required of a guilty suspect, and the Executive Committee oversees the fulfillment of these decisions. The length of sentences is not fixed in advance and can include up to one year of community service (typically, labor in village public-works projects), with meals provided by the community and nights spent in jail. Care is taken to exclude both corporal punishment and large cash or property reparations and to emphasize rehabilitation and reintegration of convicts to their communities. This is no doubt in part a reflection of the influence of the regional, independent human-rights group, Centro de Derechos Humanos, Tlachinollan (Center for Human Rights, Tlachinollan), which is supported by the Catholic diocese of Tlapa de Comonfort and has promoted the development of the *policía comunitaria* since their founding. The Council of Elders in each of the communities where the prisoner is sentenced to work for fifteen days at a time offers instruction on good behavior and responsibility. Each council also writes a letter of evaluation for the prisoner, and on the basis of these letters, the Executive Committee decides whether to free the prisoner or to extend his sentence. Once a prisoner is freed, he is taken to his village of origin and turned over to his family in the presence of the whole community, as formal testimony to his or her rehabilitation.

This system of justice is obviously designed primarily for transgressions by local residents, and the treatment for suspects from outside the indigenous communities can be problematic, especially if these complain that their human rights are violated by virtue of being detained by nongovernmental agents. On the other hand, the degree of acceptance of the *policía comunitaria* has been so great that not only do residents seek them to resolve crimes, but also, on occasion, the state police have asked for their intervention in investigating, detaining, and judging suspects in cases they fear may erupt in violent conflict.

OPPOSITION TO THE *POLICÍA COMUNITARIA*

In spite of the apparent success of the *policía comunitaria*, both in community satisfaction and cost effectiveness, the government of the state of Guerrero has shifted from quiet support to active opposition to these efforts, which threatens the future of this approach. In part, the state's disapproval is on legal grounds, but other issues may also be in play. For example, if members of the state police are in fact involved in organized crime, the *policía comunitaria* may reduce their profit margins. At the same time, any autonomous organization in the Costa Chica and Montaña regions may still represent an intolerable threat to traditional forms of political control by state elites (this argument is documented for a different region of Guerrero in Bartra 1996). Indeed, the degree of disagreement between local and state authorities on even some basic points of fact about the *policía comunitaria* suggests high levels of difficulty in working together, as well as minimal levels of mutual trust. This situation is not new to the region, but certainly presents an impediment to research. The political atmosphere at the time of our research was polarized and tense, and statements by officials and other actors at any level were often not verifiable in documents or by other informed opinions.

State authorities we interviewed insisted that the *policía comunitaria* should be disbanded for several reasons. They noted that prosecution and the administration of justice are not municipal—and much less, community—functions and that the *policía comunitaria* are not officially recognized authorities. In addition, sources in the state public-security ministry argued that the *policía comunitaria* do not conform to statewide plans and programs for public security.

In essence, the claim is that state government in fact does support efforts to reduce crime and improve policing in the Costa Chica and Montaña regions, principally by building a state-police headquarters for one hundred officers in Tlapa de Comonfort, the regional capital of the Montaña, in 2000, and by sending state police to work under the command of municipal forces, with their salaries paid by the state. In addition, state authorities insist that no police officer or *comisario municipal* has been arrested as a result of complaints to the State Human Rights Commission about violation of individual liberties put forth by people detained by state police and that only warrants have been issued in these cases.

Media coverage of the zone is limited, but reporters of at least one newspaper disagree with this version of events.[9] Still, whether *policía comunitaria* officers are in jail or are simply subject to arrest because of outstanding warrants, it is reasonable to suggest that these actions constitute a threat to the officers and the programs as a whole, especially given the documented history of state abuses against rural and indigenous populations within its jurisdiction. The fact that military forces routinely confiscate the firearms of the *policía comunitaria* only helps foster local perceptions of official persecution.

The question of whether the *policía comunitaria* force is a legal organization, and whether its activities are lawful, has yet to be resolved. Supporters insist that Article 9 of ILO Convention number 169 refers explicitly to this kind of organization in the clause that protects traditional methods of dealing with offenses committed by members of indigenous groups. In addition, Article 2 of the Mexican constitution (whose relevant parts were moved from Article 4 in 2001) is also cited as support for the *policía comunitaria*, in spite of continued controversy over what many consider the inadequacies of the Ley Indigena (legal-reform efforts to provide more explicit protection for indigenous individuals and communities; see Hernández and Ortíz Elizondo 2003). The debates over the degree of legal protection offered by these documents form an integral part of the wider questions of indigenous rights in Mexico and elsewhere (see Dandler 1999; Davis 1999), and they are unlikely to be resolved to the satisfaction of all sides for the purposes of the *policía comunitaria*. In the meantime, local supporters zigzag between defiance of the state government's interference and efforts to promote legal reform at the national level to shelter the *policía comunitaria* and their officers. A proposal for these legal reforms is being drafted by members of the Coordinadora Regional.

Toward an Evaluation of the *Policía Comunitaria*

Evaluation of a police reform that, on the one hand, is supported by local residents, and on the other, is the object of scorn and legal objections by state officials is difficult. Community satisfaction with the *policía comunitaria*, as indicated by the reports of local officials as well as the lack of any organized local protest, suggests that this initiative provides a useful public service in a reasonably effective way. In addition, the effort not only continues to operate, in spite of attacks from the state administration, but is being expanded at the request of residents of other villages in the region.

Police reform in rural areas, of course, is only one aspect of the public-security problem in Mexico, and programs such as the *policía comunitaria* are still in their infancy. It remains to be seen whether this effort will prove feasible in the long run, especially in the current climate of violence and risk of incarceration of community police officers. Nor is it clear that these types of programs are suitable and feasible for other villages and towns, especially where social cohesion is not as great. Indeed, where populations are more diverse and undergoing more rapid change, it may be preferable for residents to work through official channels to improve municipal and state approaches to public insecurity instead of launching their own *policías comunitarias*. However, results in the Costa Chica and the Montaña de Guerrero suggest that the regional and cultural diversity of a large country like Mexico would be better served by a more flexible approach to local efforts, especially where these are supported by local residents.

Several elements contribute to this success. First, the *policía comunitaria* operate on an apparently simple premise: the willingness of local community members to subject themselves to other residents in the name of mutual protection. Officers' work depends on widespread agreement about acceptable behavior, which in turn is facilitated by the small size and high cohesiveness of communities in the region, as well as the perception of a common threat from outside authorities. As with neighborhood-policing initiatives elsewhere, the level of preexisting community organization is probably a precondition for success.

A second, related factor is the low financial cost that this initiative represents for overburdened local governments. The service of nonsalaried officers is the basis of the *policía comunitaria* and reflects the particular social structure of their communities. In addition, the willingness of participating municipalities to channel federal grants for supporting police forces to administrative support for this program is also crucial to its continuity.

A final component of success is the visibility of the *policía comunitaria* as a force not only for public order but also for justice in regions all but abandoned by state and federal government. This is a persistent issue throughout Mexico, since the criminal-justice system is widely agreed to be riddled with incompetence and corruption. Villagers of the Costa Chica and Montaña de Guerrero argue that previously, even when municipal or state police caught a suspect, he or she was invariably released for lack of proof or as the result of bribery. With the *policía comunitaria,* this is no longer the case: a sense of justice in the treatment of those who offend community standards has been restored.

As of 2004, the main immediate dangers to the existence of the *policía comunitaria* stem from opposition by the government of the state of Guerrero. Continued hostility on the part of the current governor not only undermines the possibility of improving administration and training of these forces but also puts the very lives of their officers in danger, in part because of the potential for clashes with state-police agents (in the line of legitimate duty or otherwise) and in part because of the ever-present threat of incarceration for agents of the *policía comunitaria* who have been accused of human-rights violations by suspects they detain. Both the brief history of this policing effort and a longer view of Guerrero's government conduct (Bartra 1996) suggest that a new state administration, scheduled to take office in 2005, could reverse the informal policy of antagonism toward the *policía comunitaria*. However, things may just as easily go in the other direction, with increased harassment and persecution becoming the norm.

The underlying problem is that the institutional foundations of the *policía comunitaria* are weak: essentially, they depend on a controversial interpretation of a relatively new article of the national constitution and on international agreements whose mechanisms for implementation within the country are not obvious. This precariousness is likely to persist even if a state government administration more sympathetic to the *policía comunitaria* were to take control. Faced with a wide variety of social and political challenges, such an administration would not necessarily give priority to the development of a legal reform to support this program.

The *policía comunitaria,* as a response to local crime problems, is not without other risks and limitations. In municipalities where indigenous groups and mestizos live in close contact, the latter often complain about being subject to a form of policing in which their own preferences are not considered. In addition, outside observers cannot help but notice the limited role of women in this system. While defenders of the *policía comunitaria* argue that women participate in village and regional assemblies, this participation does not always encompass the right to vote. In addition, in spite of the inclusion of women in the Executive Committee for cases that involve female suspects, they do not rule on other cases, nor is any woman part of the policy decision-making process of the Coordinadora Regional. These concerns highlight the complexity of balancing local indigenous practices with the defense of individual rights and the liberal democratic principle of equal protection under the law.

Still, it is important to keep in mind that the genesis of the *policía comunitaria* is precisely the lack of effectiveness and indeed the alleged abuse of residents by state and national police as well as members of the military. Improved governmental performance in meeting local concerns and respecting human rights might make the *policía comunitaria* unnecessary.

But this observation begs the question of whether any other form of policing as currently practiced in Mexico could be effective in the setting of the Costa Chica and the Montaña de Guerrero, as well as similar zones throughout the country. The rugged topography and insufficient and poorly maintained road and telecommunication infrastructure, combined with the cultural and linguistic differences of local residents from the majority of state and national populations, present a complex scenario for any outside agency to confront. The literature on community policing argues that police officers who are intimately familiar with local conditions and who are accepted by local residents as legitimate forces of public order may be the most appropriate for the prevention and basic detection work needed to combat most forms of crime. The only police who fit this description in the villages of the Costa Chica and Montaña de Guerrero are the *policía comunitaria.*

The ineffectiveness of government police forces and their low levels of legitimacy among residents, as well as complex terrain in rural and urban areas, characterize much of Mexico. However, the federal structure of the country, in policing as well as other sectors, offers potential advantages in the ability to adjust practices to diverse local preferences. In many cases, the municipality is the most appropriate institution to undertake police-reform efforts, since funding and oversight mechanisms are already in place and the police affiliated with municipal government enjoy at least basic (if limited and at times problematic) legal protections. In addition, most Mexicans are not members of indigenous communities and therefore cannot claim the right to traditional forms of dealing with offenses that are protected by ILO Convention number 169.

Still, the evident success of the *policía comunitaria* in responding to community concerns in a region underserved by municipal and state forces is significant enough to merit consideration in national and state legislation. Why should a single model of policing continue to be imposed on an increasingly diverse country? Officers of the *policía comunitaria* assume substantial personal risk in carrying out their duties, not only because of the inherent danger of their work but also because their work lacks legal protection. Formally recognizing the possibility of this type of local police reform—particularly in remote rural areas, where cultural norms may differ substantially from those of the national majority—could help protect the human rights of both officers and suspects. The experience of the *policía comunitaria* in the Costa Chica and Montaña de Guerrero suggests that even if this type of arrangement is nominally protected by international agreements, it needs to be spelled out in national and state legislation. Given the magnitude of crime and fear of crime in Mexico, flexibility in incorporating local solutions to crime problems should be encouraged rather than suppressed.

From Law and Order to Homeland Security in the United States

John Bailey

Homeland security in the United States is being shaped in its early years by two conflicting national projects. On the one hand, over the course of two centuries the United States developed strong ideological and institutional foundations for individual liberties and democratic practices. On the other hand, more than sixty years of defense mobilization in World War II and the Cold War led to a heightened awareness of national-security threats originating almost entirely from abroad and to a global commitment to anti-Soviet containment. In a context in which internal subversion was relatively unimportant, the protection of democracy and individual liberties within U.S. borders justified a range of anti-Soviet practices abroad, even antidemocratic practices. The terrorist attacks of September 11, 2001, were a historic watershed in bringing vital threats inside U.S. national borders: the sources of the threats are not state-based agencies, but rather networks of terrorists motivated by religion or ideology, and the targets of the threats are primarily civilians. The gravity of the threats creates new levels of tension in domestic politics between democratic liberties and security preparedness.

In the century after the Civil War of 1861–1865, the United States developed different notions of security for its foreign policy, as opposed to domestic affairs. Foreign relations was the realm of national security, in which the United States as a regional, then global, power set about developing the various capabilities to compete internationally. Domestic security was characterized by commitments, at least in principle, to protection of lives, property, and civil liberties in a highly decentralized federal system operating within a checks-and-balances presidential regime characterized by a strong, independent judicial system. Episodes such as anti-German sentiment in World War

I, the internment of Japanese Americans in World War II, and McCarthyite anticommunism in the early 1950s linked concerns about external threats with internal subversion. Also, largely domestic protest movements in the late 1950s and 1960s (e.g., the racial-desegregation and civil-rights campaigns) were closely scrutinized by authorities for foreign connections.

These episodes were transcended and absorbed by the relatively stronger forces of civil liberties and decentralization. Internal security was predominantly an issue of domestic crime and violence, to be dealt with by the regular police and judicial system. Involvement by U.S. military forces in domestic law enforcement was carefully limited by legislation (e.g., the 1878 Posse Comitatus Act), and efforts were undertaken, notably in the wake of the Church hearings and the Watergate scandals of the 1970s, to separate foreign military and intelligence activities from domestic law enforcement operations.[1]

American English itself is revealing. The concept *public security* was little used or understood in the United States before September 11. Rather the more prevalent term was *law and order,* which reflected the focus on the repression of crime and violence in a country that suffered from high rates of violent crime, especially from the 1960s to the early 1990s. *Law and order* was the term applied as well to the repression of political dissent. A different term, *public safety,* referred typically to fire protection, disaster relief, transportation safety, public health measures, and the like.

This situation changed significantly with the terrorist attacks of September 2001. While many other countries had suffered large-scale internal wars and terrorism, this was the first time in 136 years that U.S. lives and property, in large numbers and on a grand scale, were threatened within national borders. Most important, the boundaries between crime and warfare and between external and internal were blurred or erased. The federal government responded with the doctrine of homeland security, which is an approach that combines public security with national security (see table 1.4 in chapter 1), with special emphasis on antiterrorism. Thus, homeland security is integrated with national-security doctrine in foreign policy, in which preemption was added to deterrence and containment as central organizing concepts. As a counterpart in public security, prevention is added to prosecution with respect to crimes related to terrorism.

As crime and warfare became blurred by terrorism, the roles of police, judiciary, military, and intelligence are being redefined in ways that reduce or remove long-standing distinctions. Domestically, fundamental changes are being introduced that affect law (e.g., passage of the USA Patriot Act, new uses of military courts), organizations (e.g., creation of the Department of Homeland Security and the Northern Command; new arrangements between police, military, and intelligence agencies at the federal level; changing relations between the federal government and state and local governments), and a broad array of policies (e.g., air-transport regulations, reports on financial transactions, insurance coverage, migration and refugee status, and the like).

The dichotomies of internal versus external threats and civil liberties versus antiterrorism preparedness are complicated by rapid globalization. Flows of travel, commerce, finance, and communications reached historic highs in the 1990s, taken in absolute terms. The United States shares 7,500 miles of land and air borders with its contiguous neighbors, Canada and Mexico. More than 500 million persons are admitted into the country annually, of whom 330 million are noncitizens. Some 11.2 million trucks and 2.2 million rail cars enter the country, while 7,500 foreign-flag ships make fifty-one thousand port calls annually (Bush 2002b, 1). In 1999, for example, more than two hundred thousand ships docked in U.S. ports and harbors, unloading approximately 4.4 million containers and 4 billion tons of cargo. The U.S. Customs Service was able to inspect less than 3 percent of the goods arriving (Tomisek 2002, 5). The new awareness of this degree of openness aggravates feelings of insecurity in the United States.

As an especially important dimension of globalization, immigration into the United States in the 1990s reached historic highs, also in absolute terms.[2] Immigration, in turn, further complicates both the internal-external and crime-warfare dichotomies. The complete menu of procedure-related constitutional guarantees attaches fully only to U.S. citizens. They apply to lesser degrees to different categories of noncitizens (e.g., permanent residents, tourists, foreign students, and the estimated 8–10 million undocumented residents). Though native-born terrorists have perpetrated catastrophes (e.g., the Oklahoma City bombing of 1995), the post-9/11 antiterrorism policies have focused more on immigrant communities, with higher proportions of noncitizens. Most scrutinized among these groups are young Islamic males of Arabic origins.

The concepts of full citizenship and complete civil liberties point to another issue related to homeland security. U.S. civil society is quite diverse, and there is a sense that some groups' civil rights are better protected than others. A 2002 survey asked whether respondents believed their civil rights were protected and found that affirmative responses varied across groups: 82 percent believed that the rights of whites were protected and 73 percent that Asians' rights, 62 percent that blacks' rights, 63 percent that Hispanics' rights, 55 percent that Muslims' rights, and 53 percent that Arabs' rights were protected. But taken as a subsample, only 33 percent of blacks believed their rights were protected (Carlson 2002, 1, 3). It follows that racial and ethnic minorities, especially African Americans, are apprehensive about the impacts of new internal-security measures on their own civil liberties. While they are full citizens in a formal sense, many members of minority groups, because of the legacies of discrimination—including allegations of racial profiling in law enforcement—will likely be skeptical about security programs that involve heightened police activity.[3]

The central dynamic shaping U.S. security policy is the tension between measures taken to protect the homeland versus concerns about protecting civil liberties. The extent and durability of the changes brought by homeland security are uncertain because of the ambivalence of public opinion about the severity of terrorist threats versus limitations to civil liberties implied in the government's responses. This ambivalence is reflected in the stands taken by political parties and public officials. Deeply ingrained commitments to civil liberties and decentralized law enforcement present a number of challenges to the Bush administration's attempts to implement homeland security policies.

The added element of uncertainty is that homeland security is driven by shocks, such as terrorist attacks, that cannot be predicted. Absent a shock, one would expect culture and ideology to moderate government security initiatives over time. But, likewise, a single additional shock would accelerate them. Thus, as a crude working hypothesis, we might posit that the longer a shock is delayed, that is, the longer the period between September 2001 and the next significant attack, the more opportunities are created for those advocating civil rights to create buffers and cushions in order to moderate the design and implementation of antiterrorism measures.

Law and Order before 9/11

Before the terrorist attacks of September 11, drug trafficking and abuse were arguably the most contentious issues in U.S. federal law enforcement.[4] Drug abuse and the associated crime and violence remain an enforcement priority. The illicit drug market was estimated at about $65 billion in 2000, but was far smaller than the market for licit drug sales, if one includes caffeine, alcohol, nicotine, and both prescription and over-the-counter products.[5] The overall public health costs of licit drugs arguably outweigh those of proscribed drugs. Even so, the crime, violence, and social disorganization associated with illegal drugs make these prime causes of public insecurity. Further, from a subjective perspective, drug trafficking and abuse are linked in U.S. culture to national-security threats in ways that reinforce punitive responses.

The federal government began in the 1990s to pay more attention to problems of transnational crime beyond drug trafficking. The government's *International Crime Control Strategy* (May 2000) and *International Crime Threat Assessment* (December 2000)[6] identified transnational crime as a direct and immediate threat to the national security of the United States and presented extensive analysis, policy prescription, and administrative coordination mechanisms. International terrorism and drug trafficking were ranked at the top of a long list of international crimes affecting U.S. interests.

In overall crime rates, the U.S. pattern over time differs from those in Latin America and the Caribbean. The dramatic increases in crime came in the 1960s through the 1980s, leveling off—although at historically high rates—in the 1990s. According to the FBI Uniform Crime Reports, the overall rate of reported property and violent crime more than tripled, from 1,887 per one hundred thousand population in 1960 to a peak of 5,898 in 1991, after which it dropped steadily to 4,160 in 2001 (see http://www.fbi.gov/pressrel02/02ciusprelim.htm). The trends in reported crime are mirrored in the National Crime Victimization Survey, which showed violent crime down 10 percent in 1999, to the lowest levels since the survey began in 1973. Property crime dropped 9 percent in 1996 and 6 percent in 2001, continuing a long-term downward trend (see http://www.albany.edu/sourcebook/1995/toc_2.html).

Another difference from most of the Latin American cases is that U.S. law enforcement is quite decentralized. In 2000 there were approximately 800,000 full-time, sworn police officers, of whom only about 11 percent (88,496) were civilian federal (national-level) officers authorized to carry firearms and make arrests. More than half of the national total (440,920) worked in 12,666 local police departments, and another 264,472 worked for 4,495 state, county, or special-district departments (see http://www.ojp.usdoj.gov.bjs/lawenf.htm).

Similarly, the great bulk of legal-prosecution activity takes place at the state and local levels. In 2001, 2,341 state court prosecutors employed about seventy-nine thousand attorneys, investigators, and support staff, a 39 percent increase over 1992. The trend is toward the employment of full-time prosecutors, more than three-quarters in 2001, compared with about half in 1990.

In fiscal 1999, federal, state, and local governments spent more than $146 billion for civil and criminal justice, up nearly 80 percent over 1995, to a per capita expenditure of $521. The great bulk of the money, 85 percent, was spent at the state and local levels ($50 billion by state governments, $35 billion by counties, and $39 billion by municipalities; see http://www.jop.usdoj.gov/bjs/eande.htm).

With increased investment in law enforcement came an overall upward trend in arrests and convictions at all levels of government after 1990. Felony convictions rose 12 percent in state courts between 1990 and 1998 and 11 percent in federal courts between 1994 and 1996. State courts convicted almost 928,000 adults of a felony in 1998 (compared with about 667,000 in 1988), and federal courts convicted another 52,000 that same year (see http://www.ojp.usdoj.gov/bjs/stssent.htm).

The result was a burgeoning prison population, the largest per capita among industrialized countries. From 1995 to 2001, the prison population grew an average of 3.6 percent annually. Increases in incarceration rates in 2001 over the previous year were significantly lower in state prisons (up 0.4 percent) and in local jails (up 1.6 percent) than in previous years. At the end of 2001, some 6.6 million persons, roughly 3.1 percent of all U.S. adult residents, were on probation, in jail or prison, or on parole. State and federal prison authorities had 1,406,301 inmates under their jurisdictions; local jails held or supervised 702,044 persons for short-term sentences or awaiting trial. Overall, after dramatic increases in the 1980s and 1990s, the incarceration rate has begun to level off (see http://www.ojp.usdoj.gov.bjs.pros.htm).

Obviously, the U.S. approach to law and order emphasizes enforcement and punishment. If recent incarceration rates continue, an estimated one of every twenty residents (5.1 percent) will serve time in a prison during his or her lifetime. The chances for a prison term are higher for men (9 percent) than for women (1.1 percent). Race and ethnicity lie at the heart of law enforcement. Chances for imprisonment are much higher for African Americans (16.2 percent) and Hispanics (9.4 percent) than for European Americans (2.5 percent). "Based on current rates of first incarceration, an estimated 28 percent of black males will enter State or Federal prison during their lifetime, compared to 16 percent for Hispanic males and 4.4 percent of white males" (http://www.ojp.usdoj.gov/bjs/crimoff.htm).

Overall, the general trend in subjective perceptions of security is favorable. Annual Gallup polls find a continuous decline after 1992 (from 89 to 41 percent) in those who answer "more" to the question, "Is there more crime in the U.S. than there was a year ago, or less?"

In sum, we can characterize the U.S. pattern as a dramatic increase in crime rates from the 1960s to the 1990s, when the rates leveled off. The overall U.S. response was an enormous escalation of police hiring, arrests, convictions, and imprisonment, which also began to level off in the late 1990s. The leveling off of crime was helped along by a decade of robust economic growth after 1991. Subjective perceptions of security, at least as measured by perceptions of crime, improved steadily after 1992. There was increased attention to problems of transnational crime and growing awareness—though still rather abstract—about problems of terrorism. This was the context of law and order when the terrorist attacks took place in September 2001.

Public Security after 9/11

There can be little doubt that the terrorist attacks of September 11 mark a watershed. President Bush's top priority became security, understood as fighting terrorism. His commencement address at the U.S. military academy in June 2002 set out themes he would repeat frequently. The president emphasized the danger when radicalism acquires lethal technology: "When the spread of chemical and biological and nuclear weapons, along with ballistic missile technology . . . occurs, even weak states and small groups could attain a catastrophic power to strike great nations. Our enemies have declared this very intention, and have been caught seeking these terrible weapons. They want the capability to blackmail us, or to harm us, or to harm our friends—and we will oppose them with all our power" (Bush 2002a). For these reasons, containment and retaliation are inadequate, and anticipation and preemption are essential. Old ideas and practices must be radically revised to combat terrorism both domestically and internationally.

Thus there is an overall logic that links antiterrorism policies to domestic and foreign policies. In *The National Strategy for Homeland Security*, homeland security itself is defined as "a concerted national effort to prevent terrorist attacks within the United States, reduce America's vulnerability to terrorism, and minimize the damage and recover from attacks that do occur" (Office of Homeland Security 2002, 2). Terrorism is defined as "any premeditated, unlawful act dangerous to human life or public welfare that is intended to intimidate or coerce civilian populations or governments" (2). The emphasis is on preventing or reacting to catastrophic threats, those involving mass casualties and massive property destruction. In this sense the fight against terrorism approximates public security's concern with the protection of lives, property, and democratic institutions from threats posed by nonstate actors. The strategy organizes security functions into six broad categories: "intelligence and warning, border and transportation security, domestic counterterrorism, protecting critical infrastructure and key assets, defending against catastrophic terrorism, and emergency preparedness and response" (4). In turn, the homeland security strategy was integrated with the logic of the *National Security Strategy of the United States,* issued in 2002.[7] These, in turn, were integrated with more specific policies relating to terrorism, weapons of mass destruction, secure cyberspace, money laundering, and drug control.

When terrorism is defined primarily as an unlawful act, a police and law-enforcement approach is emphasized. When terrorism is viewed as an act of war, which is the Defense Department's definition, a military response is called for. These differences in perspectives complicate the ways new organizations and policies are crafted to combat terrorism. They also lie at the heart of the debates about civil liberties versus antiterrorism measures. In essence, civil libertarians support the legal approach and urge the government to deal with terrorism through the established courts and legal processes; the Bush administration, however, has been willing to treat terrorists, especially those who are not U.S. citizens, as military combatants. Both citizens and noncitizens can then be subject to military law and tribunals. The difference is that criminal courts put stronger emphasis on presumption of innocence and stricter rules of evidence. Adherence to such rules, the government argues, could jeopardize sources of information and provide information to adversaries about the government's antiterrorism operations.

Thus, the tension between protection of civil liberties and the protection of homeland security operates at several levels and raises serious questions: What steps should the government take to acquire information and act to prevent terrorist attacks at home and abroad? What are implications of these steps for police, justice, military, and intelligence in a highly decentralized, open society and economy? How can these steps be taken with least damage to civil liberties?

New Policies and Organizations

The USA Patriot Act (P.L. 107-56, 115 Stat. 272 [2001]) is the principal statutory response by the federal government to the September 11 attacks. Enacted in a little over a month (September 20–October 24, 2001) the law

1. grants additional powers to federal authorities to monitor communications and gather information within the United States to investigate suspected terrorists;[8]

2. lowers the wall separating foreign intelligence gathering from domestic law enforcement as these are conducted within the United States;

3. actively encourages information sharing between law enforcement and intelligence officers;

4. strengthens anti-money-laundering sanctions and enforcement capacity and adds these to antiterrorism provisions;

5. extends extraterritorial application of U.S. law in several respects, e.g., the serving of warrants related to terrorist crimes or application of sanctions against foreign banks involved in money laundering;

6. substantially enlarges the list of foreign crimes that can lead to money-laundering prosecutions when the proceeds from those crimes are laundered in the United States.[9]

In recognition that the act responds to an emergency, a number of its provisions carry sunset clauses: after a specific period (usually five years) the provision lapses, unless Congress explicitly renews it.

An extended commentary on this remarkable law lies beyond the scope of this chapter, and its technical details are quite complex. The first three points listed are especially important. The act facilitates surveillance and information gathering by making it easier for the government to monitor telephone and electronic communications (e.g., by targeting an individual rather than physical equipment and by making a warrant valid throughout the United States, rather than only in the district in which it is issued) and eases government access to databases protected by privacy regulations (e.g., records kept for purposes of health care, credit, banking and financial transactions, and education). Information gathered for purposes of foreign intelligence can, under restricted circumstances, be made available for criminal investigations. And, going in the other direction, information acquired through grand jury hearings can be made available for intelligence-gathering purposes, again with various restrictions.[10] Finally, one of the themes running through the act is the need to promote cooperation in information sharing between intelligence and law-enforcement agencies. That is, the long-standing prohibition against cooperation has been reversed.

Just as the USA Patriot Act introduced significant changes at the federal level, most of the fifty states adopted provisions designed to strengthen state and local police powers. The state of Maryland, for example, adopted a series of laws aimed at preparing the state for a terrorism emergency. The bills strengthen the governor's hand in limiting state residents' personal freedoms and in keeping state government activity secret when the state is threatened. The most controversial of the measures expands state-police power to use wiretaps. It also strengthens the state's control over air space and seaports.[11]

The Patriot Act, accompanied by changes in security doctrines and programs, coincided with significant bureaucratic innovations and changes in administrative procedures at all levels of government. The goals are to shift the emphasis toward combating terrorism and to improve coordination and effectiveness.

The most significant organizational change is the creation of the Department of Homeland Security (DHS) in June of 2002. As the most massive reorganization since the creation of the Department of Defense and National Security Council in 1948, DHS acquired some twenty-two agencies and 170,000 employees. The new department organizes the six functions identified in *The National Strategy for Homeland Security* into four major divisions or directorates (excluding the management division):

1. Border and Transportation Security, responsible for land, sea, and air borders, as well as national transportation systems

2. Emergency Preparedness and Response, which prepares for and coordinates responses to terrorist attacks and natural disasters

3. Science and Technology, which prepares for a full range of terrorist threats, including weapons of mass destruction

4. Information Analysis and Infrastructure Protection, charged with coordination of intelligence gathering and assessment related to threats to the homeland as well as with making the appropriate preventive and protective responses

In addition to the core directorates, DHS acquired several other important agencies that retain their organizational identities, including the U.S. Coast

Guard, the Secret Service and the Bureau of Citizenship and Immigration Services.[12]

The main goal in creating DHS was to improve coordination among agencies at the federal, state, and local levels and between government and civil society in anticipating and responding to threats. Even so, reorganization on this scale entails enormous difficulties in integrating diverse bureaucratic cultures and modes of operation. To cite only one example, improved information sharing is a key objective. Complex bureaucracies find it difficult to share information among their own offices internally and even more so among external agencies. Turf protection, legal mandates, and competition for resources explain parts of the problem, but complex technical issues are important as well. For example, the twenty-two agencies adopted diverse computer applications over the past twenty years, many of which handle highly classified information. Retrieving the information, some of which has become corrupted with age; integrating it into a manageable number of applications; and reorganizing it into systems that can be shared among diverse users present significant problems.

To cite one example, the navy faces the challenge of sifting through thirty-one thousand computer applications and reducing them to a manageable number, ideally no more than five thousand, to develop the Navy–Marine Corps Intranet. Even the simple Social Security number, a nine-digit number, is used in sixteen different ways by the different systems. The integration of all these agencies into a single department requires an audit of existing applications and a series of decisions about which computer applications to retain and how to identify and undertake migration of caches of data, much of it quite sensitive, to the new systems (Schwartz 2002).

A central issue in the creation of DHS is the structure and role of intelligence gathering and analysis and their relation to law enforcement and military uses. An especially cogent analysis (Treverton 2002) identifies several "oppositions" in the shift from Cold War practices to combating terrorism. One opposition concerns law enforcement versus intelligence. The former involves investigation and prosecution following a specific act; it is especially concerned about assembling cases that can withstand the rigors of criminal court procedures, such as precise evidence, chain of custody, and the like. The latter is anticipatory and attempts to predict events and their relationships to policy; it is less concerned about precise evidence and more focused on patterns and probable causation.

A second opposition concerns foreign versus domestic, and the new arrangements need more fluid exchanges across barriers that were constructed to prevent abuses of civil rights in the Cold War days. The third opposition concerns public versus private. As Treverton puts it, "Safeguarding critical infrastructures, such as communications or electric power, from terrorist attack means protecting public goods that are mostly in private hands. Across the country, there are three times as many 'police' in the private sector as in government. Thus, private companies will be drawn more deeply into fighting terrorism than they were into fighting communism" (2002, 3). Other challenges Treverton cites are the need for information collectors to become more sophisticated analysts and for supple and fluid ways to share information among some eighteen thousand governmental entities and the many thousands more businesses, corporations, and nongovernmental organizations (6–7).

An effective antiterrorism strategy combines intelligence and law enforcement with military support. All three actors bring different mixes of prevention and reaction. The central challenge is how to design information systems that can gather and analyze information in ways that are useful to effective action. The problems are not only in acquiring information (e.g., language, technical, and cultural skills and penetration of hard targets, such as terrorist cells), but also in the appropriate analysis and routing of information to enable useful responses. A lesson drawn from 9/11 is that useful intelligence was known to authorities (e.g., that suspicious persons were receiving pilot training in the United States), but a system of coordination and cooperation was not in place to allow analysts to connect the dots, that is, to recognize a suspicious pattern of behavior.

In sum, the challenge for Homeland Security is threefold: (1) acquire appropriate skills and technologies, (2) design an intelligence apparatus that can make best use of information, and (3) link the intelligence to effective actions, both preventive and responsive. For a variety of reasons, DHS failed in its early months to acquire sufficient standing in relation to other agencies to allow it to acquire access to raw intelligence or to assemble the human or technical resources to interact effectively with its larger and more firmly established counterparts in the intelligence community.

The focus on intelligence and law enforcement traditionally falls most directly on the Justice Department's FBI and the Central Intelligence Agency (CIA), an independent entity that reports directly to the president. The FBI is charged with both law enforcement and intelligence/counterintelligence within the United States. The bureau, which was already severely criticized for a number of perceived blunders and scandals, suffered renewed attacks following September 11.[13]

1. The agency places long-standing priority on conventional law enforcement, and this works against the shift to anti-terrorism.

2. The conventional law-enforcement approach reinforces the lack of an analytic capacity and the relatively low status granted intelligence specialists.

3. The case-by-case approach to law enforcement and prosecution impedes the broader strategic planning needed for terrorism prevention.

4. Public criticism has led to a rigid, risk-averse culture in which agents perceive that one mistake can ruin a career.

5. The agency's computer system is antiquated and not up to the task of sophisticated information processing.

FBI director Robert S. Mueller III successfully resisted efforts to transfer the bureau's intelligence function to DHS or to an independent domestic agency, perhaps modeled along the lines of the United Kingdom's MI-5. As part of the shift in priorities, Director Mueller transferred 2,500 of the Bureau's approximately 11,500 agents to antiterrorism duties and began the process of hiring eight hundred additional analysts, including twenty-five to be transferred from the CIA. By mid-May 2002, the bureau claimed that it had formally shifted its priorities from conventional law enforcement to fighting terrorism. But some members of Congress and independent observers remain skeptical that the bureau can make the radical transition from traditional law enforcement to the intelligence-intensive orientation of terrorism prevention. Also, the shift has drawn resources away from the bureau's law-enforcement responsibilities in other areas, for example, drug trafficking, armed robbery, and white-collar crime (GAO 2003).

The CIA also came under close scrutiny after September 11 because of its failure to prevent the attacks. Even so, President Bush gave the agency a lead role in the U.S. antiterrorist response against al Qaeda and the Taliban in Afghanistan. The agency's paramilitary forces could respond quickly to the unconventional challenge there. As described by Woodward (2002), the operations in Afghanistan inspired new mixes of intelligence units with U.S. military special forces and local militias. In the months before the U.S. attack on Iraq in March 2003, senior administration officials gave intelligence reports as a main justification for their charges that Iraq possessed weapons of mass destruction. As of December 2004, however, such weapons had not been discovered. The shortcomings in intelligence gathering or administration mis-use of intelligence put the agency in a difficult position and contributed to the resignation of director George Tenet in June 2004.

Intelligence is the key capability in antiterrorism responses by the federal government. The various agencies are under considerable pressure to acquire skills and capabilities in languages and cultures that are challenging (e.g., Arabic, Pashto, Urdu, Chinese, etc.) and to gather and make usable information from a variety of sources. It appears from press accounts that interagency coordination has improved somewhat, although turf disputes continue to appear from time to time. One development that appears significant is the merger of FBI and CIA antiterrorism specialists in the Terrorist Threat Integration Center in May 2003.[14] This was granted stronger bureaucratic status and renamed the National Counterterrorism Center in August 2004.

Military involvement in domestic law enforcement, a common occurrence in many Latin American countries, is governed in the United States by the Posse Comitatus Act of 1878. The act does not prohibit such involvement, as is often wrongly asserted. Rather, it specifies that the army and air force (and, by extension, the other armed forces) can assist in law enforcement only on the direct order of the president. In fact, the army has assisted in law enforcement on many occasions over the years, for example, in helping repress riots in Los Angeles in 1991. But the regular armed forces generally seek to avoid involvement in domestic affairs. More usual is the involvement of the National Guard in law enforcement or disaster relief. The 450,000-member National Guard is a complex military reserve system organized at the state level and—in normal times—commanded by the state governors. In declared emergencies, the guard can be placed under presidential command.

In the Department of Defense, the shift toward an antiterrorism emphasis coincided with Secretary Donald Rumsfeld's efforts to transform the deeply entrenched Cold War mindset and operational habits of the armed forces. The U.S. Army, for example, continued to organize itself and develop weapons systems suited for large-scale conventional warfare envisioned against the Soviet Union. Rumsfeld used the terrorism emergency to push for more mobile, flexible, and cooperative arrangements among the armed forces themselves and with intelligence operations, as was demonstrated in the operations in Afghanistan against the Taliban and al Qaeda. He also used the emergency to strengthen the department's independent intelligence capacity, by creating an undersecretary for intelligence.

One interesting organizational innovation is the creation of the Northern

Command, whose geographic scope includes the mainland United States (extending five hundred miles into the Atlantic and Pacific oceans), Canada, Mexico, and some parts of the Caribbean. The Northern Command is one of nine unified commands, which integrate the various armed forces under a single commander to either protect a geographic region (e.g., European Command, Southern Command) or carry out a particular function (e.g., Special Operations or Joint Forces). The former specializes in nonconventional warfare in any geographic region, and the latter focuses on training and devising new techniques and methods of warfare. The main task of the Northern Command is to coordinate military operations (e.g., combat air patrols) in North America and to support first responders (e.g., firefighters, police, medical personnel, etc.) from all levels of government in case of emergencies in U.S. territory. The latter task brings the military into closer cooperation with law enforcement, an area little explored outside relatively limited experience in antidrug operations.

The U.S. military is a principal actor in the intelligence field as well. Each of the services maintains its own intelligence agency, and the Defense Intelligence Agency coordinates the services' activities and interacts with the CIA and DHS. Recognizing the importance of intelligence in the new challenges of terrorism prevention, Secretary Donald Rumsfeld created a high-level unit in the Defense Department to coordinate intelligence activities.

The government's antiterrorism strategy relies heavily on private-sector cooperation, especially in intelligence gathering. In the financial sector, for example, banks, securities firms, and other enterprises have long been required to report suspicious transactions as well as any cash transaction exceeding ten thousand dollars. The Patriot Act pushes the cooperation much further. It encourages financial institutions to share information among themselves about customers suspected of laundering money and grants them protection from legal liability for doing so. As the *Washington Post* reported, "In addition, it gives law enforcement and intelligence agencies greater access to confidential information without a subpoena while also requiring that credit bureaus secretly turn over credit reports to the CIA, National Security Agency and other intelligence agencies when presented with a request signed by a senior agency official." The suspicious-activity reports filed by financial institutions contain a variety of information, including telephone and Social Security numbers. The number of these reports increased substantially following 9/11, up nearly 50 percent (to 125,000) in the period October 1 to March 31, 2002, over the same period in the preceding year.[15] Presumably, these types of information will be coordinated with data banks that include other types of data (e.g., visa applications, entry/exit records, health, housing, and education records, motor vehicle applications, etc.) to identify and track suspicious persons and activities.

The homeland security emergency has generated a whole host of changes that are being adopted in a piecemeal, ad hoc fashion by existing or newly created agencies at the federal, state, and local levels. Though most state and local jurisdictions have followed the federal lead, a number have resisted. "To date, at least 142 communities and three states, encompassing more than 16 million people, have passed pro-civil-liberties resolutions that speak out against the Patriot Act, many of which call for specific fixes to the bill" (see http://baltimorechronicle.com/jul03_aclupatriots.shtml). Beyond the public sector, complex adjustments are rippling through the economy and civil society.

Civil-Society Perceptions and Responses

Public opinion is important because it is monitored by government and civil-society actors and it creates a context that influences their choices. Five trends are noteworthy: (1) terrorism ranks at the top of public concerns in terms of salience of the issue, (2) the public believes the terrorist threat within the United States will last for some time into the future, (3) there is general support for the government's response to the threat, (4) there is strong specific support for the armed forces and police, and (5) there is a strong tilt toward the Republican Party as better able to deal with the issue than the Democrats.

Gallup uses an item periodically to test for issue salience: "How important is it to you that the president and Congress deal with each of the following issues in the next year?" It lists fourteen issues and gives four response options, from "extremely important" to "not that important." For terrorism, the combined responses extremely/very important have declined only slightly, from 95 percent in October 2001 to 90 percent in January 2003, when the issue dropped just behind the economy, with 91 percent. But the salience of terrorism, that is, the proportion who considered the issue to be extremely important, remained at the top, a full ten points above the economy in January 2003 (59/49 percent; http://www.gallup.com/poll/content/login.aspx?ci= 7531).

Furthermore, terrorism is seen to be an enduring challenge. When asked, "How likely is it that there will be further acts of terrorism in the United

States over the next several weeks?" the "very likely" or "somewhat likely" response shows an erratic but generally declining trend: 83–85 percent in October 2001 to 40 percent in July 2003. A poll taken in September 2002 showed 86–88 percent giving a positive response when asked, "Just your best guess, do you think there are terrorists associated with Osama bin Laden who are currently in the United States and are capable of launching a major terrorist attack against the U.S., or not?" A third of those who gave the positive response estimated the attack would happen in less than a year; another quarter estimated less than two years (http://www.gallup.com/poll/content/login.aspx?ci=7531).

A strong majority of the public responds positively to the question: "How much confidence do you have in the U.S. government to protect its citizens from future terrorist attacks?", with the rates for the combined responses of "great deal" and "fair amount" ranging from 88 percent in September 2001 to 82 percent in February 2003 (http://www.gallup.com/poll/content/login.aspx?ci=7531).

In contrast to patterns throughout most of Latin America (Colombia and Chile are exceptions), in the United States the public in 2003 expressed greatest confidence in the military (82 percent "great deal/quite a lot") and the police (61 percent), ranking them at the top of the fifteen institutions listed. Compared with a decade earlier (March 1993), confidence in both institutions had risen fairly consistently, up from 68 percent for the military and 52 percent for the police (http://www.gallup.com/poll/content/login.aspx?ci=8668).

Finally, in partisan terms, the public leans toward the Republican party with respect to security issues. "When asked which party in Congress would do a better job of dealing with each of the issues, the public clearly favored the Republicans over Democrats in three areas, all dealing with international concerns: terrorism (55% to 27%), the situation in Iraq (53% to 29%), and foreign affairs in general (51% to 34%)" (http://www.gallup.com/poll/content/login.aspx?ci=7531). The Republicans held a roughly thirty-point advantage over the Democrats on the terrorism issue from May 2002 to January 2003 (ibid.).

Obviously, polls are volatile and event driven. One would expect sharp public reactions to a significant terrorist event within the United States or to a foreign-policy emergency. Also, one would expect perceptions of U.S. success in its occupation of Iraq to influence opinion about terrorism more generally. Even so, four inferences might be drawn from this brief review: (1)

there is strong public concern about terrorism, and the threat is expected to endure for some time; (2) there is substantial support for the government's response to the challenge; (3) there is strong confidence in the armed forces and police; and (4) the Republicans tend to benefit politically from the public's concern about security. While these trends would seem to provide support for the government's antiterrorism initiatives, we should recall that the public also places strong emphasis on protection of civil liberties.

Effects of Security Policies

Unlike with crime, in which rising or falling rates are the measure of success or failure, the difficulty with antiterrorism efforts is that the standard of success is fully 100 percent. While government may use the language of risk management, which suggests less than perfection, the public standard is that any significant terrorist act on U.S. territory or against U.S. assets throughout the world is unacceptable. A further problem is that much of the government's strategy and many of its actions and results must be kept secret. Therefore, claims and counterclaims can be brought, but the public has little basis on which to gauge them. Regarding program development, a most important criticism is that the new Department of Homeland Security's component agencies have failed to define standards and indicators by which to evaluate performance.[16]

One of the more interesting effects of antiterrorism initiatives is to strengthen law enforcement against common crime. U.S. Customs and Border Protection (CBP) claimed that its new Integrated Automated Fingerprint Identification System proved to be a valuable tool. "From October 1, 2003 through August 31, 2004, CBP agents have arrested: 138 homicide suspects; 67 kidnapping suspects; 226 sexual assault suspects; 431 robbery suspects; 2,342 suspects for assaults of other types; and 4,801 involved with dangerous narcotics as a direct result of (the new) technology" (CBP 2004).

The combination of continued fear of terrorist attacks, strong legitimacy of police and military, and support for government antiterrorism measures, alongside long-standing support for civil liberties, creates a struggle between those who would expand the new antiterrorism powers and those who seek to restrain or even reduce them. On the one side, the administration, particularly the Justice Department, is expanding its use of Patriot Act powers to investigate nonterrorist crimes, such as white-collar fraud and drug trafficking.

On the other side, congressional opponents of the broad new powers are working to improve oversight and to shorten the period of their applicability. A (still-small) number of cities have registered opposition to Patriot Act provisions, and their efforts are supported by civil-rights advocates such as the American Civil Liberties Union.

While these opposing forces compete inconclusively, the distance traveled from the initial shock of September 11 continues to grow. With time, public opinion can gain perspective on the nature of the terrorist threat and the likely success of public and civil-society measures that are possible to counter it. Presumably, the implementation of concrete measures will focus public debate on ways to achieve a new equilibrium between security preparedness and protection of civil liberties. This new balance will be achieved through democratic political processes, as courts rule on specific cases and candidates test their positions in electoral contests at various levels of government.

September 11 was clearly a watershed between law and order and homeland security. The massive trauma produced a dramatic reaction, setting in motion significant changes in U.S. doctrines, laws, and institutions related to security. The main theme in the changes is the removal of the long-standing difference between the external and the internal spheres in security concerns. Military and intelligence instruments were largely shaped to operate in external matters, while law enforcement was sufficient for internal order. The homeland security focus is remixing security instruments and measures that will be applied to both domestic and foreign spheres. The outcome of that process is indeterminate.

The simplistic hypothesis suggested here is that over time a new equilibrium between security preparedness and protection of civil liberties will emerge. The longer the gap between September 11, 2001, and the next (inevitable?) attack, the more opportunity for government and civil society to craft a workable and acceptable balance between the imperatives of civil liberties and societal security. This suggests, however, that the process is quite fragile. Another significant terrorist attack will immediately tilt the balance back toward security.

In the broader perspective, the period 2001–2004 can be compared to 1946–1948 with respect to strategic security policy. In the immediate post–World War II period, U.S. foreign policy had a variety of possible roads to travel, from multilateral cooperation to isolationism. Events and decisions drove the policy down the road of alliance building and a half-century of anti-

Soviet Cold War. The Cold War's end in 1989 opened a twelve-year interlude of adjustment and inertia in foreign policy, which ended abruptly in the September 11 attacks. Again, as in 1946–1948, there is no grand design or strategy for long-term policy. Rather, we are living through a series of specific reactions and decisions, which—over time—will add up to such a strategy. At some point in the future, some label will be invented and accepted to suggest overarching purpose and logic to the policy that ultimately resulted from many specific reactions and initiatives.

Police-Community Conflict and Crime Prevention in Cincinnati, Ohio

John E. Eck and Jay Rothman

In Cincinnati City Hall on April 12, 2002, a historic agreement was signed in the presence of the attorney general of the United States. The signatories were the mayor of Cincinnati, the president of the local police union, the head of the Ohio chapter of the American Civil Liberties Union, and the president of the Cincinnati Black United Front. This unprecedented agreement simultaneously encapsulated the goals of the citizens of Cincinnati and the most advanced social-science research on police effectiveness. Most important, it called for a complete revision of policing strategy in Cincinnati that could simultaneously reduce crime and situations leading to police-community conflict. This was the collaborative agreement.

The collaborative agreement was the result of a year of intense negotiations that included consultation with more than 3,500 citizens of Cincinnati. Its origins were rooted in a federal lawsuit sparked by allegations of police racial profiling and misuse of force. The efforts were given further momentum by three days of rioting that followed the shooting death of an unarmed African American shortly after the lawsuit was filed. The key player in moving the suit from litigation to collaborative problem solving was Judge Susan Dlott of the U.S. District Court, Southern District of Ohio.

The collaborative agreement promises to be an important touchstone in the progress of democratic policing. The agreement is notable both for the manner in which it was forged—negotiations sponsored by strong federal court oversight—and what it proposes—a shift from a notion of police as law enforcers to the idea of police as crime preventers and problem solvers. The development of the collaborative agreement was not simple or easy. In fact, at a number of points the negotiations almost failed.[1]

A History of Police, Race, and Force

In the period 1967–2000, the Cincinnati Police Department was the subject of seventeen reports investigating racial issues.[2] These ranged from the shootings of African Americans to the hiring and promotion of African American police officers. There was not a five-year period during this third of a century in which the Cincinnati Police Department was not examined as part of a lawsuit, a city government–appointed commission, or a state-appointed authority. These investigations resulted in a total of 214 recommendations. The most frequently mentioned recommendations involved ways to improve informing the public about police actions, policies, or procedures. These were closely followed by recommendations concerning external oversight, police involvement with the community, and the promotion and assignment of African American police officers. Unfortunately, few of these recommendations were implemented (Bostaph, Eck, and Liu 2002).

Though police-community conflict had been a long-standing issue in Cincinnati, for many African American activists the recent history of police abuses began with the killing of Harvey Price on February 1, 1995. Price was the first of fourteen men killed by the police between 1995 and the filing of the federal lawsuit in April 2002. He was shot after advancing with a knife on officers during the investigation of a murder he committed. Typically, emphasis is placed on the fact that these fourteen men were all African Americans. Particular attention was drawn to the deaths of four of these, all of whom were unarmed, and two others who were lightly armed.

On April 7, 2001, just after 2:00 a.m., off-duty police officers spotted Timothy Thomas, who was wanted by the police for fourteen outstanding warrants for failure to appear in court on traffic-related infractions. They reported this to on-duty officers. Thomas fled with several officers in pursuit. One pursing officer ran down a dark alley with his gun drawn. He did not know the minor nature of Thomas's warrants, nor did he expect to suddenly confront Thomas. When he did, he fired, fatally wounding Thomas. The officer at first claimed he saw what looked like a weapon and fired in self-defense. Later he claimed it was an accident. To many in the African American community it looked like murder, and yet another example of police overuse of force against them.

Many in the African American community believed that the police investigation of these deaths was inadequate, resulting in culpable officers not being held accountable. Indeed, in 1981 one of the seventeen investigations of the police practices resulted in the creation of a new city investigative agency, the Office of Municipal Investigations (OMI), to examine allegations of serious police misconduct, including misuse of force. OMI had its own investigators and was independent of the police department. In 1999, another examination of police practices resulted in the establishment of the Citizen Police Review Panel (CPRP) to examine the adequacy of investigations of police use of force by OMI and the police. Though this panel was composed of citizens, it did not have its own investigators and only reviewed the investigations of OMI and the police department's Internal Investigations Section (IIS). This meant that by spring 2001 three completely separate units were responsible for investigating the police: IIS, OMI, and CPRP.

Further, there was the nagging concern by African Americans that the police were more likely to stop them than they were to stop European Americans. In their federal lawsuit, the plaintiffs presented testimony from African Americans of police racial profiling. A newspaper article around this time presented data showing that more than 60 percent of those stopped by the Cincinnati police were African Americans, even though African Americans compose about 40 percent of the city's population, according to the 2000 census.[3] The Cincinnati City Council, following a year of discussion, passed an ordinance about the same time as the lawsuit mandating that the police record the race of people stopped and that an independent analysis of these data be conducted for evidence of racial profiling.[4]

Many police officers and officials felt threatened following the deaths of two police officers on December 6, 1997. Their killer was an African American, who committed suicide when confronted by other police officers. Shortly after the deaths of these two officers, another tragedy befell Cincinnati. On the evening of February 2, 1998, an African American male shot a police officer four times while she was sitting in her parked police vehicle. The wounded officer, who survived, shot and killed her assailant. The assailant became the fourth African American killed since 1995, but the first armed with a gun.

By the spring of 2001, there were two opposing public explanations for the high number of African Americans stopped by the police and the police record of use of force against African Americans. Many in the community believed it was a callous attitude by the police toward African Americans that allowed rogue cops to act as they saw fit and ignore repeated complaints from the African American community. If only the police department would hold officers more accountable and make meaningful efforts to engage community members in a dialogue over how policing should be conducted, then these problems would decline.

Many in the police community, on the other hand, pointed to the high victimization and arrest rates among African Americans to bolster their perspective that the underlying cause of the stops and uses of force had to do with high crime rates in the African American community. Indeed, if the police did not aggressively enforce even minor laws, crime would be higher, particularly in poor African American neighborhoods where crime was concentrated. From this perspective, good police work gave the appearance of discrimination only because antipolice community activists worked to produce tension. If the police were left alone to do their difficult job, crime rates would be brought down further and the necessity for aggressive law enforcement would abate.

A third perspective, receiving no press attention, held that the problem lay with the implicit strategy of the Cincinnati Police Department. The strategy was loosely based on a zero-tolerance policing model calling for strict enforcement of minor as well as major infractions on the principle that this simultaneously deters offenders, removes offenders who cannot be deterred, and encourages good citizens to take back the streets (Harcourt 2001).

Aggressive enforcement does not appear to be an explicit policy—publicly available strategic plans make no mention of it, for example—but a strategy based on a shared understanding of crime and policing. In fact, some members of the police department advocated a COMPSTAT style of policing and even created a crime-analysis approach for targeting enforcement.[5] However, the system was never used because district commanders resisted this intrusion into their autonomy. Rather than explicitly focus police efforts on trouble spots, police commanders, with at least the tacit support of some senior officials, appear to have encouraged a general aggressive stance toward deviancy in high-crime neighborhoods.

Another component of this third perspective was the inexperience of patrol officers. Efforts to expand the size of the police department coincided with many police officials reaching retirement age. This meant that many police officers on the streets in high-crime areas during high-crime times were the least experienced, as these were the areas and times that more senior officers chose to avoid.

Finally, the deaths of two police officers and the wounding of a third reinforced the idea that policing is highly dangerous and that officers need to act decisively and quickly to assure their own safety.

So from this third perspective, young and inexperienced patrol officers were encouraged to follow an aggressive law-enforcement strategy but were not given any focus to their efforts. This was reinforced by the idea that officers needed to be aggressive to be safe, particularly in neighborhoods with the most crime. And these neighborhoods were largely populated by African Americans. These factors, coupled with the fact that residents of these neighborhoods had a strong preexisting suspicion of police, made conflicts virtually inevitable.

The solution, from this third perspective, was to find a safer and more effective policing strategy for reducing crime and disorder and to find ways to build trust between the police and the community. In contrast to the perspective of many in the police community, the police could no longer be left to decide things on their own. In contrast to the perspective of many in the African American community, it would not be sufficient to hold officers accountable and build trust. Though accountability and trust needed to be addressed, unless the police department applied an effective crime-reduction strategy, police-citizen conflicts would still emerge and serious crime would go unaddressed. It was this third perspective that guided much of the research that led to the agreement.

The Collaborative Agreement

On March 15, 2001, the Ohio chapter of the American Civil Liberties Union joined forces with the Cincinnati Black United Front on behalf of Bomani Tyehimba, an African American businessman who claimed that two police officers had violated his civil rights by handcuffing him and unjustifiably pointing a gun at his head during a traffic stop two years earlier. Together they filed a class-action suit in District Court for the Southwestern District of Ohio alleging that the police department had treated African American citizens differently than other racial groups for more than thirty years. As evidence, they cited the seventeen investigative commissions, ad hoc committees, and other suits dealing with allegations of discrimination by the Cincinnati Police Department. In short, the plaintiffs claimed that recent deaths of African Americans at the hands of the police and the disproportionate police stopping rate for African Americans were not an aberration, but part of a pattern and practice of discrimination by the Cincinnati Police Department.

The federal judge assigned to the case, Susan Dlott, did not believe that traditional litigation was the answer to the problems of alleged racial profiling.[6] In her view, court action would only further polarize the parties and would not solve the social issues underlying the police-community conflict. Indeed, the plaintiffs preferred a negotiated settlement as well. The attorneys involved had successfully litigated discrimination suits against the police in the past, only to find that the reforms they were advocating were blocked. Further, attorneys for the city also felt that negotiations would be preferable to protracted legal proceedings, risking large monetary losses and increasing loss of public support.

Through Judge Dlott's efforts, all parties eventually agreed to set aside normal litigation efforts and instead pursue an alternative path of collaborative problem solving and negotiation on the wider issue of police-community relations. In addition, the city and the plaintiffs agreed to invite the local chapter of the Fraternal Order of Police, the local police union, to participate in the negotiations.

Collaborative processes have grown in popularity and application in recent years. They are being increasingly applied to complex social issues in which "getting all the stakeholders together to explore their concerns in a constructive way allows them to search for a solution they can all accept and averts the potential for escalation of the conflict" (Gray 1991, 5). However, applying collaborative procedures to such a large-scale dilemma—the nature and future of police-community relations in the context of mutual mistrust and animosity—was unprecedented.

In April 2001, the parties to the suit retained Jay Rothman as special adviser to the court to help mediate and guide the parties along this new path. Rothman was invited to guide this process because of his reputation and experience in resolving "identity-based conflict" in both international and domestic settings (Rothman 1997, 1999). His expertise overlapped well with the judge's view that the social conflicts at the root of the controversies over perceived or actual racial profiling needed a broader and deeper process than could be afforded by a win-lose court battle. Rothman began holding regular meetings with leaders from the three sides—the police union, city and police administration, and the plaintiffs to the suit. He first proposed a problem-definition process, suggesting to the parties that without a common definition of the problem, they would have difficulties finding a common solution. However, the police leadership strongly resisted this approach. They argued that focusing on problems would only result in finger pointing—at them! Moreover, the police and city attorneys were unwilling to engage in an effort to define a problem—racial profiling—that they simply did not agree existed.

In response to these concerns, Rothman suggested that the parties under-take a broad-based visioning process focused on improving police-community relations. The city and police department accepted this proposal because it seemed to be a constructive process in which representatives from all parties could work collaboratively. The leaders of the Black United Front found this approach appealing largely because it was to be conducted within a framework that promised some form of judicial oversight during the process and after its conclusion. Such a process, it was hoped, would foster collaborative relationships. Such relations are defined as those that "evolve toward commitment to common mission, comprehensive communication and planning, pooled resources, and shared risks and products. Authority is vested in the collaborative, rather than in individuals or an individual agency" (Taylor-Powell, Rossing, and Geran 1998, 5).

This set of ambitious goals led to a year-long process of unprecedented proportions in which thousands of Cincinnatians, dozens of lawyers, and a research team, all under federal court oversight, conducted an inclusive and ultimately successful large-scale collaborative effort.

The process consisted of five interlocking elements. As shown in Figure 13.1, the first element was establishing an authoritative framework that established legitimacy. Second was a process for gaining widespread participation and acceptance from the public and media in the form of a visioning or goal-setting process for the future of police-community relations. A third and parallel process was launching systematic research on best practices. The goals and best practices were then combined into a single text to guide negotiations toward an agreement. As figure 13.1 illustrates, the agreement is actually just the beginning, as it requires implementation that should lead to outcomes that address the goals and underlying conditions that created the original conflict. Implementation and outcomes are in the future as of this writing.

Stakeholders' Goals

A few weeks after the initial discussions about a collaborative process, Thomas was shot and Cincinnati was engulfed in riots. Despite this, the Cincinnati Black United Front, The American Civil Liberties Union, the city and police administrations, and the Cincinnati Fraternal Order of Police continued to meet as the advisory group to Rothman. The formal establishment of the collaborative was catalyzed when a New York–based foundation, the Andrus Family Fund, challenged the city to commit to the court-sponsored explo-

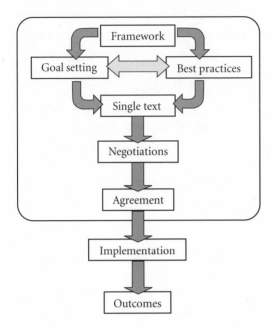

FIGURE 13.1 Process used to reach an agreement

ration of this alternative dispute-resolution process, by matching the fund's proffered grant of one hundred thousand dollars and signing on as a formal sponsor and member of the collaborative. At a rancorous city council meeting on May 2, 2001, the collaborative, and the city's financial and moral contribution to it, was narrowly approved by a five-to-four vote, with several amendments regarding transparency of the process.

Judge Dlott stated the purpose of the collaborative in her subsequent court order:

> The proposed amended complaint alleges social conflict of great public interest to the community. To the extent possible, the collaborative will include an opportunity to receive the viewpoints of all persons in the Cincinnati community regarding their goals for police-community relations. The participants will state their goals for police-community relations, why these goals are important, and how they would achieve these goals. . . . The collaborative will include an opportunity for dialogue about these responses in structured group sessions. . . . The collaborative will also include a process for expert analysis of the current practices of the Cincinnati Police Division and [best] practices in other communities. (Dlott 2001a)

Now formally launched and officially legitimized, though with strong and significant opposition, the next task for the collaborative was to gain legitimacy through wide-scale public participation. As its first act, the advisory group determined to invite participation from all citizens of the city in the goal setting/visioning process. Based on previous studies of tensions in police-community relations, the advisory group organized the population into eight stake-holding groups (African American citizens, city employees, police and their families, white citizens, business/foundation/education leaders, religious and social-service leaders, youth, and other minorities). It then invited, with considerable help from the news media, everyone who lived or worked in the city, or was closely associated with the city (e.g., those in the suburbs), to answer a questionnaire and participate in feedback groups. Thirty-five hundred people responded and some seven hundred of those respondents engaged in nearly three thousand hours of follow-up dialogue and agenda setting.

The views of these participants were summarized in a series of goals. In addition to establishing principles, the stakeholders also articulated thousands of specific implementation ideas. Five summary goals were established:

1. Police officers and community members will become proactive partners in community problem solving.

2. Build relationships of respect, cooperation, and trust within and between police and communities.

3. Improve education, oversight, monitoring, hiring practices, and accountability of Cincinnati Police Division.

4. Ensure fair, equitable, and courteous treatment for all.

5. Create methods to establish the public's understanding of police policies and procedures and recognition of exceptional service in an effort to foster support for the police. (Dlott 2002)

The media played a constructive role in this outreach. Perhaps as part of an effort to restore the city's reputation following the unrest, the collaborative was portrayed in print, radio, and television in very positive terms.[7] For example, nearly a dozen supportive editorials appeared in local and regional papers. Stories inviting participation appeared regularly in the media from the launch of the collaborative to its conclusion.

Best Practices

The second decision made by this advisory group was to hire John Eck to serve as policing expert. Eck's job was to research the most relevant best police practices and model programs to provide recommendations to the negotiating parties (Dlott 2001b). To do this, Eck drew on the social-science research on police effectiveness conducted over the past quarter of a century. A consistent body of research demonstrates that traditional police practices have little or no impact on reducing crime. Another body of research points to an alternative set of police strategies that can prevent crime. Unfortunately, these findings are largely unknown to the public and nonpolice policy makers. Further, when asked, the public is likely to demand the old ineffective strategies rather than the newer effective ones. This posed a serious risk that a police-public partnership would be created but would be unable to deliver the basic services the public wanted. As police are often skeptical of public demands for community policing on the grounds that it does little to reduce crime, it was important that police effectiveness be directly addressed within the collaborative agreement.

Throughout the summer and fall of 2001, Eck and three graduate students examined the existing strategy of the Cincinnati Police Department, through interviews and document review, and collected information on research and practices in other police agencies. They also met with other community groups working on related issues. This research was facilitated by Eck's work with the Cincinnati Police Department prior to joining the collaborative process, and by his experience in conducting research on police effectiveness since 1977.

Policing Strategies That Do Not Work

The standard model for policing applies four generic approaches to addressing crime. The first is random patrol. The theory is that if police provide a visible presence, this will deter offenders and assure the public. This idea was tested in the late 1970s in Kansas City, Missouri, by varying the level of patrolling in different beats. Whether measured by crimes reported to the police or by surveys of citizens, the study found no differences in crime or citizen fear of crime or in public satisfaction with the police (Kelling et al. 1974). In addition, the evidence supporting the idea that the addition of police officers will reduce crime is far from settled. Several studies suggest that small-to-modest increases in police strength have no impact, though a few recent studies suggest otherwise (Sherman and Eck 2002; National Research Council 2004).

The second generic approach to addressing crime is rapid response to calls about crimes. This is supposed to reduce crime by apprehending offenders and deterring people considering crime. Again, the evidence contradicts this idea. Most crimes are reported long after they occur because, as in the case of burglaries, offenders strike when no one is around. Except for the relatively few violent crimes, the odds are against an arrest because of delays in citizen reporting to the police. Rapid response makes a difference only in a very small proportion of the crimes (Spelman and Brown 1981).

Investigation is the third generic approach to crime control. The low arrest productivity of detectives has been noted for more than thirty years. Most property crimes have so little evidence that it is impossible to catch the offender, thus precluding any crime reduction through deterrence or imprisonment. The solution rate for violent street crimes is higher, but only because there is more likely to be a witness. Even in the best cases, the solution rates are insufficient for investigations to have an impact on crime rates (Sherman and Eck 2002).

In recent years, a fourth generic approach has been promoted: zero-tolerance policing. The idea here is that by continuously cracking down on minor violations, offenders will not engage in more serious offenses. There is little scientific evidence backing this proposition (National Research Council 2004).[8] There is also concern that zero-tolerance policing may unnecessarily widen the scope of criminal-justice sanctioning, reduce police legitimacy, and thus undermine public support for police and erode police effectiveness (Harcourt 2001, National Research Council 2004).

Policing Strategies That Do Work

A highly effective strategy is focusing on hot spots—very small areas with exceptionally high levels of crime or disorder. Hot-spots patrols have been found to have large impacts on disorder and modest but important impacts on serious crime (Braga 2001). It is important to note that hot-spots patrolling does not require large numbers of arrests to be effective. In short, encouraging proactive enforcement in hot spots, though effective, is not a requirement.

Considerable evidence from Great Britain suggests that focusing on "hot victims" is also effective. Though most people who have been a victim of crime in a given year are victims only once, a few are victimized multiple times. When the police concentrate on helping these repeat victims, substantial crime reduction can be achieved (Farrell and Sousa 2001).

Community policing that increases direct contacts between police and citizens appears to reduce the public's fear of crime, but it probably does not have much effect on crime itself. However, much community policing is implemented along with problem-oriented policing, which is effective (Sherman and Eck 2002).

Problem-oriented policing focuses police attention on various crime patterns, including, but not limited to, hot spots and repeat victims. Officers and community members identify problems, conduct careful and detailed analysis of the local immediate causes, undertake a broad search for a solution tailored to the details of the problem, and then evaluate whether the solution was effective. Problem-oriented policing has been used effectively to reduce youth homicides (Braga et al. 2001), violent and property crime (Eck and Spelman 1987), fear of crime (Cordner 1988), and various forms of disorder, including prostitution and drug dealing (Capowich and Roehl 1994; Eck and Spelman 1987; Hope 1994). Randomized experiments of problem-oriented policing and problem-solving strategies consistently show large crime-reduction effects (Braga et al. 1999; Mazerolle, Roehl, and Kadleck 1998; Eck 1998; National Research Council 2004).

Problem-oriented policing had several advantages for Cincinnati. First, there was consistent research evidence (Sherman and Eck 2002) that if it were implemented well, it could prevent crime. Second, it is highly compatible with community policing, hot-spots tactics, and repeat-victimization approaches. In fact, many police agencies in the United States and Great Britain had combined these approaches. Third, a problem-oriented approach (as well as community policing and repeat victimization) places far less emphasis on enforcement as the means for reducing crime (Goldstein 1990). Rather it attempts to reduce opportunities for committing crime (Clarke 1997). This reduces aggressive law enforcement and thus could reduce negative police-citizen encounters and the chances of injuries to officers and citizens. Finally, a problem-oriented approach as well as community policing can bring police and community members together to solve meaningful crime problems. In short, adopting a problem-oriented approach would address many of the major issues identified by critics of the force's zero-tolerance strategy.

HANDLING INVESTIGATIONS OF ALLEGATIONS OF POLICE MISUSE OF FORCE

Though there was considerable scientific evidence on which to build a new crime-reduction policing strategy for Cincinnati, there was virtually no scientific evidence on which to design a new way of handling citizen complaints of police misuse of force. The American Civil Liberties Union and the Black United Front saw this as a major issue, and citizens in the stakeholder meetings consistently raised it. While there was no research pointing to a form of investigation that would reduce such complaints, anecdotal information suggested that citizen review boards, outside of police agencies, sometimes improved citizen confidence in the investigation processes.

Three different processes were supposed to investigate police misuse of force allegations. The IIS investigated excessive use of force and serious criminal or sexual misconduct allegations against police officers, as well as incidents in which officers used their guns. For lesser complaints, the police department applied its Citizen Complaint Resolution Process. This process required complaints to be handled by police district commanders. Outside the police department, but reporting to the city manager, OMI conducted investigations parallel to IIS. CPRP was charged with reviewing the adequacy of IIS and OMI investigations, but unlike OMI it had no investigators, only a volunteer board. It was clear from press accounts, interviews, and meetings attended by Eck and his students that this amalgam of processes virtually guaranteed long delays in coming to resolutions and the production of contradictory results that undermined any legitimacy the external reviews were designed to enhance.

For sound reasons, the police chief argued that the police department could not give up its ability to investigate its own officers. At the same time it was also clear that an outside investigation process was required. Therefore, Eck recommended that a new agency be created that combined the roles of OMI and CPRP. This Citizen Complaint Authority would have an independent director, an appointed board, and its own investigative staff.

POLICE POLICIES AND PRACTICES

Shortly after the riots, the mayor invited the U.S. Department of Justice's Civil Rights Division to examine the police department's use-of-force policies, training, and practices. The Justice Department conducted this review over the summer of 2001 and into the fall. As this review progressed, the city became anxious that it would be subjected to a court-imposed settlement as a result. So the city hired an outside law firm to negotiate with the Justice Department. It was hoped that the results of the investigation and negotiations could be combined with the collaborative agreement. Consequently, the collaborative process did not undertake a separate examination of police use-of-force issues. However, it was not clear until the last weeks of the negotiations whether combining the Justice Department's requirements with the collaborative agreement would be possible.

As part of the best-practices development process, Eck and his students attended meetings of other groups working on related matters. These included regular meetings sponsored by the local chapter of the National Council for Community and Justice, as well as meetings of Cincinnati Community Action Now (CCAN). CCAN had been established following the riot to look at a broad array of issues related to economic and social justice within the city. The law and justice subcommittee focused on practices within the police, prosecution, and court systems. Police officials and a diverse array of community members participated in both groups. These discussions informed the best-practices recommendations on handling investigations of allegations of police misconduct and on ways recruitment and promotion polices could be altered. Interestingly, the police and many community members agreed that changes needed to be made in the way the police recruited, but the police felt stymied by the city's civil-service board. With the encouragement of CCAN and the National Council for Community and Justice, ideas from these discussions were included in the recommendations.

The repeated failures of prior attempts to address police-race issues suggested that there needed to be a mechanism for evaluating the effect of any agreement on police-community relations, officer morale, use of force, and other issues. Eck's team examined evaluation mechanisms used in other cities and devised a set of annual data collection processes involving official police data and surveys of the public, police officials, and people who had contact with the police. The objective was to show whether the city was making progress, independent of the degree of implementation of the agreement.

The best-practices report to Rothman outlined recommendations for six areas: problem solving, community engagement (both aspects of problem-oriented policing), use of force (from the U.S. Department of Justice), promotion and hiring, citizen review, and evaluation. These were then checked against the stakeholder goals to ensure that each goal was addressed by at least one set of recommendations. As can be seen in table 13.1, each goal was addressed by at least three recommendations.

13.1 Combining stakeholder goals with best practices

	Best practices recommendations					
Stakeholder goals	Problem solving	Community engagement	Use of force	Hiring and promotion	Citizen review	Evaluation
Partners in problem solving	X	X	X			
Relationships of respect and cooperation	X	X	X		X	X
Oversight and accountability	X	X	X	X	X	X
Fair treatment for all	X	X	X	X	X	X
Public under-standing	X	X	X			X

Negotiating an Agreement

Within complex, multiparty negotiations, mediators often use a single-text process. This process is most helpful when the settlement issues to be resolved are varied, complex, and highly charged and it is anticipated that there will be a great deal of negotiation over precise settlement terms and language.

Usually, a single-text process begins with the mediator's private consultation with each of the disputing parties concerning possible settlement terms and acceptable structure and language for an agreement. In these conversations, the mediator attempts to understand and gather in oral or written form each party's specific objectives, concerns, and restraints regarding possible terms of settlement. With this information, the mediator produces a single text of possible settlement terms, drafted from a third-party perspective.

In the Cincinnati process, the single-text drafting process was guided by the five summary goals articulated in Judge Dlott's order (2002). These principles represented a formula established by these stakeholders, which was to be followed by the details the parties to the proposed lawsuit would seek to reach agreement on.[9]

The mediator's drafts were based on

1. a formula established by the parties to the lawsuit, based on intergroup goals;

2. parties' confidential proposals shared with the mediator;

3. Eck's research on details of agreement;

4. input from other community groups in the city.

These drafts did not constitute the mediator's recommendation or opinion of what fair or correct settlement terms might be. That was left up to the parties to decide. Rather, the drafts reflected the mediator's analysis, based largely on the formula constituted of the stakeholders' goals and the research team, of what terms and implementation details might be acceptable to all parties.

While drafting the single text, the mediator shared drafts with all parties for comment, criticism, and revision. Each party communicated privately and confidentially with the mediator regarding which terms were acceptable and which were not and suggested alternatives for terms that were not acceptable. The mediator then revised the single text. Face-to-face meetings between parties were launched by early February 2002, approximately two months after the single-text negotiation process was initiated. The process continued until a collaborative settlement agreement emerged that was acceptable to all parties.

This process allowed the mediator to

- act as a buffer when tensions escalated
- keep the parties focused on finding ways to effectively implement their agreed-upon formula through specific agreements about who will do what, when and how
- supply a neutral memory on the spirit and basic structure of the settlement when the parties' recollections diverge
- suggest new language where the parties agree on concepts but not on their articulation,
- facilitate agreement on any new issues that arose
- keep track of and confine the package of unresolved issues

This single-text process formed the basis of settlement negotiations. All of the recommendations were closely examined, resulting in multiple revisions.[10] At any time during this process any one of the parties, the judge, or the mediator himself could have called the process off, and indeed, this almost occurred, as several serious disagreements had to be resolved. Nevertheless, the process ultimately succeeded in producing a collaborative settlement agreement between the parties on April 5, 2002, almost exactly a year after the riots.

The final agreement was based on the stakeholder goals and the best-practices recommendations. The goals were explicitly stated in the final court order, and the recommendations were codified in the five operating conditions:

- Implementation of Community Problem-Oriented Policing

- External evaluation of the implementation of the agreement

- Incorporation of the use-of-force agreement between the city and the U.S. Department of Justice

- Parties' collaboration to ensure fair, equitable, and courteous treatment for all citizens

- City establishment of a citizen-complaint authority (Dlott 2002)

In addition, the final agreement's sixth section describes a detailed process for monitoring compliance with the agreement and for settling disputes among the parties should conflicts arise over compliance. Ultimately, the federal courts have jurisdiction. The parties have various responsibilities to carry out provisions within the agreement, with the largest burden being shouldered by the city and its police department. The parties also select an independent monitor who reports on implementation compliance, thus assuring all sides of an impartial overseer. If disputes cannot be resolved at these stages, a federal magistrate judge acts as the conciliator to resolve the conflict. Finally, if this fails, Judge Dlott can examine the dispute and force a resolution. This process covers both the collaborative agreement and the Department of Justice agreement. Consequently, the Department of Justice has a role in selecting the monitor and examining compliance.

Police, Race, and Crime

The agreement reached on April 12, 2002, allowed the parties involved in the lawsuit, and the citizens of Cincinnati, to step back from the crisis and begin working in a common direction. The city set aside $5 million for implementation of the agreement, and the plaintiffs to the lawsuit are raising another $8 million in private money to fund a community-based problem-solving partnership. But there were delays in selecting the monitor and in funding the evaluation. The independent monitor was selected in December 2002 and issued his first report on the implementation of the agreement three months later.[11] As of late 2004 the agreement is being implemented, though the various parties differ in their assessment as to how much progress is being made. It is clear from various public statements of high-ranking police and city officials that they believe the agreement has been largely, if not fully, implemented. The attorneys who brought the suit see only grudging progress. They often urge the independent monitor to make stronger statements in his reports.[12]

A notable sign of progress has been the creation of the Community Policing Partnering Center. The center is a community-based organization with its own field staff, funded by corporate and other private donations. It is the brainchild of the plaintiffs' attorneys, who saw it as a bridge between the police and the community, a mechanism for educating and involving the public, and a method for ensuring an independent voice in crime problem solving. The center's executive director is a recently retired assistant police chief.

After a year of negotiations and more than two years of implementation, there are no overt public objections to the agreement's content, though the parties still have difficulty working together to implement it. Disagreements between the city and the plaintiffs typically center around what precise action is called for in the agreement. As one might expect, the police and city favor a rather narrow interpretation, whereas the plaintiffs take a broader view. Some of the objections to the agreement are more a matter of pride than substance; the mayor and some senior police officials appear to view the agreement as insulting and an unnecessary intrusion into their professional work.

A major test of the agreement was expected in late 2005 with the city council and mayor's election. The mayor during the negotiations and implementation announced he would not run again. Some of the most vocal city council opponents to the agreement left the council, and most new council members expressed strong support for the agreement. The leadership of the Black United Front also changed. Its most public and articulate leaders during the negotiations left the organization to enter mainstream politics. One leader came very close to being elected a city councilman in 2003 and was likely to run again in 2005. It is also possible that the command ranks of the police department will change in the next few years. As of fall 2004, two of the four assistant police chief positions are vacant. But a new mayor or city council cannot fire the police chief, so it is unclear how political changes might affect police leadership.

Despite its slow start and uneven progress, the agreement shows surprising vitality, probably for two reasons. First, the agreement itself raised expectations for the city and its police. The fact that no one voiced objections to the agreement's substance speaks to the political necessity of carrying out the content, or at least pretending to endorse it. Second, the collaborative agreement is court enforceable. Legally, the city cannot withdraw from the agreement without costly and uncertain litigation before a judge who supported it. And though the city might prevail on appeal, this would take years and would jeopardize a great deal of public support for the mayor and council.

This agreement differs from other attempts to address police-race conflicts, and several factors may make it more successful than other approaches.

First, directly soliciting the views of stakeholders and incorporating them into the agreement required the conflicting parties to frame their interests within the larger community's interest. Rather than litigants pursuing their own ends, the parties had to show how their interests addressed a larger set of goals. The stakeholder meetings created a new political reality. Once stakeholders had a voice and could articulate their goals, it would have been difficult for the parties in the lawsuit to pursue alternatives. In short, although the court served as a venue for the negotiations, the negotiations were no longer a simple matter of law and of winning and losing. Indeed, the one thing the various parties appear to agree on is the agreement itself.

Second, the agreement addresses the core strategy of the Cincinnati police. Prior attempts at dealing with these issues in Cincinnati focused on the results of the policing strategy—primarily the disproportionate impact of enforcement on African Americans—without addressing the underlying strategy itself. The idea of law enforcement as the core strategy was never seriously challenged. Many efforts to apply community policing did not work because both the police and members of the public rapidly came to realize that behind the meetings and other trappings, policing proceeded as before. The police saw little being accomplished, and members of the public deeply resented being simply the eyes and ears of the police. This was particularly true when community policing was relegated to specialist squads, and the rest of the police department followed a traditional law-enforcement approach.

Third, the agreement includes an innovative and bold attempt to engage community members in problem solving, independent of the police. If this can be accomplished, community problem-solving partnerships will educate and train members of the public in new methods for addressing crime and disorder problems in their neighborhoods. Putting communities on a more equal footing with the police enables them to work with their police more effectively. In addition, when community members have experience with problem solving, they have a different set of expectations for policing. This provides external constituencies for police problem solving that may help this strategy withstand changes in police administrations and elected officials.

Fourth, the agreement is enforceable by the federal court. Trust among the parties is extremely tenuous. Yet trust is required to implement this agreement. The combination of an independent monitor, conciliator, and ultimately the federal court substitutes trust in the process for trust among the parties. This is not a permanent arrangement. In the end, the police and communities of Cincinnati must develop an ongoing collaboration built on trust. But this is an important temporary arrangement, much like scaffolding and bracing that are needed during construction but are removed once a building can stand on its own.

Finally, the evaluation component provides measures of overall goal attainment. Compliance with the agreement is no guarantee of success. The agreement is a codified working hypothesis based on the best available information, but it does not come with a guarantee. Evaluating the success of the agreement by its impact on the public, police officers, and crime should provide information to the collaborative partners and the court that will permit adjustments to the agreement, should they be found necessary. Evaluation information also protects various parties to the agreement from unsupported declarations about public opinion. Like the stakeholder meetings, the evaluation process puts the public's perception of success first and foremost. And like the search for best practices, the evaluation uses social-science methods to ensure effectiveness.

Other communities faced with similar issues may be able to benefit from the Cincinnati agreement. The social-science research supporting much of the agreement is highly generalizable. Where there is little or no conflict, Cincinnati's findings could simply be adopted. But even then, discussions with community members and elected representatives would be needed. When the legitimacy of policing is under attack from its own communities, however, it is vitally important to engage communities in discussions of police strategies. Engagement of stakeholders should be accompanied by consideration of social-science research. Engaging public discussion in a vacuum of reliable information is unlikely to lead to much progress, because the public is largely unaware of scientific evidence regarding effective police strategies. Ultimately, the most important implication from the Cincinnati experience is that science and community goals can be brought together in a process that leads to a clear, positive vision for the future of policing. The influence of this vision on politics, and politics on this vision, are yet to be realized.

Assessing Responses to Public Insecurity in the Americas

John Bailey and Lucía Dammert

The contributions to this volume explore the common theme of heightened concerns about the various challenges to public security in the hemisphere, and they analyze the ways in which governments and civil society in the region are attempting to respond. Police reform is a priority throughout the region. The case studies here offer insights that can help assess which responses are more useful and which are less so and the reasons for success or failure.

Lessons Learned about Public Security and Police Reform

The case studies, drawn from various national and local contexts, show us broadly similar sets of problems and policy initiatives, with two exceptions. The Colombian case is a clear outlier in the scope and complexity of its political and criminal violence. Also, in the United States common crime is actually declining, but concern about terrorism remains high. Even so, many of the findings from the exceptions are relevant to the other cases.

PUBLIC SECURITY AND POLICE REFORM AS POLITICAL PROCESSES

It is a truism that politics governs police reform and other public-security issues. Politics in the broadest sense is about system legitimacy or—in our cases—about the legitimacy of democracy. In the periods of authoritarian rule, citizens' views about public safety mattered less than the regimes' views of national security. Also, under authoritarianism problems of crime and violence could be veiled by government censorship. In democratic politics citizens' views are paramount. Security is not the only factor influencing the public's support for democracy, but it usually ranks among the top three concerns in public-opinion polls.

Overall, the picture is mixed. The experiences of Brazil, El Salvador, and Mexico are generally negative. That is, the evidence suggests that citizens view their governments as unsuccessful in confronting criminality. The connection is most explicit in the Salvadoran case, where public-opinion polls show an apparent linkage between declining trust in police and declining support for democracy. Opinion data from Mexico also suggest a generally negative opinion about the police and justice systems. Impunity, or the sense that only a small fraction of criminal acts are prevented, investigated, or punished, is the dominant problem. More generally, data presented in chapter 1 show a decline in support for basic institutions throughout the region over a five-year period.

Chile presents a different situation since its police still enjoy a relatively high standing in public opinion, even given their repressive role in the Pinochet regime and in the face of increasing crime rates. Interesting here is the Carabineros' effective leadership in shaping their public image and in taking the initiative in the public debate. Colombia conveys a sense of some limited progress in confronting the worst security conditions in the region, especially in the three largest urban areas and particularly in Bogotá. It teaches that a continuous deterioration of security is not inevitable, even in the gravest situation in the hemisphere. Here again, much is owed to institutional leadership by the national police in pushing through internal reforms and to political leadership at the national and local levels. The U.S. case is also generally positive, where favorable public views toward military forces, judiciary, and police reinforce overall system support.

Politics is also about power. How power is distributed and employed in a society and who benefits from it permeate public security and police reform. In the abstract, security is supposed to be a public good, one whose benefits are enjoyed by the whole society. In fact, this is far from the case. Interest groups influence how security policy is developed and implemented. Pressures by lawyers, bureaucrats, police, army, drug traffickers, the media, and other groups constrained security reforms in Brazil to "what the context allows." Conflicts related to race and class—often overlapping—also figure in most of the cases. In the U.S. case, racial tension lies at the heart of citizens' confidence in police and justice generally. Minorities, especially African Americans, indicate much less confidence in the police and justice system. The Cincinnati case provides a lesson of partial success in how a police-reform process might be structured to confront the profound lack of trust by African Americans. Race, in the sense of Indian-mestizo conflict, figures importantly in tensions between state officials and villagers in Guerrero, Mexico. There the indigenous groups found special constitutional provisions and international legal doctrine to support their efforts to organize extraofficial police forces.

Income distribution in Latin America is more unequal than in any other region of the world. The police-reform case of São Paulo shows how business interests can promote initiatives that may privilege their concerns. Class conflict is also emphasized in the Chilean case—where an age and gender bias by police against lower-strata young men is also noted. Class tension is also stressed in the Salvadoran case, where the security forces historically served the economic elites. Businessmen in El Salvador addressed their concerns by helping finance the public police assigned to antikidnapping duties. On the other hand, class actors, such as left-wing parties and labor unions, constituted an important factor in constraining police abuses in El Salvador. Perhaps the more interesting finding, however, is their relative absence in most of the other cases. That is, the general sense of fear and insecurity about criminal violence or terrorism tilted public concern away from due process and the vulnerability of marginal groups and toward strengthening the police and justice system.

Politics involves partisan conflict. In Chile, the center-right opposition coalition in Congress was able to block the governing center-left's initiatives to reduce the Carabineros' ties to the military. In the Salvadoran case, the party representing the former guerrillas was more interested in its partisan agenda than in insisting on strict compliance with the 1992 accords. The Mexico case emphasizes the reach of the political parties into security policy in appointments and in program initiatives. The Republican Party in the United States has benefited from a general public opinion that associates the party with strength on security issues.

Partisan conflict typically carries over to bureaucracy and administration. For example, the bureaucratic location of policing is a sensitive issue. Interior ministries handle varieties of political problems, for example, conflicts between the central government and provincial governments. Defense ministries typically give less priority to policing but can more successfully resist partisan conflict. In Colombia, the police were shifted from interior to defense because of partisan interference during *la violencia*. In Chile the police resisted greater control by interior for fear of partisan manipulation. Confronting the same dilemma, in the Salvadoran and Mexican cases policing was located in newly created ministries of public security.

Finally, politics is about images and symbols. Citizens look to government for reassurance about the safety of their persons and property. Unable to deliver the quality of security and justice administration in the time frame that citizens demand, governments typically offer up symbolic reassurance. This can take many forms. Governments—for example, Chile and Mexico—may designate anticrime programs as state policy, something of great importance and therefore above partisan conflicts. It can take the form of tough-sounding language denouncing crime, unveiling tougher laws, or announcing military-type campaigns against crime, as in Brazil, or color-coded warning alerts about terrorism, as in the U.S. case. Leaders show off impressive-looking technologies or launch impressive-sounding plans or consultative mechanisms. Presumed miracle workers, such as Mayor Rudolph Giuliani of New York, are flown to major cities for very visible consultations.

Symbolism should not be dismissed out of hand. Lasting improvements in security and justice administration take decades to accomplish. Symbols can help mobilize public support. They at least convey to audiences that leaders understand the urgency of the problem and are trying to respond. Symbolism, however, works mainly in the short term. It may buy time for governments to undertake substantive reforms

THE INFORMATION CHALLENGE

Accurate, reliable, useable information is universally in short supply. This scarcity hampered policy making in all cases. Virtually all governments throughout Latin America operate in a fog of distorted and incomplete information about criminality and about the principal actors and agencies involved. Comparative time-series data on criminal trends were fragmentary or lacking in all cases. With respect to official data, all of the cases report a substantial *cifra negra* (black number). That is, a large fraction of crimes are not formally denounced. The most usual reason for citizens' not filing formal complaints is their conviction that nothing will come of them. Or worse, that denouncing crimes will entangle the complainants in complex and time-consuming procedures that ultimately produce little or no result—or may even endanger their personal safety. While survey data are increasingly available, periodic victimization surveys, which can be a useful corrective to official data, are beginning to be used only in limited cases, such as Colombia and Chile.

When governments cannot produce credible, timely, and accessible data on trends in crime and policing, the public responds to political rhetoric or mass media coverage—often inaccurate, if not inflammatory. Misinformed fear, in turn, can be manipulated to support hard-line anticrime policies. This situation, as the Brazilian, Chilean, and Salvadoran cases show, can benefit the antireform agenda of traditional elites and established interest groups.

Even where victimization data are available, however, there is a disconnect between real trends in crime and public perceptions. Generally, the public's fear of crime was out of proportion to real trends (at least as estimated through surveys and official data). This is most evident in the Chilean and Salvadoran cases. On the other hand, perceptions of security improved in the largest Colombian cities, lagging behind but in line with indicators of real trends. The hypothesis developed most clearly in the Chilean case is that the fear generated by perceptions of insecurity explains the gap between perceptions and what is known or can be found out from existing data.

In the Latin American cases, accurate information about the principal actors and agencies involved in security policy making is quite limited as well. Data on prisons and prisoners are scarce, and rather little is known about who are actually convicted of crimes.[1] Data on police give quantitative guides about numbers, territorial distribution, and the like. But little is known about internal organization and functioning or about the attitudes and values of police personnel. Much more research is needed that combines extensive interviewing of police and justice officials with careful analysis of institutional arrangements and procedures. The analysis of the Colombian police reform can serve as a useful model with its combined use of interviews and documentary analysis.

Furthermore, we see how organizational dynamics can distort information or limit its usefulness. Incentive systems that emphasize arrests lead police to increase that activity, leading, in a fraction of cases, to arbitrary detentions and civil-rights abuses, as in El Salvador. In Cincinnati, police commanders at the precinct level had available the COMPSTAT technology, which combines event reports with mapping, but they resented its intrusion into their decision-making authority and preferred to rely on their own instincts in assigning priorities and resources. In Colombia, centers for crime information were established in six cities but were not sufficiently integrated with other agencies to develop anticrime strategies or operations.

The public-security situation at the national level in the United States was different but even more problematic. In that case, the information requirements of an antiterrorism policy far exceeded those for anticrime policy. An antiterrorism program requires information covering national, transnational, and foreign contexts. The volume and complexity of the information are overwhelming. Much of the information must be translated from various different languages. Data must be gathered from routine financial, commercial, educational, and transportation organizations within the United States and in a variety of foreign countries. Sophisticated technologies must be developed to "fish" those rivers of data for relevant patterns and to communicate the findings to street-level law-enforcement personnel. Furthermore, for ordinary crime, the data deal with ongoing patterns of activity, such as armed robbery or kidnapping. Information needed in combating terrorism may relate to a single event and must be provided to the relevant authorities before a specific terrorist act takes place.

GAPS BETWEEN KNOWLEDGE AND POLICY

A gap exists between ways of knowing and ways of doing. In the best of all worlds, accurate ways of knowing should help shape useful ways of doing. But, as James Q. Wilson (1983) has pointed out, social-science knowledge does not automatically translate into useful policy knowledge. The presumption that success in the United States in reducing crime is somehow linked to empirical science may be misguided. As in Cincinnati, policing throughout the United States typically follows custom rather than scientific knowledge. The success in introducing problem-oriented policing in Cincinnati was an exception to the rule. And the fact that allegations of police abuse recurred after the introduction of problem-oriented policing will very likely reopen debates in that city about the effectiveness of the technique. Another important example of the knowledge-practice gap is the consistent finding that simply adding more police to existing forces is not a cost-efficient, or perhaps even useful, anticrime measure. Most of the cases followed a pattern of more is better, that is, either hire more new police or purge the allegedly corrupt officers first and then hire replacements, plus additional new officers.

Some characteristics of criminology and social science in Latin America seem particularly remote from policy thinking.[2] Criminology in the region tends to lack strong disciplinary identity and evolved, until very recently, as an isolated appendage of criminal law. Law programs, by and large, tend to be formalistic and have not developed policy studies to an important degree. The weak empirical orientation of criminology has meant limited attention to and information about actual police and judicial behavior. Despite these weaknesses, criminologists have exercised extensive influence on legal reforms, development of criminal policies, and the design of law-enforcement agencies and practices.

In social science more generally, varieties of Marxist thought—for example, the work of Michel Foucault (e.g., 1995) and critical criminology—have been particularly influential, especially in the Argentine and Brazilian academic communities. The latter approach emphasizes the gap between profound social inequality and the expectation of equality before the law. Two implications follow. First, explanations of crime emphasize class inequality, and prescriptions point toward extensive social reforms in a broad strategy to put crime prevention ahead of repression and punishment. Second, police repression of crime suffers the stigma of the illegitimacy of a political order that tolerates—even promotes—inequality. Critical-criminology approaches intrinsically appeal to anyone troubled by the profound social inequalities of the region. In several of the cases—for example, Mexico, El Salvador, and Brazil—implicit (but sometimes explicit) reservations were expressed about whether the state should impose force and punishment in repressing crime. While influential in academic debates, however, Marxism and critical criminology exercise relatively little influence on policy debates. There, the academic contributions tend to be attacked as *garantista* (rights focused), that is, overly concerned about protecting the rights of the accused, coddling minors, or pampering prison inmates.

Arguably, the main source of policy ideas in Latin America is foreign experience, as in Chile for police reform. However, there are interesting cases of local innovation in Brazil (the São Paulo Institute against Violence) and Mexico (the community police in rural Guerrero). Still, the search for policy ideas abroad is standard procedure and has intensified in the age of international professional associations, abundant information, and easy communication. Policy diffusion can be useful when the foreign experience is clearly comprehended and when local realities and requirements are well understood. Several ideas have been drawn from U.S. experience with the thought that these represent best practices. But the English experience, which shaped U.S. practices, is fundamentally different from the continental European experience, from which Latin American countries drew their models.[3] Further, to be effective, the ideas drawn from abroad need to be tailored to fit local circumstances. This requires that local conditions be accurately described by appropriate data and methods. With few exceptions (e.g., several Colombian cities have made important advances in data collection and analysis), this is seldom the case.

In the Latin American countries examined here, a variety of foreign ideas have been imported. Neighborhood watch, *koban* (neighborhood police posts), community policing, probation, community tipsters, total quality management, zero tolerance/broken windows, internal-affairs units, COMPSTAT, crime mapping, task forces, and 911-type emergency telephone service appear in a variety of adaptations in most of the countries. Unsurprisingly, the imported ideas have produced diverse, sometimes unexpected outcomes. For example, adversarial proceedings (as opposed to inquisitorial proceedings) introduced recently in Chilean criminal courts led to higher rates of citizens' reporting of crimes. Community policing provides a more widely applicable example.

A wide range of possible interpretations exists about what community policing means. In some cases, community policing is a new label for long-standing practices. Illustrative is the Chilean Carabineros' claim to do community policing because they are the community's police! The Chilean case, and arguably the Colombian as well, show that community policing can increase the public's trust in the police, which might serve as the first step toward more substantial improvements in crime prevention. Thus, in Chile there is a symbolic discourse that focuses on the importance of police-community relations and the improvement of crime-prevention strategies. However, issues such as decentralization of police organization and operations, typical of community policing elsewhere, are not on the agenda. In the Colombian case (more specifically in Bogotá) community policing was limited to a part of the police force that would enhance police-community relations, while the rest of the force focused on traditional modes of crime control and prevention. As a very different interpretation, the Mexican case shows how community policing could be understood as a way in which the local community organizes its self-protection, partially from state-level police forces. Also, community policing works best when combined with a problem-oriented approach, as in Cincinnati.

In short, community policing is a transplanted concept that needs to be addressed in imaginative and creative ways in countries in which, in most cases, police agencies are highly corrupt; lack public trust; operate in hierarchical, almost military, organizations; and lack resources. We believe there is evidence—for example, in the discussions of Chile and Colombia—that community policing programs may improve the public's perception of police efforts to prevent crime. But there are no strong grounds on which to argue that such programs actually have an impact on crime rates, on reducing fear of crime, or on improving the administration or management of police forces.

THE ELUSIVE LOGIC OF REFORM

Public security and justice administration involve several functions that are closely interconnected. Limiting the focus to common crime and justice administration, the functions might be viewed as a series of phases that involve complex webs of actors from government, civil society, and the international system. The functions/phases include (1) crime prevention, (2) investigation and prosecution, (3) judicial action (indictment, prosecution), (4) sanction (acquittal, fines, probation, imprisonment), and (5) rehabilitation-reintegration. Reforms introduced in any of the phases have multiple impacts throughout the overall process. The most frequent pattern reported in the cases is a response to public demands for security by intensifying the activity in the middle phases (investigation, prosecution, and sanction). This often took the form of hiring more police personnel (and purging existing ranks); criminalizing more activities, for example, organized-crime legislation and money laundering; and hardening penalties, for example, increasing sentences or lowering the legal age to be tried as an adult. Such responses have the effect in all cases of overloading the police, courts, and prisons; diverting resources from prevention; and further weakening efforts at rehabilitation and reintegration into society.

This is not to say, however, that crime-prevention policies are completely absent. Community policing appeared in different guises in all of the cases, with prevention as its main goal. Several other common prevention practices were used as well, such as neighborhood watch, crime mapping, improved lighting, and the like. As something of an overall exception, the Lagos administration in Chile invested considerable resources in a prevention strategy.

A related lesson is that in the context of the broader policy-making sequence, prevention works best when the supportive civic culture and civil-society organizations are already present. As underlined in the discussions of public security in Mexico and El Salvador, a culture of legality has yet to take firm root and participation in social organizations is relatively weak. A theme recurring in other cases—for example, El Salvador and Brazil—is that the public is willing to allow the police to bend or break the law if doing so helps combat violent crime. Their rather understandable viewpoint is that violent criminals present more of a human-rights problem than do aggressive police. Absent a culture of legality and robust webs of pro-civil-rights community organizations, there is a weak basis for the positive police-community dynamics that are essential to prevention policies. Put differently, a culture that is indifferent or hostile toward legality can easily engender a climate of permissiveness toward abusive policing.

Problems of sequencing appear not only among the various phases of policy making but also within them. The story of police reform in El Salvador notes that the internal-control units were organized and launched late in the process, which allowed problems of indiscipline and police misconduct to escalate.

The cases highlight the sequence problem, but provide no guidance about whether there is an internal logic of reform that might serve as a general guide. One infers that reform of public security is an integral whole and that all parts need to be addressed simultaneously within a framework of planning.[4] The reality, however, is that no country has the human or material resources, much less the overall wisdom, to carry out an integral reform. Therefore, the puzzle of where to begin deserves priority. The negative lesson is that reforms are most unlikely when the stakeholders are excluded or worse, when the main actors resist change. On the other hand, the Brazilian police-reform story offers two positive lessons: start the reform effort in the most change-oriented agency, and reform is more likely when a political initiative connects with a useful idea. The São Paulo police in the 1990s were themselves promoting change, and the idea of using an NGO as catalyst proved successful.[5]

COORDINATION PROBLEMS

For policy formulation and implementation, a constant challenge is managing the complexity of the multiple agencies operating in public security and justice administration. Part of the issue is legal-constitutional, with the courts operating as a separate and—formally at least—coequal branch of government. In Chile, the Carabineros made a claim to constitutional standing. For the narrower question of administrative coordination within the executive branch, the recurring lesson is the need to overcome interagency overlap, confusion, and lack of effective coordination.

As expected, the three federal cases present the most daunting problems of coordination. Formal-legal rules governing distribution of powers and functions among the levels of government complicate policy coordination. The United States is especially interesting because of its size and complexity and its long tradition of decentralized justice and policing. In response to the threat of terrorism, the U.S. federal government created the Department of Homeland Security in 2002, its most complex reorganization since the creation of the Department of Defense in 1949. Mechanisms and procedures to coordinate security policies with state and local governments in the new context of combating terrorism are at a very early stage of development. Mexico created a Secretariat of Public Security in 1999, a public-security council composed of a variety of federal agencies, and a complicated National System of Public Security to manage coordination with states and municipalities. Absent an independent evaluation, we have no sense of whether the system promotes consultation and coordination or serves mainly as a symbolic response. Brazil also created a National Secretariat for Public Security, but subordinated it to the Justice Ministry. Brazil appeared to rely mainly on its national planning system to coordinate activities.

Effective coordination is also a problem in the unitary systems. In Chile, for instance, there are several government institutions that do not work closely together, such as the Gendarmería (from the French Gendarmerie, people in arms; the agency is in charge of the prison system) and the Servicio Nacional de Menores (National Service for Minors), which oversees juvenile justice, or the Carabineros and the investigative police. Similar problems in cooperation appeared between prosecutors and investigative police in Colombia. El Salvador established a National Council on Public Security, but it failed in its primary task of coordination.

Two additional coordination issues affect government capacity throughout the region. First is the central-local dynamic. In general, policing is over-centralized throughout Latin America. Part of the dynamic is related to the organizational model, since most police institutions are structured along hierarchical, military lines. In most cases policing strategies are adopted in the capital cities without sufficient attention to the special realities of local and regional contexts. Much of the actual crime fighting takes place at the local level, however, and citizens expect effective local responses. In most cases, local governments lack sufficient resources and skills and tend to rely on situational crime-prevention measures such as better lighting. Decentralization as part of the overall democratic deepening is the dominant trend throughout the region, and local governments are seeking (or being assigned) more policy-making authority. In Colombia, for instance, local governments are beginning to play an important role in policy design and implementation in security, and in many cases these efforts are not coordinated with the national government. Initiatives by local governments in Chile and El Salvador are beginning as well. In sum, better central-local coordination is needed in both the federal and unitary cases.

A different coordination issue is the public-private dynamic. Citizens generally perceive that governments have not responded effectively to crime, and they have turned to self-help in the form of private security. For those who can afford them, private security companies of a wide range of competence and professionalism have mushroomed over the past decade. Private security, however, has evolved with little effective coordination with the public sector, especially the police. Here is where an innovation such as the São Paulo Institute for the Prevention of Violence can play an important consultative role.[6]

These few items suggest that better coordination is a high priority. Coordination mechanisms can take a variety of forms at the tactical or strategic levels: for example, task forces, search blocs (in the Colombian case), a presidential adviser, an office within the presidency, a coordinating ministry, or a policy-making council. Whatever the particular form, coordination mechanisms are needed that can bring to the table the relevant organizations and stakeholders and that can assign responsibilities and evaluate programs and initiatives. This is not to suggest that coordination can magically produce policy success. The Cincinnati case emphasizes relatively effective coordination of stakeholders. The jury is still out on policy success.

PLANNING DEFICIENCIES

All the governments analyzed here adopted some form of planning in response to the security challenge. Yet there is no clear instance of best practice, no case of a strong planning performance. Planning is defined as a set of more or less coherent and measurable policy goals related to a strategy of implementation that connects specific activities to agencies, that links the strategy and agencies to budgeting and resource allocation, and that provides for performance indicators and adjustment mechanisms. In some respects the U.S. performance succeeded at the strategic level by linking homeland-security concepts and priorities to the semiannual national-security overview and then connecting these to the logic that guided the construction of the Department of Homeland Security and the reforms of relevant agencies. The connection of these, however, to the budget process and to performance indicators is yet to be accomplished, although we can expect targeted forms of evaluations by agencies such as the Government Accounting Office.

The Brazilian case provides the most interesting discussion of planning

largely as a symbolic exercise. The announcement of a national public-security plan was apparently prompted by a national scandal. The plan itself
lacked a clear concept, strategy, or workable connections between goals, programs of implementation, performance indicators, and the like. Planning was
opportunistic, a response to a specific crisis to address the public's demands
for effective action against violence and insecurity.

In Chile, a so-called comprehensive plan for citizen security appeared at
the end of the 1990s. In Colombia, a central theme was the government's tendency to improvise, to react to security problems, at least until Plan Colombia, also in the late 1990s, set out a general strategy (though not a plan in the
sense that we use the term). In El Salvador the Consejo Nacional de Seguridad Pública was created to plan and coordinate policies, but its recommendations were often ignored by the relevant government ministries. Though the
Salvadoran plan adopted utterly unrealistic goals, these were at least clearly
specified and measurable. Mexico also adopted complicated planning and
consultative mechanisms.

Neglect of program evaluation is widespread. Certainly bad information
and weak coordination are serious problems. But policy learning about
efficiency and effectiveness can best be gained when programs set measurable
(and realistic) goals and provide useful indicators by which to assess progress.
Typically, indicators adopted relate to processes or activities (e.g., numbers of
patrol hours in an area, or numbers of complaints processed) that are assumed to be relevant to improving security. Mexico, while employing evaluation indicators, emphasized those that are easily quantifiable rather than
those that can measure quality, such as the effects of better training on work
performance. Much more difficult—and more useful—to assess are the connections between actual trends in crime and specific government programs
and activities.

MILITARY INVOLVEMENT IN POLICING

Civilian policing is more consistent with community-oriented practices that
emphasize problem solving, minimum violence, and maximum respect for
civil and human rights. Our cases generally report strong military involvement in domestic affairs as a historical pattern (with the U.S. exception) and
serious obstacles to the transition to civilian policing. Democracy advocates
and human-rights and civil-liberties organizations have pushed for reducing
the role of the military in police activities. In four of the cases, however, there
is a countertrend toward greater military involvement.

Before the terrorist attacks of September 2001, military participation in domestic policing in the United States was largely limited to technical-support activities (e.g., training, communications) in antinarcotics programs. Even this was aimed at deterring smuggling. The National Guard (normally under the command of state governors) is closer to local communities and performs policelike duties in cases of natural disasters or large-scale disruptions or violence. After September 11, however, the regular military forces were assigned domestic duties in combating terrorism. A joint command—the Northern Command—was established to coordinate military activities in the mainland United States and with respect to Canada and Mexico, and the military was assigned more extensive duties to support first responders (e.g., fire fighters, police). Although the specific roles and duties remain to be determined, the increased involvement of the military reversed a long-standing balance and sent signals that might affect civilian-military dynamics in other countries in the region.[7]

A central theme in the Mexican case is the strong trend since the 1980s toward militarization, not only in policing but in justice administration as well. Military personnel and organizational style shape the newly created Federal Preventive Police. Military officers make up the top leadership of the attorney general's office. Not mentioned in the analysis, but important as well, are the hundreds of military personnel on leave or retired who provide leadership and technical skills to state and local police forces throughout the country.

Brazil shows strong military organization of the preventive police itself (even in the name, *policia militar* [military police]). Failures of the regular preventive and investigative police to deal with widespread violence, mostly associated with drug trafficking, are prompting political leaders to call on the regular army to restore order. This is evident in the military operations in the shanty towns of São Paolo and Rio de Janeiro.

Part of the supposed success of the police reforms in El Salvador was the reconstitution of the civilian police and the separation of the military from policing. That trend, however, has been reversed in recent years. Military forces have been assigned to civilian patrols, especially in the rural areas. More important, public opinion seems to support military involvement in law enforcement.

Apart from these four, Colombia's situation of extreme violence due to the mix of common crime, drug trafficking, and guerrilla and paramilitary conflicts has meant that close cooperation between military and police forces continues. An effort was made to increase civilian influence by involving the

Ministry of the Interior in the police chain of command. But the priority of dealing with guerrilla and paramilitary conflicts requires that the Ministry of Defense retain ultimate control over the resources and operations of both the police and armed forces.

Something similar holds in Chile, where since the Pinochet era (1973–1990) the Carabineros were a formal component of the armed forces. Efforts to increase civilian control by involving the Ministry of the Interior have been successfully resisted by the Ministry of Defense, the armed forces, and the Carabineros themselves. These agencies and their supporters in the legislature and in civil society have been successful in controlling the public debate about the civil-military balance in policing.

The most important lesson is that the police-military issue remains a prisoner of the history of the human-rights abuses of the 1970s and 1980s. Scholars and human-rights activists view the relationship with suspicion. In no case was fresh thinking discovered about the ways in which the two sets of institutions could better cooperate to improve public security in ways that protected civil rights.

MIXED RESULTS FROM INTERNATIONAL ASSISTANCE

Though several international actors influence security policy throughout the region, the United States is the dominant actor (e.g., Nadelmann 1997). A potential problem in technical-bureaucratic cooperation is that the availability of U.S. resources can create dependencies in Latin American police and intelligence agencies that can distort their own priorities. Colombia is a case of extensive U.S. involvement in combating drug trafficking, and much knowledge and experience gained in that endeavor have strengthened police effectiveness more generally. Even so, as Gonzalo de Francisco notes, "It is inexpedient . . . to create the kind of dependency that appears when things are done or encouraged only because of the availability of resources from the United States."

On the political-ideological side, the important new issue is terrorism. The strong U.S. emphasis on this issue raises two key questions. What precisely is terrorism, and who are the terrorists? This label was applied in the Salvadoran case to youth gangs and to certain labor unions. The terms lend themselves to manipulation and, as in the Cold War with Communism, one can easily imagine how governments or other political actors will try to apply the terrorist label to whatever groups they oppose in order to enlist U.S. support. The real significance of terrorism as a security issue in Latin American countries is also an open question. With the exception of Colombia, terrorism would seem to be a secondary issue in comparison with the high levels of conventional forms of crime and violence. Procedural safeguards are needed to monitor human and civil rights as security forces are strengthened. Democratic transitions have been under way for some time in the region, but dissatisfaction with economic growth and concerns about crime and violence could tip the scales toward hard-line policies that are less attentive to human and civil rights. Finally, safeguards are also needed to protect national sovereignty. The U.S. claim of a security imperative could lead to practices that violate conventional notions of sovereignty.

Progress or Retreat?

A mixed picture of relative success in confronting the challenges of crime and violence emerges in these studies. The problems seemed to spike upward in the mid-1980s in Latin America and in 2001 in the United States. Thus, governments and societies have had relatively little time to respond effectively. At this point there is little experience to generalize from. Rather, we have the potential for a mixed stream of influences that point to different scenarios. Also, analysts viewing the same general set of problems may see more cloud or more silver lining. The public-security analysis of Brazil is decidedly pessimistic, whereas the story of police reform is optimistic. There is cause for cautious optimism about the overall direction of change. One factor in this optimism is the sense that pessimism stifles imagination and effort, but the record justifies some hope as well.

In Latin America, there is a shared commitment to creating more efficient, effective, and professional police and justice systems. Also, protection of civil and human rights has become more institutionalized than in the 1960s and 1970s, and webs of national and transnational groups have grown up to support these more effectively.

In all of the Latin American cases, energetic efforts were made to improve public security, most dating from the mid-to-late 1990s. Varieties of technologies and programs are being tried out, and personnel are receiving better training. By the late 1990s, most of the countries were shifting from ad hoc responses to efforts toward more coherent planning. Similarly, civil society in most of the countries is responding. Though some forms of response might be considered negative—for example, walled communities or vigilante justice—many others are positive. One of the implications of the deepening of democracy in the region is that civil-society involvement in security and justice administration will become more active and will assume forms that we cannot foresee. To note merely one example, the diffusion of public-policy programs and the improvement in legal education in the region will produce new generations of talent that can improve the quality of both government and societal responses to insecurity.

An important positive lesson learned throughout the region is that human-rights organizations, both governmental and nongovernmental, have taken root in varying degrees in many different settings, strengthening both security and democracy. Even though these organizations operate with multiple constraints, their presence affects security policy making in all its phases. Put another way, the established legitimacy of human rights and the local-national-international webs of public and civil-society organizations create a context of policing and justice administration in the twenty-first century that is substantially different from the authoritarian contexts of 1970s and 1980s. For example, human-rights organizations acted to help constrain the counterreform campaign in El Salvador. They also provided additional tools to indigenous groups in their struggle against abusive state officials in the most backward regions of Mexico. We need to know more about the ways in which concepts of human rights, which have widespread legitimacy, can reinforce norms and practices of citizenship and civil rights as individuals confront the overall system of law enforcement and justice.

Finally, in the United States, the threat of terrorists with potential access to weapons of mass destruction gives rise to a new set of challenges. Here as well signs of progress are seen, in the sense of government moving as quickly as possible to reorganize itself and to pursue innovative responses in the intelligence, defense, diplomatic, and law-enforcement fields. Civil society is also cooperating with government initiatives while remaining vigilant about civil liberties. The more worrisome possibility is that the U.S. initiatives against terrorism may create risks for progress toward better protection of civil rights in societies with relatively weak democratic institutions and values.

NOTES

1. The literature on the dual transition is extensive. See, for example, Haggard and Kaufman (1995), Chalmers et al. (1997).

2. Colombia is an exception in the sense that it preserved formal democracy in the 1980s and 1990s at the same time that criminal and guerrilla violence accelerated dramatically.

3. Data compiled by authors from Web sites of Secretarias Estaduais de Segurança Pública (State Secretariats of Public Security) http://www.mj.gov.br/senasp/institucional/inst_sspestados.htm.

4. In Argentina surveys have been implemented by the Ministry of Justice and Human Rights since 1999 as a part of the National Criminal Justice Informational System (http://www.jus.gov.ar/polcrim/snic.htm). In Chile surveys are implemented by the Ministry of Interior, also since 1999. There is no information available to the public, however. In Colombia the Departamento Nacional de Estadística has carried out four national victimization surveys, with the last wave in 2003. In El Salvador, the Ministry of Government has done several nationwide surveys; also, useful surveys have been done by academic institutions such as the Instituto Universitario de Opinión Pública (IUDOP). For information on victimization surveys in the United States, the Bureau of Justice is an excellent resource (http://www.ojp.usdoj.gov/bjs/).

5. In Colombia, another source about fear of crime can be found in public opinion surveys conducted periodically in the four major cities (Bogotá, Cali, Medellín, and Barranquilla) by a prestigious private think tank, Fedesarrollo (www.fedesarrollo.org.co). In Brazil, several universities have done surveys, among them the universities of São Paulo, Rio de Janiero, and Minas Gerais. Also, institutions such as Fundación Sistema Estadual de Análise de Dados (State System for Data Analysis), Instituto Latinoamericano de las Naciones Unidas para la Prevencion del Delito (Latin American Institute of the United Nations for the Prevention of Crime), Organización Panamericana de la

Salud (Panamerican Health Organization), and United Nations Development Program do useful work. In Mexico, the Instituto Ciudadano sobre la Inseguridad has done two nationwide surveys. Also, universities such as Universidad Nacional Autónoma de México and El Colegio de México have done local and regional surveys.

6. The implications of such low trust are well analyzed in Teresa P. R. Caldeira's *City of Walls* (2000), an anthropological study of crime, segregation, and citizenship in the city of São Paulo.

7. For present purposes we exclude natural disasters from the discussion, while recognizing the enormous importance of earthquakes, hurricanes, floods, epidemics, and the like on private lives and political systems.

8. The separation meant that law enforcement officials could communicate with intelligence officials only under strictly limited circumstances.

9. In El Salvador, for example, the army and police conduct joint patrols in rural areas. A Salvadoran colleague who works with the combined army-police patrols in that country put it starkly in a scholarly meeting. In answer to his question about standard patrol practice by the army, a soldier commented that he kept the rifle safety off and his finger on the trigger. Seminar on Research and Teaching of Defense and Security, Santiago, Chile, October 2003.

10. Bayley (2001, 25) emphasizes that "if the incidence of crime and disorder is thought to be unacceptable or increasing, police reform will be inhibited." Reform in such cases may be seen as a distraction from law enforcement.

11. Controversy in that city flared again. A recent incident of alleged police brutality in the death of an African American (videotaped and televised) angered civil rights activists and prompted calls for the resignation of the police chief (William Branigin, "Struggle with Police Killed Man, Coroner Says," *Washington Post*, December 4, 2003).

CHAPTER 2 • BRAZIL'S PUBLIC-SECURITY PLANS

1. On June 12, 2000, a single assailant, Sandro do Nascimento, hijacked a bus in Rio de Janeiro in a middle-class neighborhood. The kidnapping was widely televised. The Special Operations Battalion (Batalhão de Operações Especiais) of the Military Police was sent in, but not the Antihijacking Division (Divisão Anti-sequestro) of the Civil Police. The governor would not authorize the use of an elite sharpshooter. The episode ended with the death of a bus passenger and of the assailant himself, who was caught by the Military Police and later strangled by three of its officers in a police vehicle. The governor, who throughout the crisis had praised the police, changed his opinion once the results were known: "[The governor] says that the conduct of the police was mediocre given the investments made and he said the policemen were criminals" (*O Globo On-line*, June 14, 2000). A survey revealed the general disrepute of the police: 72

percent of those interviewed answered that they mistrusted the police ("A fear statistic," *O Globo On-line,* June 18, 2000). The connection the governor made between the investments made and the performance of the police is notable.

2. See James G. March and Herbert A. Simon (1958, 169): "The simplifications have a number of characteristic features: 1) Optimizing is replaced by satisfying—the requirement that satisfactory levels of the criterion variables are attained."

3. This expression suggests that, without a planned direction, it is still possible to arrive at (some sort of) conclusion for a given task, despite incompetence, inefficiency, and existing obstacles. In relation to problems that are difficult to solve, politicians often launch programs with objectives that are far beyond available competencies. Consequently, administrators charged with implementing them end up defining and seeking their own goals.

4. On November 1, 1994, the army occupied and controlled some critical slum areas in the city of Rio de Janeiro, after a series of violent assaults and kidnappings, in the so-called Operação Rio. The practical results, as predicted by several members of the federal and civil police, faded away a couple of weeks after the army evacuated. This kind of intervention by the army was repeated later several times, with noticeably decreasing results (see Caldeira 1994, 1996, 1998).

5. See http://www.senado.gov.br/web/codigos/const88/const88i.htm for the English version of the 1988 Constitution.

6. Responsibility is a polysemic concept, and it is not clear in which sense(s) it is used nor how it is qualified. It might mean, for example: (1) the quality of someone who is responsible; (2) obligation to answer for one's own acts or those of another; (3) civic responsibility, legal responsibility, and so on. The relationships between the state and civil society are very confused even within the constitutional text itself.

7. See Law 9637, May 15, 1998.

8. The law of October 15, 1827, creates the post of *juiz de paz* (justice of the peace), who had wide investigative and police powers in his area (Holloway 1997, 61). Today this situation is different: judges do not have investigative powers; these remain exclusively with the police.

9. The *Plano Plurianual Avança Brasil 2000–2003 (Plan Avanza Brasil)* includes fifty-four strategic priorities that have as a premise the creation of a favorable environment for sustainable development. It agrees with the strategic goals established for the Justice Ministry in objective no. 28, to mobilize the government and civil society to reduce violence (http://www.abrasil.gov.br).

10. This point was roundly criticized, especially within the agencies themselves.

11. Brazil has a uniformed and very visible military police force and a plainclothes force, the civil police, that conducts investigations.

12. According to Article 4, the FNSP supported projects in public security aimed at, among other goals, (1) equipping state police forces, (2) training and evaluating police officers at various levels, (3) establishing information systems and police statistics, (4) supporting community policing, and (5) strengthening scientific and technical policing.

13. Luiz Eduardo Soares "said that there is no one single explanation for the problem, but he tied the weak bureaucratic performance to administrative incompetence and corruption" ("Las Provincias apenas gastan 7% de los recursos en seguridad," *O Globo*, July 1, 2003).

14. "Governo só gastou 14% da verba da segurança," *O Globo*, December 14, 2003.

15. "The mayor [of Rio de Janeiro], Cesar Maia, criticized yesterday the delays by the federal and state governments in completing the decrees related to the task force for Rio. The Security Plan released six days ago, the so-called 'ten commandments of public security,' in Rio called for delegating the authority to coordinate the task forces, which still has not happened. . . . Maia fears that the task force was announced only as a response to critics of public security in the state." "Operação policial," Editorial, *O Globo On-line*, March 7, 2002.

16. During a television interview, Renato Hottz, commander general of the military police, said that political issues and lack of political will led to the dissolution of the task forces. He called for adopting other operations in the political arena in the Rio metropolitan area (Joana Ribeiro, "Poder paralelo," *O Globo On-line*, February 26, 2003).

17. Soares opposes the idea of reactivating the federal task forces to combat organized crime. Coordinated by Commisioner Getulio Bezerra of the federal police, the task force was deactivated three months after its introduction. According to the secretary, it is necessary to convince society of the need to change the structure of the Rio police. "He criticized what he called 'palliative measures' taken in cases such as that which occurred in Rio" ("Luis Eduardo afirma que ajudará a reformar a policía," *O Globo On-line*, February 26, 2003).

18. For a close examination of political influence in public-security policies, see Soares 2000.

19. "In practice the text begins the process of unifying the military and civilian police. . . . 'Those that do not adopt these measures will not get one cent in federal aid from now on,' justice minister Jose Gregori advised. He alluded to three of the ten items: unified command of the two police forces, creation of a common training program, and installation of an integrated operations center" (*O Estado de São Paulo On-line*, August 8, 2002). Recent data show that federal funds were received by the states, but federal guidelines were not applied, nor were all the funds actually spent (barely 7 percent).

20. In Bahia state, the police strike left the population unprotected, and there were instances of looting and violence.

21. "FHC busca nova saída para garantir segurança pú," *AN Agora* (Joinville), January 31, 2002.

22. Some sectors of civil society went into action. A privately owned (but with a council with public officials) system called Tipster Hotline (Disque Denúncia) was initially developed in Rio de Janeiro after a wave of kidnappings. Citizens contact the system anonymously to provide information about crimes.

23. "Elias Maluco fax novo desafio," June 21, 2002; "Escolas permanecem fechadas por medio da guadrilha de Elias Maluco," June 22, 2002; "Retratos do Brasil," June 20, 2002.

24. Material obtained from "Tendências/Debates," *Folha de São Paulo*, February 24, 2003.

25. Justice minister Thomaz Bastos has not always accepted the Workers Party proposal. For example, he disagreed about the subordination of the federal police to the National Public Security Secretariat. According to the proposal, that secretariat would be connected directly to the executive office. Thomaz Bastos canceled that plan. *Correio Braziliense* (Brasília), January 3, 2003.

26. Summary of presentation by Luiz Eduardo Soares to the World Social Forum, Porto Alegre, Brazil, January 29, 2001. The book mentioned is Soares 2000.

27. "Sem motivo para comemorar," *O Globo*, November 14, 2004.

CHAPTER 3 ▪ PUBLIC-PRIVATE PARTNERSHIPS FOR POLICE REFORM IN BRAZIL

In this chapter I develop ideas explored initially at the Global Meeting on Public-Private Partnerships for Police Reform, in Nanyuki, Kenya, January 12–15, 2003, organized by the Vera Institute of Justice and the Nairobi Central Business District Association, and funded by the Ford Foundation. I thank the participants of the meeting, particularly Renato Aldarvis, from the Military Police of the State of Paulo, for their comments, suggestions, and contributions to those proceedings.

1. In the states of Pernambuco, Rio de Janeiro, Espírito Santo, and São Paulo, homicide rates reached 52.3 per one hundred thousand, 50.9 per one hundred thousand, 46.7 per one hundred thousand, and 42.2 per one hundred thousand, respectively, in 2000.

2. For a discussion of the multiple relationships between public and private policing, see Bayley and Schearing 2001.

3. Municipal guards frequently perform police activities, even though they are not legally authorized to do so. They sometimes cooperate with the military and civilian

police, or they may compete with them. There is an ongoing debate about the advantages and disadvantages of changing the law to permit the municipal guards to perform police activities, even transforming municipal guards into municipal police agencies. In 2001, there were approximately 48,000 officers in 307 municipal guard units in Brazil, of which 32,000 officers and 134 municipal guard units were in the state of São Paulo.

4. Data compiled by author from an agency Web site that is no longer accessible.

5. In the state of São Paulo, the police ombudsman agency was created by government decree in 1995 (decree 39,900/95). In 1997, the Legislative Assembly passed a law institutionalizing the police ombudsman (complementary law 826/97).

6. Globo Television is the main television network in Brazil. The Center for the Study of Violence at the University of São Paulo is the leading research institution in the areas of public security and police reform. The papers presented at the conference were published in Pinheiro (1998).

7. An example is Ethos Institute, www.ethos.com.br.

8. A collective-action problem arises when some beneficiaries of a service try to avoid paying for it. They are "free riders."

9. The ISPCV's Web site provides current information on its activities: www.spcv.org .br.

10. Information provided by Institute São Paulo Against Violence.

11. The project report is available at the Web site of the Center for the Study of Violence: www.nev.prp.usp.br.

12. The six states capitals are São Paulo, state of São Paulo; Rio de Janeiro, state of Rio de Janeiro; Vitória, state of Espírito Santo; Salvador, state of Bahia; Recife, state of Pernambuco (and the city of Pesqueira); and Belém, state of Pará. Information on the observatories is available at www.nev.prp.usp.br/observatorio.

13. Data from the Institute São Paulo Against Violence, based on crime data from the state secretary of public security and population data from the Brazilian Institute of Geography and Statistics.

CHAPTER 4 • FROM PUBLIC SECURITY TO CITIZEN SECURITY IN CHILE

This chapter was substantially improved thanks to suggestions by Jorge Burgos, Gonzalo García, Patricio Tudela, and John Bailey. Liliana Manzano helped with data collection and editing.

1. State policy is understood as an intersectoral plan (i.e., one that connects various groups of agencies) of an ongoing nature, which is not related solely to priorities de-

fined by the administration in power but rather by a political consensus involving the opposition political parties in the interest of realizing long-term actions.

2. It should be noted that during the military regime information on crimes reported to the police was not subject to any analysis.

3. The rehabilitation policy for the prison population is not analyzed in depth here because of the lack of public information. During the three periods analyzed, the programs dealing with resocialization of prisoners apparently had little or no effect.

4. Public expenditure on the police falls under the justice and security (*justicia y seguridad*) line item, which implies that the budget for the Defense Ministry (to which the Carabineros are subordinated) does not have a line item specifically for the police. On the other hand, in this section of the budget, there is a line item for the Public Ministry (Ministerio Público), whose importance has increased notably since the penal system reform.

5. The penal-process reform is considered one of the main public policies developed in the last decades. The political consensus about the need for this reform generated an agreement in the Senate about the budget for justice and police agencies.

6. This process can be explained in part because the media did not cover it; also, the government took the plan out of public discussion. This was apparently because the initiatives were not changes that the public would connect with a decline or increase in crime.

7. Rodrigo Barria, "Propuesta en verde. ¿Rumbo a Carabineros S. A.?" interview with the director general of the Carabineros Cienfuegos, *El Mercurio*, January 12, 2003.

8. Its full name is *Plan de Seguridad Vecinal Integral y Plan Nacional de Difusión de Acciones Policiales Preventivas* (Plan for Integral Neighborhood Security and National Plan for Diffusion of Preventive Police Activities).

9. On this point, it should be noted that community participation in crime prevention is a concept that, as yet, lacks a definite meaning. Thus, some view it as merely a process of logistical support for police operations, whereas for others it is the backbone of those same prevention initiatives.

10. The *alcalde* (mayor) heads this council and among its members are the two councilmen who have received the most votes, the chiefs of police from the Carabineros and Investigative Police, a representative of the Public Ministry, a representative of the drug-prevention program, three representatives from neighborhood organizations, and one representative each from the security committees, the Chamber of Commerce and Industry, and the Parent-Teacher Association. Membership of the council can be increased to a maximm of twenty-one, whenever the council feels it is appropriate.

CHAPTER 5 • THE INSTITUTIONAL IDENTITY OF THE CARABINEROS DE CHILE

1. The Web site for the Carabineros claims, "Almost 1,000 martyrs have fallen in the line of duty, making it the national uniformed organization that has given in peacetime the greatest number of lives for the sake of the nation" (www.Carabineros.cl).

2. The bibliographic references on this subject are extensive. At an institutional level, there are studies financed by international institutions such as the Inter-American Development Bank, the Washington Office on Latin America, and the Ford Foundation. In Chile, the Fundación Paz Ciudadana and SUR Profesionales have funded studies.

3. For a good definition of the various actors involved in these reforms, and for the priorities that various groups place on different police-reform issues, see Neild and Zeigler 2002, 17.

4. On September 5, 1938, a group of sixty National-Socialist youth were massacred in the Seguro Obero (Worker Security) building, very near the La Moneda, the government palace. This was part of a failed coup d'état, and the police riddled them with bullets.

5. The Caso Degollados (Case of the Beheaded Men) was emblematic. It was proved that officers in the Dirección de Comunicaciones de Carabineros (Communications Directorate of the Carabineros) had participated in the 1985 kidnapping, murder, and beheading of three professionals who were communists. This cost then–director general César Mendoza his position in the governing junta.

6. "La Dependencia de Carabineros," *Diario La Tercera*, October 28, 2001.

7. María Pía Guzmán was also the first administrator of the Fundación Paz Ciudadana, founded in 1992.

8. Joaquín Lavín was president of the political party Unión Demócrata Independiente (Independent Democratic Union), mayor of the municipality of Las Condes and candidate of the right in the 1999 presidential elections. Currently, he is mayor of the Santiago Centro, which is in the business, administrative, and political center of the metropolitan region of Chile.

9. As Ignacio Cano (2001) has noted, the difference in these two terms is vital in the case of the police. The ways in which police carry out their work directly affect security and the life of people, including the officers themselves.

CHAPTER 6 • ARMED CONFLICT AND PUBLIC SECURITY IN COLOMBIA

1. In July 2002, a Gallup poll reported that 72 percent of Colombians approved of the National Police. Only the Catholic Church, with 76 percent, and the armed forces, with 79 percent, did better (Ministerio de Defensa 2002).

2. One of the first tasks of the military government of General Gustavo Rojas was to create the Armed Forces General Command, which incorporated the National Police as a fourth branch, pulling it out of the Interior Ministry (Echeverri 1993, 224).

3. One cannot claim that Colombian society is antimilitary. To the contrary, consistently over many decades, the public has recognized and supported the role that the military plays, above all in the armed conflict. However, it is also apparent that it would not be acceptable to Colombians if the military, whatever its role may be in the armed conflict, were to become involved in the government or influence the evolution of democracy in the country. An exception was the application of the National Security Doctrine during the liberal administration of Julio César Turbay (1978–1982). In that instance, the attempt to prepare the government to provide national security in the context of the guerrilla confrontation ended in frustration. The failure led to a search for a negotiated solution, an option that is still available today. Concerning the subordination of the armed forces to the political regime, see Leal (1984).

4. Guerrilla warfare and phenomena such as the peasant struggle for land rights and the student movement of the 1960s and 1970s led all administrations to rely on the State of Siege laws, which the 1991 constitution calls Conmoción Interior (domestic disturbance) laws. Among the various tools is operational control, that is, the police are subject to the military authority in specific areas (see Leal 1994).

5. I am aware of the polemical nature of this claim. Having participated in the negotiations with the M-19, the Ejèrcito Popular de Liberación (People's Liberation Army), the Partido Revolucionario de los Trabajadores (Workers' Revolutionary Party), Quintín Lame Command, Corriente de Renovación Socialista (Socialist Renovation Movement), and Milicias Populares de Medellín (Peoples' Militias of Medellín), I am completely convinced of the positive effects that the commencement of civil and democratic life brought to these organizations. Here, I simply want to point out a contradiction that the so-called negotiated political solution creates in the long term when the outcome is viewed as an inevitability, that is, something of a consensus and consequently a government policy in essence.

6. The term paramilitary does not imply an organization associated with or complementary to the military institution itself. Colombians use the word to identify a variety of armed organizations opposed by the National Police and the armed forces.

7. The role of the National Police in rural areas is not limited to municipal capitals that are population centers. The 1992 reform created a rural police force, the Policía de Carabineros, whose mission extends beyond the population centers. However, the lack of manpower has impeded its development.

8. It is not enough to mention the murders of politicians, such as Luis Carlos Galán, of journalists, such as Guillermo Cano, and of police officers, such as Baldemar Franklin

Quintero. What happened in Colombia between 1984 and 1993 constitutes a tragedy because of the lives lost, including many anonymous individuals who died in indiscriminant terrorist bomb attacks. For more on this period, see Pardo (1996, chap. 7, 8).

9. Following negotiations, on June 14, 1991, Pablo Escobar entered La Catedral prison, specially and luxuriously outfitted for him, in the suburbs of Medellín. Shortly thereafter, the rumors began that he was continuing to run his organization even though he was in prison. On July 21, 1992, when the Gaviria administration tried to dismantle the prison and move Escobar to Bogotá, he fled (Pardo 1996, 425–47).

10. On August 18, 1991, President Gaviria appointed Rafael Pardo as the first civil defense minister.

11. To act rapidly and forcefully, the Samper administration granted special powers to the then-chief of the National Police, which led to the dismissal of approximately five hundred members of the force (see Serrano 1999b).

12. Although the public never understood it in this way, in the four components beside the Initiative against Drug Trafficking are the unsuccessful negotiation process with the FARC and the ELN, the strengthening of government institutions, and social and economic aid for the sectors most affected by the economic crisis that began in 1998. The U.S. law on Plan Colombia centers on funding and support, especially for the antidrug initiative, but it also includes aspects relating to institutional strengthening.

13. The urban population grew from 38.7 percent in 1951 to 70.7 percent in 1995. In contrast to most Latin American countries, the Colombian population resides in more than three urban centers or regional capitals.

14. The Gaviria administration proposed the reform, which appeared in Law 62 (August 12, 1993). The Cultural Transformation refers to the changes that the National Police experienced under the leadership of General Rosso José Serrano (1994–1999).

15. In 2000, a comparison of Latin American capitals with the seven largest cities in Colombia—Bogotá, Medellín, Cali, Barranquilla, Pereira, Manizales, and Armenia—showed that those cities had 131.2 robberies of businesses per one hundred thousand inhabitants, fewer than Caracas and Lima, with 335.6 and 275.1, respectively, but more than Mexico City, with 93.8, and Santiago, with 72.4. The Colombian cities had a rate of 98.7 car thefts per one hundred thousand inhabitants, whereas both Mexico City (335.6) and Caracas (287.8) were significantly higher. Homicide rates are very high in Colombia, but, notably, Bogotá, had a rate of thirty homicides per one hundred thousand inhabitants in 2000, lower than Washington, DC, Brasilia, Caracas, San Salvador, and São Paulo. This was the result of a multiyear preventive policy the mayor's office implemented, in which the National Police played a fundamental role (Acero 2002).

16. For an understandable historical reason (linked, undoubtedly, to Colombia's rural character), arms control has been in the hands of the Armed Forces, which have always

been obstinate, even about experimenting with periods of full prohibition against carrying weapons in major cities.

17. These data were provided to the author by the Dirección General de la Policía, April 2002.

CHAPTER 7 · DEMILITARIZATION IN A WAR ZONE

1. During that period, the General Command of the Armed Forces was created, comprising the police, as a fourth force, alongside the army, the navy, and the air force.

2. Particularly relevant is the 1960 institutional reform during the first Frente Nacional administration. Under it, the highest-ranking police officers retook command of the force. The institution also reassumed its original name (Policía Nacional) and ceased to be a fourth member of the armed forces (Llorente 1999, 403).

3. Notably, when the first Colombian police force was organized in the nineteenth century, antecedents to the modern criminal-investigation units appeared in the form of officers assigned investigative tasks and serving as assistants to the courts. However, the first laws establishing jurisdictions for the judicial police did not appear until 1964 and 1966 (Londoño and Diettes 1993, 305–20).

4. The CAI, inspired by the Japanese *koban,* are small police posts that decentralize basic police patrolling services to cover geographic areas smaller than those served by a station. This gives the police more direct contact with the residents of a jurisdiction. In 1987, 85 centers were created, most of them in Bogotá; in 1994, the Policía Nacional calculated that there were 480, two-thirds of which were in urban areas.

5. As the then minister of defense, Rafael Pardo, noted, "This provision was very significant in giving legal status to the [Policía Nacional] since the 1886 Constitution had established the army, at the time the only force in existence, as the nation's sole armed body" (Pardo 1996, 337).

6. At the municipal level, the advances in institutional structure made in Bogotá during the 1990s to address public safety are well recognized (see Acero 2003, 48–51). Progress was also made in Cali and Medellín but to a lesser degree (Guzmán 1999).

7. Data in this section are from the Human Resources Office, Policía Nacional.

8. The police-to-population ratios for Colombia are comparable to many developed countries, including the United States, Australia, Canada, and Japan. However, the ratio is not good when compared to countries that face similar domestic-security problems, such as Peru or Northern Ireland. In the Latin American context, in contrast, the size of the Colombian police force is relatively large, being surpassed only by Uruguay, Panama, Cuba, Peru, Brazil, and Venezuela (Llorente 1999, 437).

9. In August 2002, at least 160 *municipios* (townships) out of 1,098 in Colombia had no police (data from the Operational Office, Policía Nacional).

10. The *campesino* soldiers are young rural men conscripted into the army at age eighteen to serve in their native areas. This modality was created by the Uribe administration as part of its strategy aimed at increasing police and military presence in rural areas in order to take control of areas pressured or influenced by outlaw armed forces.

11. Two other Colombian institutions share criminal investigation functions with the police: the Departamento Administrativo de Seguridad (Administrative Security Department), an intelligence agency created in the 1950s, and the Cuerpo Técnico de Investigaciones (Technical Investigative Corps) of the Attorney General's Office, created in 1991.

12. Until recently, the armed forces were on the margins of the anti-drug-trafficking efforts. Many military personnel felt that the danger of internal corruption would be extremely high were they to get involved (Dávila 1999, 310–16). However, at the end of the 1990s, as part of Plan Colombia, financed by the U.S. government, the army created the Brigada Antinarcóticos (Antinarcotics Brigade) and it became involved in the eradication of illicit crops.

13. Francisco Leal, "Policía Nacional a debate," *El Espectador*, April 11, 1993.

14. Between 1990 and 1993, I worked at the Office of the President's Advisor for National Defense and Security, where this particular request was discussed in several meetings.

15. According to the former minister of defense Rafael Pardo, about seven hundred police officers died between 1990 and 1993 as a consequence of this conflict (1996, 344).

16. "Prueban requeza ilícita de exdirector de La Policía," *El Tiempo*, December 30, 1989.

17. "Purga en La Policía tumba a 174 uniformados," *El Tiempo*, October 22, 1994.

18. In the 1980s almost 690 officers died in this conflict, and in the next decade this figure increased to 1,730 (from data on personnel injured and killed in the line of duty, as reported annually in the Policía Nacional's *Revista Criminalidad* [Crime Magazine], for the years 1980 to 2000). For comparison, in Northern Ireland, during the period of the worst confrontations with the Irish Republican Army (1969–91), 284 police officers lost their lives (Weitzer 1995), about one-third the losses in Colombia in the 1980s alone, and one-sixth of those between 1990 and 2000.

19. The Bogotá daily *El Tiempo* published a three-part series (August 15–17, 1999) on localities from which the police had retreated as a consequence of guerrilla attacks. These reports revealed that after the police withdrawal, guerilla groups or paramilitaries took over these cleared-out zones.

20. Significantly, the increase in police personnel during the 1980s was primarily in the rank and file, without a corresponding increase in supervisory personnel.

21. The Estrategia Nacional contra la Violencia (National Strategy Against Violence), as this government initiative was called, was published along with most relevant policy documents from the Gaviria administration in Presidencia de la República (1994b, 1994c).

22. The law allows municipalities to contract with the Policía Nacional to increase the number of officers serving their area. The contracts can include both career officers and police assistants (Presidencia de la República 1994d, 50–86). This law remains in force but has not yet been used by any municipality.

23. Operational control over the police by the military was a common practice within counterinsurgency operations.

24. On the details of the discussion and the results of the work of both commissions, see Presidencia de la República–Consejería Presidencial para la Defensa y Seguridad Nacional (1994d) and Serrano (1999b).

25. This discussion about the reform's content is taken from the main publications on the topic: Goldsmith (1993), Camacho (1993), Torres (1994), Leal (1994), Llorente and Bulla (1994), Pardo (1996), and Llorente (1999).

26. In the creation of this office, international experiences were taken into account, particularly those of English-speaking democracies (see Goldsmith 1991).

27. The criminal investigation specialty is not discussed here because an office within the Policía Nacional had already been created for that purpose in the 1980s.

28. Until then the rank-and-file officers were not promoted. They entered as police agents and remained as so until the end of their career.

29. The Colombian case demonstrates that a basic requisite for successful, relevant institutional change is the active involvement of the police-force leadership, not only in the implementation of the reform but especially in its design (see, for example, Goldsmith 1991; Bayley 1994).

30. For a thorough discussion on this experiment in the Colombian case, see Goldsmith (2000).

31. The *Procuraduría General de la Nación* (Procurator General of the Nation) exercises the principal responsibility for discipline of public officials, including the military and the police, and the protection of human rights, with the assistance of the *Defensor del Pueblo* (or Ombudsman Office, created in the 1991 constitution). At that time, members of the military forces and the police viewed both the *Procuraduría* and the *Defensor* as an obstacle to carrying out operations against the guerrillas and organized

crime. Unfortunately, both supervising agencies were the model initially used to design the *comisionado's* office.

32. In countries such as Japan, Australia, Great Britain, Canada, and the United States, the correlation between supervisors and the base oscillates between 1:1.3 and 1:6.4 (Bayley 1994, 60).

33. "Asumió nuevo director de la Policía," *El Tiempo*, December 7, 1994.

34. Dismissals were used in 1993, but only against rank-and-file police officers. That year more than three thousand officers were dismissed with this discretionary power (data from the Human Resources Office, Policía Nacional).

35. Figures calculated on data supplied by the Human Resources Office, Policía Nacional.

36. These sorts of statements by Serrano appeared in various press reports, for example, *El Tiempo*, September 14, 1995; *El Espectador*, February 2, 1996; *Vanguardia Liberal*, February 5, 1996.

37. "Entra en liquidación la oficina del Comisionado," *El Tiempo*, September 14, 1996.

38. For further discussion on the failure of the *comisionado's* office, see Goldsmith (2000, 182–86); Misión Especial para la Policía Nacional (2004, 21–24).

39. From mid-2002 to late 2003 numerous press reports revealed a series of incidents linking police officers with narco-trafficking and with paramilitary and guerrilla groups, as well as cases of high-ranking personnel involved in kidnappings, robberies, and the irregular handling of police funds—including U.S. antinarcotics aid. For example, *Semana*, June 24, 2002; *Revista Cambio Colombia*, June 11, 2002, June 23, 2003, July 21, 2003; *El Tiempo*, Editorial, August 24, 2003, August 24, 2003, September 10, 2003; *Revista Semana*, September 14, 2003, September 21, 2003. By mid-2003 police integrity was once again at the top of the Colombian public agenda. A new corruption scandal involving a significant number of officers of one police department (with jurisdiction over the Atlántico province) was widely discussed in the Congress and the media. For a brief analysis of this period, see Llorente (2003).

40. This commission had five civilian members appointed by the minister of defense for a five-month period (see *El Tiempo*, September 23, 2003).

41. The most substantive aspects of this reform are explained in Policía Nacional (1996, 1997).

42. Data from the Operational Office, Policía Nacional.

43. From the outset, the community-policing program in Bogotá involved nine hundred police officers out of the city's sixteen thousand (Llorente 2004, 79). Even though the current commander of the police in Bogotá has shown great interest in this form of

service and has maintained the program, the number of uniformed officers dedicated has not increased.

44. Between 1996 and 2002, the police abandoned more than seventy rural posts as a consequence of guerrilla harassment. In contrast, during the ten previous years, slightly more than thirty posts were abandoned, which is troublesome enough (data from the Operational Office, Policía Nacional).

45. Nevertheless Colombian armed forces have always been popular and continue to be, with a current rating near 76 percent.

46. "Colombia enferma (I)," *El Tiempo,* January 26, 2003. This high number can be explained by the fact that during the same period the survey was carried out, several corruption scandals surfaced involving high-ranking officers. See note 34.

47. Data compiled by author from *Revista Criminalidad,* produced by the Policía Nacional, 2000–2002, and Fedesarrollo, which publishes annual surveys, 1999–2003.

48. It is important to emphasize the magnitude of the effort that the police have made, given that their training schools have a capacity for only seven thousand new students each year.

49. See note 34.

CHAPTER 8 ▪ SECURITY POLICIES IN EL SALVADOR, 1992–2002

1. The transformation of El Salvador's public security sector is a special case since it involved dismantling the security apparatus and substituting an entirely new one, completely different from what existed before.

2. Notably, a principal feature of the Salvadoran political transition is that the presidential administration that negotiated and signed the peace accords also initiated the implementation of the transition. This facilitated input from hard-liners in the ruling party, who were given a say in government decision making concerning the implementation of the peace accords. The Alianza Republicana Nacionalista (Nationalist Republican Alliance) party, in power since 1989, with major representation in the Legislative Assembly, falls on the right of the political spectrum. It is the primary representative of Salvadoran conservatives and the national economic and business elite, a coalition that is reproduced organizationally in the government bureaucracy (Paniagua 2002, 689). The management of security policy passed from the hands of the military to the hands of an elite with representation in the government, whose members have managed it for their own benefit.

3. An oversight mechanism on police misconduct (Control Unit and Disciplinary Investigation Unit) was not created until 1994. Its work was evaluated as slow and inefficient; its fairness and impartiality were also questioned (Aguilar and Amaya 1998).

In 1997, the Consejo Nacional de Seguridad Pública (National Council on Public Security, CNSP) revealed high levels of impunity because of the weakness of criminal investigation (CNSP 1997).

4. In contrast to the period before the signing of the peace accords, these violations lacked political motivation. Instead, they arose because of police practices that resulted not only from substandard training, operational supervision, and personnel selection but also from a lack of institutional will to address violations and impunity due to ineffective mechanisms of police control.

5. Regarding the police institutional crisis in 2000, a prominent member of the CNSP commented that it was due to the lack of attention and implementation of the CNSP's recommendations (La Prensa Gráfica, June 19, 2000; see also Aguilar, Amaya, and Martínez 2001, 35).

6. The institutions involved were the PNC, Fiscalía General de la República (National Attorney General's Office), and the criminal courts. Until 1998, inquisitorial proceedings were used in criminal trials. The criminal judges were in charge of both the investigation and judgment of cases, with the PNC and attorney general serving as their auxiliaries. After April 1998, adversarial proceedings were adopted in which the Attorney General's Office takes charge of the investigation of crimes, assisted by the PNC.

7. The sensitivity of members of the elite to the problem of crime is explained by their vulnerability to certain crimes, such as kidnapping and robbery of imported merchandise (Martínez 2002, 102).

8. Between 1998 and 2002, almost 190 amendments were made to the Criminal Code and Criminal Procedure Code (Marchelli and Martínez 2002, 60). These reforms were oriented primarily to toughening sentences, creating new categories of crime, and broadening police powers in regard to detention and investigation (Martínez 2002, 93–96; FESPAD 2002, 79).

9. According to Paul Chevigny (2002, 61), these initiatives for tougher measures gave politicians and the security administration an image of strength but did not address the structural problems behind the situation. Such discourse is effective because it appeals to the fears of broad social sectors, among them the elite, and that provides important political support.

10. The government presented the Alliance for Security as the systematization of a broad process of multisectorial consultation. However, it was shown that the alliance was a more or less recycled version of a 1996 document produced by the CNSP, called *Elementos básicos para una estrategia de Seguridad Pública* (Basic Elements for a Public Security Strategy) (FESPAD 2001, 10).

11. A FESPAD (2002) study that monitored police conduct toward youths and minors revealed a tendency to systematically detain youths with gang connections or those

from poor neighborhoods in order to search them or book them as suspects. Youth roundups also occurred.

12. The patrolling system facilitated improved organization of police patrols (whether in vehicles, on bicycles, or on foot) in specific geographic areas. During the patrols, searches and booking of suspects took place, and routine activity and crime statistics for the area were tabulated daily. This was a different paradigm from the one the PNC had been operating with, which favored deployment and more police stations (FESPAD 2001, 29; Aguilar, Amaya, and Martínez 2001, 96). EFICACIA involved periodic meetings to measure crime statistics in specific regions of the country. This also served to measure the performance of police chiefs in terms of reducing crime rates and increasing arrests, in an imitation of business practices that measure productivity (Aguilar, Amaya, and Martínez 2001, 40; FESPAD 2002, 8).

13. Police statistics on reported crimes should be viewed with caution because most crimes are not reported by victims. (In Latin America, these unreported statistics are called the *cifra negra*.) A quantitative reduction in crime does not necessarily imply a reduction in criminal activity; it may mean, instead, a loss of confidence in the police. The quality of data collection, classification, and systematization of information must also be considered (Aguilar 2002), as well as the arbitrary and manipulative use of statistics by the police (Loveday 2000; FESPAD 2002, 9).

14. For example, the new law favored cases with long periods of pretrial detention. This reduced the time of imprisonment that many people served following sentencing, because time served in pretrial detention was deducted from their sentences. Later, because of the criticisms of the perceived weakness of the new law, more categories of crimes were created and the requirements for imprisonment were reduced. At the same time, the police favored as an institutional goal an increase in the number of arrests.

15. In most cases, union members arrested during protests for acts of terrorism were freed by the courts because the cases lacked legal merit. Nevertheless, even though these arrests were groundless, the police could use them to send a warning.

16. *Diario Oficial* 184, vol. 353, October 3, 2002. Available at www.asamblea.gob.sv.

17. The creation of this law coincided with a context of increasing political and social tension, as seen in frequent public demonstrations and protests during which there was a systematic presence of the PNC's antiriot unit. Far from preventing confrontations, police intervention was provocative, by limiting or restricting the free movement of the marchers (FESPAD 2002, 81).

18. This criticism of limits on public involvement in decision making arose because security policy involved a heavy investment of material and financial resources in the police. This is expensive and unsustainable, and thus calls for a model that can be effective with existing resources.

19. Ample and detailed reporting on the involvement of certain PNC members in various criminal activities led President Flores to order a massive and extraordinary purge in 2000 and 2001 (Aguilar, Amaya, and Martínez 2001, 53). Pressure from journalists and other organizations in civil society also led to the removal from the National Defense Law of those dispositions that would have affected press freedoms.

CHAPTER 9 • VIOLENCE, CITIZEN INSECURITY, AND ELITE MANEUVERING
IN EL SALVADOR

I am grateful for comments and suggestions from Laurence Whitehead, Commissioner Jaime Vigil-Recinos, Stephanie Kitchen, Nicole Mottier, Edgardo Amaya, and Viktoria Åberg.

1. This is true not only for transitional or new democracies, but for established and "old" democracies as well.

2. Foundational democracies are what Garretón and Newman (2002) and Torres Rivas (2001) have called democratic foundings, when democracy is installed for the first time after civil wars or revolutions.

3. For an excellent work analyzing the different causes of postwar violence in El Salvador, see PNUD (2000).

4. A study done in 2002 showed that more than 70 percent of the population reported feeling very insecure because of crime (FUNDAUNGO and IUDOP 2002).

5. The military stripped the installations before giving them to the academy. Doors, light bulbs, and windows were removed, forcing the authorities to reconstruct the premises. Furthermore, the location was an inhospitable zone of the country, near the coastline, where average temperature is 35 degrees Celsius with 95 percent humidity throughout the year.

6. The National Guard would be integrated into the military police and the treasury police would be absorbed by the Guardia de Fronteras (border patrol).

7. Costa (1999) stresses the role of the United Nations in the implementation of the peace accords. He emphasizes its oversight over the parties and facilitation of negotiations.

8. The national police force was finally terminated in December 1994, but only after a bank assault perpetrated by the chief of its Criminal Investigations Unit. The armed robbery was broadcast by national media and showed uniformed officers perpetrating the crime.

9. It is interesting that even after the peace accords and public-security reforms, the relationship between the army and the elite landowners continued working. The reluctance to withdraw the military as the protectors of the landowners' property remains

up to this writing (February 2003), and the military are still committed to protecting coffee harvests.

10. The Grupo Conjunto para la Investigación de Bandas Armadas Ilegales con Motivaciones Políticas en El Salvador (Joint Group for the Investigation of Illegal Bands with Political Motives in El Salvador) was a commission created in 1994 to investigate the murders that occurred after the cease-fire. This commission found strong links between organized crime and political assassinations. Some of these bands of criminals included members of the army and the public-security corps, and some of them received support from government agencies (Grupo Conjunto 1994).

11. I thank Commissioner Vigil Recinos for stressing this point. He also suggests that apart from the pressures of the deployment, the reasons for the delay in initiating those units can be found in the absence of adequate disciplinary processes and the holdover of the old framework rules. In the first two years of deployment of the police, three different sets of *reglamentos* (rules) were approved to regulate disciplinary processes. This meant that when the units were beginning to get used to a specific regulation, they had to start learning a new one. This in effect delayed taking additional cases (see also Vigil Recinos 2003b; Aguilar and Amaya 1998b).

12. According to the police director's statement, the inspectorate was reformed to avoid a duplication of functions that the previous code entailed. Since several police units had similar disciplinary and control tasks (the Control Unit, the Disciplinary Investigations Unit, and the Disciplinary Court), the purpose of the reform was to assign a new coordinating role to the inspectorate in disciplinary issues within the police. To fulfill the role of a unit independent from the police, the Reforma de la Ley Orgánica de la Policía (Reform of the Police's Basic Law) established a Consejo de Ética Policial (Council of Police Ethics). However the council has not been activated, because the government has not appointed any of its members. So, the police still lack autonomous surveillance. Some independent analysis has pointed out that the relocation of the inspectorate and the absence of an external overseer of police performance have eroded the capacity of the institution to control its disciplinary problems (Aguilar, Amaya, and Martínez 2001).

13. Legislative decree 101 allowed the director of the police to expel, without process, any member of the PNC assessed by a commission appointed by the president, on the basis of suspicion and mistrust (Aguilar, Amaya, and Martínez 2001).

14. For an excellent account of this dilemma, see Stanley, Vickers, and Spence (1996).

15. This was one of the cases investigated by the organized-crime unit. The investigators succeeded in identifying the suspects and sending them to jail. Some of the suspects happened to be police officers and supervisors, and the departmental governor as well. But, because of political pressures and judicial misconduct, they were subsequently freed.

CHAPTER 10 • PUBLIC SECURITY AND POLICE REFORM IN MEXICO

1. The Public Ministry is a principal component of the Procuraduría General de la República (General Procuracy of Justice, PGR), whose head is procurator general. The roughly counterpart entities in the United States are the Department of Justice and the attorney general. In the Mexican case, investigative police work is under the supervision—at least in principle—of the prosecuting attorneys. General Macedo took leave from active army duty to assume his new post. Key positions in Mexico's federal Public Ministry—including the private secretary, the Counselors' Office, the Center for Planning on Drug Control, and the main office for the Policía Judicial Federal (Federal Judicial Police, today the Federal Investigation Agency), among others—were placed under the direction of military personnel.

2. The extent of impunity is even greater when one considers that most crimes are never brought to the attention of the authorities. During 2001, slightly more than 2.8 million crimes were not reported, as reflected in a national poll (Instituto Ciudadano de Estudios sobre la Inseguridad 2002). In 2001, 4.4 million Mexicans were crime victims, 14 percent of all households suffered at least one crime during the year, 75 percent of the population perceived that crime had increased from 2000 to 2001, 67 percent of those who thought that crime was increasing attributed that to drug trafficking and related crime, 44 percent of the crimes were violent, 47 percent of those polled said that living in their neighborhood made them feel somewhat or very insecure, 23 percent of the population had given up certain daily habits out of fear or insecurity, and 66 percent of the crimes were never reported to any authority.

3. Mexico, with 3.6 points, shares the sixty-fourth position with Ghana and Thailand. The point system ranges from 10 (highly clean) to 0 (highly corrupt).

4. As the increase in insecurity and its relationship to state failure in law enforcement has become visible, society has chosen to distance itself from government out of mistrust or fear (Poder Ejecutivo de la Federación 1995, 18). Thus, Mexicans indicated least confidence in political parties (24 percent), the federal legislature (26 percent), and the police (23 percent; Secretaría de Gobernación 2001). In contrast, the Catholic Church and television, followed closely by the armed forces, are among the few institutions in which Mexicans do indicate confidence (University of Michigan 2000; Latinobarómetro 2001).

5. This is defined as a type of crime that occurs when three or more people agree to organize, or organize themselves, to carry out in an ongoing or reiterated fashion such conduct that, by itself or together with other activities, has as its objective or result to commit any of the following crimes: terrorism; drug trafficking; counterfeiting or altering of money; money laundering; trafficking in weapons, illegal aliens, minors, or

body organs; assault; kidnapping; or car theft (Ley Federal contra la Delincuencia Organizada 1996, art. 2).

6. Areas to be coordinated include entrance requirements; training, tenure, promotion, and retirement of police officers; disciplinary, promotion, and compensation systems; organization, administration, operation, and technological modernization of public-security institutions; contracting out for services; information management; joint police actions; regulation and control of private security services and other auxiliaries; community relations and promotion of a culture that prevents crimes and misdemeanors (Ley General de Seguridad Pública 1995, art. 10).

7. The following discussion draws primarily on the founding legislation and internal regulation that structured the PFP (Ley de la Policía Federal Preventiva 1999; Reglamento de la Policía Federal Preventiva 2000).

8. The law endows the PFP with the power to obtain and process information (Ley de la Policia Federal Preventiva 1999, article 4, section IX), for which purpose the Office of Coordination of Preventive Intelligence was created. This organization constitutes an intelligence agency within the PFP, dedicated to the collection, assessment, and exploitation of criminal information. It consists of personnel previously employed by CISEN and by Section 2 Intelligence of SEDENA. Experienced analysts and operations personnel were transferred from both agencies. As a corollary, since the PFP's creation in 1999, CISEN no longer carries out operative or policing functions; its mission is now limited to the generation of strategic national intelligence (see www.cisen .gob.mx).

9. The commissioner is the head of the PFP and makes decisions based on the analysis provided by the Central Office on Intelligence for Prevention.

10. The agreement was renewed a year later, at the beginning of 2001, this time between the secretary of public security and SEDENA; as of 2003, there were 5,332 soldiers supporting the PFP (Presidencia de la República 2003b).

11. For example, the National Defense Plan is officially defined as having the goal of preparing the armed forces to respond effectively to foreign aggressors, domestic disturbances, disasters, and any other similar eventuality that might disturb the peace, security, or domestic order (Secretaría de la Defensa Nacional 2001, 326–37).

12. The executive secretary of the SNSP is a mechanism for the coordination of programs and policies on public security (Secretaría de Seguridad Pública 2002c).

13. At a symbolic level, the transformation of the Federal Judicial Police into the AFI also included a redesign of the organization's emblem and philosophy, which included the reintroduction of the principles of the *caballeros aguila y jaguar* (knights of the eagle and jaguar). In Aztec folklore, these animals represented day and night, and the

symbols were incorporated into the Mexican military tradition to symbolize the protection of Mexico's territory, people, and institutions both night and day.

14. This process ended June 25, 2003, when the PGR expedited new regulations that finally established the AFI as the auxiliary organ of the Public Ministry of the Federation.

CHAPTER 11 • LOCAL RESPONSES TO PUBLIC INSECURITY IN MEXICO

The information presented here was gathered from 2001 to 2003 in numerous interviews with leaders in the region, attendance at community meetings, and informal conversations with residents and others familiar with the region. I express special gratitude to Crispin de la Cruz Morales, Abel Barrera Hernández, and Raúl López Vargas, for their generous help in answering my questions about the region and putting me in contact with key actors. Part of the research was financially supported by the *Comisión Nacional de Ciencia y Tecnología* (National Commission for Science and Technology) and undertaken by Luis Gómez, as part of his master's thesis at the *Centro de Investigación y Docencia Económicas* (Center for Research and Teaching of Economics). The opinions expressed are my own, except where noted otherwise.

1. An extensive body of work in the early 1970s, principally from anthropology and from law, focuses on comparative and indigenous legal systems (for a review of this literature, see Merry 1992), but interest is centered more on civil justice and dispute resolution than on policing.

2. I am referring here to common crime and perceptions of personal safety and not the resolution of disputes over land ownership, electoral processes, or other civil issues.

3. The Montaña municipality of Metlatónoc ranks as the most marginalized of more than 2,400 municipalities in the country (CONAPO 2000); municipalities ranked number seven, twelve, sixteen, and nineteen are also found in these regions. Within Guerrero, all ten of the state's most marginalized municipalities are found in the Costa Chica and the Montaña regions.

4. The first of these victories was in 1979, when the municipality of Alcozauca was won by the *Partido Comunista Mexicano* (Mexican Communist Party), during the administration of then-president José López Portillo. His successor, Miguel de la Madrid, agreed to continue to recognize consecutive victories of the left-wing opposition in the same municipality (in recent years, represented by the Partido de la Revolución [Party of the Democratic Revolution]). During this presidency, much of the region's conflict was attributed to a shadowy group affiliated with the Partido de la Revolución Institucional (Institutional Revolutionary Party), known as *Antorcha Campesina*, which is also active in rural and semiurban areas in other states of central and southwest Mexico, and was rumored be sponsored by Salinas's brother, Raúl.

5. In one well-documented incident, in El Charco, in the municipality of Ayutla de los Libres, soldiers opened fire on residents who were attempting to surrender, killing eleven people (CNDH 2000).

6. A single voluntary village police force had been formed about a month earlier, in the village of Cuanacaxtitlán, municipality of San Luis Acatlán, as a result of discussions in the community assembly. The names of fifty-one victims of violent death from 1991 to 1995 are listed in the assembly's report (this, in a village of about three thousand residents), along with the names and circumstances related to assaults on sixty-one villagers from 1993 to 1995, ranging from rape to robbery and beatings.

7. Since reform in 2001, the relevant text is now found in Article 2 of the Mexican constitution.

8. Interview with Juan Carlos Tellez Guerrero, secretario ejecutive del Consejo Estatal de Seguridad Pública de Guerrero (executive secretary of the State Council on Public Security of Guerrero), conducted by Luis Gómez, June 1, 2001.

9. Rosa Rojas, "Enardece a guerrerenses de la Montaña y Costa Chica la detención de cinco policías comunitarios," *La Jornada*, Feb 13, 2002; Rosa Rojas, "Promete el gobierno de Guerrero no desarmar ni arrestar a agentes de la policía comunitaria," *La Jornada*, March 30, 2002; Misael Habana, "Otorgan libertad total a los policías comunitarios de la Montaña, Guerrero," *La Jornada*, February 14, 2002; Misael Habana, "Exige el alcalde de San Luis Acatlán, Guerrero, liberar a 2 policías indígenas," *La Jornada*, January 21, 2003.

CHAPTER 12 ▪ FROM LAW AND ORDER TO HOMELAND SECURITY IN THE UNITED STATES

1. Hearings chaired by Senator Frank Church (1975–1976) were instrumental in developing a variety of restraints on defense and intelligence-related activities, especially within the United States.

2. The Center for Immigration Studies, an anti-immigration think tank, reports, "The number of immigrants living in the United States has more than tripled since 1970, from 9.6 million to 28.4 million. As a percentage of the U.S. population, immigrants have more than doubled, from 4.7 percent in 1970 to 10.4 percent in 2000. By historical standards, the number of immigrants living in the United States is unprecedented. Even at the peak of the great wave of early-twentieth-century immigration, the number of immigrants living in the United States was less than half what it is today (13.5 million in 1910)" (Camarota 2001, 1).

3. Racial profiling refers to the practice of greater police scrutiny toward categories of persons, for example, young, male African Americans. Gallup (2001, 19) reports that "nearly nine out of ten whites feel that they are treated fairly by state or local police,

compared to just over half of blacks—over a 30 point gap in perceived treatment. . . . 'Racial profiling' is believed to be widespread by 55% of whites, but by 83% of blacks. This large gap in perceptions between whites and blacks underscores the broad sense from our data that the law enforcement establishment is associated with perceptions of racial division."

4. This section updates data presented in Bailey and Chabat (2002, 25–31).

5. Office of National Drug Control Policy, March 2003, http://clinton4.nara.gov/WH/EOP/NSC/html/documents/pub45270/pub45270index.html.

6. See http://www.state.gov/g/inl/rls/nrcrpt/2002/html and http://www.clinton4 .nara.gov/wh/eop/nsc/html/documents/pub45270/pub45270index.html, respectively.

7. Discussion of the changes in national security strategy lies beyond the scope of this chapter. Useful commentaries include Gaddis (2002) and Litwak (2003).

8. For purposes of the statute, which opts for the legal approach, "the term 'international terrorism' means activities that—(A) involve violent acts or acts dangerous to human life that are a violation of the criminal laws of the United States or of any state, or that would be a criminal violation if committed within the jurisdiction of the United States or of any state; (B) appear to be intended—(i) to intimidate or coerce a civilian population; (ii) to influence the policy of a government by intimidation or coercion; or (iii) to affect the conduct of a government by mass destruction, assassinations or kidnapping; and (C) occur primarily outside the territorial jurisdiction of the United States, or transcend national boundaries in terms of the means by which they are accomplished, the persons they appear intended to intimidate or coerce, or the locale in which their perpetrators operate or seek asylum." Domestic terrorism, according to the statute, has the meanings of A and B, but constitutes acts committed within the territorial jurisdiction of the United States (Doyle 2002, 42, fn. 86).

9. "The additional crimes include all crimes of violence, public corruption, and offenses covered by existing bilateral extradition treaties. The Committee intends this provision to send a strong signal that the United States will not tolerate the use of its financial institutions for the purpose of laundering the proceeds of such activities" (quoted in Doyle 2002a, 35).

10. "Although both criminal investigations and foreign intelligence investigations are conducted in the United States, criminal investigations seek information about unlawful activity; foreign intelligence investigations seek information about other countries and their citizens. Foreign intelligence is not limited to criminal, hostile, or even governmental activity. Simply being foreign is enough" (Doyle 2002a, 12). A grand jury is a mechanism by which the government presents evidence to a body of citizens, who then decide whether a crime has been committed and whether an indictment is warranted.

11. See Matthew Mosk, "Anti-Terror Bill becomes Law: Measure Boradens Md. Powers," *Washington Post*, April 10, 2002.

12. Useful websites for extensive information on the department include http://www .dhs.gov, http://www.homelandsecurity.org, and http://www.govexec.com.

13. The litany of scandals included, for example, the bureau's role in the fatal confrontations at Ruby Ridge, Idaho, and the Branch Davidian compound at Waco, Texas; its perceived heavy-handed investigation of nuclear scientist Wen Ho Lee; the arrest of senior counterintelligence agent Robert P. Hanssen on charges of spying for Russia; and the loss of internal documents related to the investigation of the Oklahoma City bombing of 1993 (Don Van Natta Jr. and David Johnston, "Wary of Risk, Slow to Adapt, F.B.I. Stumbles in the Terror War," *New York Times*, June 2, 2002).

14. David Lichtblau, "F.B.I. and C.I.A. Set for a Major Consolidation in Counterterror," *New York Times*, February 15, 2003.

15. Robert O'Harrow Jr., "In Terror War, Privacy vs. Security," *Washington Post*, June 3, 2002.

16. Siobhan Gorman, "Agencies Urged to Set HS Standards," October 14, 2003, http://www.govexec.com/dailyfed/1003/101403nj1.htm; Siobhan Gorman, "HS Still Seeking to Define, Measure Performance," March 5, 2004, http://www.govexec.com /dailyfed/0304/030504nj1.htm.

CHAPTER 13 · POLICE-COMMUNITY CONFLICT AND CRIME PREVENTION IN CINCINNATI, OHIO

1. We are observers and participants in the process we describe, but we relied on documents prepared during the negotiations, internal memorandums, and newspaper accounts for this narrative. And though we can speak with expertise about the agreement, and believe we can claim neutrality relative to the contesting parties, we cannot claim neutrality relative to the final agreement itself. Jay Rothman thanks the Andrus Family Fund for timely financial support.

2. Before 2001 the Cincinnati Police Department was called the Cincinnati Police Division, as it was part of the Public Safety Department. Following the 2001 riot, the Public Safety Department was disbanded and the police were given department status. To avoid confusion, however, we refer to it as a department.

3. See Jennifer Edwards, "Police Stop Blacks More Often," *Cincinnati Post*, June 23, 2001, http://www.cincypost.com/2001/jun/23/copcrd062301.html.

4. The city held a competitive bid for the analysis of the police-stops data. A team from the University of Cincinnati, led by John Eck, won this bid. The analysis of the data was presented to city council in the fall of 2003. The results were inconclusive, though

there was some evidence that tended to refute the idea that the disproportionate stopping of African Americans was due to police bias. The report is available at http://www .uc.edu/criminaljustice/ResearchReports.html or at http://www.cincinnati-oh.gov/ police/pages/-5111-/.

5. COMPSTAT is the name of an information intensive style of policing created by the New York City Police Department that uses crime data and maps to quickly identify crime and disorder patterns and focus police resources on them (McDonald 2002). Some credit COMPSTAT with the decline in homicides in New York City during the 1990s (Silverman 1999), while others claim the evidence does not support such a conclusion (Eck and Maguire 2000; Karmen 2000).

6. The role of the federal courts in regulating local police conduct has expanded over time, but is still controversial. Whether or not the federal courts should play the role they did in this case is beyond the scope of this narrative.

7. For an archive of this, see http://ariagroup.com/cinti.html. The full agreement can be found at http://www.ariagroup.com/FINAL_document.html.

8. The popularity of a zero-tolerance approach is in part based on a misreading of Wilson and Kelling's (1982) "broken windows" article, in which the authors argue that inattention to small disturbances of the social order of a neighborhood can lead to widespread criminality and that police should address disorder to prevent crime.

9. Zartman and Berman (1982) recommend a formula-detail process, by which they suggest that before details of agreements can be negotiated, the parties should define an overarching formula to ensure a collaborative momentum.

10. Among a number of important substantive changes, the parties added provisions calling for the expedited investigation of accusations that police pointed guns at citizens and establishing an independently funded and operated police-community problem-solving center.

11. The reports of the Cincinnati police monitor can be found at http://www.cincinnati -oh.gov/police/pages/-5111-/ and http://www.cincinnati-oh.gov/police/pages/-5122-/.

12. The observations in this section are based on Eck's conversations with various parties involved with the implementation and oversight of the collaborative agreement.

CHAPTER 14 • ASSESSING RESPONSES TO PUBLIC INSECURITY
IN THE AMERICAS

1. An exception is the survey of prisoners carried out in Mexico under the general supervision of Marcelo Bergman at the Center for Research and Teaching of Economics in Mexico City. A recent edition of *Renglones* (Guadalajara, Mexico) is devoted to "El

mundo de la carcel" (The World of Prison). Barros Lezaeta (2001) is an exemplary study of the psychology of youth offenders in Chile.

2. This paragraph draws on Llorente and Rubio (2003, 5–6), who draw, in turn, on Birkbeck and Rincones (1992).

3. In an early draft of her chapter on Colombia, María Victoria Llorente described the two distinct traditions that evolved in Europe, influenced especially by France and Great Britain. The former emphasized a centralized, top-down imposition of policing over subjects, while the latter evolved more decentralized traditions of police as problem solvers in their local communities, a form of policing by consent.

4. Probably the United States, with its massive undertaking to reformulate its internal and external security doctrines, reorganize its federal bureaucracy, and rearrange central-state and government–civil-society relations, comes closest to integral reform. That enormous process is in its early stages, however, and we cannot yet evaluate its success.

5. Marcos Pablo Moloeznik (personal communication, December 2004) hypothesizes that priority should go to reform of justice administration, with emphasis on prosecution and defense attorneys, judicial staff, and judges. Improvements at this stage could act to promote reform both upstream (prevention and police behavior) and downstream (prison administration and rehabilitation). Chile under President Lagos should be something of a test, since funding priority has gone to justice administration.

6. The São Paulo story also suggests the lesson that too much coordination and cooperation might not be a good thing. A certain amount of competition among agencies and between the government and private sector might produce more effort and innovation and better-quality service. That said, a surplus of coordination was a problem found nowhere in the region.

7. A press report from November 17, 2004, Sixth Defense Ministerial of the Americas in Quito, Ecuador, noted U.S. defense secretary Donald Rumsfeld's comment on this issue. "Since the September 11, 2001, terrorist attacks on the United States, Rumsfeld said, 'we have had to conduct an essential reexamination of the relationship between our military and our law enforcement responsibilities in the U.S. The complex challenges of this new era and the asymmetric threats we face require that all elements of state and society work together' " ("Rumsfeld Says America's at 'Unique Moment' for Democracy," November 18, 2004, http://www.usembassy.it/file2004_11/alia/a4111804 .htm).

REFERENCES

AAVV (American Academy of Arts and Sciences). 2000. "Brazil: The burden of the past; the promise of the future." Special issue, *Daedalus* 129(2).

Acero, Hugo. 2002. "Reducción de la violencia y la delincuencia en Bogotá, 1994–2002." In *Reducción de violencia y delincuencia en Bogotá*, ed. Hugo Acero. Bogotá, Colombia: Alcaldia de Bogota, Subsecretaría de Asuntos de Convivencia y Seguridad Ciudadana.

———. 2003. "Violencia y Delincuencia en Contextos Urbanos." In *La experiencia de Bogotá en la reducción de la criminalidad 1994–2002*. Bogotá, Colombia: Alcaldía Mayor de Bogotá–Subsecretaría para Asuntos de Convivencia y Seguridad Ciudadana.

Acuerdo del Poder Ejecutivo. 1994. "Acuerdo que crea la Coordinación de Seguridad Pública de la Nación." *Diario Oficial de la Federación*, April 26.

Adorno, Sérgio. 2002. "Monopólio estatal da violência na sociedade brasileira contemporânea." In *O que ler na ciência social brasileira*, ed. Sérgio Miceli, 267–307. São Paulo, Brazil: ANPOCS.

Aguila, Ernesto, and Carlos Maldonado. 1996. "Orden público en el Chile del S. XX. trayectoria de una policía militarizada." In *Justicia en la calle: Ensayos sobre la policía en América Latina*, ed. P. Walkman, 73–183. Buenos Aires, Argentina: Konrad Adenauer.

Aguilar, Jeannette. 2002. *Metodologías para la cuantificación del delito*. San Salvador, El Salvador: FESPAD.

Aguilar, Jeannette, and Edgardo Amaya. 1998a. "Mecanismos oficiales de control sobre la Policía Nacional Civil." *Revista Pena y Estado* 3:367–93.

———. 1998b. *Mecanismos oficiales de control sobre la Policía Nacional Civil*. San Salvador, El Salvador: Fundación de Estudios para la Aplicación del Derecho.

Aguilar, Jeannette, Edgardo Amaya, and Jaime Martínez. 2001. *Información y gestión policial en El Salvador*. San Salvador: FESPAD.

Alcaldía Mayor de Bogotá, Secretaría de Gobierno. 2000. "Caracterización de la violencia homicida en Bogotá." Unpublished report, Universidad de los Andes.

Aldarvis, Renato. 2003. "Public-private partnerships for police reform." Presentation at the Global Meeting on Public-Private Partnerships for Police Reform, Nanyuki, Kenya, January 12–15.

Alvarenga, Patricia. 1996. *Cultura y ética de la violencia. El Salvador 1880–1932.* San José, Costa Rica: EDUCA.

Amaya, Edgardo. 1999. *Cifras del delito y del sistema penal.* San Salvador, El Salvador: FESPAD.

———. 2002. "Violencia y sistema penal." *Revista Entorno* 26(August–October):38–41.

Amaya, Edgardo, and Gustavo Palmieri. 2000. "Debilidad institucional, impunidad y violencia." In *Violencia en una sociedad en transición,* ed. United Nations Development Program (UNDP), 75–114. San Salvador, El Salvador: UNDP.

Americas Watch. 1990. "The drug war in Colombia." Mimeo. Washington DC: Americas Watch.

———. 1993. *La violencia continúa.* Bogotá, Colombia: Tercer Mundo-IEPRI.

Amnesty International. 1994. *Colombia: Political Violence.* New York: Amnesty International Publications.

———. 1999. *Mexico: Urgent need for new direction and judicial reform.* New York: Amnesty International Publications.

———. 2002. *Informe 2002: "Ahora que es la hora de saber."* New York: Amnesty Internacional Publications.

Araya, Andrés, Hugo Frühling, and Luis Sandoval. 1998. "Temas policiales." *Cuadernos del CED* 27.

Araya Moya, Jorge. 1999. "Experiencias de participación ciudadana en la prevención local del delito. Éxitos y dificultades." *Cuadernos del CED* 30.

Arriagada, Irma, and Lorena Godoy. 1999. *Seguridad ciudadana y violencia en América Latina: Diagnóstico y políticas en los años noventa.* Santiago, Chile: CEPAL, ONU.

Arriagada Valdivieso, Humberto. 1938. "Order Público." *Revista de Carabineros,* no. 81.

Ayres, Robert L. 1998. *Crime and violence as development issues in Latin America and the Caribbean.* Washington DC: World Bank.

Bailey, John, and Jorge Chabat. 2002. "Transnational crime: Trends and issues." In *Transnational crime and public security: Challenges for Mexico and the United States,* ed. John Bailey and Jorge Chabat, 1–50. La Jolla, CA: Center for U.S.-Mexican Studies, University of California at San Diego.

Bailey, John, and Roy Godson. 2000. *Organized crime and democratic governability: Mexico and the U.S.-Mexican borderlands.* Pittsburgh, PA: University of Pittsburgh Press.

BANAMEX-ACCIVAL. 2000. *Examen de la situación económica de México. Estudios económicos y sociales* 75. Mexico City: Grupo Financiero BANAMEX-ACCIVAL.

Barros Lezaeta, Luis. 2001. *Planificacion de la actividad delictual en casos de robo con vilencia e intimidación.* Santiago, Chile: CESC.

Bartra, Armando. 1996. *Guerrero bronco: Campesinos, ciudadanos y guerrilleros en la Costa Grande.* Mexico City: Ediciones Sinfiltro.

Bayley, David H. 1990. *Patterns of policing: A comparative international analysis.* New Brunswick, NJ: Rutgers University Press.

———. 1994. *Police for the future.* New York: Oxford University Press.

———. 2001. *Democratizing the police abroad: What to do and how to do it?* Washington DC: National Institute of Justice.

Bayley, David H., and Clifford D. Schearing. 2001. *The new structure of policing: Description, conceptualization, and research agenda.* Washington DC: National Institute of Justice.

Bazdresch Parada, Miguel. 1994. "Gestión municipal y cambio político." In *En busca de la democracia,* ed. Mauricio Merino, 25–60. Mexico City: Colegio de Mexico.

Beato, Claudio, and Luiz Antonio Paixao. 1997. "Crimes, vítimas e policiais." *Revista de Sociología da Universidade São Paulo* 9(1). http://www.crisp.ufmg.br/cvitpol.pdf.

Benjamin, Cid. 1998. *Hélio Luz: Um xerife de esquerda.* Rio de Janeiro, Brazil: Contraponto Relume-Dumará.

Berumen y Asociados. 2002. Séptima encuesta nacional telefónica. June 28. (unpublished).

Bettancour Valparaíso, Joaquin. 1937. "Las multitudes y nasotros." *Revista de Carabineros,* no. 68.

Birkbeck, Christopher, and J. Martínez Rincones, eds. 1992. *La criminologia en America Latina: Balance y perspectivas.* Merida, Venezuela: Universidad de los Andes.

Blumstein, Alfred, and Joel Wallman. 2000. *The crime drop in America.* Cambridge: Cambridge University Press.

Boeninger, Enrique. 1998. *Democracia en Chile: Lecciones para la gobernabilidad.* Santiago, Chile: Andrés Bello.

Bostaph, Lisa, John Eck, and Lin Liu. 2002. "Racial profiling and police vehicle stops: The Cincinnati data." Paper presented at the annual meeting of the American Society of Criminology, Chicago, IL, November 13.

Botella, Joan. 1996. "Transiciones democráticas en América Central: 1979–1995." *Revista Papers* 49:9–15.

Bowden, Mark. 2001. *Killing Pablo: The hunt for the world's greatest outlaw.* New York: Atlantic Monthly Press.

Braga, Anthony A. 2001. "The effects of hot spots policing on crime." *Annals of the American Academy of Political and Social Science* 578:104–25.

Braga, Anthony A., David M. Kennedy, Elein J. Waring, and Anne Morrison Piehl. 2001. "Problem-oriented policing, deterrence, and youth violence: An evaluation of Boston's operation ceasefire." *Journal of Research in Crime and Delinquency* 38(3):195–225.

Braga, Anthony A., David L. Weisburd, Elin J. Waring, Lorraine G. Mazerolle, William

Spelman, and Frank Gajewski. 1999. "Problem-oriented policing in violent crime places: A randomized controlled experiment." *Criminology* 37(3):541–80.

BRASIL. 2000. Lei n. 989, de 21 de julho de 2000. "Dispõe sobre o plano plurianual para o periodo de 2000/2003." *Diario Oficial da República Federativa do Brasil,* Brasilia, Brazil, 1, anexo 1.

Briceño-León, Roberto, Leandro Piquet Carneiro, and José Míguel Cruz. 1999. "O apoio dos cidadãos a acão extrajudicial da policia no Brasil, en El Salvador e na Venezuela." In *Cidadania, justica e violencia,* ed. D. Chaves Pandolfi, J. Murilo de Carvalho, L. Piquet Carneiro, and M. Grynszpan, 117–27. Rio de Janeiro, Brazil: Fundacão Getulio Vargas Editora.

Burgos, Jorge. 2000. "De la tolerancia cero al compromiso 100: Reflexiones sobre políticas preventivas de seguridad ciudadana." In *Conversaciones públicas para ciudades más seguras.* Santiago, Chile: SUR Profesionales.

Bush, George W. 2002a. "Remarks by the President at 2002 graduation exercise of the United States Military Academy." Office of the Press Secretary, June 1.

———. 2002b. "Securing America's Borders Fact Sheet: Border Security." http://www. whitehouse.gov/news/releases/2002/01/print/20020125.html.

Buvinic, Mayra, Andrew Morrison, and Michael Shifter. 1999. *Violence in Latin America and the Caribbean: A framework for action.* Washington DC: IADB.

Cabrero Mendoza, Enrique. 1995. *La nueva gestión municipal en México: Análisis de experiencias innovadoras en gobiernos locales.* Mexico City: Miguel Angel Porrúa.

———, ed. 1996. *Los dilemas de la modernización municipal: Estudios sobre la gestión hacendaria en municipios urbanos de México.* Mexico City: Miguel Angel Porrúa.

Caldeira, Cesar. 1994. "Seguridad pública e cidadania: Las instituições e suas funções no Brasil Pós-Constituinte." *Revista Archè* 9:5–25.

———. 1996. "Operação Rio e Cidadania: las tensões entre o combate à criminalidade e la ordem jurídica." In *Política e Cultura: visões do passado e perspectivas contemporâneas,* ed. Elisa Reis, Maria Hermínia Tavares de Almeida, and Peter Fry, 50–74. São Paulo, Brazil: Hucitec–ANPOCS.

———. 1998. "Política de segurança pública no Rio: apresentação de um debate público." *Revista Archè* 19:13–37.

Caldeira, Teresa P. R. 2000. *City of walls: Crime, segregation, and citizenship in Sao Paulo.* Berkeley: University of California Press.

Calderón Mólgora, Marco Antonio. 1994. *Violencia política y elecciones municipales.* Mexico: El Colegio de Michoacán and Instituto Mora.

Call, Charles T. 2000. *Sustainable development in Central America: The challenges of violence, injustice and insecurity.* CA 2020: Working Paper no. 8. Hamburg: Institute for Latinoamerika-Kunde.

Camacho, Alvaro. 1993. "La reforma de la Policía: Realidades inmediatas y objetivos estratégicos." *Análisis Político* 19(May–August):50–62.

————. 1995. "El problema central de una política de seguridad ciudadana." In *Violencia urbana e inseguridad ciudadana. Memorias del Seminario Internacional. Santa Marta, Colombia, March 6–7, 1994*. Bogotá, Colombia: Plan Nacional de Rehabilitación (PNR) and United Nations Development Program.

Camacho, Alvaro, and Alvaro Guzmán. 1990. *Colombia: Ciudad y violencia*. Bogotá, Colombia: Ediciones Foro Nacional.

Camacho Leyva, Bernardo. 1993. "Frente Nacional y era contemporánea." In *Historia de la Policía Nacional de Colombia*, ed. Alvaro Valencia Tovar, 239–84. Bogotá, Colombia: Planeta.

Cámara de Diputados del H. Congreso de la Unión. 2000. Dictamen sobre la Iniciativa de Decreto que Reforma, Adiciona y Deroga diversas disposiciones de la Ley Orgánica de la Administración Pública Federal, de la Comisión de Gobernación y Seguridad Pública de la Cámara de Diputados del H. Congreso de la Unión, November 16.

————. 2002. Dictamen de la iniciativa de Ley Orgánica de la PGR de las Comisiones Unidas de Justicia y Derechos Humanos y de Gobernación y Seguridad Pública, LVIII Legislatura de la Cámara de Diputados del H. Congreso de la Unión, October 24.

Camarota, Steven A. 2001. "Immigrants in the United States—2000: A snapshot of America's foreign born population." Center for Immigration Studies, *Backgrounder January 2001*. http://www.cis.org/articles/2001/back101.html.

Cano, Ignacio, and Nilton Santos. 2001. *Violência letal, renda e desigualdade no Brasil*. Rio de Janeiro, Brazil: 7Letras.

Capowich, George E., and Janice A. Roehl. 1994. "Problem-oriented policing: Actions and effectiveness in San Diego." In *The Challenges of community policing: Testing the promises*, ed. Dennis Rosenbaum, 127–46. Thousand Oaks, CA: Sage.

Carlson, Darren K. 2002. "Civil rights: A profile in profiling." Gallup Organization, Gallup Poll Tuesday briefing, July 9, 2003.

Casas, Pablo. 1994. "Vigencia y futuro de la Policía Nacional." *Política Colombiana* 4(4):21–24.

Castro-Morán, Mariano 1984. *Función política del ejército salvadoreño en el presente siglo*. San Salvador, El Salvador: UCA Editores.

Centro de Derechos Humanos, Tlachinollan. 1995. *Informe anual 1994–95*. http://www.laneta.apc.org/tlachinollan.

————. 1996. *Informe anual 1995–96*. http://www.laneta.apc.org/tlachinollan.

Chalmers, Douglas A., Carlos Vilas, Katherine Hite, Scott Martin, Kerianne Piester, and Monique Segarra, eds. 1997. *The new politics of inequality in Latin America: Rethinking participation and representation*. New York: Oxford University Press.

Chevigny, Paul. 1996. "Changing control of the police violence in Rio de Janeiro and Sao Paulo, Brazil." In *Changing police, policing change: International perspectives*, ed. Otwin Marenin, 23–35. New York: Garland Publishing.

———. 2002. "Definiendo el rol de la policía en América Latina." In *La (in)efectividad de la ley y la exclusión en América Latina,* ed. Juan E. Méndez, Guillermo O'Donnell, and Paulo Sérgio Pinheiro, 59–78. Buenos Aires, Argentina: Paidós.

Cienfuegos, Alberto. 2002a. "Integración Carabineros de Chile-Comunidad: Pasado, presente y futuro." Presentation to the conference on Policía y Comunidad: Los nuevos desafíos para Chile, Santiago, Chile, December.

———. 2002b. Keynote speech for the 75th anniversary of Carabineros de Chile, April.

CISEN. 2002. "Palabras de Eduardo Medina-Mora Icaza, Director General del Centro de Investigación y Seguridad Nacional (CISEN), durante la presentación a los medios de los resultados del proceso de evaluación del CISEN." http://www.cisen .gob.mx.

Clarke, Ronald V. 1997. *Situational crime prevention: Successful case studies.* 2nd ed. Albany, NY: Harrow and Heston.

CNDH. 2000. *Recomendación 20/2000.* (Comisión Nacional de los Derechos Humanos). http://www.cndh.org.mx/Principal/document/recomen/fr_rec00.htm.

CNSP (Consejo Nacional de Seguridad Pública). 1996. *Elementos básicos para una estrategia de seguridad pública.* San Salvador, El Salvador: CNSP.

———. 1997. *Resultados y conclusiones del seminario sobre políticas de seguridad pública organizado por el Consejo Nacional de Seguridad Pública.* San Salvador, El Salvador: CNSP.

———. 1998. *Diagnóstico de las instituciones de seguridad pública.* San Salvador, El Salvador: CNSP.

Collier, Jane Fishburne. 1995. *El derecho zinacanteco: procesos de disputar en un pueblo indígena de Chiapas.* Mexico City: UNICACH and CIESAS.

Comisión Consultiva para la Reforma de la Policía Nacional. 1994. "Informe Final." In *La nueva policía para Colombia,* ed. Presidencia de la República-Consejería Presidencial para la Defensa y la Seguridad Nacional, 111–89. Bogotá, Colombia: Imprenta Nacional.

Comisión de Estudios sobre la Violencia. 1987. *Colombia: violencia y democracia.* Bogotá, Colombia: Universidad Nacional-Centro Editorial.

Comisión de la Verdad. 1993. *De la locura a la esperanza. Informe de la Comisión de la Verdad y Reconciliación para El Salvador.* New York: United Nations.

CONAPO. 2000. *Índices de marginación 2000.* http://www.conapo.gob.mx.

Consejería Presidencial para la Convivencia y Seguridad Ciudadana. 1998. *Estrategia Nacional para la Convivencia y Seguridad Ciudadana.* Bogotá, Colombia: Presidencia de la República.

Constitución política de los Estados Unidos Mexicanos. 2002. México: Editorial Porrúa.

Cordner, Gary W. 1988. "A problem-oriented approach to community-oriented policing." In *Community policing: Rhetoric or reality,* ed. Jack R. Greene and Stephen D. Mastrofski, 135–52. New York: Praeger.

Correa Sutil, Jorge. 2002. "La Investigación Académica y su Importancia para la

Política del Gobierno en Materia de Seguridad Ciudadana." Presentation to the first international conference on Nuevos Métodos y Antiguos Desafíos en la Investigación sobre la Policía. Vera Institute of Justice and Centro de Estudios en Seguridad Ciudadana, Universidad de Chile, November 18.

Costa, Gino. 1999. *La nueva Policía Nacional Civil de El Salvador (1990-1997)*. San Salvador, El Salvador: UCA Editores.

Courbet, Jaume. 1983. "La Policía y la Prevención de la Criminalidad." In *Policia y sociedad democrática*, ed. José María Rico. Madrid: Ministerio del Interior, Direccion de la Seguridad del Estado.

Crozier, Michel. 1997. "The transition from the bureaucratic paradigm to a public management culture." *Revista del CLAD. Reforma y Democracia* 7(January). http://www.clad.org.ve/rev07/0029601.pdf.

Crozier, Michel, and E. Friedberg. 1977. *L'acteur et le système*. Paris: Éditions du Seuil.

Cruz, José Miguel. 1997. "Los factores posibilitadores y las expresiones de la violencia en los noventa" *Revista Estudios Centroamericanos* 588:977-92.

———. 2003. "The peace accords ten years later. A citizens' perspective." In *El Salvador's democratic transition ten years after the peace accords*, ed. Cynthia J. Arnson, 5-13. Washington DC: Woodrow Wilson International Center for Scholars, Latin American Program.

Cruz, José Miguel, and María Antonieta Beltrán. 2000. *Las armas de fuego en El Salvador. Situación e impacto sobre la violencia*. San Salvador, El Salvador: IUDOP-UCA and Fundación Arias.

Cruz, José Miguel, Ricardo Córdova, and Mitchell Seligson. 2000. *Auditoria de la Democracia. El Salvador 1999*. San Salvador, El Salvador: UCA.

Cruz, José Miguel, and Luis Armando González. 1997. "Magnitud de la violencia en El Salvador" *Revista Estudios Centroamericanos* 588:953-66.

Cruz, José Miguel, Álvaro Trigueros, and Francisco González. 2000. *El crimen violento en El Salvador. Factores sociales y económicos asociados*. San Salvador, El Salvador: Instituto Universitario de Opinión Pública and World Bank.

Dammert, Lucía. 2002. Participación comunitaria en la prevención del delito en América Latina ¿De qué participación hablamos? Cuadernos Area Seguirdad Ciudadana, Chile.

Dammert, Lucía, and Alejandra Lunecke. 2002. *Victimización y temor en Chile: Análisis teórico-empírico en doce comunas del país*. Chile: Serie Estudios del CESC, Universidad de Chile.

Dammert, Lucía, and Mary Malone. 2003. "Fear of crime or fear of life? Public insecurities in Chile." *Bulletin of Latin American Research* 22:79-101.

Dandler, Jorge. 1999. "Indigenous peoples and the rule of law in Latin America: Do they have a chance?" In *(Un)rule of law and the underprivileged in Latin America*, ed. Juan E. Méndez, Paulo Sérgio Pinheiro, and Guillermo O'Donnell, 116-51. South Bend, IN: Notre Dame Press.

Dávila, Andrés. 1999. "Ejército regular, conflictos irregulares: La institución militar en los últimos quince años." In *Reconocer la Guerra para Construir la Paz*, ed. Malcolm Deas and María Victoria Llorente, 284–345. Bogotá, Colombia: Editorial Norma, Ediciones Uniandes, FESCOL.

Davis, Shelton H. 1999. "Comments on Dandler." In *(Un)rule of law and the underprivileged in Latin America*, ed. Juan E. Méndez, Paulo Sérgio Pinheiro, and Guillermo O'Donnell, 152–59. South Bend, IN: Notre Dame Press.

Debrun, Michel. 1983. *La Conciliação e outras estratégias*. São Paulo, Brazil: Brasiliense.

Delgado, César. 1985. "Las Relaciones Públicas y su aplicación en Carabineros de Chile." *Informativo INSUCAR* (Instituto Superior de Carabineros) 5.

Dellasoppa, Emilio E. 2000. "Structure of social relations and collusion processes in Brazilian society." *Revista Internacional de Estudos Políticos* 2(3):535–56.

———. 2002a. "Estratégias e Racionalidade na Polícia Civil do Estado do Rio de Janeiro." In Violencia, sociedad y justicia en Amèrica Latino, ed. Roberto Briceño-León, 201–28. Buenos Aires, Argentina: CLACSO.

———. 2002b. "Violencia: Planos, oportunidades e o centro radical." *Polêmica* 5 (May–June). UERJ http://www2.uerj.br/~labore/violencia_dellasopa.htm.

———. 2003. "Corruption in post-authoritarian Brazil: An overview and many open questions." Discussion paper F-107, Institute of Social Science, University of Tokyo.

Díaz, Elías. 1985. *Estado de Derecho y sociedad democrática*. Madrid: Taurus.

Díaz Montes, Fausto, Gloria Zafra, and Salomón González Mechor. 1994. "Oaxaca: diversidad municipal y participación ciudadana." In *En busca de la democracia municipal*, ed. Mauricio Merino, 135–62. Mexico City: Colegio de México.

Dlott, Susan. 2001a. In re Cincinnati: Federal Court Order. Case no. C-1-99-317. United States District Court, Southern District of Ohio, Western Division, May 3, 2–3.

———. 2001b. In re Cincinnati: Federal Court Order. Case no. C-1-99-317. United States District Court, Southern District of Ohio, Western Division, June 18.

———. 2002. In re Cincinnati: The Collaborative Agreement. Case no. C-1-99-317. United States District Court, Southern District of Ohio, Western Division.

Dobry, Michel. 1986. *Sociologie des crises politiques*. Paris: Presses de la Fondation Nationale des Sciences Politiques.

Donolo, Carlo. 2001. *Disordine*. Rome: Donzelli Editore.

Donoso Pérez, Carlos. 1985. "La doctrina institucional y su relación con el order público." *Revista de Carabineros*.

Doyle, Charles. 2002. "The USA Patriot Act: A legal analysis." Library of Congress, Congressional Research Service, *CRS Report for Congress*, order code RL31377. Washington DC: CRS, April 15, 2003.

Drucker, Peter. 1996. *The executive in action: Managing for results*. New York: Harper Collins.

Echandía, Camilo. 1999a. *El conflicto armado y las manifestaciones de violencia en las regiones de Colombia*. Bogotá, Colombia: Oficina Alto Comisionado para la Paz—Presidencia de la República.

———. 1999b. "Expansión territorial de las guerrillas colombianas: Geografía, economía y violencia." In *Reconocer la Guerra para Construir la Paz*, ed. Malcolm Deas and María Victoria Llorente, 99–149. Bogotá, Colombia: Editorial Norma, Ediciones Uniandes, FESCOL.

Echeverri, Bernardo. 1993. "Tres décadas turbulentas." In *Historia de la Policía Nacional de Colombia*, ed. Álvaro Valencia Tovar, 145–239. Bogotá, Colombia: Planeta.

Echeverría, Mónica. 1993. *Anti Historia de un luchador (Clotario Blest 1823-1990)*. Santiago, Chile: LOM Ediciones.

Eck, John E. 1998. "Preventing crime by controlling drug dealing on private rental property." *Security Journal* 11(4):37–43.

Eck, John E., and Edward Maguire. 2000. "Have changes in policing reduced violent crime? An assessment of the evidence." In *The crime drop in America*, ed. Alfred Blumstein and Joel Wallman, 207–65. New York: Cambridge University Press.

Eck, John E., and William Spelman. 1987. *Problem-solving: Problem-oriented policing in Newport News*. Washington DC: Police Executive Research Forum.

Elias, Norbert. 1988. "Violence and civilization: The state monopoly of physical violence and its infringement." In *Civil society and the state*, ed. John Keane, 129–46. London: Verso.

———. 1995. *O processo civilizador*. Vols. 1 and 2. São Paulo, Brazil: Jorge Zahar Editores.

———. 1997. *Os Alemães*. São Paulo, Brazil: Jorge Zahar Editores.

Ellacuría, Ignacio. 1991. "La seguridad nacional y la Constitución salvadoreña." In *Veinte años de historia en El Salvador (1969-1989)*. Vol. 1, ed. Ignacio Ellacuría, 247–66. San Salvador, El Salvador: UCA.

Elster, Jon. 1990. *The cement of society*. New York: Cambridge University Press.

Fajnzylber, Pablo, Daniel Lederman, and Norman Loayza. 1998. *Determinants of crime rates in Latin America and the World: An empirical assessment*. World Bank Latin America and the Caribbean Studies. Washington DC: World Bank.

Farrell, Graham, and William Sousa. 2001. "Repeat victimization and hot spots: The overlap and its implications for crime control and problem-oriented policing." In *Repeat Victimization*, ed. Graham Farrell and Ken Pease, 221–40. Crime Prevention Studies, vol. 12. Monsey, NY: Criminal Justice Press.

Fedesarrollo. 2003. "Encuesta Social—Etapa VII." Mimeo. Bogotá, Colombia, February.

FESPAD (Fundación de Estudios para la Aplicación del Derecho). 1998. *Informe Seguridad Pública y Derechos Humanos. El Salvador 1997*. San Salvador, El Salvador: FESPAD.

——. 1999. *Informe Seguridad Pública y Derechos Humanos. El Salvador 1998.* San Salvador, El Salvador: FESPAD.

——. 2001. *Estado Actual de la Seguridad Pública y la Justicia Penal en El Salvador (junio 1999 – marzo 2001).* San Salvador, El Salvador: FESPAD.

——. 2002. *Estado de la Seguridad Pública y la Justicia Penal en El Salvador 2001.* San Salvador, El Salvador: FESPAD.

Foucault, Michel. 1995. *Discipline and punish: The birth of the prison.* New York: Vintage.

Frühling, Hugo. 1996. "Políticas públicas y seguridad ciudadana en un proceso de paz: La necesidad de un orden." Presentation to the Forum on Justice, Inter-American Development Bank, Guatemala.

——. 2001. "Las estrategias policiales frente a la inseguridad ciudadana en Chile." In *Policía, Sociedad y Estado. Modernización y reforma policial en América del Sur,* ed. Hugo Frühling and Azun Candina, 13–38. Santiago, Chile: CED

——. 2002. "Policía y Sociedad. Tres experiencias sudamericanas." Presentation to the International Conference on Policía y Comunidad, los nuevos desafíos en Chile, Santiago, Chile, December 4–5.

Fuentes, Claudio. 2002. "Resisting Change: Security Sector Reform in Chile." *Journal of Conflict, Security, and Development* 2(1):121–31.

——. 2003. "Denuncias por Violencia Policial en Chile, 1990–2000." *Boletín Policía y Sociedad.* Centro de Estudios para el Desarrollo, CED, March 11.

FUNDAUNGO and IUDOP (Fundación Dr. Guillermo Manuel Ungo and Instituto Universitario de Opinión Pública). 2002. *Encuesta sobre la percepción ciudadana a nivel nacional, municipal y zonal.* San Salvador, El Salvador: Ministerio de Seguridad Pública y Justicia.

Gaddis, John Lewis. 2002. "A grand strategy of transformation." *Foreign Policy* (November/December): 50–57.

Gallup Poll. 2001. "Black-white relations in the United States: 2001 update." *Gallup Poll Social Audit.* Washington DC, July 10.

GAO (U.S. Government Accountability Office). 2003. "FBI reorganization: Progress made in efforts to transform, but major challenges continue." Report no. GAO 003-759T, June 18.

Garretón, Manuel Antonio, and Edward Newman. 2002. Introduction. In *Democracy in Latin America: (Re)constructing political society,* ed. Manuel Antonio Garretón and Edward Newman, 3–15. New York: United Nations University Press.

Giddens, Anthony. 2001. *O Estado-nação e a violência.* São Paulo, Brazil: Edusp.

Goldsmith, Andrew, ed. 1991. *Complaints against the police: The trend to external review.* Oxford: Clarendon Press.

——. 1993. "Informe al Consejero Presidencial para la Defensa y Seguridad Nacional sobre la reforma a la Policía Nacional Colombiana." Mimeo. Bogotá, Colombia.

——. 2000. "Police accountability reform in Colombia." In *Civilian oversight of policing: Governance, democracy and human rights,* ed. Andrew Goldsmith and Colleen Lewis, 167–94. Oxford, UK: Hart.

Goldstein, Herman. 1990. *Problem-oriented policing.* New York: McGraw-Hill.

González, Luis Armando. 1996. "Cruzada contra la delincuencia: ¿Democracia versus autoritarismo?" *Estudios Centroamericanos* 576. http://www.uca.edu.sv/publica/eca.htm.

González Jorquera, Iván. 2001. *Proyecto de Reforma Constitucional referido a "Carabineros de Chile."* Mimeo. Santiago, Chile: Centro Nacional de Estudios del Orden.

Government of El Salvador. 1999. *La Nueva Alianza.* San Salvador, El Salvador: Government of El Salvador.

Gray, Barbara. 1991. *Collaborating: Finding common ground for multiparty problems.* San Francisco: Jossey-Bass.

Greene, Jack R., and Stephen D. Mastrofski, eds. 1988. *Community policing: Rhetoric or reality?* New York: Praeger.

Grupo Conjunto de Investigación de Grupos Armados Ilegales Armados con Motivación Política en El Salvador. 1994. *Informe.* Pamplet. San Salvador, El Salvador.

Guillén, Tonatiuh. 1996. *Gobiernos municipales en México: entre la modernización y tradición política.* Mexico City: Miguel Angel Porrúa.

Guzmán, Alvaro. 1999. "Teorías y políticas de seguridad ciudadana" In *Armar la Paz es Desarmar la Guerra,* ed. Alvaro Camacho and Francisco Leal. Bogotá, Colombia: IEPRI-Universidad Nacional de Colombia, FESCOL, and CEREC.

Guzmán, Juan Andrés. 2000. "El rap del desencanto." *Revista Paula,* June.

Guzmán Campos, Germán. 1986. *La violencia en Colombia: Estudio de un proceso social.* Bogotá, Colombia: Carlos Valencia Editores.

Haggard, Stephan, and Robert Kaufman. 1995. *The Political Economy of Democratic Transitions.* Princeton, NJ: Princeton University Press.

Harcourt, Bernard E. 2001. *Illusion of order: The false promise of broken windows policing.* Cambridge, MA: Harvard University Press.

Hernández, Rosalva Aída, and Héctor Ortíz Elizondo. 2003. "Diferentes pero iguales: Los pueblos indígenas en México y el acceso a la justicia." Paper presented at the Reforming the Administration of Justice in Mexico conference, Center for US-Mexican Studies, University of California, San Diego, May 15–17, 2003.

Holloway, Thomas H. 1997. *Polícia no Rio de Janeiro.* Rio de Janeiro: Editora Fundação Getúlio Vargas.

Hope, Tim. 1994. "Problem-oriented policing and drug market locations: Three case studies." In *Crime Prevention Studies,* ed. Ronald V. Clarke, 2:5–31. Monsey, NY: Criminal Justice Press.

Huezo, Miguel. 2000. "Cultura y violencia en El Salvador." In *Violencia en una sociedad en transición: Ensayos,* ed. PNUD, 115–37. San Salvador, El Salvador: Programa de las Naciones Unidas para el Desarrollo.

Human Rights Watch. 2001. *Military injustice: Mexico's failure to punish army abuses.* Vol. 13:4(B). http://hrw.org/reports/2001/mexico/mexi1201-02.htm.

Instituto Cidadanía. 2002. *Projeto Seguarança Pública para o Brasil.* Brasilia, Brazil: Instituto Cidadanía.

Instituto Ciudadano de Estudios sobre la Inseguridad, A.C. 2002. *Encuesta Nacional sobre Inseguridad Pública en las Entidades Federativas.* http://www.icesi.org.mx/icesi-org-mx/images/pdf/Inseguridad_01.pdf.

IUDOP (Instituto Universitario de Opinión Pública). 1992. "Visión del cumplimiento de los Acuerdos de Paz y valoraciones políticas de los salvadoreños." *Serie de informes 32.* San Salvador, El Salvador: IUDOP-UCA.

———. 1993a. "La delincuencia urbana: Encuesta exploratoria." *Estudios Centroamericanos* 534–35:471–82.

———. 1993b. "Los salvadoreños y la evaluación de 1993: Una consulta de opinión pública." *Estudios Centroamericanos* 541–42:1141–54.

———. 1994. "La delincuencia como problema nacional." *El Salvador Proceso* 629:14–16.

———. 1995. *Sondeo sobre la Procuraduría para la Defensa de los Derechos Humanos.* Serie de informes 50. San Salvador, El Salvador: IUDOP-UCA.

———. 1996. *Encuesta sobre Derechos Humano y el sistema judicial.* Serie de informes 57. San Salvador, El Salvador: IUDOP-UCA.

———. 1997. "La violencia en El Salvador en los Noventa: Magnitud, costos y factores posibilitadores." *Material del seminario "Promoviendo la convivencia ciudadana."* Cartagena, Colombia: Banco Mundial.

———. 1998. "Delincuencia y opinión pública." *Revista Estudios Centroamericanos (ECA)* 599:785–802.

———. 1999. *Normas culturales y actitudes hacia la violencia: Estudio Activa.* San Salvador, El Salvador: UCA.

———. 2002. *Evaluación del país a finales de 2002 y perspectivas electorales para 2003.* http://www.di.uca.edu.sv/publica/iudop/principal.htm.

Karmen, Andrew. 2000. *New York murder mystery: The true story behind the crime crash of the 1990s.* New York: New York University Press.

Kelling, George, Tony Pate, Duane Dieckman, and Charles E. Brown. 1974. *Kansas City preventive patrol experiment: A summary report.* Washington DC: Police Foundation.

Kravetz, Katharine. 1998. "Vigilando a la Policía: El Control de la Policía en los Estados Unidos." In *Control Democrático en el Mantenimiento de la Seguridad Interior,* ed. Hugo Frühling, 176. Santiago, Chile: Ediciones Segundo Centenario, Centro de Estudios para el Desarrollo.

Lagos, Marta. 2001. "How people view democracy: Between stability and crisis in Latin America." *Journal of Democracy* 12(January):137–45.

Latinobarómetro. 1998. *Informe de Prensa 1998*. http://www.latinobarometro.org/infopre98nr.htm.

———. 1999. *Encuesta Latinobarómetro*. Santiago, Chile: Mori.

———. 2001. *Encuesta Latinobarómetro*. Santiago, Chile: Mori.

———. 2002. *Informe de Prensa 2002*. www.latinobarometro.org/ano2002.htm.

———. 2003. *Encuesta Latinobarómetro*. Santiago, Chile: Mori.

Leal, Francisco. 1984. *Estado y Política en Colombia*. Bogotá, Colombia: CEREC–Siglo XXI.

———. 1994. *El Oficio de la Guerra. La Seguridad Nacional en Colombia*. Bogotá, Colombia: Tercer Mundo Editores–IEPRI, Universidad Nacional.

Lemoine, Carlos. 1997. *Iberoamérica habla*. Bogotá, Colombia: Organización de Estudios Iberoamericanos (OEI).

———. 2003. "El barómetro de la gobernabilidad." *Lecturas Dominicales-El Tiempo*, March 23.

Ley de la Policía Federal Preventiva. 1999. *Diario Oficial de la Federación* 544(1):6.

Ley Federal contra la Delincuencia Organizada. 1996. *Diario Oficial de la Federación* 518(5):6.

Ley General que Establece las Bases de Coordinación del Sistema Nacional de Seguridad Pública. 1995. *Diario Oficial de la Federación* 507(8):7.

Ley Orgánica de la Procuraduría General de la República. 2002. *Diario Oficial de la Federación* 591(19):20.

Lindblom, Charles E. 1978. "Defining the policy problem." In *Decisions, organizations and society,* ed. Francis G. Castles, David C. Potter, and D. J. Murray. New York: Penguin Books/Open University.

———. 1980. *The policy-making process*. Englewood Cliffs, NJ: Prentice Hall.

———. 1995. "The science of 'muddling' through." In *Public policy: The essential reading,* ed. Stella Theodoulou and Matthew Can, 113–17. New York: Prentice Hall.

Litwak, Robert. 2003. "The new calculus of pre-emption." *Survival* 44(4):1–27.

Llorente, Maria Victoria. 1999. "Perfil de la Policía Colombiana." In *Reconocer la Guerra para Construir la Paz,* ed. Malcolm Deas and María Victoria Llorente, 390–473. Bogotá, Colombia: Editorial Norma, Ediciones Uniandes, FESCOL.

———. 2003. "La Honda Crisis de la Policía." *Revista Semana Especial Issue: Colombia y el Mundo en el 2003* (December 22):84–86.

———. 2004. "La Experiencia de la Policía Comunitaria de Bogotá. Contexto y Balance." In *Calles más Seguras. Estudios de Policía Comunitaria en América Latina,* ed. Hugo Frühling. Washington DC: Banco Interamericano de Desarrollo.

Llorente, Maria Victoria, and Patricia Bulla. 1994. "En qué va la reforma de la Policía Nacional." *Política Colombiana* 4(4):15–20.

Llorente, María Victoria, and Mauricio Rubio, eds. 2003. *Elementos para una criminología local: Políticas de prevención del crimen y la violencia en ambitos urbanos*.

Bogotá, Colombia: Alcaldía de Bogotá, Ediciones Uniandes y Centro de Estudios sobre Desarrollo Económico.

Londoño, Fabio, and Guillermo Diettes. 1993. "Dependencias orgánicas mayores: Surgimiento y evolución." In *Historia de la Policía Nacional de Colombia*, ed. Alvaro Valencia Tovar, 285–364. Bogotá, Colombia: Planeta.

Londoño, Juan Luis, and Rodrigo Guerrero. 1999. *Violencia en America Latina: Epidemiología y Costos—Documento de Trabajo R-375.* Washington DC: Banco Interamericano de Desarrollo.

Loveday, Barry. 2000. "Managing crime: Police use of crime data as an indicator of effectiveness." *International Journal of the Sociology of Law* 28:215–37.

Loveman, Brian. 1999. *For la Patria: Politics and the armed forces in Latin America.* Wilmington, DE: Scholarly Resources Books.

Lyons, William. 1999. *The politics of community policing: Rearranging the power to punish.* Ann Arbor: University of Michigan Press.

Maldonado, Carlos. 1998. "Temas policiales chilenos." http://www.maldonado.de.vu.

March, James G., and Herbert A. Simon. 1958. *Organizations.* New York: Wiley and Sons.

Marchelli, Xochitl, and Jaime Martínez. 2002. *Acuerdos de Paz y Reforma Penal.* San Salvador, El Salvador: FESPAD.

Marenin, Otwin. 1996. *Changing police, policing change: International perspectives.* New York: Garland.

Martínez, Jaime. 2000. *Beneficios penitenciarios de las personas privadas de libertad.* San Salvador, El Salvador: FESPAD.

———. 2002. *La Policía en el Estado de Derecho Latinoamericano: Estudio sobre El Salvador.* San Salvador, El Salvador: Friedrich Ebert Stiftung/FESPAD.

Martínez, Javier, and Margarita Palacios. 1996. *Informe sobre la Decencia.* Santiago, Chile: Ediciones SUR, Colección Estudios Urbanos.

Mazerolle, Lorraine Green, Jan Roehl, and Colleen Kadleck. 1998. "Controlling social disorder using civil remedies: Results from a randomized field experiment in Oakland, California." In *Civil remedies and crime prevention*, ed. Lorraine Mazerolle and Jan Roehl, 141–60. Crime Prevention Studies, vol. 9. Monsey, NY: Criminal Justice Press.

McDonald, Phyllis Parshall. 2002. *Managing police operations: Implementing the New York crime control model—CompStat.* Belmont, CA: Wadsworth.

Méndez, Juan E., Guillermo O'Donnell, and Paulo Sérgio Pinheiro, eds. 1999. *The (Un)rule of law and the underprivileged in Latin America.* Notre Dame, Indiana: University of Notre Dame Press.

———. 2000. *Democracia, Violência e Injustiça. O Não-Estado de Direito na América Latina.* São Paulo, Brazil: Paz e Terra.

Menéndez Carrión, A. 2001. "The transformation of political culture." In *Democracy in*

Latin America. (Re)constructing political society, ed. Manuel Antonio Garretón and Edward Newman, 249–77. New York: United Nations University Press.

Merry, Sally Engle. 1992. "Anthropology, law, and transnational processes." *Annual Review of Anthropology* 21:357–79.

Mesquita Neto, Paulo de. 2001. "Crime, violence and political uncertainty in Brazil." In *Crime and policing in transitional societies—seminar report 8,* ed. Mark Shaw, 77–91. Johannesburg: Konrad Adenauer Stiftung and South African Institute of International Affairs.

Ministério da Justiça. 2000. *Plano Nacional de Seguarança Pública.* Brasilia, Brazil: MJ.

———. 2001. *Balanço de 500 dias de PNSP- Balanço Consolidado de Destaques.*

Ministerio de Defensa. 2002. "Fuerzas Armadas con el Concepto mas Favorable." http://www.mindefensa.gov.co/fuerza/fpconcepto.html.

Ministerio de Gobernación, Government of El Salvador. 2002. Crime statistics. http://www.gobernacion.gob.sv/web-Penales/Estadisticas-Penales.htm.

Ministerio del Interior Chile. 2004a. *Diagnóstico de la Seguridad Ciudadana en Chile.* Santiago, Chile: Foro de Expertos en Seguridad Ciudadana.

———. 2004b. *Resultados preliminares de la Encuesta Nacional de Seguridad Ciudadana.* Santiago, Chile: Foro de Expertos en Seguridad Ciudadana.

Misión Especial para la Policía Nacional. 2004. "Informe final entregado al Ministro de Defensa Nacional." Mimeo. Bogotá, Colombia, March 2.

Nadelmann, Ethan A. 1997. "The Americanization of global law enforcement: The diffusion of american tactics and personnel." in *Crime and law enforcement in the global village,* ed. William F. McDonald, 123–38. Highland Heights, KY, and Cincinnati, OH: Academy of Criminal Justice Sciences and Anderson Publishing.

Nader, Laura. 1990. *Harmony ideology: Justice and control in a Zapotec mountain village.* Stanford, CA: Stanford University Press.

National Research Council. 2004. *Fairness and effectiveness in policing: The evidence.* Washington DC: National Academies Press.

Neild, Rachel. 2002. *Sustaining reform: Democratic policing in Central America.* Washington DC: Washington Office on Latin America.

Neild, Rachel, and Melissa Zeigler. 2002. *From peace to governance: Police reform and the international community.* Washington DC: Washington Office on Latin America.

O'Donnell, Guillermo. 1994. "Delegative democracy." *Journal of Democracy* 5(1):55–69.

———. 1997. *Contrapuntos. Ensayos escogidos sobre autoritarismo y democratización.* Buenos Aires, Argentina: Paidós.

———. 1999. "Horizontal accountability in new democracies." In *The self-restraining state,* ed. Andreas Schedler, Larry Diamond, and Marc Plattner, 29–52. Boulder, CO: Lynne Rienner.

Office of Homeland Security. 2002. *National strategy for homeland security* (July). http://www.whitehouse.gov/homeland/book.

Oviedo, Enrique. 2002. "Democracia y seguridad ciudadana en Chile." In *Violencia, sociedad y justicia en América Latina,* ed. Roberto Briceño León, 313–38. Buenos Aires, Argentina: FLACSO.

Oviedo, Enrique, and Ximena Abogabir. 2000. "Participación ciudadana y espacio público." In *Espacio público y ciudadanía,* ed. Ofelia Segovia and Guillermo Dascal, 27–45. Santiago, Chile: SUR.

Oxhorn, Philip D., and Graciela Ducatensziler, eds. 1998. *What kind of democracy? What kind of market? Latin America in the age of neoliberalism.* College Park: Pennsylvania State University Press.

Paniagua, Carlos. 2002. "El bloque empresarial hegemónico salvadoreño." *Revista Estudios Centroamericanos (ECA)* 645–46:609–93.

Pardo, Rafael. 1996. *De primera mano. Colombia. 1986-1994 entre conflictos y esperanzas.* Bogotá, Colombia: Norma-CEREC.

Pinheiro, Paulo Sérgio. 1998. *São Paulo Sem Medo: Um diagnóstico da violência urbana.* Rio de Janeiro: Garamond.

———. 2001. "Transição política e não-estado de direito na República." In *Brasil, un século de transformações,* ed. Ignacy Sachs, Jorge Wilhem, and Paulo Sérgio Pinheiro, 260–305. São Paulo, Brazil: Companhia de las Letras.

Pizarro, Eduardo. 1991. *Las Farc (1949–1966). De la Autodefensa a la Combinación de Todas las Formas de Lucha.* Bogotá, Colombia: Tercer Mundo Editores.

PNC (Policía Nacional Civil). 2000. *La Alianza por la Seguridad y el nuevo modelo de seguridad pública. El combate al crimen organizado en El Salvador. Situación actual, planes y proyectos.* San Salvador, El Salvador: Dirección General PNC.

PNUD (Programa de las Naciones Unidas para el Desarrollo). 2000. *Violencia en una sociedad en transición. Ensayos.* San Salvador, El Salvador: PNUD.

Poder Ejecutivo de la Federación. 1995. *Plan Nacional de Desarrollo 1995–2000.* http://www.cddhcu.gob.mx/bibliot/publica/otras/pnd/pndind.htm.

———. 2001. *Plan Nacional de Desarrollo 2001–2006.* See esp. "Orden y Respeto." http://www.pnd.presidencia.gob.mx.

Polícia Militar do Estado de São Paulo, Conselho Geral da Comunidade, Grupo de Trabalho de Polícia Comunitária. 1993. "Projeto Polícia Comunitária." São Paulo, Brazil: Polícia Militar do Estado de São Paulo, Conselho Geral da Comunidade.

Policía Nacional. 1996. *La fuerza del Cambio No. 2.* Bogotá, Colombia: Imprenta Fondo Rotatorio de la Policía Nacional.

———. 1997. *La Fuerza del Cambio No. 3.* Bogotá, Colombia: Imprenta Fondo Rotatorio de la Policía Nacional.

Portes, Alejandro, and Kelly Hoffman. 2003. "Latin American class structures: Their composition and change during the neoliberal era." *Latin American Research Review* 38(1):41–82.

Presidencia de la República. 2000. *Sexto Informe de Gobierno.* Mexico City: Presidencia de la República.

————. 2001. *Primer informe de gobierno.* Mexico City: Presidencia de la República.

————. 2002. *Mensaje del C. Vicente Fox Quesada, Presidente de la República, con motivo de la presentación de su Segundo Informe de Gobierno.* Mexico City: Presidencia de la República.

————. 2003a. *Anexos Tercer Informe de Gobierno.* Mexico City: Presidencia de la República.

————. 2003b. *Tercer informe de gobierno.* Mexico City: Presidencia de la República.

Presidencia de la República–Consejería Presidencial para la Defensa y Seguridad Nacional. 1994a. La *nueva policía para Colombia.* Bogotá, Colombia: Imprenta Nacional Press.

————1994b. *Una política de seguridad para la convivencia.* Vol. 1. Bogotá, Colombia: Imprenta Nacional.

————. 1994c. *Una política de seguridad para la convivencia.* Vol. 2. Bogotá, Colombia: Imprenta Nacional.

————. 1994d. *Una política de seguridad para la convivencia. Instrumentos legales.* Tomo III. Bogotá, Colombia: Imprenta Nacional.

Presidencia de la República and Ministerio de Defensa Nacional. 2003. "Política de defensa y seguridad democrática." http://www.mindefensa.gov.co/politica/documentos/seguridad_democratica.pdf.

PRODH. 1995. *Guerrero 95: Represión y muerte.* Centro de Derechos Humanos "Miguel Agustín Pro Juárez," A.C. http://www.sjsocial.org/PRODH.

————. 1997. *Informe sobre la presunta implicación del ejército mexicano en violaciones a los derechos humanos en el Estado de Guerrero.* Centro de Derechos Humanos "Miguel Agustín Pro Juárez," A.C. http://www.sjsocial.org/PRODH.

Programa Nacional de Procuración de Justicia 2001–2006. 2002. *Diario Oficial de la Federación* 583(16):47.

Programa Nacional de Seguridad Pública 1995–2000. 1996. *Diario Oficial de la Federación* 514(14):37.

Programa Nacional de Seguridad Pública 2001–2006. 2003. *Diario Oficial de la Federación* 592(9):46.

Ramírez Sáiz, Juan Manuel, ed. 1998. *¿Cómo gobiernan Guadalajara? Demandas ciudadanas y respuestas de los ayuntamientos.* Mexico City: Miguel Ángel Porrúa, UNAM.

Ramos, Carlos Guillermo. 2000. "Marginación, exclusión social y violencia." In *Violencia en una sociedad en transición: Ensayos,* ed. PNUD, 65–82. San Salvador, El Salvador: Programa de las Naciones Unidas para el Desarrollo.

Ramos, Marcela, and Juan A. Guzmán. 2000. *La guerra y la paz ciudadana.* Santiago, Chile: LOM.

Ranum, Elin Cecilie. 2000. "Violence in post-war El Salvador: The impact on state-society relations." Master's thesis in Latin American politics, Institute of Latin American Studies, University of London.

———. 2002. *Violent crime in post-war El Salvador: An obstacle to the consolidation of democracy?* Trondheim, Norway: Hovedoppgave i historie, Historisk Institutt.

Rauch, Janine. 2000. "Police reform and South African transition." Paper presented at the South African Institute for International Affairs conference. www.csvr.org.za/papers/papsaiia.htm.

Reglamento de la Policía Federal Preventiva. 2000. *Diario Oficial de la Federación* 559 (18):36.

Revista de Carabineros. 1927a. "Conferencia del Colonel Armando Romo." No. 4.

———. 1927b. Editorial. No. 3.

———. 1932. Editorial. No. 18.

———. 1965. "Disciuso del Colonel Jorge Aranda en el funeral del Lt. Merino." Special section. No. 127.

———. 1981. "Misión y roles de Carabineros de Chile." No. 316.

———. 1987. Editorial. No. 385.

Reyes Heroles, Federico. 1999. *Memorial del mañana.* Mexico City: Editorial Taurus.

Rodés, Jesús. 1991. "Informe de la misión técnica de las Naciones Unidas para la creación de la Policía Nacional Civil de El Salvador." Unpublished manuscript.

Rodríguez, Alfredo. 2001. "La vivienda privada de ciudad." *Temas Sociales* 39. Working paper. Santiago, Chile: Sur.

Rojas, Carlos E. 1996. *La violencia llamada "limpieza social."* Bogotá, Colombia: CINEP.

Rosenbaum, Dennis P., ed. 1994. *The challenge of community policing.* Thousand Oaks, CA, London, and New Delhi: Sage.

Rothman, Jay. 1997. *Resolving identity based conflict in nations, organizations and communities.* San Francisco: Jossey-Bass.

———. 1999. "Conflict and creativity: Opening windows on new ideas." http://www.ariagroup.com/paper_training.html.

Rothstein, Bo, and David Stolle. 2002. "How political institutions create and destroy social capital: An institutional theory of generalized trust." Paper presented at the 98th meeting of the American Political Science Association, Boston, MA, August 29–September 2.

Rotker, Susana. 2000. *Ciudadanías del miedo.* Caracas, Venezuela: Nueva Sociedad.

Rowland, Allison M. 2001. "Population as a determinant of variation in local outcomes under decentralization: Illustrations from small municipalities in Bolivia and Mexico." *World Development* 29(8):1373–89.

———. 2003a. "Assessing decentralization: What role for municipal government in the administration of justice?" Center for U.S.-Mexican Studies, Project on Reforming the Administration of Justice in Mexico. http://repositories.cdlib.org/usmex/prajm/rowland.

————. 2003b. "La seguridad pública local en México: Una agenda sin rumbo." In *Gobiernos municipales en transición,* ed. Enrique Cabrero, 339–71. Mexico City: Miguel Angel Porrúa.

Rubio, Mauricio. 1999. *Crimen e impunidad: Precisiones sobre la violencia.* Bogotá, Colombia: Tercer Mundo Editores-CEDE.

Sánchez, Fabio, María Victoria Llorente, Jairo Nuñez, Marta Badel, Gustavo Salazar, and Carina Peña. 2001. "Investigación sobre Atraco Callejero, Robo de Automotores, Hurto a Residencias y a Establecimientos Comerciales en Bogotá. Informe Final." Bogotá, Colombia: CEDE-Uniandes y Alcaldía de Bogotá.

Sandoval, Ricardo. 2002. "Los modelos de policía comunitaria, como cambio doctrinario y procesos de modernización de las policías." Presented at Policía y Comunidad: Los nuevos desafíos para Chile Seminar, December 2002.

Schwartz, Karen D. 2002. "The data migration challenge." December 15. http://www. GovExec.com.

Secretaría de Gobernación. 2001. *Resultados Preliminares de la Encuesta Nacional de Cultura Política y Prácticas Ciudadanas 2001.* Mexico City: Dirección General de Desarrollo Político, Secretaría de Gobernación.

Secretaría de la Defensa Nacional. 2001. *Glosario de Términos Militares.* Mexico City: Colección Manuales del Ejército Mexicano.

Secretaría de Seguridad Pública. 2002a. *Boletín de Prensa.* Mexico City, February 3.

————. 2002b. "Convocatoria para Ocupar Grados de Suboficiales y Oficiales en los Agupamientos de las Fuerzas Federales de Apoyo." www.ssp.gob.mx/_h_pricipal/mar_pfp_2.html.

————. 2002c. "Reglamento del Secretariado Ejecutivo del Sistema Nacional de Seguridad Pública." *Diario Oficial de la Federación* 594(3):8.

SENASP. 2001. *SENASP Management Report for 2000.* Brasilia: MJ.

Sepúlveda, Daniela. 1996. "Violencia Urbana desde la perspectiva de miembros de Carabineros de Chile." Presentation to the Social Policies Workshop, Instituto de Sociología, Pontificia Universidad Católica de Chile, Santiago, Chile.

Serrano, Rosso José. 1999a. *Jaque Mate.* Bogotá, Colombia: Norma.

————. 1999b. "La Policía Comunitaria." *Revista Policía Nacional* 85 (January–March):238.

Sherman, Lawrence W., and John E. Eck. 2002. "Policing for crime prevention." In *Evidence-based crime prevention,* ed. Lawrence W. Sherman, David Farrington, Brandon Welsh, and Doris Layton MacKenzie, 295–329. New York: Routledge.

Sherman, Lawrence W., Denise Gottfredson, Doris MacKenzie, John Eck, Peter Reuter, and Shawn Bushway. 1997. "Preventing crime: What works, what doesn't, what's promising: A report to the United States Congress." http://www.ncjrs.org/works/.

Sieder, Rachel. 2001. "War, peace, and memory politics in Central America." In *The politics of memory: Transitional justice in democratization societies,* ed. Alexandra

Barahona de Brito, Carmen González-Enríquez, and Paloma Aguilar, 161–89. Oxford: Oxford University Press.

Silverman, Eli B. 1999. *NYPD battles crime: Innovative strategies in policing.* Boston: Northeastern University Press.

Skogan, Wesley G., and Susan M. Hartnett. 1997. *Community policing, Chicago style.* New York: Oxford University Press.

Smulovitz, Catalina. 2003. "Citizen insecurity and fear: Public and private responses in Argentina." In *Crime and violence in Latin America: Citizen security, democracy and the state,* ed. Hugo Frühling and Joseph Tulchin, 125–52. Washington DC and Baltimore: Woodrow Wilson Center Press and The Johns Hopkins University Press.

Soares, Luiz Eduardo. 2000. *Meu Casaco de General; 500 dias no front da Seguridad pública do Rio de Janeiro.* São Paulo, Brazil: Companhia de las Letras.

———. 2003. "Entrevista Aziz Filho." *Revista Isto É,* March 12, 2003. http://www.luizeduardosoares.com.br/docs/como_enfrentar_o_caos.1.doc.

Spelman, William, and Dale Brown. 1981. *Calling the police: Citizen reporting of serious crime.* Washington DC: Police Executive Research Forum.

Spence, Jack, David Dye, Mike Lanchin, and Geoff Thale. 1997. *Chapultepec: Five years later.* Washington DC: Hemisphere Initiatives.

Stanley, William. 1996. "International tutelage and domestic political will: Building a new civilian police in El Salvador." In *Changing police, policing change: International perspectives,* ed. Otwin Marenin, 37–77. New York: Garland.

Stanley, William, George Vickers, and Jack Spence. 1993. *Risking failure: The problems and promise of the new civilian police in El Salvador.* Boston and Washington DC: Hemisphere Initiatives and Washington Office on Latin America.

———. 1996. *Protectores y perpetradores. La crisis institucional de la Policía Nacional Civil Salvadoreña.* Boston and Washington DC: Hemisphere Initiatives and Washington Office on Latin America.

Stone, Christopher, and Chitra Bhanu. 2003. "Framework paper: Public-private partnerships for police reform." Paper presented at the Global Meeting on Public-Private Partnerships for Police Reform, Nanyuki, Kenya, January 12–15, 2003.

Stone, Christopher, and Heather Ward. 1998. "Country overview: Chile. Focus on Santiago." Presented to the Workshop on Police in Democratic Societies: Advancing Public Safety and Accountability, Vera Institute of Justice, Arden Conference Center, New Jersey.

Suprema Corte de Justicia de la Nación. 1996. Tesis del Pleno de la Suprema Corte de Justicia de la Nación (Tesis XXV/96, XXVII/96, XXVIII/96, XXIX/96 y XXX/96) in *Semanario Judicial de la Federación y su Gaceta.* Ninth Session. Vol. 3 (March). Mexico City: Suprema Corte de Justicia de la Nación.

Taylor-Powell, Ellen, Boyd Rossing, and Jean Geran. 1998. *Evaluating collaboratives: Reaching the potential.* Madison: Program Development and Evaluation of the University of Wisconsin Extension.

Tironi, Eugenio. 1990. *Autoritarismo, modernización y marginalidad.* Santiago, Chile: SUR.

Tomisek, Steven J. 2002. "Homeland security: The new role for defense." *Strategic Forum* 189(February):1–8.

Torres, Javier. 1994. "La ciudadanía pacta con su policía: El proceso de modernización de la Policía Nacional de Colombia." In *Orden mundial y seguridad,* ed. Francisco Leal and Juan Gabriel Tokatlián, 173–205. Bogotá, Colombia: Tercer Mundo Editores-SID-IEPRI.

———. 2002. "Se necesita una reforma!" *Revista Semana,* June 2. http://www.semana.com.

Torres Rivas, Edelberto. 1996. "La gobernabilidad centroamericana en los noventa. Consideraciones sobre las posibilidades democráticas en la posguerra." *Revista Papers* 49:17–31.

———. 2001. "Foundations: Central America." In *Democracy in Latin America: (Re)constructing political society,* ed. Manuel Antonio Garretón and Edward Newman, 99–125. New York: United Nations University Press.

Treverton, Gregory F. 2002. "Intelligence, law enforcement, and homeland security." Report prepared for the Century Foundation's Homeland Security Project. http://www.homelandsec.org./publications.asp?pubid=278.

Tudela, Patricio. 2001a. "Seguridad, policía y comunidad." *Revista Detective ANEPE,* May.

———. 2001b. "Seguridad y políticas públicas." *Revista Detective ANEPE,* May, 65–69.

Turbiville, Graham H., Jr. 2001. "Las múltiples misiones de la Fuerza de Seguridad Interna de México." *Military Review* [Hispano-American] 81(2):49–58.

UNDP (United Nations Development Program). 1998. *Desarrollo Humano en Chile: Las paradojas de la modernización.* http://www.desarrollohumano.cl/textos/sin1998/informes/2cop1.pdf.

———. 2002. *Informe de Desarrollo Humano 2002: Profundizar la democracia en un mundo fragmentado.* Madrid: Editorial Mundi-Prensa Libros, S.A.

———. 2003. *Armas de Fuego y Violencia.* San Salvador, El Salvador: Programa Sociedad sin Violencia.

United Nations. 1997. "Informe de evaluación del sector Seguridad Pública presentado por ONUSAL el 28 de septiembre de 1995 a solicitud del Presidente de la República." In *Ejecución de los Acuerdos de Paz en El Salvador. Recalendarizaciones, acuerdos complementarios y otros documentos importantes,* 93–113. San Salvador, El Salvador: Oficina de Apoyo de las Naciones Unidas en El Salvador.

Universidad de Antioquia-Instituto de Estudios Políticos. 1994. "La imagen social de la policía en Medellín." *Institución policial y crisis, Estudios Políticos* 5(December):47–67.

University of Michigan. 2000. World Values Survey 2000. Ronald Inglehart, coordinator. http://wvs.isr.umich.edu/ques4.shtml.

U.S. Customs and Border Protection. 2004. "U.S. Customs and Border Protection announces staggering arrest numbers using anti-terror technology." Press release, October 7. http://www.chp.gov/xp/cgov/newsroom/press_releases/10072004.xml.

Vargas, Mauricio, Jorge Lesmes, and Edgar Téllez. 1996. *El presidente que se iba a caer.* Bogotá, Colombia: Planeta.

Velásquez, Jorge Enrique. 1993. *Cómo me infiltré y engañé al Cartel.* Bogotá, Colombia: Editorial Oveja Negra.

Vigil Recinos, Jaime. 2003a. "El Salvador's National Public Security System. An overview." Unpublished manuscript.

———. 2003b. "The more police reform, the more democracy in El Salvador." Unpublished manuscript.

Villaroel Altamirano, Jorge. 2002. "La asociación entre investigadores y policías." In *Violencia o intimidacion,* ed. Villaroal Altamirano. Santiago, Chile: Instituto de Asuntos Publicos, Universidad de Chile.

Wacquant, Loïc. 2000. *Las cárceles de la miseria.* Madrid: Alianza Editorial.

Waiselfisz, Jacobo. 2002. *Mapa da Violência III.* Brasília: Unesco, Instituto Ayrton Senna, and Ministério da Justiça/State Secretary for Human Rights.

Walklate, Sandra. 1998. "Crime and community: Fear or trust?" *British Journal of Sociology* 49(4):550–69.

Ward, Heather. 2001. "Police reform in Latin America: Current efforts in Argentina, Brazil, and Chile." Presented to the working group on citizen security, Woodrow Wilson International Center for Scholars, Washington DC.

Weitzer, Ronald. 1995. *Policing under fire: Ethnic conflict and police-community relations in Northern Ireland.* Albany: State University of New York Press.

Whitehead, Laurence. 2002. *Democratization: Theory and experience.* Oxford: Oxford University Press.

Wieworka, Michael. 1997. *Une societé fragmentée.* Paris: La Découverte.

Wilson, James Q., ed. 1983. *Crime and public policy* . San Francisco: Transactions.

Wilson, James Q., and George L. Kelling. 1982. "The police and neighborhood safety: Broken windows." *Atlantic Monthly,* March.

Woodward, Bob. 2002. *Bush at war.* New York: Simon and Schuster.

World Health Organization. 2002. *Report on violence and health.* New York: Vintage Books.

Zartman, William, and Maureen Berman. 1982. *The practical negotiator.* New Haven, CT: Yale University Press.

Zepeda Lecuona, Guillermo. 2002. "Las cifras de la impunidad. La procuración de justicia penal en México." *Renglones* (Revista del ITESO, Guadalajara) 51(May–August):63–71.

Ziccardi, Alicia, ed. 1995. *La tarea de gobernar: Gobiernos locales y demandas ciudadanas.* Mexico City: Miguel Ángel Porrúa.

CONTRIBUTORS

EDGARDO ALBERTO AMAYA is an academic researcher in criminal justice, public security, and human rights in the Centro de Estudios Penales de El Salvador (Center for Penal Studies of El Salvador) of the Fundación de Estudios para la Aplicación del Derecho (Foundation of Studies for Law Enforcement).

JOHN BAILEY is professor of government and foreign service at Georgetown University.

AZUN CANDINA is assistant professor in the Historical Sciences Department, Universidad of Chile, and at Citizen Security Area, Centro de Estudios de Desarrollo (Center of Development Studies), Santiago, Chile.

JOSÉ MIGUEL CRUZ has been director of the University Institute of Public Opinion at Universidad Centroamericana since 1994. He is a member of the editorial staff for the *Central American Journal of Studies* and a researcher for various international organizations.

LUCÍA DAMMERT is a researcher at the Facultad Latinoamericana de Ciencias Sociales, Chile.

GONZALO DE FRANCISCO Z. is currently vice president of community relations at Dattis.com, a Colombian enterprise dedicated to strategic communication, and senior aide of the Municipality of Bogotá in the design of a public-security model.

EMILIO ENRIQUE DELLASOPPA is professor and board member of the Public Policies Laboratory at the State University of Rio de Janeiro.

PAULO DE MESQUITA NETO is a senior researcher at the Center for the Study of Violence at the University of São Paulo and executive secretary at the Institute São Paulo against Violence.

JOHN E. ECK is professor of criminal justice at the University of Cincinnati.

MARIA VICTORIA LLORENTE has been coordinator of the Public Peace Program of the Center for Development Studies at the University of the Andes in Bogotá since 1998.

MARCOS PABLO MOLOEZNIK is a research professor at the Main Campus of Social Science and Humanities of the University of Guadalajara, Mexico.

JAY ROTHMAN is president of the ARIA Group, Inc., a conflict-resolution training and consulting company, and founder and research director of the Action Evaluation Research Institute.

ALLISON M. ROWLAND is a specialist in local government and public policy in the Department of Public Administration at Centro de Investigación y Docenia Econòmicas, in Mexico City, where she has worked since 1997.

ZORAIA SAINT'CLAIR BRANCO has been delegado de polícia of the Civil Police in the state of Rio de Janeiro since 1994.

INDEX

Afghanistan, 217–18

Agencia Federal de Investigación. *See* Federal Investigation Agency (AFI)

Agreement of Chapultepec, 153–54, 160–61

al Qaeda, 217–18

Alckmin, Geraldo, 50

Alessandri, Arturo, 82

Altamirano, Jorge Villaroel, 89

American Civil Liberties Union, 223, 225, 229, 231, 237

Andrus Family Fund, 231

Anticrime Plan (Chile), 71

antiterrorism measures, 211–17, 250; coordination of, 215–18; evaluation of, 222; intelligence gathering and 217; personnel and 217; public perception of, 223. *See also* terrorism

At-Risk Neighborhoods (Chile), 68, 72

Attorney General's Office (PGR), 174, 176, 181–85

Aylwin, Patricio, 62–3, 70, 85, 87

Barco, Virgilio, 99–100

Barrios Vulnerables. *See* At-Risk Neighborhoods (Chile)

Bastos, Márcio Thomaz, 37, 43

Blest, Clotario, 81

Block Watch Plan (Chile), 71, 81, 91

Bloque de Búsqueda. *See* Search Bloc

Bogotá, 10, 105–6, 112, 114, 128

Brazil: 246–58; community policing, 48; constitution, 25–26, 32, 47, 265n6; drug trafficking, 28; government, 5, 26, 34, 45–46; gun control, 28; homicide rates, 8, 44, 55, 267n1; human rights, 53–54; interagency coordination, 40–41; organized crime, 42–43, police, 33, 45–47, 264n1, 265n8, 266n11, 267n3; police misconduct, 47–48, 54; police reform, 24, 34–35, 44–45, 48–50, 56, 266n19; police training, 29–30; public perception of security in, 26–27; public security, 35, 41, 47; security reform, 33, 49, 266nn15–17; victimization surveys, 8; violence, 38

Brizola, Leonel, 46

Bureau of Judicial and Investigative Police (DIJIN), 107

Bush, George W., 208, 211–12, 217

Business Against Crime (South Africa), 55

Cali (city), 114

Cali cartel, 98, 100–102, 118, 125, 129

campesino soldiers, 116, 274n10

Cano, Guillermo, 100

Carabineros (Chile), 19, 22, 61, 73, 246–47, 252–55, 259, 270n1; anthem, 75–76; and community policing in, 90–91; conflict in, 88; criticism of, 79–80; description of, 76, 86; evaluation of, 71; financial aspects of, 64–65, 87–88; identity in, 75–76, 81–83, 86, 91–92; misconduct in, 84–85, 92, 270n5; origins of, 80–81; politics in, 70, public perception of, 61–62, 79–81, 84–85; purpose of, 75–76, 81–83, 90; reform, 65, 68–70, 88–89, 92–93; studies of, 79

Carabineros (Colombia), 116, 122–3, 131, 271n7

Cardoso, Fernando Henrique, 24, 28–35, 39–42, 50

Center for Development Studies, 87

Center for Research and National Security (CISEN), 177–78, 283n8

Center for Social Studies (SUR), 79, 87

Center for Strategic Police Information (CIEP), 105–7

Center for the Study of Violence (Brazil), 49–53, 268n6

Central de Inteligencia de la Policía Nacional. *See* Police Intelligence Agency

Central Intelligence Agency (CIA), 216–19

Centro de Estudios para el Desarrollo. *See* Center for Development Studies

Centro de Estudios Sociales. *See* Center for Social Studies (SUR)

Centro de Información Estratégica Policial. *See* Center for Strategic Police Information (CIEP)

Centro de Investigación y Seguridad Nacional. *See* Center for Research and National Security (CISEN)

Cerqueira, Nilton, 25, 41

Chiapas (Mexico), 188

Chile, 246–59; citizen security, 58, 73, 93; community policing, 90; constitution, 61; crime rates, 59, 69; criminal justice system, 67; democracy, 62–63; government, 5; human rights 61, 63, 70; military dictatorship, 60–63; national security, 83; National Security Doctrine, 61; police, 60, 64, 75–93; police misconduct, 79–80, 84–85; police reform, 22, 65, 74, 77–78, 91, 269n6; politics, 61; prisons, 269n3; security policy, 60, 64, 68–69, 74, 268n1; security reform, 62–63, 66–69, 93; victimization surveys, 8, 59. *See also* Carabineros (Chile)

Cincinnati, 246, 249–52, 264n11; police-citizen conflict, 227–32, 243; police miscon-duct, 226–29, 237–38; police reform, 225, 230–34, 240, 288n10

Cincinnati Black United Front, 225, 229, 231, 237, 242

Cincinnati Community Action Now (CCAN), 238

Cincinnati Fraternal Order of Police, 230–31

Cincinnati Police Department, 226, 229, 234, 287n2; race relations, 225–29, 238; training, 228–29

Citizen Complaint Authority, 237

Citizen Peace Foundation (Chile), 68, 73, 87

Citizen Police Review Panel, 227, 237

Citizen Protection Committees (Chile), 66

Citizen Security Division (Chile), 68–69

citizen security, 14, 257; Chile, 58, 66, 73, 87, 93; Colombia, 95, 103–6; community involvement in, 58, 66–68, 71–74 108–10, 120–24, 127–29, 269n9; evaluation of, 71; financial aspects of, 64–65, 73, 296n5; interagency coordination and, 101, 106; legislation and, 63; public perception of, 129–30; reform, 58, 63, 68–70

citizens: involvement in intelligence gathering, 219–20; involvement in security, 173, 186

civil liberties, 5, 10–13, 18, 254, 260; public perception of, 206–8; in United States, 206, 212–13, 222–23

civilian police, 258

coca base, 96–98, 102

cocaine, 96–98, 102, 175, 193

Cold War, 205, 224

collaborative agreement (Cincinnati), 225, 240–44

Colombia, 245–49, 252, 258; citizen security in, 103–6; community policing in, 128; constitution of, 273n5; drug trafficking in, 96–105, 110, 125; government of, 263n3, 271n3; guerrillas in, 96–105, 112–13, 118–19, 122, 128–30; gun control in, 105, 272n16; homicide rates in, 99, 105, 119; human rights in, 118; insecurity in, 10, 117; kidnapping in, 96–97, 104, 111; national police, 94, 97–98, 101–3, 107, 271n4, 273n1, 273n3; paramilitaries, 97–98,

100–105, 122; police, 94, 271n4, 273n1, 273n3; police misconduct, 119–20, 125–26; police reform in, 22, 104–30, 272n14, 273n2; public security, 111, 274n11; security reform, 121–22, 271n2; and the United States, 109–10; victimization surveys, 8, 119. *See also* Carabineros (Colombia); Policía Nacional (Colombia)

Comisión Investigadora de Hechos Delictivos. *See* Commission to Investigate Criminal Acts (CIHD)

Commission to Investigate Criminal Acts (CIHD), 156–57

Community Policing Partnering Center, 242

Community Policing Program, 106

community policing, 57, 111, 140, 203, 234–36, 243, 252–53, 257, 276n43; Brazil, 46–48, 52; Chile, 90–91; Colombia, 128; El Salvador, 143, 279n12; Mexico, 188

COMPSTAT, 107, 140–41, 228, 249, 252, 288n5

Comuna Segura Compromiso 100. *See* Safer Cities Program (Chile)

Concertación, 85–86

Concha, Marcial Rafael Macedo de la, 170

Consejo de Seguridad Pública. *See* Public Security Council (Chile)

Correa, Hernán Merino, 83

Costa Chica (Mexico), 188–91

Covas, Mario, 48, 50

crime: Mexico, 190, 193; surveys, 8, 263n5; trends, 8–9

crime rates, 1, 6–7, 272n15; Chile, 59, 69; El Salvador, 279n13; Mexico, 282n2; United States, 209, 211

Crime Stoppers, 51, 54–55

criminology, 250–51

Cristiani, Alfredo, 134, 155

Cuerpos de Seguridad Pública. *See* Public Security Forces (CUSEP)

da Silva, Luis Inâcio Lula, 30–32, 37–39, 41–42, 50

democracy, 2, 50, 148–51

Democratic Party, 220–21

Democratic Security proposal, 111

Department of Homeland Security (DHS), 214–19, 222, 255–56

Dirección de Policía Judicial e Investigación. *See* Bureau of Judicial and Investigative Police

Dirty War (Mexico), 192

Disque-Denúncia. *See* Crime Stoppers

División de Seguridad Ciudadana. *See* Citizen Security Division (Chile)

Dlott, Susan, 225, 229–32, 239, 241

domestic security: United States, 205–6

drug trafficking, 15, 22, 31, 99–105, 117–18, 258, 274n12; Brazil, 28; Chile, 72; Colombia 96–98, 110, 125; Mexico 174–75, 193–94; United States, 208–9

Eck, John, 234, 238

EFICACIA, 140

Ejército de Liberación Nacional. *See* National Liberation Army (ELN)

Ejército Popular Revolucionario. *See* Popular Revolutionary Army

El Salvador, 247–361; civil war, 132, 148, 152; community policing in, 143, 279n12; constitution of, 135; crime rates in, 137–39, 279n13; government, 5–6, 277n2; gun control in, 145; homicide rates, 145, 152; human rights in, 134–35; judicial reform, 136; paramilitaries, 133; parapolice, 133; police, 140; police misconduct, 157–59, 278n4, 278n11, 280n8, 281n10, 281n13, 281n15; police reform, 22, 138–68, 278n9, 281nn11–12; politics, 135, prisons, 141; public security, 135, 153, 168, 277n1; security, 133; security reform, 134–35, 138–40, 145–47, 154, 164–67, 278n8, 278n10, 278nn14–15; and the United States, 142; victimization surveys, 8, 137; violence, 152–53. *See also* National Civil Police (PNC)

Escobar, Pablo, 99, 101, 118, 272n9

Escuelas de Seguridad. *See* Security Schools

Espírito Santo, 31, 35–36, 42–43

Farabundo Martí Front for National Liberation (FMLN), 132–34, 154–55, 167

Federal Bureau of Investigation (FBI), 216–18, 287n13

Federal Investigation Agency (AFI), 173, 181–86, 283n13, 284n14

Federal Preventative Police (PFP), 173–81, 185–86, 258, 283n7–10

Ferreira, Aloysio Nunes, 34

Fondos Locales de Seguridad. *See* Local Security Funds

Foucault, Michel, 251

Foundation for Law Enforcement Studies (FESPAD), 135, 160

Fox, Vicente (Quesada), 169–74, 185–86

fracasomanía, 20, 23

Frei, Eduardo, 63, 68, 70

Frente Farabundo Martí para la Liberación Nacional. *See* Farabundo Martí Front for National Liberation (FMLN)

Frente Nacional. *See* National Front

Frentes de Seguridad. *See* Neighborhood Security Fronts

Frentes de Seguridad Local. *See* Local Security Fronts

Fuerzas Armadas Revolucionarias de Colombia. *See* Revolutionary Armed Forces of Colombia (FARC)

Fundación de Estudios para la aplicación del derecho. *See* Foundation for Law Enforcement Studies (FESPAD)

Fundación Paz Ciudadana. *See* Citizen Peace Foundation (Chile)

Fundo Nacional de Segurança Pública. *See* National Public Security Fund (FNSP)

Gacha, Gonzalo Rodriguez, 99

Galan, Luis Carlos, 100

Gallup poll, 211, 220–21

Garotinho, Anthony, 42

Gaviria, César, 100, 119–20

Giuliani, Rudolph, 248

Globo Television, 49, 51, 53, 268n6

Gomes, Paulo César Hartung, 43

government, 5–6, 26, 34; Brazil, 45–46; Colombia, 263n3, 271n3; El Salvador, 277n2; Mexico, 189–90

Gratz, José Carlos, 42–43

Guerrero (Mexico), 187, 191–92, 247, 251, 284n3

guerrillas, 15, 19, 258–59; Colombia, 95–105, 111–13, 118–19, 122, 128, 130, 274n19

gun control: Brazil, 28; Colombia, 105, 272n16; El Salvador, 145

heroin, 193

homeland security, 14, 205–12, 220, 223

homicide rates, 7–8; Brazil, 44, 55, 267n1; Colombia, 99, 105, 119, 271n8; El Salvador, 145, 152; Sao Paulo, 55

hot spot policing, 235–36

human rights, 2, 13–25, 18, 191, 254–61; Brazil, 40, 53–54; Chile, 61–63, 70; Colombia, 118; El Salvador 134–35; Mexico, 170–72, 187, 194; and police misconduct, 150, 161–62; policía nacional and, 118; and policing, 77–78; public perception of, 165; and public security, 163

Ibáñez, Carlos, 80–82

Immediate Service Centers (CAIs), 114, 120, 273n4

immigration: to the United States, 207, 285n2

import substitution industrialization, 4

indigenous populations: Mexico, 187–204

insecurity, 1, 4–7, 10–11, 22–23; Colombia, 117; public perception of, 39, 59–60, 137, 220, 247; United States, 207

Instituto Libertad y Democracia. *See* Liberty and Democracy Institute (Chile)

Instituto São Paulo Contra a Violência. *See* São Paulo Institute Against Violence (ISPCV)

Insulza, José Miguel, 70

intelligence gathering, 213–20, 250

Interior Ministry (SEGOB), 179–81, 185–87

Internal Investigation Section (IIS), 227, 237

Iraq, 217–18, 221

Jorquera, Iván González, 86

judicial system: United States, 209–10

Juntas Vecinales. *See* Neighborhood Councils

kidnapping, 31, 43; Colombia, 96–97, 104, 111

la violencia, 94–95, 112, 347
Lagos, Ricardo, 66, 68, 70, 253
Las Condes, 89
Lavin, Joaquin, 89, 270n8
law and order, 206
law enforcement: military involvement in, 218–19
Liberty and Democracy Institute (Chile), 68
Local Security Fronts, 128
Local Security Funds, 107
Lopes, Tim, 31
Luz, 41
Luz, Hélio Tavares, 24, 41

Maluco, Elias, 31
Maranhão (state), 46
marijuana, 98, 175, 193
Martínez, Maximiliano Hernández, 133
Marxism, 251
mass media, 6, 59, 144, 233
Massacre of Carandiru, 47
Medellín (city), 114, 118
Medellín cartel, 98–102, 118
mediation, 239–40
Merchant Chamber (India), 55
Metropolitan Forum for Public Security, 53
Mexico, 246–48, 251–58, 262; community policing, 188; constitution 169–70, 175, 189, 195, 200–202, 285n7; crime, 190–93; crime rates, 170–72, 282n2; criminal justice system, 183–84; drug trafficking, 174–75, 193–94; government, 5–6, 189–90; human rights, 170–72, 187, 191, 194; indigenous populations, 187–204; military, 180; organized crime, 174–75; police, 187–204; police misconduct, 194, 285n5; police reform, 177–204; politics, 192, 196, 284n4; poverty, 172–73; prisons, 176–77; public security, 169–76, 181–82, 185–91, 203, 282n1; security reform, 184–86, 283n6, 283n11; victimization surveys, 8; police reform, 204. *See also* Federal Preventative Police (PFP); policía comunitaria (Mexico)
military: involvement in public security, 170,

186, 257–58, 264n9, 280n9; relation to police, 15, 18, 83–4, 280n5
Minas Gerais (state), 46, 48
Miranda, Rodney, 43
Montaña de Guerrero (Mexico), 188–92
Montoro, Franco, 46
Mueller, Robert S., III, 217
municipios, 189–91

Nairobi Central Business District Association, 55
National Civil Police (PNC), 132–68, 278n6, 279n17, 280n19
National Council for Community and Justice, 238
National Council on Public Security (CNSP), 135, 139, 143–45, 277n3, 278n5
National Counterterrorism Center, 218
National Defense Law, 142–43, 146
National Defense Secretariat (SEDENA), 177–80, 283n8, 283n10
National Front (Colombia) 95, 112
National Guard, 218, 258
National Liberation Army (ELN), 95–96, 104, 272n12
National Plan for Public Security (PNSP), 24–37
national police (El Salvador), 153–56, 162
National Police Corps, 112
National Public Security Fund (FNSP), 30–31, 266n12
National Public Security System (SNSP), 173–81, 185, 283n12
National Secretariat for Public Security (SENASP), 25, 27, 30, 37, 255
National Security Doctrine (Chile), 61
national security: Chile, 83; definition of, 1–2, 11; El Salvador, 133; United States, 205–6
National Strategy for Homeland Security, 211–14
Nato, Arthur Virgílio, 34
Neighborhood Councils, 164
Neighborhood Security Fronts, 108
Neighborhood Security Program (Chile), 66
neighborhood watch, 252–53
Neves, Tancredo, 46

New Orleans Police Foundation, 55

nongovernmental organizations, 50–53, 144, 254

O Globo, 35

Office of Municipal Investigations (OMI), 227, 237

Open Door Program (Chile), 65

Orejuela, Rodríguez, 102

organized crime, 2, 31, 35; Brazil, 42–43; definition of, 282n5; Mexico 174–75

paramilitaries, 100–105, 258–59, 271n6; Colombia, 97–98, 122, 274n19; El Salvador, 133

parapolice: El Salvador, 133

Pastrana, Andrés, 102, 111

Perez, Francisco Flores, 138

Pinilla, Gustavo Rojas, 95

Pinochet, Augusto, 64, 246, 259

Plan Antidelincuencia. *See* Anticrime Plan (Chile)

Plan Avansa Brasil, 27, 265n9

Plan Colombia, 102–3

Plan Cuadrante. *See* Block Watch Plan (Chile)

Plano Nacional de Segurança Pública. *See* National Plan for Public Security

police: Brazil, 45–47, 265n8, 266n11, 267n3; Chile 60, 64, 75–93; Colombia, 94, 271n4, 273n1, 273n3; definition of, 19; description of, 76–77; El Salvador, 140; evaluation of, 71; financial aspects of, 45, 72, 269n4; indigenous, 20, 187–204; Mexico, 187–204; militarization of, 61; public perception of, 9–10, 19–20, 160–62, 246, 264n1, 270n1 (chap. 6), 282n4; purpose of, 94, 149–51; and racial profiling, 225; relation to military, 15, 18, 83–84, 280n5; strikes, 48, 267n20; training, 29–30, 109; United States, 206, 209, 216. *See also individual police forces by country*

Police Intelligence Agency, 125

police misconduct, 250, 254, 276n39; Brazil, 47–48, 54; Carabineros (Chile), 84–85, 92, 270n5; Chile 79–80, 84–85; Cincinnati, 225–29, 237–38; Colombia, 119–20, 125–26; El Salvador, 157–59, 278n4, 278n11, 280n8, 281n10, 281n13, 281n15; human rights and, 150, 161–62; Mexico, 194, 285n5; public perception of, 166

Police Ombudsman (Brazil), 48

police reform, 2–3, 18–22, 245–49, 254, 261, 264n10, 275n29, 275n31; Brazil, 24–57, 266n19; business involvement in, 45–57; Chile, 22, 65, 74, 77–78, 91, 269n6; Cincinnati, 225–40, 288n10; Colombia, 22, 104–30, 272n14, 273n2; El Salvador, 22, 138–68, 278n9, 281nn11–12; evaluation of, 201–2, 241–42, 260; coordination, 47–57; Mexico, 177–204; objectives of, 44–45; public perception of, 23; South Africa, 56; United States, 22, 56. *See also individual police forces by country*

police-citizen conflict: Cincinnati, 227–32, 243

police-civilian cooperation, 13

policía comunitaria (Mexico), 187–204, 270n9, 285n6; evaluation of, 201–2; financial aspects of, 196–98; judicial system and, 198–99; legality of, 200–202; opposition to, 199–202; origin of, 195–96; personnel, 197; public perception of, 194; structure, 188–89, 197; weaknesses of, 203

Policía Federal Preventiva. *See* Federal Preventative Police (PFP)

Policía Nacional (Colombia), 95–110, 113–31, 271n7, 275n22, 277n44; criticism of, 119; deaths 274n15, 274n18; and drug trafficking, 117; effectiveness, 120; and human rights, 118; identity, 113, 128–31; misconduct, 118–20, 125–26; personnel, 115–17, 122–24, 130–31, 272n11, 273n8, 275n20, 275n28, 276n32, 276n34; public perception of, 117–18, 129; reform, 114, 120–30; structure, 114–17, 123–24, 127, 273n6; training, 113, 124, 127, 131

policing: and human rights, 77–78; models, 77, 252, 289n3; strategies, 234–36, 243; studies, 77–78

politics: Chile, 61; and public security, 32

Popular Revolutionary Army, 194

poverty: Mexico, 172–73
Price, Harvey, 226
prisons, 249; Chile, 269n3; El Salvador, 141; Mexico, 176–77
private security, 45, 49, 256; Mexico, 177
problem-oriented policing, 236, 250
Procuraduría General de le República. *See* Attorney General's Office (PGR)
Program for Shared Security (Chile), 65
Programa Puertas Abiertas. *See* Open Door Program (Chile)
Programa Seguridad Compartida. *See* Program for Shared Security (Chile)
public safety: United States, 206
Public Security Council (Chile), 63
Public Security Forces (CUSEP), 132–34
Public Security Secretariat (SSP), 173, 179–81, 185
public security, 13, 245, 253, 259; Brazil, 35, 41, 47; business involvement in, 50; citizen involvement in, 186; Colombia, 111, 274n11; community involvement in, 143, 173, 267n22; definition of, 1–2, 11, 25–26; El Salvador, 135, 153, 168, 277n1; evaluation of, 181, 260–61; financial aspects of, 176; and human rights, 163; and intelligence gathering, 264n8; and interagency coordination, 40–41, 45, 50–53, 255–56; Mexico, 169–76, 182, 185–91, 203, 282n1; military involvement in, 170, 180, 186; models, 141; policies, 18–19, 23, 38–42; and politics, 32, 144–47, 245–49; public perception of, 26–27, 136–37, 153–54, 161–64, 171–72, 249; symbolism, 248; United States, 206; use of military forces, 135–36

race relations: Cincinnati, 225–29, 238
racial profiling, 20, 225–30, 285n3, 287n4
Reale, Miguel, 35, 42
Rebouças, João Batista, 36
repeat victims, 235–36
Republican Party, 220–22, 247
Revista de Carabineros, 80, 84
Revolutionary Armed Forces of Colombia (FARC), 95–97, 104, 272n12

Ribeiro, Paulo de Tarso, 42
Rio de Janeiro (city), 41, 258
Rio de Janeiro (state), 31, 35, 42, 46, 48
Rio Grande do Sul (state), 48
Rivero, Ángel Aguirre, 195, 198
Rothman, Jay, 230–31
Rumsfeld, Donald, 218–19, 289n7

Safer Cities Program (Chile), 68, 73
Salinas, Carlos, 192
Salvadoran Communist Party, 133
Samper, Ernesto, 101–2, 124–25
San Salvador, 166
Santiago, 67, 71–73, 79–80, 88–89
São Paulo (city), 54, 258
São Paulo (state), 43–56
São Paulo Institute against Violence (ISPCV), 20, 46, 49, 50–56, 251
Sarney, José, 46
Search Bloc, 100–102
Secretaría de Gobernación. *See* Interior Ministry (SEGOB)
Secretaría de la Defenso Nacional. *See* National Defense Secretariat (SEDENA)
Secretaría de Seguridad Pública. *See* Public Security Secretariat (SSP)
Secretaría Nacional de Segurança Pública. *See* National Secretariat for Public Security (SENASP)
Secretariat of Public Security, 255
security policy: Chile, 74, 268n1; El Salvador, 132
security reform, 14–15, 251–53, 289nn4–6; Brazil, 33, 49, 266nn15–17; Chile, 62–69, 93; citizen involvement in, 279n18; Colombia, 121–22, 271n2; El Salvador, 134–35, 138–40, 145–47, 154, 164–67, 278n8, 278n10, 278nn14–15; financial aspects of, 269n10; and interagency coordination, 254; and mass media, 144; Mexico, 184–86, 283n6, 283n11; politics of, 85–86; public perception of, 189, 246; United States, 206–24
Security Schools, 128
Seguro Obrero massacre, 82, 270n4
Serrano, Rosso José, 124–30

Sistema Nacional de Seguridad Pública. *See* National Public Security System (SNSP)

Soares, Luiz Eduardo de Mello, 31–32, 35–38, 266n13, 266n17

Sol, Armaudo Calderón, 155–56

Sombra Negra, 164–65

South Africa: police reform, 56

Stange, Rodolfo, 84–85

Sutil, Jorge Correa, 87

Taliban, 217–18

Tenet, George, 218

terrorism, 1–2, 15, 255, 259–60; Chile, 63; Colombia, 111; definition of, 211–12; public perception of, 220–22; United States, 205–6. *See also* antiterrorism measures

Thomas, Timothy, 226, 231

Thousand Days War, 112

Truth and Reconciliation Commission (Chile), 85

Truth Commission, 133

Tyehimba, Bomani, 229

U.S. Customs and Border Patrol, 222

U.S. Department of Justice: Civil Rights Division, 237–38, 241

Uniformed Municipa: Inspectors corps (Chile), 89

Unión Patriótica, 99

United States, 245–55, 258–61; antiterrorism measures, 211–17; civil liberties, 206, 212–13, 222–23; and Colombia, 109–10; crime rates, 1, 209–11; domestic security, 205–6; drug trafficking, 208–9; and El Salvador, 142; foreign policy, 223–24; homeland security, 205; immigration to, 207, 285n2; insecurity, 3, 10, 207; intelligence gathering, 213–15, 218, 250; judicial system, 209–10; law and order, 206; military, 206, 216; national security, 205–6; police, 206, 209, 216; police reform, 22, 56; prisons, 210; public safety, 206; public security, 3, 206; security reform, 206–24; terrorism, 205–6; victimization surveys, 8

Uribe, Alvaro, 111, 123, 131

USA Patriot Act, 207, 213–14, 219–23, 286nn8–9

Vera Institute of Justice, 45

victimization surveys, 8–10, 248–49, 263n4; Chile, 59; Colombia, 119; El Salvador, 137

violence: Brazil, 49; El Salvador, 152–53; legitimate, 38–42

Workers Party (Brazil), 37–39, 267n25

World Bank, 53

World War II, 205

Zapatista National Liberation Army, 187–88, 194

Zedillo, Ernesto, 170, 184–86

zero-tolerance policing, 4, 141, 228, 235–36, 252, 288n8